The Ku Klux Klan in Mississippi

The Ku Klux Klan
in Mississippi
A History

MICHAEL NEWTON

McFarland & Company, Inc., Publishers
Jefferson, North Carolina, and London

LIBRARY OF CONGRESS CATALOGUING-IN-PUBLICATION DATA

Newton, Michael, 1951–
The Ku Klux Klan in Mississippi : a history / by Michael Newton.
p.   cm.
Includes bibliographical references and index.

ISBN 978-0-7864-4653-7
softcover : 50# alkaline paper ∞

1. Ku-Klux Klan (19th cent.) — Mississippi — History.   2. Ku Klux Klan
(1915–) — Mississippi — History.   3. Mississippi — History.   I. Title.
HS2330.K63N496   2010   322.4'209762 — dc22   2009039298

British Library cataloguing data are available

Front cover: *eyes at top* Samuel Bowers led Mississippi's most militant
Klan faction in the 1960s (National Archives); Klansmen bombed
scores of homes, churches, and other targets in the 1960s (HCUA)

Manufactured in the United States of America

*McFarland & Company, Inc., Publishers
Box 611, Jefferson, North Carolina 28640
www.mcfarlandpub.com*

Table of Contents

Preface

Since 1866 the Ku Klux Klan has been a force to reckon with in Mississippi. Enduring through repeated cycles of expansion and decline, Klansmen have rallied, marched, elected civic leaders, infiltrated law enforcement, and committed crimes ranging from petty vandalism to assassination and mass murder. Despite Mississippi's 142-year history as one of the Klan's most persistent and violent realms, surveys of "Klannishness" in the Magnolia State have thus far been restricted to vignettes and footnotes within broader histories of Reconstruction or the long campaign for civil rights by African Americans. *The Ku Klux Klan in Mississippi* intends to fill that gap in scholarship, examining the Mississippi KKK, its allies, and its long-suffering victims in the context of their changing times.

I owe thanks for assistance to the following: Yvonne Arnold at the University of Southern Mississippi's McCain Library and Archives; Laura Lipsey Bradley; Cindy Brown at the University of Mississippi Alumni Association; Sean Farrell at the Library of Hattiesburg, Petal and Forrest County; Christine Fletcher at the Mississippi State University libraries; David Frasier at Indiana University; Shaun Howard at the New York Public Library; Jerry Mitchell at the *Jackson Clarion-Ledger*; Mark Potok at the Southern Poverty Law Center; Peter Rinaldi at the *Natchez Sun*; Marianne Sweeney-Raley at the Natchez-Adams-Wilkinson Library Service; Linda White at the Clarksdale Public Library; and Christine Wilson at the *Journal of Mississippi History*.

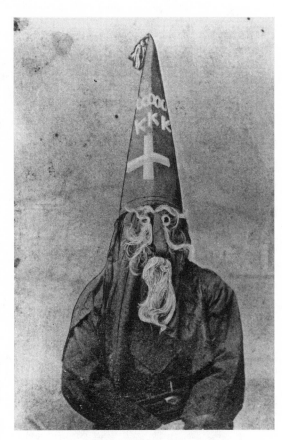

Early Klan costumes were often elaborate (National Archives).

Introduction

In spring 1866, six young Confederate veterans met secretly in Pulaski, Tennessee. Their purpose was to found a "hilarious social club," to "have fun, make mischief, and play pranks on the public." They called themselves *ku klux*—a corruption of the Greek *kuklos* (circle)—and added *clan,* spelled with a *k* for uniformity. In keeping with the lodge's mystic name, they made up titles for themselves—grand cyclops, lictor, magi, night hawk—and persuaded their womenfolk to stitch up suitable regalia. Henceforth, life was never dull around Pulaski as the ghost-garbed Klansmen gamboled after dark, impersonating victims of the recent Civil War. Their antics were alleged to be no more than boyish pranks.[1]

That much is "common knowledge"—which should never be confused with truth. The order's name and rituals were borrowed more or less intact from the wholly respectable Kuklos Adelphon collegiate fraternity—"Old Kappa Alpha," the "Circle of Friends"—founded at the University of North Carolina in 1812 and dissolved sometime during the Civil War. Kuklos Adelphon, in turn, was heavily influenced by Masonic ritual. Pulaski boasted eight Masonic lodges in the postwar years, and Klan founder James Crowe subsequently served as Masonic Grand Master for Tennessee.[2] In short, the fledgling KKK had all the makings of a stodgy social club.

Unfortunately, Kappa Alpha and the Masons represented only part of the new order's ancestry. Pulaski had been dominated in the years before secession by a faction of the xenophobic "Know-Nothing" movement, constituted as the Supreme Order of the Star-Spangled Banner. Members of that order called their local chapters "clans," and they were not confined to Tennessee. A Natchez, Mississippi, unit plotted an abortive invasion of Cuba in 1854, while Woodville's *Wilkinson Whig* proclaimed, in June of that year, "Deride, scoff, malign and traduce; it will avail nothing. Ere many suns have sunk in the west, the 'Know-Nothings' will be the most powerful party in the land—the bodyguard of our liberties and rights." Lafayette County alone boasted 1,200 members, and Know-Nothing candidates swept Vicksburg's municipal elections in 1855, confirming William Percy's later observation that "of all things hated in the South, more hated than the Jew or the Negro or sin itself, is Rome [Catholicism]."[3]

Not that the cause of white supremacy was overlooked, by any means. The Klan was racist from day one, playing its "pranks" exclusively on blacks. One of its founders later told congressional investigators that "the impression sought to be made upon" freedmen "was that these white-robed night prowlers were the ghosts of the Confederate dead, who had arisen from their graves in order to wreak vengeance on an undesirable class" of people. The ghostly raiment and tactics—extending skeletal hands to be shaken, guzzling buckets of water with aid of funnels and bladders—were borrowed with little or no alteration from antebellum overseers and slave patrols. Indeed, most of the Klan's nocturnal behavior echoed that of the dreaded "patter-rollers" who had terrorized southern blacks before emancipation. Slaves described patrol members as "the worst fellows that can be found; as bad as any you could pick up on the wharves," and "nothing but poor white trash.... [I]f they didn't whip some slaves, every now and then, they would lose their jobs." Prewar observers noted that patrols "armed with arbitrary power, and frequently intoxicated, break into the houses of the colored people, and subject them to all manner of outrages." Mississippi's patrols, established long before secession, became increasingly violent after slaves were accused of plotting to burn Natchez in 1861.[4]

The KKK and antebellum slave patrols resembled each other so closely, in fact, that some freedmen could not differentiate between the two. Several ex-slaves, interviewed long after the fact, claimed contact with a Ku Klux Klan *before* the Civil War, while others cited raids by "patter-rollers" during Reconstruction. The Klan's young, affluent founders in Pulaski were almost certainly slave patrol veterans, and historian Wyn Wade suggests that some local patrol units may have joined the KKK en masse. Whatever the case, their spirit lived on in the Klan, as described by one Alabama Klansman whose Greensboro den raided black communities "in regular old style."[5]

From such beginnings sprang an instrument of terror, but the Klan did not immediately turn to violence. It took time to grow and shed the trappings of a social club. Meanwhile, the war-torn South was changing too.

Presidential Reconstruction

President Abraham Lincoln, sixteen months before Appomattox and Ford's Theater, had announced a program for readmission of secessionist states to the Union "with malice toward none." That plan's only conditions of forgiveness were acceptance of the new Thirteenth Amendment's ban on slavery and a loyalty oath pronounced by 10 percent of 1860's registered electorate. Lincoln's successor, Andrew Johnson, was even more lenient, offering readmission to any state wherein "that portion of the people ... who are loyal" produced a constitution and established a new government. On 13 June 1865 Johnson named Vicksburg unionist William Sharkey as Mississippi's provisional governor, directing him to call a constitutional convention that would formally abolish slavery and nullify the Magnolia State's Ordinance of Secession. Johnson also suggested (but did not insist on) extension of suffrage to literate freedmen, while ordering a general election for state officials to be held in October 1865.[6]

Governor Sharkey dutifully echoed that plea for black suffrage at the August convention, where it fell on deaf ears. Instead, the delegates grumbled at federal demands and quarreled ad infinitum over precise wording of the ban on slavery (described by one attendee as "ceaseless wrangling over an immaterial issue"). Some delegates challenged President Johnson's authority to order emancipation, while others clung to hopes of compensation for their liberated slaves. Judge William Yerger warned his colleagues that the North "was not to be trifled with," and while the convention finally acknowledged slavery's demise, its members disclaimed responsibility "for whatever honor there may be in abolishing it." In closing, the assembly urged Mississippi's next legislature to pass laws that would "guard [freedmen] and the State against any evils that may arise from their sudden emancipation."[7]

On 2 October, Mississippi's white voters chose former slaveholder and unpardoned Confederate brigadier general Benjamin Humphreys as their governor. Rebel officers and sympathizers also dominated the new state legislature, which appointed William Sharkey to the U.S. Senate and rejected the Thirteenth Amendment as a legally redundant tool of "radicals and demagogues." President Johnson demanded ratification, but Mississippi Democrats stood firm. ("Shall Mississippi ratify the Thirteenth Amendment?" asked the *Vicksburg Herald*. "We answer, no, ten thousand times no.") Nonetheless, Johnson pardoned Humphreys on 26 October, clearing the way for his inauguration as governor. At that ceremony, Sharkey reaffirmed his pledge "that ours is and it ever shall be, a government of white men." To that end, he called for legislation that would forestall "anarchy" among freedmen.[8]

The Black Codes

Between 20 and 25 November 1865, Mississippi enacted the first southern "Black Codes," designed to restore antebellum race relations. That battery of statutes was preceded by a three-man committee's report proclaiming slavery "the happiest and best system ever devised for a laboring class," deficient only in its failure to regulate black fornication. Strict laws were needed, the committee said, to protect white Mississippians from the "innate bestiality" of freedmen. The *Jackson Daily News* agreed, proclaiming, "We must keep the ex-slave in a position of inferiority. We must pass such laws as will make him *feel* his inferiority."[9]

With that injunction in mind, state legislators produced a series of laws circumscribing every aspect of life for "freedmen, free Negroes or mulattoes." To preserve Mississippi's labor pool, all nonwhites above age eighteen were required to obtain written proof of employment by 8 January 1866. Those caught without such evidence were branded vagrants, as were all those "found unlawfully assembling themselves together, either in the day or night time, and all white persons so assembling with freedmen, free Negroes or mulattoes, or usually associating with freedmen, free Negroes or mulattoes on terms of equality, or living in adultery or fornication with a freedwoman, free Negro or mulatto." Penalties included fines of ten dollars for nonwhites and two hundred dollars for whites, plus jail terms of six days (for nonwhites) to six months (for white "vagrants"). Black adults who found work were bound to their employers by law, subject to forfeiture of wages and summary arrest if they broke their contracts. Any white who offered alternate employment to a worker under contract faced a fine of five hundred dollars. "Every person" was empowered to arrest delinquent workers, thereby earning rewards of five dollars plus ten cents per mile for transportation. That reward was charged against the prisoner, as was a fifty-dollar fine. For those who could not pay the added debts, the penalty was peonage.[10]

Nonwhite adults were not the only ones required to labor in conditions tantamount to slavery. County sheriffs were commanded to make semiannual surveys of nonwhite minors and "apprentice" to white masters without pay all those whose parents "have not the means, or who refuse to provide for and support said minors." In selecting masters, preference was granted to "the former owner of said minors," with approval of the court. Blacks were further barred from renting any property outside of an incorporated town or city, thus ensuring that they had no independent farms. No law forbade the outright sale of farmland to blacks, but as freedmen in Claiborne County observed, "not one of us out of a thousand" could afford even a paltry quarter-acre.[11]

To remedy the perceived moral failings of antebellum slave codes, Mississippi's lawmakers recognized black marriages and legitimized the children of black couples living together as husband and wife. The flip side of that benevolent coin was a mandatory sentence of life imprisonment for both partners in any mixed marriage. Furthermore, the state imposed a ten-day jail term and a hundred-dollar fine on the following:

> All rogues and vagabonds, idle and dissipated persons, beggars, jugglers, or persons practicing unlawful games or plays, runaways, common drunkards, common night-walkers, pilferers, lewd, wanton, or lascivious persons in speech or behavior, common railers and brawlers, persons who neglect their calling or employment, misspend what they earn, or do not provide for the support of themselves or their families, or dependents, and all other idle and disorderly persons, including all who neglect all lawful business, habitually misspend their time by frequenting houses of ill-fame, gaming-houses, or tippling shops.[12]

While that statute seemingly applied to all Mississippians, special restrictions were placed on freedmen. They could sue whites or file criminal charges, but any charge judged "false and malicious" by white authorities burdened the plaintiff with court costs, twenty days in jail, and a fifty-dollar fine. Unless a soldier of the U.S. Army, no black was permitted to "keep or carry firearms of any kind, or any ammunition, dirk, or bowie-knife," under penalty of confiscation and a ten-dollar fine. Thirty-day jail terms and fines ranging from ten to one hundred dollars awaited any freedman "committing riots, routs, affrays, trespasses, malicious mischief and cruel treatment to animals, seditious speeches, insulting gestures, language or acts, or assaults on any person, disturbance of the peace, exercising the functions of a minister of the gospel without a license from some regularly organized church, vending spiritous or intoxicating liquors, or committing any other misdemeanor." In every case where fines remained unpaid, white planters were at liberty to "hire" slave labor from the state. No more would white Mississippians fear blacks like the ex-slave who responded to a planter's "Howdy Uncle" with an angry "Call me Mister."[13]

In case the import of the Black Codes still eluded anyone, Mississippi lawmakers declared that "all the penal and criminal laws now in force in this State, defining offenses, and prescribing the mode of punishment for crimes and misdemeanors committed by slaves, free Negroes or mulattoes, be and the same are hereby enacted, and declared to be in full force and effect, against freedmen, free Negroes, and mulattoes, except so far as the mode and manner of trial and punishment have been changed or altered by law." In sum, though slavery was theoretically abolished, most of its procedures were retained intact.[14]

While other southern states hastened to mimic Mississippi's Black Codes, native freedmen were the first to protest. Claiborne County blacks petitioned Governor Humphreys, asking whether slavery's abolition was permanent or simply "a policy for the present." They acknowledged the existence of some "good and honest" white employers, but deemed them "not the majority," expressing fears that even decent planters would be easily intimidated and "put down as a negro spoiler." As for various offenses listed in the Black Codes, they declared, "Now we are free, we do not want to be hunted by negro runners and their hounds unless we are guilty of a criminal crime." White critics of the codes were rare, but their number included ex–Governor Sharkey, who deemed the ban on blacks renting farmland "foolish," and the *Columbus Sentinel,* which branded Mississippi's lawmakers "as complete a set of political Goths as were ever turned loose to work destruction upon a state. The fortunes of the whole South have been injured by their folly."[15]

The northern response was predictable. While President Johnson accepted the Black Codes, General Oliver Howard ordered his Freedmen's Bureau to ignore restrictions on black rental of farmland and Mississippi's on-site military commander declared all racially discriminatory statutes null and void. On 1 December the *Chicago Tribune* declared, "We tell the white men of Mississippi that the men of the North will convert the State of Mississippi into a frog pond before they will allow such laws to disgrace one foot of soil in which the bones of our soldiers sleep and over which the flag of freedom waves." Five days later, Charles Sumner thundered in the U.S. Senate, "Strike at the Black Codes as you have already struck at the Slave Codes. Strike at once; strike hard. You have already proclaimed Emancipation; proclaim Enforcement also."

Over the next six months, Congress rejected the South's newly elected senators and representatives, passed a sweeping Civil Rights Bill over President Johnson's veto, and wrote a Fourteenth Amendment to the Constitution guaranteeing "equal protection of the law" without regard to race. Belatedly, one Mississippi planter lamented, "We showed our hand too soon. We ought to have waited till the troops were withdrawn and our representatives admitted to Congress; then we could have had everything our own way."[16]

Drawing Battle Lines

There was another way, however, which had served the South for better than a century: brute force. In May 1866, one month after passage of the Civil Rights Bill, in a three-day "race war" in Memphis forty-seven blacks were slaughtered and eighty more were wounded, while arsonists burned twelve black schools and four black churches. Two months later in New Orleans, a similar outbreak left forty freedmen dead, and more than two hundred blacks and white Republicans wounded.[17]

Racist violence was commonplace in Mississippi, where Governor Sharkey had reported "an unprecedented amount of lawlessness" in summer 1865. By early 1866, General Augustus Chetlain counted an average of one freedman murdered per day in the counties surrounding Jackson, while his troops once found seven blacks "wantonly butchered" during a forty-mile ride from the state capital. Spokesmen for the Freedmen's Bureau claimed two or three murders per day, statewide, with black army veterans singled out as particular targets. A freedman suspected of rape in Oktibbeha County was bailed out of custody, then "run to death by hounds." In Carroll and Montgomery counties, gangs of armed whites repeatedly scoured their districts for "troublesome negroes." Increasingly, the violence sprang from organized bands of self-styled "regulators" who "shoot freedmen without provocation, drive them from plantations without pay, and commit other crimes." Ex-governor Sharkey predicted genocide, warning Congress that Mississippi's freedmen "are destined to extinction, beyond all doubt." The *Natchez Democrat* agreed, declaring, "The child is already born who will behold the last Negro in the State of Mississippi." Even the "hilarious" Ku Klux Klan had lost its sense of humor by October 1866, with reports of "numerous revolting outrages" spreading from the mother den in Tennessee to other counties and adjoining states.[18]

Republicans in Washington retaliated with new legislation to suppress the rising tide of southern violence. On 2 March 1867 Congress passed the first Reconstruction Act, dividing the late Confederacy into five military districts ruled by army generals. Two weeks later, a second statute spelled out the details of military occupation and imposed an "ironclad" loyalty oath upon prospective voters (though in practice it was seldom used). In mid–July a third statute gave military commanders sweeping power to remove civil officials in Dixie and ordered voting registrars to "investigate" the loyalty of white applicants. Mississippi and Arkansas comprised the fourth military district, overseen in turn by Generals Edward Ord and Alvan Gillem. Over the next two years, Mississippi was occupied by a total of 716 officers and men (all white), including 129 stationed at Vicksburg and 59 in Natchez. A dozen of those soldiers were detailed to serve as agents of the Freedmen's Bureau, since the bureau had no budget of its own for personnel. Mississippi sought an injunction to bar enforcement of the Reconstruction Acts, but the U.S. Supreme Court declined to intervene.[19]

The southern Democrat view of Reconstruction may be swiftly summarized. Dispatched by Radical Republicans in Congress, hordes of venal northern "carpetbaggers" inundated Dixie, teaming with traitorous native-born "scalawags" to loot the prostrate South. Responsible Democrats— now labeled "Conservatives"—were disfranchised en masse, while illiterate freedmen were herded like sheep to the polls and bribed or coerced into voting Republican. State governments were mired in corruption, infested with black officeholders and propped up by black troops. The South became a veritable hell on earth. Its natural aristocrats were driven from their land and left destitute, while white women languished in constant fear of rape by lecherous, subhuman freedmen. It would take no less than armed rebellion to restore God's order in a world turned upside down.

The Klan Reorganized

It hardly matters that the classic view of Reconstruction was a work of Gothic fiction, almost comically distorted, for the year-old Ku Klux Klan had no intention of allowing such a nightmare to be realized. Six days before the "radicals" in Congress overrode President Johnson's veto on the first Reconstruction Act, Klansmen began arriving in Nashville, Tennessee. No less than thirty ranking members were in town by 11 April, their secret meeting at the Maxwell House hotel "coincidentally" occurring at the same time as a state convention of Conservatives. Those in attendance included such Confederate icons as General John Brown of Tennessee, Major General John Gordon of Georgia, and Lieutenant General Nathan Bedford Forrest, who had joined the Klan in Memphis during autumn 1866.[20]

The Nashville delegates were furious at recent news from Washington and they stated their purpose:

> To reorganize the Klan on a plan corresponding to its size and present purposes; to bind the isolated Dens together; to secure unity of purpose and concert of action; to hedge the members up by such limitations and regulations as are best adapted to restrain them within proper limits; to distribute authority among prudent men at local centers and exact from them a close supervision of those under their charge.[21]

According to the prescript penned in Nashville and revised in 1868, the "present purposes" of those who gathered to reorganize the KKK involved creating "an institution of Chivalry, Humanity, Mercy, and Patriotism; embodying in its genius and its principles all that is chivalric in conduct, noble in sentiment, generous in manhood, and patriotic in purpose."[22] Its goals were threefold:

> First: To protect the weak, the innocent, and the defenseless, from the indignities, wrongs, and outrages of the lawless, the violent, and the brutal; to relieve the injured and oppressed; to succor the suffering and unfortunate, and especially the widows and orphans of Confederate soldiers.
>
> Second: To protect and defend the Constitution of the United States, and all laws passed in conformity thereto, and to protect the States and the people thereof from all invasion from any source whatever.
>
> Third: To aid and assist in the execution of all constitutional laws, and to protect the people from unlawful seizure, and from trial except by their peers in conformity to the laws of the land.[23]

All these were noble aims, at least on paper, but the rub came when they were reviewed through Ku Klux eyes. To members of the Klan, the "injured and oppressed" were southern whites, condemned to suffer in a world where blacks could vote. "The violent and brutal" were officials who enforced black civil rights, no matter how reluctantly. "Constitutional" laws were the Black Codes, relegating freedmen to virtual slavery. "Unlawful seizure" was a catchall term for any so-called Radical activity, from raising taxes in support of schools to the arrest of racial terrorists.

In fact, the KKK was overhauled in April 1867 as a paramilitary movement to defend the sacred Southern Way of Life. Authority within the Klan's "Invisible Empire" was divided as follows: each "realm" (state) was ruled by a grand dragon and his eight hydras; each "dominion" (congressional district) by a grand titan and his six furies; each "province" (county) by a grand giant and his four goblins; each local "den" by

General Nathan Bedford Forrest was the Klan's first leader (Library of Congress).

a grand cyclops and his two night hawks, commanding rank-and-file ghouls. The empire at large would be administered by a grand wizard and his ten genii.[24]

Selection of the grand wizard was critical, and the convention's choice of Nathan Bedford Forrest determined to a large extent how Klansmen would conduct themselves in their ensuing battle to "redeem" the South. That choice would also make the imminent guerrilla war intensely personal for Mississippi and her citizens.

CHAPTER 1

Reconstruction and "Redemption" (1866–1877)

Mississippi was inured to violence long before the Ku Klux Klan arrived. A century of racist propaganda, slave patrols and rumored uprisings, lynchings and executions, kidnapping and torture all helped fertilize the soil. Four years of civil war cost Mississippi 50,000 lives and left much of the state a scorched-earth "forest of chimneys."[1] Still, many restless and embittered veterans found the wartime killing habit hard to shake.

No individual better personified that spirit of impulsive, rough-and-ready mayhem than the Klan's grand wizard, Nathan Bedford Forest. A Tennessee native, born 13 July 1821, Forrest moved to Tippah County, Mississippi, with his family as a young teenager. By 1842 he was a livestock dealer in DeSoto County. Three years later Forrest shot two men in a street fight that left his uncle dead and ironically resulted in his election to serve as Hernando's constable. He inherited a debt-ridden mercantile business from his late uncle and subsequently moved to Memphis as a slave trader. His slave mart collapsed during a January 1860 rainstorm, killing eight of its hapless inmates, but Forrest persevered. Two months after the shelling of Fort Sumter, Forrest joined the 7th Tennessee Cavalry as a private. Promotion to lieutenant colonel followed three weeks later, launching Forrest on the fast track to near-mythic status.[2]

Southern partisans hailed Forrest as a "genius" and "the Wizard of the Saddle," but his wartime record was checkered at best. While leading whirlwind cavalry attacks that showcased his personal courage, Forrest also executed Union prisoners of war and once publicly threatened his commanding general's life — a lapse in military discipline that somehow won him an independent command. At Fort Pillow, Tennessee, on 12 April 1864, troops led by Forrest and Brigadier General James Chalmers captured an integrated garrison of 580 Federal soldiers. A massacre ensued, leaving 193 black prisoners and 101 whites "bayoneted, beaten, and shot to death" in a "cold-blooded and persistent ... slaughter." Three days later, Forrest voiced his hope that the massacre would "demonstrate to the Northern people that negro soldiers cannot cope with Southerners."[3]

Forrest's crime went unpunished and he finished the war as a lieutenant general. May 1865 found him settled in Coahoma County, Mississippi, but debtors hounded him back to Memphis four months later, where Forrest established himself as a sharecropper and cotton trader, subsequently pursuing a new career in railroad construction that saw him travel widely throughout the South. By then, he had already joined the KKK, praising the order as "a damned good thing" useful "to keep the niggers in their place." Publicly, Forrest would only admit to joining "a different order" called the Pale Faces, which he described as "[s]omething like Odd Fellowship, Masonry, orders of that sort, for the purpose of protecting the weak and defenseless, &c." In fact, the Pale Face order was founded by Klansmen in Columbia, Tennessee, who used the name interchangeably with "Ku Klux." Forrest's April 1867 promotion to serve as grand wizard sent a message to Klansmen everywhere. They were prepared for war, mindful of Forrest's motto that "War means fightin,' and fightin' means killin.'"[4]

Mobilizing for Resistance

Deliberate confusion surrounds the Klan's initial appearance in Mississippi. The Magnolia State's first Klan-like group was Heggie's Scouts, reputedly organized in Carroll County "right after the surrender," and later spreading into Holmes and Montgomery counties. Although the group was reportedly named for its leader, "Major Heggie of Vaiden," multiple sources name Nathan Forrest as its founder. While conducting railroad business in Aberdeen, Forrest was "frequently consulted by the native white people as to what they might do to protect themselves" against freedmen. As historian Stanley Horn explains, "[I]t did not take much persuasion to win them over to the Ku Klux idea; and in that part of Mississippi subject to Forrest's influence the Ku Klux Klan soon began to make itself felt as a force in the community."[5]

In fact, Heggie's Scouts may have been a proto–Klan. Although their stated purpose matched the KKK's—"to make the negroes humble by visiting terrible punishment upon them"—the Scouts operated in daylight and without traditional Klan disguises, various "captains" commanding an estimated 100 members divided into six- and eight-man companies. On one occasion, members crushed a rumored "negro uprising" by murdering 116 blacks and dumping their corpses into the Tallahatchie River. Later, the Scouts "participated in a few small riots" and "often whipped negroes who refused to work." Federal officers arrested forty-eight reputed members in 1866, transporting them to Oxford for trial, where prominent attorneys James Z. George and Edward Walthall represented the defendants free of charge. Judge Robert Hill proved sympathetic, releasing the accused after fining them one dollar each. When a sheriff asked if he should actually collect the fines, Judge Hill replied, "Not on your life."[6]

Heggie's Scouts disbanded soon after that trial, absorbed by Mississippi's first recognized Ku Klux den in 1866. Several other counties sprouted dens in 1867, their formation spurred by a proclamation from Governor Humphreys alleging black "combinations and conspiracies" to seize white property. Grand Wizard Forrest

Governor Adelbert Ames opposed the early Mississippi Klan (Library of Congress).

traveled widely through the state, promoting sale of railroad stock, pausing long enough to organize dens in DeSoto, Lafayette and Pontotoc counties. His Lafayette recruits included a physician, two leaders of the Democratic Party, and ten other "worthy citizens of the community." Grenada's den made do without the wizard and was organized by seven prominent citizens, meeting at the local bank, above a barber's shop.[7]

As during later incarnations, Mississippi's early Klan disguised itself with other names whenever possible. One such "front" was the Robinson Club, also known as the Jack Robinsons, active at various times in Chickasaw, Monroe, Newton, Pontotoc and Tippah counties. Described by sympathetic historians as a coalition of "Democratic clubs" created to topple Republican rule, the Robinsons allegedly numbered 1,200 to 1,500 men at peak strength. Sheriff Tom Saddler led the Robinsons in Pontotoc County, where members used the password "Old Coon" and a silent recognition sign required initiates "to pull at their trousers." Historian Ruth Watkins names Thomas Gathwright as the group's statewide leader, reporting that the Robinsons "would decree in council the punishment of offenders, whether chastisement or death, and the decrees of the council were always carried out." T.M. Scanlan, a prominent Newton County Democrat, spent three months in jail for refusing to name his comembers. Some accounts describe the Robinsons as Klan allies, "another secret order of like character," but Deputy U.S. Marshal Henry Clark told congressional investigators that the club — which he called the "Robertson Family"— used "precisely the same oath as the ... oath of the Ku Klux of South Carolina."[8]

A more transparent front was Mississippi's Knights of the Black Cross, active in Franklin and Lawrence counties. The group took its name from the black crosses adorning its white robes, a ruse designed to let members "truthfully" deny Klan membership if questioned under oath. State legislator J.F. Sessions demonstrated that duplicity when he testified before Congress in July 1871. Sessions denied any knowledge of the Klan but admitted joining the KBC three years earlier, describing it as "a political organization ... in which they wore disguises," created solely to "organize and electioneer" during the 1868 presidential campaign. While pleading faulty memory, Sessions recalled that KBC members swore "an oath of fidelity to the Constitution, to prevent innovations upon the Constitution, and to endeavor to secure the success of the conservative party."[9]

Other Klan-like groups active in Mississippi during this period included Leake County's Washington Brothers and the White Line, but no details of their activities are presently available. Anonymous groups also flourished, such as the band of Confederate veterans led by W.H. Gilmer and J.H. Welch in Lafayette County, whose members roamed at large disarming freedmen, sometimes employing "harsh means to achieve their purpose."[10]

The Mississippi Klan preserved no records to identify its first grand dragon, but two candidates emerge from study of the period. The first, named by Pulaski Klan founder John Lester, is James Zachariah George, a Georgia native whose family emigrated to Mississippi when he was still a child. George served briefly in the Mexican War, then returned to study law, was admitted to the bar in 1847, and was elected reporter to the state supreme court seven years later. He was a member of Mississippi's secession convention and joined the 20th Mississippi Infantry after Fort Sumter, rising to the rank of brigadier general by war's end. His sympathy with postwar terrorists was established by his pro bono defense of Heggie's Scouts in 1866; Lafayette County Democrats subsequently organized a James Z. George Club to disrupt Republican meetings. During the chaotic election campaign of 1875, while serving as chairman of the Democratic state central committee, George pretended to negotiate a white cease-fire that ultimately offered no relief to black and Republican targets. Author Stetson Kennedy dubs George "the commandant of the terrorist militias" during that campaign.[11]

If George was not the Klan's grand dragon during Reconstruction, the dubious honor may belong to his friend and fellow lawyer Lucius Quintus Cincinnatus Lamar. Another Georgia native, Lamar moved to Oxford, Mississippi, in 1849 and taught mathematics at the state university for a year before returning to Georgia. Lamar came back to Mississippi in 1855 and served in the U.S. House of Representatives from March 1857 to December 1860, when he resigned to join the state's secession convention. He drafted Mississippi's secession ordinance, then served in the Confederate army as a lieutenant colonel until 1862, when he retired to join the Rebel diplomatic service for a tour of England, France and Russia. After Appomattox, Lamar resumed legal practice and served as a delegate to successive state constitutional conventions in 1865 and 1868.

While no published source names Lamar as a Klansman, his actions are suggestive. With law partner Edward Walthall, he defended KKK defendants at their federal trial in Oxford, during June 1871. In court, Lamar assaulted deputy U.S. marshals while his clients cheered and threatened spectators. A belated apology spared Lamar from a contempt citation, and he won election to Congress the following year. During the 1875 election campaign Lamar toured Mississippi with Georgia grand dragon John Gordon, delivering a series of incendiary speeches. Author Albert Kirwan names Lamar and George as joint leaders of the violent campaign that "defied the federal laws and over[threw] the government of the state without regard for statutory law or the constitution."[12]

While the identity of Mississippi's grand dragon remains in question, other Ku Klux officers have been identified beyond a reasonable doubt. The most prominent was Samuel Jameson Gholson, a former state legislator and congressman, member of the state secession convention and a Confederate brigadier general who was widely recognized as the top-ranking Klansman in Monroe County. Gholson was also an attorney, sharing duties as co-counsel with L.Q.C. Lamar and Edward Walthall at the Oxford trial in June 1871. Another ex-state legislator, Dr. William Compton, doubled as Marshall County's grand giant and editor of a Democratic newspaper in Holly Springs before turning Republican in 1871, emerging as editor of the *Jackson Leader* and superintendent of the state asylum. Lafayette County's Klan ranked leading Democrats B.F. Goolsby, J.M. Gilmer, W.T. Ivey, R.W. Phipps and J.H. Welch among its officers. Judge T.B. Graham first opposed Scott County's Klan, then served as its grand cyclops, aided by *Forest Register* editor James Glanville. Col. M.D.L. Stephens, yet another state lawmaker, served as grand cyclops of Yalobusha County's northern district. Neighboring dens in the county were led by Capt. James Taylor (Coffeeville) and Capt. John Powell (Grenada). Attorney Henry Lowndes Muldrow brought his experience as a Confederate cavalry officer to the Oktibbeha County den, which he served as grand cyclops. Insiders named DeSoto County's Klan leaders as "Grand Ghoul" Pad Myers, Jobe Day, L.L. Jones and Jim McCrowan.[13]

Despite one historian's claim that Mississippi Democrats "all ... belonged to the same class," the KKK's rank-and-file ghouls were a distinctly mixed bag. An Irishman named Lee Cole organized Lee County's Klan at Saltillo. Attala County's den consisted chiefly of "high-toned, honorable Christian men" drawn from Kosciusko's leading social and professional circles. Joshua Morris, Mississippi's attorney general, told Congress in 1871 that "very frequently young men—boys and youth—are deluded into this thing by its novelty and mystery and secrecy; there is a sort of charm in this respect to young men, and they go into it frequently without realizing the extent of their wrong-doing." At least two Mississippi dens also enlisted female members to sew Klan regalia and serve as hostesses for their respective gatherings. In DeSoto County, those early Klanswomen included the wives of L.L. Jones and Asa Doggett. Pontotoc County recruited the wife of Grand Cyclops W.B. Clark, plus Martha Benson and Mrs. W.L. Phillips.[14]

Not all recruits of Mississippi's Klan were willing volunteers—nor were all of them white. Threats of boycotts forced Pontotoc County merchants to join the KKK or its sister group, the Robinson Club, while freedmen in at least three counties were also dragooned into service. Four blacks joined the Winston County raiding party that killed Simon Triplett in December 1870. Soon afterward, forty Klansmen visited the Lowndes County home of Lewis Perkins and his wife to threaten a schoolteacher sharing their quarters. All were disguised except an elderly black man, whom Mrs. Perkins recognized as a servant of her antebellum master. Monroe County's knights drafted freedmen Joseph Davis, Michael Forshee and Henry Hatch under threat of death, while brothers Burrill and Jefferson Willis donned Klan robes voluntarily. All five took the Ku Klux oath before participating in the 1871 murders of freedmen Jack Dupree and Alexander Page. Davis, Forshee and Hatch later turned state's evidence against their fellow Klansmen.[15]

The Public Klan

While the Ku Klux prescripts of 1867–1868 extolled the order's dedication to chivalry and the U.S. Constitution, Mississippi Klansmen spoke more bluntly of their purposes. Attala County's knights punished both "obstreperous" freedmen and white "bushwhackers," whose depredations sparked "a worse terror than even the negro." Marshall County Klansmen swore an oath "to suppress the negro and keep him in the position where he belongs, and to see that the Democratic party controls this country." In Yalobusha County, night riders vowed "to keep unruly whites and negroes under control" and "to put down negro supremacy." Panola County Klansmen rallied "to counteract the influence which the nefarious reconstruction principles had upon the negroes, particularly the evil effects of the loyal leagues and the work of the carpetbaggers." Noxubee's ghouls pledged themselves "to take the avenging of a wrong against a white man by colored men into the hands of the people, and away from the law."[16]

Ku Klux regalia was diverse throughout the state, as in the South at large. Klan robes were stitched from simple cloth, calico or "domestic," in white, red, or black. Most were ankle-length and slit for horseback riding, though Monroe County Klansmen preferred knee-length gowns and Lowndes County's knights combined white overalls with "these tight sacks the ladies wear, trimmed in black, that are white." Pearl buttons adorned Klan robes in Monroe County, Lafayette County's sported large tin buttons and the letters "KKK," Attala County Klansmen preferred red calico appliqués, and Lawrence County's night riders displayed black crosses. Klansmen in Chickasaw County made do with red pants and wide belts for their pistols and knives, plus "some kind of uniform hat." Head gear ranged from simple caps to conical hoods "in the shape of a dunce-cap," with horns or dangling tassels attached. Lowndes County Klansmen wore hoods stitched to the shoulders of their coats and pulled forward to hide their faces, whereas Noxubee's crafted paper masks with false beards and mustaches made from mules' tails. "Some kind of hideous design" masked Lafayette County Klansmen, while those in Chickasaw County simply blackened their faces. Klan horses were also shrouded, some with their hooves wrapped in sackcloth. Klan wives prepared some costumes, while other costumes were commissioned professionally. Samuel Gholson feigned ignorance of where Klan costumes came from, then admitted that selected tailors were commissioned to prepare them. George Picket, a U.S. Army officer stationed in Aberdeen, observed that the robe stripped from a Klansman killed in Pontotoc County was "very nicely made."[17]

As noted earlier, Klan "pranks" were freely borrowed from the tactics used by antebellum slave patrols and overseers, modified in keeping with the postwar atmosphere. When ghostly riders visited some freedman's cabin they impersonated Rebel soldiers killed at Shiloh or Manassas. Having ridden from those battlefields (or Hell itself) within the hour, they were thirsty, calling out for bucketsful of water which they "drank" with the aid of a funnel and rubber bladder. In lieu of spoken words, some Klansmen communicated via "watchwords, signs, curious sounds and whistles."

The Lowndes County raiders who terrorized Joseph Turner surrounded his home while "hollering like owls, some whippoorwills, and some talked talk I could not understand." Their "broken language" turned to English only after they dragged Turner from his home. Joseph Galloway, a white teacher in the same county, was less impressed when Klansmen "shook their heads and horns at me, and acted like cows." In Yalobusha County, where "bad negro" Percy McFarland "gave the white people much trouble," Klansmen timed their visit to coincide with a family tragedy. Shortly after the burial of McFarland's son, they snatched McFarland from home and carried him to the gravesite, where a robed knight lay concealed in a casket covered with leaves. As McFarland approached under guard, the "ghost" sprang forth, commanding his startled "father" to "behave himself and stick closely to the white people."[18]

Despite their oath of secrecy, Klansmen sometimes used Democratic newspapers to publicize their meetings and intimidate their enemies. One such public notice appeared in the *Forest Register* on 1 April 1868. Editor James Glanville claimed that some unknown visitor had tossed the note through his office window, but since he was a leader of the local Klan, it was likely his own handiwork.[19] The notice read as follows:

VENGEANCE, RETRIBUTION, TRAITORS, BEWARE!

Valley of Death, Twenty-Eight May,
Third Mortal Month, X 10.

K.K.K.'s. You are ordered to assemble at the Dark Valley on the night of the first mortal month at the hour of Silence. Come prepared. Work to do. Lamps to extinguish. Darkness to follow.

By command,
K.G.C.B.R.G.C.

S.T. 5X
EDITOR REGISTER: Refuse to publish this at your peril. You are watched. Enough!!![20]

Klansmen raid a cabin during Reconstruction (Library of Congress).

While such antics kept Klansmen amused for a time, most of their targets saw through the supernatural masquerade. Direct threats quickly followed, often in the form of letters signed "Ku-Klux" or "KKK," sometimes adorned with crude drawings of caskets and skeletons. Robed Klansmen delivered the notes on occasion, or enlisted freedmen as their messengers. Some threats were vague, as when the Klan promised to visit Robert Gleed "on the first bloody moon," while others were specific. Judge Jonathan Tarbell, in Scott County, received notice that he "would be shot through the head within a year." In Lafayette County, Democratic party leaders handpicked the recipients of Ku Klux warnings. J.J. House, a Democratic spokesman in Marshall County, reversed that trend by passing a personal death threat to Republican Sheriff Nelson Gill, then demanded the note's return under threat of a KKK whipping.[21] The letter sent to magistrate George Campbell in Shuqualak (postmarked from Carrolton, Alabama) was typical:

BIG THINGS ON ICE, October 14, 1870

Sir: You are hereby ordered to come out in your county paper, in fifteen days, and make an explanation of your conduct of hear [*sic*] lately. We would like to hear of you taking some more social drinks with your friend Marshall Allick Vandevner. We know you to be a white man in daytime and a dam negro at night, and if you fail to come out in county paper, as above ordered, and give an account of yourself, your life will be at stake. You have been waited on before this, but the lady part of your family prevented. We do not know you only by carracter [*sic*]. We hope to hear from you soon, and hope you will make a good report of yourself.

Respectfully,
K.K.K.[22]

Reign of Terror

Where threats and warnings failed to cow its enemies, the KKK soon turned to violence. While one apologist insists that Klansmen were "scrupulously opposed to the shedding of human blood," the public record proves otherwise. No final tabulation of Klan violence during Reconstruction is available, but congressional investigators compiled partial statistics during 1871. "Bodily correction"—i.e., whipping—may have been the order's most common criminal activity, with seventy-five victims specifically identified, but murder ran a close second. Federal investigators identified forty-eight homicide victims in Mississippi, but that total barely scratched the surface. We know that Heggie's Scouts killed 116 blacks in a single engagement, while Klansmen at Coffeeville subsequently ambushed and murdered 77 members of the Loyal League. Lafayette County Klansmen drowned thirty blacks at Yockana, incensing local fishermen, who dreaded hooking corpses on their lines. Historian John Kyle, an ardent KKK admirer, listed twenty-four Klan-related murders in Panola County alone between August 1870 and December 1872. "Chivalrous" Klansmen raped black women in Aberdeen and Columbus, while Ku Klux arsonists torched dozens of churches, schools, and homes. Statewide, Klan-led mobs dragged victims from jail for lynching and staged wholesale pogroms against black communities.[23]

Those who reorganized the KKK in 1867 advertised it as an order pledged to justice and enforcement of the law. That vigilante role was evident in Mississippi, where Klansmen flogged and lynched victims of both races for various presumed infractions. Lee County's knights whipped freedmen and whites alike "for the most trivial offenses," once fatally lashing "an innocent old Englishman" named Reding, near Baldwyn. Blacks accused of raping or murdering whites were always candidates for lynching, a time-honored tradition which Klansmen preserved. In July 1868, Yalobusha County's knights hanged Tom McLain and Gilbert Quinn, who were accused of killing the "noble-hearted" overseer at a local plantation.

The same knights subsequently lynched a freedman, his wife, and their twelve-year-old son for allegedly attempting to kill the county treasurer's wife. A sixth Yalobusha lynching victim, one Dr. Lott, was a white man hanged for slaying a romantic rival. In Lafayette County, after home invaders wounded Klansman Sam Ragland and murdered his wife, fellow knights went searching for "the most vicious slaves [*sic*] in the county." The unnamed killers were "justly dealt with," and Lafayette's ghouls then killed another thirty freedmen for good measure. The same den subsequently tortured several blacks accused of theft, then learned that their accuser had simply misplaced the "stolen" money. In October 1870, after Sanders Flint and his sons were jailed for assaulting a white man, Monroe County Klansmen took them from jail with a deputy's connivance; Sanders escaped outside town, but sons Joseph and Willis were murdered and dumped in the Tombigbee River. In contrast to that law-and-order zeal, Klansmen in Holly Springs liberated a white defendant awaiting extradition to Tennessee on capital charges and whisked him off to parts unknown.[24]

While neither of the first Klan's prescripts mentioned white supremacy, defense of that most sacred southern principle was foremost in the mind of every Klansman. A DeSoto County planter named T. Yancey spoke for most white Mississippians when he wrote, in 1866: "As to recognizing the rights of freedmen to their children, I will say there is not one man or woman in all the South who believes they are free, but we consider them stolen property—stolen by the bayonets of the damnable United States government." Or, as the *Natchez Courier* opined, "A monkey with his tail off is a monkey still."[25]

With those sentiments in mind, Klansmen treated any black deviation from the antebellum code of racial conduct as a criminal offense. Disarming blacks became a common ritual, and whipping was the standard punishment for any word or gesture whites considered "impudent" or "vicious." Instant death awaited any freedman who resisted such "correction." Yalobusha County's knights administered 350 lashes to Turner Nichelson for calling himself a "free man," then hanged another victim who resisted flogging. Berry Smith's whipping nearly provoked a "race war" in Scott County when fellow freedmen flocked to rescue him. Black "insurrection" was a constant fear for Mississippi's white minority. Alarmed by false reports of black militia exercises, Lafayette County Klansmen raided the home of "Captain" Jake Watson, shooting Watson and two other freedmen, burning the house, and dealing out 250 lashes to Watson's supposed "lieutenants." Still unsatisfied, the raiders drowned another thirty freedmen in the river near Yockana, while Yalobusha's knights ambushed and murdered seventy-seven unarmed members of the Loyal League.[26]

Anti-Semitism did not feature as a tenet of the Reconstruction-era KKK, but Klansmen in Attala County worried over the behavior of "a Northern Jew" named Sternberger who ran a store in Kosciusko. Rumors spread that Sternberger had told freedmen to "stand up for their rights." Klan spokesmen warned him to leave town and Sternberger complied, but soon returned with U.S. troops and warrants to arrest his persecutors. Local Klansmen proved "too wiry" for the soldiers and avoided capture, while the Kosciusko den pronounced a death sentence on Sternberger. A Klansman named Rayford subsequently ambushed Sternberger on a rural highway, escaping punishment with a plea that the murder resulted from "a private quarrel."[27]

Some of the Klan's antipathy toward blacks was economically inspired. While wealthy leaders of the order missed their "stolen property," poor whites who filled the lower ranks feared economic competition with freedmen. Subjugation of blacks to their former masters, as planned with the early Black Codes, seemed a perfect solution. Noxubee County Klansmen pledged "to keep [freedmen] from renting land, so that the majority of the white citizens may control labor," but they also punished tenants on established plantations. One den meeting in 1870 voted to "whip out" all black workers on the Wilbanks plantation for acting "rather too free." Aleck Stewart suffered flogging in Monroe County after suing his employer for back wages; the Klansmen who whipped him warned Stewart that "darkeys were through with suing white men, getting their rights in that way." Edward Holman, a white farmer in Marshall County, reported that local Klansmen "do not like to see the negro go ahead. They think his place is in the cotton-field, and that he should stay there." William Coleman offended the Winston County Klan by purchasing eighty acres of land to raise sheep

Mississippi Klansmen pose with their costumes and weapons (Library of Congress).

and hogs. The knights responded by shooting up his house, whipping Coleman, and slashing him with knives when he fought back. White men who dealt with blacks were also imperiled, as Confederate veteran Thomas Brookshire learned in Noxubee County. Brookshire purchased corn and cotton for his rural store from freedmen until Klansmen branded him "a demoralizer of the neighborhood" and threatened him with "a good deal of thrashing."[28]

Throughout the state such tactics had the general effect of driving independent freedmen from their homes. Some fled to more hospitable counties, while others left Mississippi entirely. The resultant labor shortage troubled planters and some Democratic leaders, whose concern was echoed by Grand Wizard Forrest. While traveling by train from Memphis to Jackson, Forrest briefed a reporter from the *Louisville Courier–Journal* on his plan to repopulate the Magnolia State's abandoned lands with Africans. Recalling an era when the slave ship *Wanderer* transported four hundred blacks across the Atlantic and "only six percent died," Forrest called for a new "liberal policy" of black immigration to Dixie. Africans, said Forrest, were "the most imitative creatures in the world" and "the best laborers we have ever had in the South."[29]

Railroads provided yet another realm of economic friction, wherein Forrest had a personal interest. Forrest served first as president of the Memphis, Okolona & Selma Railroad, then switched to the Selma, Marion & Memphis line when his first venture failed. He imported Chinese workers to lay track in Alabama, but stopped short of extending that plan to Mississippi, where a mere fifty-one "celestials" resided in 1880. Like everything else in Reconstruction-era Mississippi, railroad employment often hinged on race and politics. The Grand Gulf & Port Gibson Railroad fired workers who cast Republican ballots, while Klansmen in Alcorn County purged black workers from the Gulf & Ohio line. Frank Diggs, a black mail agent on the run from Selma, Alabama, to Meridian, was murdered by a masked gunman in November 1870 when his train stopped for fuel at Kewanee, in Lauderdale County. Three months later, Klansmen accosted his white replacement at the same place and warned him to stay out of Mississippi.[30]

Unlike its twentieth-century successors, the original Klan espoused no particular religious doctrine. Still, sectarian bigotry persisted, rooted in the antebellum slavery debate that had divided America's churches. Mississippi Klansmen singled out members of the Northern Methodist Episcopal Church for harassment, including a minister named Baldwin who rented land to freedmen in Noxubee County, and Anna Davis in Tupelo, sister of the sect's presiding elder for northern Mississippi. Davis offended the KKK by funding construction of a black church and treating its parishioners as human beings. A local knight named Freeman invaded Davis' home, kidnapped and raped one of her black Sunday-school students, and finally burned the "damned radical church" after announcing his plan to multiple witnesses. Freeman escaped indictment, while Grand Cyclops Samuel Gholson defended him as "a very brave man" from "a very good family." Other Klan arsonists burned black churches in Lauderdale, Lee, Monroe and Winston counties, where some houses of worship doubled as schools for freedmen. Joseph Galloway taught separate Sunday-school classes for white and black children in Monroe County, while encouraging freedmen to read. Local Klansmen accused him of "preaching false doctrine" and conducting military exercises on the side.[31]

Denials notwithstanding, much of the KKK's violence during Reconstruction was blatantly political. Mississippi historians of the early 1900s universally recognized the Klan as an adjunct of the Democratic Party and praised its efforts to overturn "carpetbag" rule. Attala County Klansmen served as poll watchers in Kosciusko, to "make the negroes vote 'right.'" Lafayette County's most conspicuous Democrats included alleged Grand Dragon L.Q.C. Lamar and three confirmed Klansmen: B.F. Goolsby, J.M. Gilmer and J.H. Welch. The same was true in Pontotoc County, where Democratic spokesmen James Fountaine and his son served respectively as grand cyclops and secretary of the local den. In Toccopola the sheriff commissioned W.B. Gilmer, a prominent Democrat and "highly honored teacher" to "devise the means necessary to put down negro uprisings and to keep the negroes in their places." Gilmer led a private posse until Klansmen organized a local den, whereupon he ceded authority to the KKK.

Klansman Thomas Keith served as Newton County's probate clerk, then won election to the state legislature before his arrest with other night riders. Luckily for Keith, his background as a friend and protégé of Judge Hill in Oxford secured his speedy release. Tippah County Klansmen lined up seventy freedmen on one plantation, promising that if any voted Republican on election day they would return and "lick the last one of them." Overall, as historian Julia Kendel observes, the KKK was "one of the most effective means for carrying elections for the Democrats, since the negroes were afraid to vote the Radical ticket, if threatened by them."[32]

Nor were those empty threats. Freedmen in various counties were whipped for casting Republican ballots; others were flogged until they swore to vote the Democratic ticket or to stay home on election day. In Noxubee County, Klan snipers killed a white magistrate in his home. Brookhaven's mayor suffered a similar fate, being fatally injured when night riders lobbed a brick through his window. Scott County's ghouls permitted freedman Sam West to serve one term on the board of supervisors, then killed him when he ran for reelection. Several black Republicans were slain in Alcorn and Monroe counties. Jack Dupree, in Monroe, served as president of a local Republican club until 10 February 1871, when sixty Klansmen dragged him from his home and stripped and flogged him in front of his family. Still unsatisfied, they marched him five miles farther on, beat him again, then disemboweled him with a knife and dumped his mutilated body in McKinley's Creek.

Three months later, in the same neighborhood, a mob of fifty to sixty Klansmen took the Rev. Abraham Wamble from his home and shot him seven times for voting the "radical" ticket. Even before that spate of homicides, in August 1869, Governor Adelbert Ames had warned Gen. John Sherman that Mississippi's rising murder rate did not represent "usual events of ordinary times." Rather, Ames wrote, the slayings were "Ku-Klux outrages mainly based on political enmity and hatred. The war still exists in a very important phase here."[33]

Such crimes were justified, according to the KKK and its apologists, because most members of Mississippi's nonwhite majority (437,404 blacks vs. 353,899 whites in the 1860 census) were simple-minded and amoral — childlike at best, "vicious" and "bestial" at worst. Universal suffrage was a "Black Peril" which Klansmen vowed to resist at all costs.[34]

The Politics of Race

Mississippi's first task, before readmission to the Union, was the preparation of a new state constitution. One hundred delegates convened in Jackson for that purpose on 7 January 1868, pilloried from day one by Democratic newspapers and orators who branded their assembly a "nigger convention" or a "black-and-tan menagerie." The *Panola Star* was typical, describing the convention as a "skunk cage" filled with "nigs," although eighty-three of the delegates were white. Republicans dominated the assemblage with seventy-nine delegates (including twenty-three northern "carpetbaggers"). Over the next four months they labored to produce a document that would, they hoped, find favor with both Congress and the state electorate.[35]

The end result, adopted by the delegates on 15 May, mirrored the U.S. Constitution in most respects, with additional provisions that banned dueling and imprisonment for debt, protected the property rights of married women, established the framework for a comprehensive public school system, granted "all persons" the right to bear arms in self-defense, and extended suffrage to black men as required by Congress. The flip side of that coin was a clause that disfranchised certain Confederate veterans, a move that brought new heapings of scorn from the Democratic press. The *Jackson Clarion* opined that the assembled delegates "have no constituency outside of the ignorant black rabble whom they are seeking to convert into convenient tools for the promotion of their own selfish ends."[36]

It still remained for Mississippi voters to ratify or reject the constitution at a special election in June. A week before those votes were cast, on 15 June, President Johnson removed Governor Humphreys from office and replaced him with Adelbert Ames, a Maine native and graduate of West Point who won a Congressional Medal of Honor at Bull Run and finished the war as a major general. Assigned to occupied South Carolina in 1866 and transferred to Mississippi the following year, Ames thus far had been engaged primarily in prosecuting white terrorists. That experience convinced him that "[f]ire still burns in the hearts of the people and our star-spangled banner or our country's uniform are only needed to fan the flames into wrath."[37]

Johnson's replacement of Governor Humphreys with a New Englander, albeit only as provisional governor, sealed the fate of Mississippi's "black-and-tan" constitution. On 22 June the people spoke, rejecting the constitution by a vote of 63,860 to 56,231. Republicans charged that Democrats had carried the election with threats, violence and fraud. Observer E.J. Lipsey, in DeSoto County, reported that on election day "every road was guarded with armed Ku Klux Klan to intimidate Union voters." Yazoo County rioters attacked Republican parades, seized party banners, and murdered a freedman at Benton. Julia Kendel, writing of Lafayette County, freely admitted that in 1868's election the KKK "was used to the furthest extent, and contributed largely to the grand result."[38]

The Klan's next political object was the election of a friendly president. Grand Wizard Forrest served as a Tennessee delegate to the Democratic National Convention in July 1868, at New York's Tammany Hall, where Horatio Seymour and Francis Blair Jr. received the party's presidential and vice-presidential nominations. Seymour had endeared himself to racists in July 1863, when he addressed rampaging lynch mobs as "my friends" during New York City's draft riots; Blair was a close friend of Forrest himself. The two had appeared arm in arm at a Memphis Odd Fellows convention, in September 1866, after which Blair wrote a letter to his brother Montgomery, extolling Forrest's "noble bearing" and lamenting "all the prejudice that has existed against him" since the Fort Pillow massacre. Blair deemed Forrest "a man perfectly sincere in the desire to accept the condition of affairs as determined by the results of the war," adding a fervent hope that Montgomery "will aid him ... to obtain his objects" in the railroad business. The *Memphis Avalanche*, in turn, called Blair "an earnest advocate of the President's policy and the recognition of the rights which ample justice demands for the South."[39]

The Democratic nominee was General Ulysses Grant, reviled by ex–Confederates from Texas to Virginia. Mississippi's failure to adopt a constitution in June 1868 barred its citizens from voting in November's presidential election — where Grant defeated the Seymour-Blair ticket by 309,584 votes.

While the KKK committed fewer crimes in the Magnolia State that autumn than in other parts of Dixie, its members still found time to persecute blacks and Republicans. One target, in Panola County, was James Alcorn, an old-line Whig from Illinois who settled in Mississippi as a young lawyer and accumulated large plantations complete with slaves and served in the antebellum state legislature. After Appomattox, Alcorn joined the Republican Party and revealed an unexpected passion for black political equality. Klansmen raided one of Alcorn's Panola County plantations on 8 December 1868 — one day after he rented it to freedmen — and inflicted an estimated six thousand dollars in damages. On 1 January 1869 Alcorn wrote to Illinois Rep. Elihu Washburne: "I thought it best to guard the remainder of my plantations as well as I can until I see what Congress may do under Genl Grant's administration. Should there be no improvement, then I will make the best disposition of my estates, and leave the State."[40]

Wizard Forrest's public support for the Democratic ticket proved "a significant negative influence" among northern voters in 1868, but all was not lost for his friend Frank Blair. The four-term former congressman won election to the U.S. Senate in 1870 and took his seat in time to aid Forrest with a federal investigation of the KKK.[41] Meanwhile, Mississippi Klansmen had a new fight on their hands, struggling to help their state win readmission to the Union without surrendering its racist principles.

No further progress could be made without a constitution capable of winning "radical" support in Congress. Aside from considering the critical document, finally stripped of eleven provisions offensive to white Democrats, Mississippi voters also would cast ballots in December 1869 for a governor, state legislators and assorted district officers. Republicans appeared to have the new black vote secured for candidate James Alcorn, but Conservatives sought to achieve through chaos what they could not win with frank appeals to white supremacy.

Three brand-new parties thus appeared in Mississippi. A Democratic White Man's Party brooked no compromise with freedmen. A Constitutional Union floated vague promises of dubious sincerity to black voters. The mainstream Conservative vehicle, christened the National Union Republican Party, nominated Louis Dent, a brother-in-law of President Grant, for governor and named a freedman as his secretary of state, with vows to perpetuate black suffrage. Still, their message smacked of old-fashioned racism, as when one party spokesman told a black audience, "You can't blame us for your slavery. Most of you were well treated as slaves."[42]

In Washington, President Grant declined the chance to support his brother-in-law, cleaving to Alcorn as the only true Republican candidate. On 5 March 1869, his first full day in office, Grant promoted Adelbert Ames to serve as military governor of the district embracing Arkansas and Mississippi. Ames also remained Mississippi's provisional governor pending election of a replacement, pursuing what his enemies dubbed a "crusade" against the Southern Way of Life. In compliance with federal law, Ames removed various state and county officials elected in 1868, replacing them with candidates who could pronounce the "iron-clad" oath of loyalty. He also slashed the state's poll tax by two-thirds, to $1.50, and extended it to Rebel veterans formerly exempt. Lastly, Ames dropped the color bar on jury service, thus enabling freedmen to "protect themselves from much oppression and injustice."[43]

Violence ensued. In June 1869 wealthy Democrat Edward Yerger fatally stabbed Lt. Col. Joseph Crane, appointed by Ames as provisional mayor of Jackson, after Crane served a tax lien on Yerger's piano. Troops arrested Yerger, but the U.S. Supreme Court dismissed the military charges, leaving him unpunished. Ames next appointed voter registrars statewide and ordered each party to supply pairs of poll watchers (one black, one white) on election day.

While James Alcorn campaigned on a pledge that "society should no longer be governed by the pistol and the Bowie knife," Ku Klux violence escalated and full-scale riots erupted in several counties. Before the final votes were cast, Ames distributed his 322 soldiers to keep the peace as best they could, warning General Sherman that Mississippi's campaign "is not between two established parties, as they are elsewhere, but between loyal men and a class of men who are disloyal." Victory for "the men who took this State from the Union," Ames wrote, would produce a "reign of terror" and leave blacks "reduced to a condition bordering on serfdom." The Democratic *People's Paper*, in DeSoto County, aired a warning of its own for Democrats, alleging Republican bribery and intimidation of freedmen.[44] Eight days before the final vote the paper ran a rousing call to arms:

> Stand by the polls until the last vote is cast. Be sure to guard against the possibility of fraud.... Look out, Conservatives, and be ready for any emergency.... To your posts every man in Desoto County.... Work! Work!! WORK!!! Look out for frauds of every character. Thieves and robbers have been imported by Ames from Memphis as managers of the elections. Watch! Watch!! WATCH!!![45]

In fact, the two-day election witnessed near-unanimous ratification of the redacted constitution, with an easy victory for Alcorn's Republican slate. Governor Ames, ruling on borrowed time, ordered the state legislature to convene on 11 January 1870. That body instantly appointed Ames to fill a U.S. Senate seat. Congress granted Mississippi's readmission to the Union one month later, and Governor Alcorn was inaugurated on 10 March.[46] A new war for control of Mississippi had begun.

Escalating Violence

Alcorn's administration pursued a program designed to reassure white Conservatives while safeguarding the civil and political rights of freedmen, including establishment of public schools for both races. While free to students, those schools created a new tax burden deemed onerous by many white residents. An economic upswing in early 1870 blunted the program's initial impact, but subsequent cotton crop failures, coupled with a legislative change in the timing of tax collections, producing dual levies before year's end, amplified white resistance.[47]

Various scholarly sources maintain that "most" of Mississippi's Ku Klux violence during Reconstruction emanated from seven counties — Chickasaw, Kemper, Lauderdale, Lowndes, Monroe, Noxubee and Winston — ranged along the Alabama border. That misconception seemingly arises from the fact that sixty-nine of eighty-one Mississippi witnesses questioned by congressional investigators during 1871 resided in those seven counties — including twenty-eight from Lowndes County and fifteen each from Monroe and Noxubee — while only two were called from Warren County and five other counties furnished one witness apiece. (Two others came from out of state.) In fact, the KKK was organized statewide, with violent acts reported from at least thirty-five of Mississippi's seventy-six existing counties. The three most lethal incidents on record, accounting for 223 murdered freedmen, occurred in Carroll, Lafayette and Yalobusha counties.[48]

That said, it is true that eleven of Mississippi's most Klan-infested counties bordered other states where the order was both well established and habitually violent. Alcorn, DeSoto, Marshall, Tippah and Tishomingo all border Tennessee, the Klan's birthplace, and Tishomingo also shares a boundary with Alabama. DeSoto County, close to Memphis, fell under particular influence from Grand Wizard Forrest throughout Reconstruction. Kemper, Lauderdale, Lowndes, Monroe and Noxubee counties all adjoin Alabama, whose border proved extremely fluid throughout Reconstruction. Cotton State Klansmen and deputies alike made frequent raids across the line, particularly in Lauderdale County, where their depredations sparked a bloody riot in 1871. Meanwhile, Adams and Warren counties border Louisiana, where the KKK and allied Knights of the White Camellia achieved four-figure body counts during 1868's presidential campaign.[49]

Along the Tennessee border, Wizard Forrest served as the "chief organizer" of DeSoto County's Klan, launching "maneuvers" around Hernando in April 1868, although reports of its "debut" in the *People's Paper* only surfaced six months later, when Klansmen stood accused of burning a cabin and terrorizing its black occupants outside Senatobia. Dr. William Compton was the order's chief propagandist in Marshall County, while cofounder Henry Myers won election as sheriff.

Ruth Watkins denies any "deeds of extreme violence" in Marshall County, then devotes her next sentence to the description of a bungled plot to assassinate Republican leader Nelson Gill. Local knights also whipped a freedman for "insolence" toward his former master and liberated a white murder suspect from jail at Holly Springs. Tippah County Klansmen threatened a federal investigator and whipped freedmen who voted Republican or otherwise forgot "their place." In Alcorn County, Congress documented floggings of six freedmen and white Republican E.J. Stubblefield, whose nephew was also pistol-whipped. In March 1870 Alcorn Klansmen dragged two prisoners from jail, shooting the black defendant to pieces and mutilating and hanging his white cohort. Knights from the same den raped Frazier Duncan's wife when they failed to catch the black Republican at home. Members of Tishomingo County's den, founded by Klansmen from neighboring McNary County, Tennessee, spent their nights "prowling through the county constantly," indulging in "whippings and killings both." Led by Capt. Joe Hicks, they shot up the home of a widow named Hunnicut (leaving her daughter crippled for life), whipped a white Republican named Richardson, and hounded from their county a Confederate veteran named Newman.[50]

Ranging southward along the Mississippi-Alabama border, congressional investigators documented seven murders and ten whippings in Monroe County, a tally that was certainly conservative. Republican Allen Huggins became the nation's best-known Ku Klux victim when his torn and bloody shirt was brandished on the floor of Congress to arouse the wrath of northern voters. Fifty Klansmen stormed the Athens jail to lynch the Flint brothers in August 1870, and Aberdeen's mayor fled the county in fear for his life, while the local *Examiner* pretended to believe that freedmen ran the KKK. A subsequent anti–Klan rally convened by Aberdeen's best citizens failed to stop night riders from burning churches and schools.[51]

Lowndes County received the most attention from congressional investigators, but the hearings were anticlimactic. While witnesses, including a Ku Klux defector, described gangs of fifty or sixty Klansmen riding "every night pretty nearly," whipping freedmen and kidnapping others who were never seen again, murdering eight to ten victims in the twelve months ending July 1871, details were meager. Testimony identified Andy Crosby as the county's grand cyclops, while Congress named sixteen specific flogging victims and three persons killed by the Klan. One of those slain, a freedman named Perkins, apparently died from a dose of poison. Klansmen shot another freedman for quarreling with his white landlord and killed a third without apparent cause. Local witnesses observed that Klansmen often seemed to be intoxicated during their nocturnal raids.[52]

In Noxubee County, investigators documented multiple arsons, eleven specific floggings, and nine murders linked to the Klan. Most victims were black, but Klansmen also whipped two white men from Chicago after jurors acquitted them of conspiring to rob a local merchant. A white victim named Shipley suffered fatal burns when Klansmen torched his home, and night riders also shot deputy U.S. marshal Charles Wissler in his house. Republican sheriff William Chisolm maintained relative order in Kemper County, after fielding troops against the KKK in 1869, but Klan defector John Taliaferro still counted seven local murders between July 1870 and June 1871. Congress identified one of those victims and heard testimony detailing the Klan's raid on a plantation owned by Lieutenant Governor Ridgeley Powers. Thomas Adams, a white Republican, also suffered flogging, as the KKK explained, to "learn him how to take a lash like a nigger." Lauderdale County's most infamous outbreak was the Meridian riot of March 1871, but Congress documented three murders before the riot and "several" more afterward. More than any other Mississippi county, Lauderdale suffered incursions by the Alabama Klan.[53]

Five counties bordering the eastern tier were also plagued by Ku Klux violence. Investigators in Chickasaw documented one murder, two nonfatal shootings, multiple arsons, and several whippings. Flogging victims included a white man accused of incest, two white Republicans and one "radical's" wife. When human victims proved elusive, Chickasaw Klansmen amused themselves by shooting horses. In neighboring Clay County, Klansmen kidnapped a white man named Cunningham who was never seen again. Three dens terrorized Oktibbeha County, led (and defended in court when need be) by Henry Muldrow. Republican sheriff Homer Powers enforced the law haphazardly, winning praise from Klan apologists as a "friend of the white man and an advocate of good government."

Winston County knights invaded the jail to kill black rape suspect Allen Bird, one of six murder victims identified by congressional researchers. Ruth Watkins calls the KKK "the most important organization" in Reconstruction-era Newton County, where it shared members and duties with the Jack Robinsons. White terrorists killed several freedmen during a "possum hunt" near Hickory, in February 1868, while Eugene Carleton—founder of the Decatur den—began a long career as chancery clerk in 1871. Watkins's history of Newton

County denies any corporal punishment by Klansmen, then acknowledges "bodily correction" of freedmen documented by "many statements ... about the whipping of negroes and other forms of violence."[54]

North-central Mississippi saw more than its share of racist mayhem during Reconstruction. Five separate dens launched raids in Panola County, briefly deterred by a half-dozen federal arrests in February 1869. But skirmishing with sheriff's deputies resumed in autumn of that year, tacitly encouraged by Democratic spokesman R.H. Taylor, who had served with General Forrest in the war. John Kyle describes Panola's Klan as "scrupulous" in avoiding bloodshed, then admits to "many brutal acts" by masked night riders, including fourteen murders committed between August 1870 and March 1871. Leading Democrats founded the KKK in Lafayette County, while members of Pontotoc County's Sarepta den provided frequent "aid" to whites in Dallas, the Yocona bottom, and surrounding areas. Julia Kendel identifies Alexander Phillips as grand cyclops of Lafayette's "Radical Ku Klux Klan" in 1870, but she fails to explain how it differed from dens led by B.F. Goolsby, W.T. Ivey, or Florida transplant R.W. Phipps.[55]

When not raiding across the county line, Pontotoc Klansmen were busy enough on their own turf, collaborating or competing with like-minded groups, including the Jack Robinsons, the Seventy-Six Society, Native Sons of the South, and the White Rose Society. Toccopola's den had a quasi-official sheriff's commission to "keep the negroes in their places." Attorney James Fountaine hosted visits by Grand Wizard Forrest and L.Q.C. Lamar while keeping an eye on local freedmen and Republicans.

The Pontotoc Klan's primary targets were Republican spokesman Robert Flournoy, publisher of the "inflammatory" newspaper *Equal Rights*, and a pair of "carpetbag" teachers who served black students. The teachers, Sarah Cole and Patty Day, compounded their offense by boarding with a black woman until Klansmen drove them from the county. Flournoy proved more obstinate, sparking a bungled murder attempt on 12 May 1871 that left one Klansman mortally wounded. (Despite claims from apologists that the night riders merely sought "fun and frolic," meaning "no harm at all," the dying man confessed their plan to kill Flournoy.) Klansman Tom Saddler, widely recognized as leader of the raid, weathered that storm and won election as sheriff six months later.[56]

Lee County's Klan followed the strange recruiting practice of drafting members without their knowledge, then informing candidates of their induction. By such means the den enlisted "men prominent in both Church and State," bound by a death-oath to preserve the order's secrets. "Vicious negroes" received marathon floggings, at least one resulting in death, and Klansmen also visited white neighbors for "the most trivial offenses." Hal Fisher, son of a judge in Grenada, led Tallahatchie County's Klan on sporadic raids, but Yalobusha County saw more action. There, knights lynched three freedmen accused of various crimes and executed an informer, Bug Green, whose testimony resulted in several indictments. It hardly mattered, though, since L.Q.C. Lamar defended the accused successfully and General Galusha Pennypacker—commanding the Department of Mississippi—showed little inclination to pursue Klansmen. (After the den's third lynching Pennypacker told the killers "that they had done right, but that ... burning [the body] was wrong.") Calhoun County's violent den, at Sarepta, drew most of its members from Pontotoc County. Grenada County, formed from Yalobusha in 1870, distinguished itself with six dens comprising "the best men in the county." Its most memorable action was the murder of John Scurlock, a seven-foot-tall "saddle colored negro" who offended Klansmen by running unsuccessfully for the state legislature.[57]

Historian Fred Witty observes that Democrats in Reconstruction-era Carroll County were "unexcelled by any in the State for genuine bravery and love of white supremacy." His history of the region first denies any Ku Klux organization, then grants the existence of an early den at Lodi (part of Montgomery County after 1871) and admits that "bands of young white men were active all over the county in regulating negroes." Lt. Gov. Ridgeley Powers spoke more emphatically, describing "a perfect reign of terror among the colored people there" in 1869. Authorities jailed Klansman Joe Tribble for killing a freedman, but attorney Edward Walthall defended him "on condition that the Ku Klux would fill the court room in order that the jury might be picked from them."

Troops briefly quelled the Carroll County violence, whereupon Montgomery County erupted, Klansmen riding from their quarters in Winona's Masonic lodge to punish "any misdemeanor of negroes." One victim received a hundred lashes for being "impudent" to a Confederate war widow. Attala County knights traced their lineage to a visit from a Kentucky organizer, and while author Edward Coleman claims that they found "no occasion for stringent measures," local Klansmen killed the merchant Sternberger (previously discussed) while terrorizing many others. Surviving victims included a St. Louis merchant who urged blacks to defend themselves and a freedman named Orange, whipped for naming a knight as a horse-thief.[58]

Central Mississippi witnessed Ku Klux violence in at least four counties. Yazoo County knights raided Republican rallies, seized banners, and terrorized black voters, encouraged by the *Yazoo Banner*'s publication of a song whose chorus ran: "If you belong to the Ku Klux Klan, here's my heart and here's my hand." Leake County Klansmen operated as, or in conjunction with, the night riding Washington Brothers. Hinds County's ghouls detested Charles Caldwell, a freedman who won election to the state senate and commanded a troop of black soldiers based in Clinton. Enemies finally lured Caldwell to a basement, shot him several times, then carried his corpse to the street, where it was "grotesquely turned completely over by the impact of innumerable shots fired at close range." Historian Forrest Cooper credits Scott County's Klan with "some valuable work" in the field of voter intimidation, noting that "hardly a month passed without some murder or assault" in the district. Besides the Klan proper, Cooper also notes the existence of several unnamed groups "whose object it was to persuade the negro to occupy his place and to vote the Democratic ticket, or not vote at all."[59]

Southwestern Mississippi produced fewer reports of Klan violence, but the order still saw action. Klansmen in Franklin and Lawrence counties sometimes styled themselves Knights of the Black Cross, but they were Ku Klux nonetheless. Lawrence spawned three active dens at Brookhaven, Hebron and Monticello, then lost the Brookhaven chapter when Lincoln County was formed in 1870. Still, the Klan carried on as elsewhere in the state, rattling chains outside the homes of freedmen after nightfall and whipping some like Bill Dotson, who stood accused of "an unmentionable crime." Brookhaven's den included "nearly all" the town's white Democrats, some of whom conspired to kill the mayor with a brick lobbed through his window.[60]

Such activities were not risk-free for Klansmen. Wesley Pulliam suffered fatal gunshot wounds in Chickasaw County when farmer John Conklin ambushed a group of Ku Klux raiders killing horses. Klansman George Evans died in a similar fashion while raiding the Kemper County plantation owned by Lt. Gov. Ridgeley Powers. In Lowndes County, a "good Union man" named Lee killed three or four of the raiders who sought to drive him from his home. John Plair, a freedman in Oktibbeah County, faced murder charges after shooting a Klansman who raided his farm. The deputies sent to arrest him made Plair ride "in front at a certain distance" for the convenience of Klan snipers who killed him en route to the county jail. Richard Dillard, mortally wounded in the foiled attempt to kidnap Robert Flournoy, issued a deathbed confession to conspiracy, yet local whites still raised donations for a monument to mark his grave. Another unnamed knight was killed by freedmen in Oktibbeah County after he burned a school near Tampico. Tippah County Klansmen posted death threats for deputy marshal Henry Clark, but got the message when Clark left a message of his own "informing them ... [that] in case any of them got tired of living they could come around and see me and I would do the best I could for them."[61]

"Disbandment" and Rejuvenation

While some Ku Klux apologists absolve the Klan of any wrongdoing, others admit that the order fell into "low and violent hands," suggesting infiltration by "ruffians" or outright usurpation of the Ku Klux name by nonmembers. On 16 January 1869, in strife-torn Tennessee, state legislators authorized widespread militia action to suppress the KKK. Nine days later, Wizard Forrest issued a dramatic but confusing order from his Memphis headquarters, the full import of which is still debated among modern students of the Klan.[62]

Two years later, in his testimony before Congress, Forrest would deny Klan membership, then claim that he suppressed the order sometime during 1868. He was deliberately vague on details, and his sworn statement conflicted with the memories of other Klansmen who recalled the order's abolition falling sometime between March and August 1869. In fact, Forrest's order of 25 January commanded that Ku Klux masks and disguises should be "entirely abolished and destroyed" in the presence of a grand cyclops. The order also banned further Klan demonstrations (unless ordered by a grand titan or higher officer) and prohibited disarming of freedmen (unless they plotted insurrection). Also forbidden were jail raids and lynchings, political floggings, and threats in the name of the Klan. That said, Forrest decreed, "This order is not to be understood to dissolve the Order of the Ku Klux Klan, but it is hereby held more firmly together and more faithfully bound to each other in any emergency that may come."[63]

Forrest's order had little impact on Tennessee Klansmen, and none at all outside of the Volunteer State. Indeed, Mississippi's Klan "took on new life" and experienced "considerable reorganization" after January 1869. Forrest himself reportedly launched a new den in Monroe County during 1869 while visiting the region with his brother on railroad business. A year later, John Cole of Saltillo was "sent to Memphis" by persons unknown "to take the required oath and to get a commission to organize the Klan in Lee County." British traveler Robert Somers, touring the Magnolia State in January 1871, observed that "the remains of the Confederate armies—swept after a long and heroic day of fair fight, from the field—flitted before the eyes of the people in their weird and midnight shape of a 'Ku-Klux Klan.'"[64]

Governor Alcorn, eager to suppress the KKK, signed three new statutes between April and July 1870. The first appropriated $50,000 for informers, detectives, attorneys, and other personnel required to prosecute the Klan; the second granted Alcorn power to raise a militia; and the third punished persons who "prowl ... travel ... ride ... walk" or otherwise appeared in public while disguised. Simply donning Klan regalia made the wearer liable to a $500 fine and indeterminate jail time; threatening while masked meant one to five years in prison; and actual assault raised the maximum term to ten years. Another round of legislation, passed in 1871, taxed Bowie knives and pistols, banned concealed weapons, and authorized removal of trials from Klan-ridden counties.[65]

Enforcing anti–Ku Klux legislation proved impossible in parts of Mississippi. Certain county sheriffs—such as those in Alcorn, Lafayette and Pontotoc—were either Klansmen or known allies of the order. Ripley's justice of the peace refused to hear testimony from freedmen victimized by the KKK, while General Pennypacker ("always very lenient towards the Southern people") warned indicted Klansmen in time for them to flee the state. Those held for trial were ably defended by the likes of Samuel Gholson, L.Q.C. Lamar and Edward Walthall. Sympathetic judges frequently dismissed all charges, while Klan-packed juries guaranteed acquittal for the remainder and hometown crowds feted "exonerated" terrorists as heroes.[66] In such an atmosphere, with justice subverted, violence could only go from bad to worse.

The War on Schools

Public education was the centerpiece of Governor Alcorn's "radical" platform, consuming more public money in 1870 than all other government programs combined. It also proved remarkably successful, establishing the state's first university for blacks and enrolling half of all Mississippi's children in elementary classes by 1875. White conservatives despised "free" education on three grounds: its cost to taxpayers, the antebellum phobia concerning educated blacks, and fear of race-mixing in public schools. Alcorn proposed no integrated schooling, but the fear remained, articulated by the *Jackson Clarion*'s warning that "a fund will be raised by taxing the property of people to build up a gigantic system of 'Public Education,' under the control of imported amalgamationists." Before year's end the Mississippi Klan surpassed all others in the South at purging public schools and teachers from the state.[67]

All public schools were bad, in Ku Klux eyes, for the tax burden they imposed on whites; but schools for blacks received more Klan attention, and black schools with white teachers suffered worst of all. Klan apologists maintained that "[e]very teacher of a negro school, supported at the expense of white people, was a radical tool and emissary to excite race hatred among the negroes." Alexander Phillips, leader of Lafayette County's Radical KKK, "poured out his wrath upon the Alcorn system of education" and declared the new black university "a nuisance," while opposing even segregated schools "in every particular." Teachers throughout the state received Klan threats, patterned on one that warned: "We can inform you that we are the law itself and that an order from these Headquarters is supreme above all others." Most were simply told to leave the state, though one — a teacher named Ebart, in Aberdeen — reported the Klan's offer to help him collect tuition if he transformed his public school into a private academy.[68]

Where threats failed, violence followed. Scott County Democrats regarded T.W. Crevette as an "arrogant, unscrupulous, sullen negro teacher" who "poisoned" the minds of his students "by doctrines of political and social equality" before Klansmen smashed his windows and drove him away. Armed knights physically prevented collection of school taxes in several counties and burned the scrip collected for Winston County's schools. Chickasaw County Klansmen kidnapped teacher Cornelius McBride, pistol-whipping him and flogging him with black-gum switches before he fought clear and escaped. Winston County teacher Nathan Cannon was less fortunate, though he survived his injuries.[69]

Allen Huggins was the most famous victim of the Mississippi Klan's protracted war on schools. An Ohio native, former Union officer and hard-line Republican, Huggins settled in Monroe County after the Civil War, serving first as sheriff, then assistant tax collector, and finally as superintendent of public schools. The Baptist church in Aberdeen refused him membership and Huggins suffered constant threats, but he endured. On the night of 9 March 1871, while he was staying at a friend's house, Klansmen called Huggins out and ordered him to leave the county. He refused and bore the ensuing seventy-five lashes with sufficient stoicism that his floggers deemed him "pretty gritty," enduring his punishment "like a little man." Despite death threats and a subsequent campaign of character assassination, Huggins remained to prosecute his assailants, while an army officer dispatched his torn and bloodied shirt to Washington. There, Massachusetts Rep. Ben Butler brandished it on the floor of Congress, the literal first example of "waving the bloody shirt."[70]

Destruction of schools was the surest way to put them out of business, and Mississippi Klansmen never shrank from arson. Local witnesses later quibbled over the number of schools burned, versus those "interrupted" or "broken up," and while no final tally exists, state legislator O.C. French counted twenty-five schools burned statewide in the year ending 3 June 1871. That estimate was clearly too conservative, since other tabulations list twenty-six burned in Monroe County alone, two more in Kemper, and one each in Oktibbeha and Yalobusha counties. No schools remained in Lowndes, Noxubee or Winston counties when Klansmen finished their work. Night riders also torched the home of Chickasaw County school superintendent A.J. Jamison. The Rev. John Avery, a Winston County teacher, identified his own brothers as the Klansmen who burned his home.[71]

The Meridian Riot

No single event of Mississippi's Reconstruction era was more notorious than the Klan-led riot at Meridian, in March 1871. The two-day pogrom enraged Republicans, guaranteed passage of anti–Klan legislation in Congress, and thereby set the stage for a new phase in the guerrilla war to rescue white supremacy.

Ironically, the outbreak had its roots in Alabama, where incessant Ku Klux raids drove many freedmen to desert their Sumter County farms and seek refuge around Meridian. White farmers deputized a former slave, Adam Kennard, and dispatched him to Mississippi with Klansmen in tow to retrieve their fugitive field hands. Kennard's "posse" made several successful forays across the state line in January 1871, before resistance organized in Meridian. When Kennard returned in February, masked men dragged him from his boardinghouse and whipped him Ku-Klux style, prompting Kennard to file charges under

Mississippi's new anti–Klan legislation. He named Daniel Price, a white Republican and teacher of an all-black school, as leader of the flogging party and filed a claim for the standing $5,000 reward. The *Meridian Gazette* promptly branded Price "Grand Cyclops of the negro Ku Klux." At Price's preliminary hearing, Kennard appeared with a gang of Alabama Klansmen, calling for blood, but the hearing was postponed, leaving the visitors to satisfy themselves by snatching three more Sumter County fugitives. Price subsequently fled the county, while Mayor William Sturgis of Meridian accused white Democrats of sponsoring the border-hopping raids.[72]

The mayor's remarks, while almost certainly accurate, inflamed his political enemies. Their first move was a call for Governor Alcorn to replace Sturgis with a Democratic mayor. Sturgis sent his own delegation to Alcorn, including freedmen William Dennis and Warren Tyler (a fellow teacher with Daniel Price at Meridian's black school, named by Kennard as one of his floggers). Alcorn denied their request for troops to repel Alabama invaders, whereupon the delegates returned and called a public meeting on Saturday, 4 March. Black speakers at that rally included the Rev. J. Aaron Moore — a blacksmith and state legislator for Lauderdale County — and militia officer William Clopton, who told his audience that "Ku Kluxing has got to be stopped." Soon after nightfall on 4 March, fire engulfed the store run by Mayor Sturgis and his brothers. The streets filled with armed whites and "turbulent negroes," but violence was averted when the freedmen returned to their homes. By Sunday, Clopton, Moore and Warren Tyler were in jail, charged with arson and disorderly conduct.[73]

Conservatives rallied on Monday, their ranks augmented by numerous "professional rioters" from Alabama. That afternoon, Judge Bramlette convened a preliminary hearing for the three defendants in a courtroom packed with armed men. Midway through the proceedings, Warren Tyler challenged the veracity of a white witness named Brantley or Patton (accounts differ), whereupon the witness rushed toward him with an upraised cane. Gunfire erupted in the courtroom, killing Judge Bramlette and several black spectators. Tyler fled to a nearby shop, pursued by a deputy sheriff and several Klansmen who murdered him there. Finding defendant Clopton wounded but alive in court, white gunmen carried him upstairs and tossed him from the second-story balcony, then cut his throat when the drop failed to kill him. The Rev. Moore escaped in the confusion, finally making his way on foot to Jackson and relative safety, while a mob of some three hundred Klansmen and allies scoured Meridian, burning Moore's home and church, killing an estimated thirty freemen and wounding many more. Trains leaving Meridian on 7 March carried visiting combatants as far eastward as Eutaw, Alabama.[74]

The Meridian massacre outraged Republicans and hastened passage of anti–Klan legislation in Congress. Mississippi Democrats who orchestrated the event then chastised "radicals" for turning the slaughter "to partisan uses." In fact, as Klan historian Allen Trelease observes, the outburst was part of a white coup d'état that caused Mayor Sturgis to flee for his life, leaving Meridian's government in Democratic hands. State legislators authorized investigation of the riot on 21 March, ultimately questioning 116 witnesses to no avail. Six whites faced preliminary charges of assault, intent to kill and unlawful assembly, but an April grand jury refused to indict them. Two months later, congressional investigators reexamined the pogrom without deciding who fired the first shot. The only person ever punished was an Alabama Klansman convicted of raping a black woman during the riot.[75]

Washington Responds

Reports of escalating southern violence evoked response from "radicals" in Congress over time. The first of three Enforcement Acts, passed on 31 May 1870, penalized public officials and private citizens who deprived any person of civil rights, while permitting use of federal troops to protect freedmen. On 28 February 1871, a second statute granted federal officers and courts control over registration and voting in congressional elections. It was the third Enforcement Act, however, which provoked the greatest storm of passion from Capitol Hill to the occupied South. Popularly dubbed the Ku Klux Act, it broadly defined typical Klan behavior as rebellion against the United States, imposing prison terms of six months to six years, with fines of five hundred to five thousand dollars on convicted offenders. Furthermore, the statute authorized declaration of martial law, with suspension of habeas corpus, in regions where the President declared a state of insurrection to exist.[76]

The Ku Klux Act infuriated Democrats on both sides of the Mason-Dixon Line. Francis Blair, Missouri's senator and longtime friend of Wizard Forrest, turned the fight against its passage into a personal war against Adelbert Ames. It was lamentable, Blair said, that his Senate colleagues had rejected William Sharkey "to give place to one of these major generals [Ames] and a vagabond negro [Sen. Hiram Revels], the twin emblems of Radical supremacy in this country." Ames, in turn, retorted, "What a remarkable spectacle! He who wore the blue in the days of rebellion now leading the rebel gray!" Blair's rhetoric could not eclipse the sight of Allen Huggins's bloody shirt, however, and the Ku Klux Act passed Congress on 20 April 1871.[77]

Passage of the Enforcement Acts did not ensure their usefulness in the Magnolia State. G. Wiley Wells, U.S. attorney for Mississippi's northern district, complained to Congress in November 1871 that key witnesses in Ku Klux cases often "were run off or somehow disappeared." Two months later, Wells told attorney general George Williams that Klansmen had murdered four grand jury witnesses. Nor were witnesses alone at risk: Charles Caldwell, one of the grand jurors who grilled terrorist leader T.M. Scanlan in Newton County, was also murdered. Other witnesses were simply bribed or threatened into silence, while Klansmen packed juries to acquit indicted comrades at trial.[78]

Despite its oath of secrecy, the KKK gave up its secrets to investigators. Henry Clark, employed by Wiley Wells, identified some leaders of the Klan, along with those of several fronts and allied groups. A Missouri native and Union veteran, imprisoned at Andersonville during the Civil War, Clark nearly infiltrated Tippah County's Klan himself before "congestion of the brain" prevented his initiation. Two informants penetrated the Yalobusha den, but assassins killed one in Coffeeville, while General Pennybacker warned leading Klansmen in time to flee before their indictment. Another spy, one "Stomy" Jordan, failed to deceive Lafayette County's knights. After the first stage of his welcome to the order featured whipping with a stirrup strap, Jordan abandoned plans to take the final oath. Where infiltration failed, victims, including Robert Flournoy, Allen Huggins and a host of freedmen, managed to identify the night riders who threatened and assaulted them.[79]

Mississippi produced the first charges filed under the Ku Klux Act, when federal grand jurors in Oxford indicted twenty-eight Monroe County Klansmen on 17 June 1871. On 29 March the defendants had whipped and hanged freedman Alexander Page without appar-

Former slaves were stripped of federal protection against racist violence in the mid–1870s (Florida State Archives).

ent motive, leaving his body in a shallow grave. Two black participants in the raid turned state's evidence against their comrades, while Page's widow identified several of the lynchers. The *Jackson Clarion* complained that "[m]en have been dragged from their homes without knowledge of the cause of their arrest, at the suggestion of malicious and procured perjurers." Lead defense counsel L.Q.C. Lamar brawled with federal marshals in court, while Klansman Samuel Gholson lent the team his legal expertise. The *Iuka Gazette* predicted that prosecution would be difficult, and so it proved.

Prosecutor Wiley Wells survived a near-fatal dose of poison on 24 June, and snipers killed deputy marshal Charles Wissler — a target of L.Q.C. Lamar's wrath in court — at his home five months later. Between those events, Wells informed attorney general Amos Akerman that "[e]very person who has acted as a United States Deputy Marshal & aided in the arrest of Ku Klux have been either imprisoned or are under indictment." Judge Robert Hill released the prisoners on bond, then accepted their guilty pleas in December and dealt suspended prison terms to all concerned.[80]

Meanwhile, in March 1871 Congress created a joint select committee to investigate the Ku Klux terror in Dixie. Its members included seven senators and fourteen representatives chaired by Pennsylvania Senator John Scott on behalf of the Republican majority, while Missouri's Frank Blair set the Democratic tone by minimizing southern violence, blaming the victims, and pursuing claims of carpetbag corruption. Public hearings on the Mississippi Klan lasted from 8 June to 4 August in Washington, then resumed in November before subcommittees in Macon and Columbus. Eighty-one witnesses described affairs in the Magnolia State, ranging from Klansmen Samuel Gholson and Dr. William Compton (who denied any role in the KKK) to Mississippi's lieutenant governor, federal prosecutors, and Sheriff William Chisolm of Kemper County. Klan victims called to testify included Robert Flournoy, Allen Huggins, and dozens more whose names had never previously reached the North. Overall, the committee documented forty-five slayings, eighteen nonfatal shootings and seventy-five whippings— while overlooking the bulk of Klan crimes.[81]

Grand Wizard Forrest addressed the committee in Washington, on 27 June 1871. Chairman Scott sought amplification of an August 1868 newspaper interview, wherein Forrest threatened a massacre of Tennessee Republicans while claiming statewide Klan membership of 40,000, with 550,000 Klansmen in the South at large. Forrest first denied that he spoke "twenty words" to the reporter, then backpedaled to claim misquotes from a twenty-minute interview. He admitted superficial knowledge of the Klan, then claimed he "had it broken up and disbanded" by speaking to various members. Forrest confessed to joining the Pale Faces—"some called them Ku Klux"— then admitted *and* denied joining the rival Knights of the White Camellia. The KKK, he claimed, had been "disorganized" in 1868, and during its existence had accepted "no man who was not a gentleman." Overall, Forrest maintained, "It was a matter I knew very little about.... All my efforts were addressed to stop it, disband it, and prevent it." Afterward, when asked about his testimony by a journalist, the wizard winked and said, "I lied like a gentleman."[82]

Back in Mississippi, federal prosecutors did their best against the Klan. Victim Robert Flournoy filed charges against various Pontotoc County knights, including "almost all the principal citizens" of Cherry Creek, but the cases were later dismissed. Twenty-six arrests followed the burning of a Republican merchant's store in Oktibbeah County, but Judge Robert Hill "showed himself the white man's friend," postponing trial of those defendants indefinitely. On 16 January 1872 Wiley Wells advised attorney general George Williams that "I cannot get witnesses as all feel it is sure death to testify before the grand jury." Nonetheless, Wells indicted 758 Klansmen during 1872–73, convicting 540. Barely 1 percent of those convicted received prison time, Judge Hill preferring a standard twenty-five-dollar fine with a peace bond of one thousand dollars to encourage future good behavior.

Frustrated but still hopeful, Wells wrote to attorney general Williams on 2 April 1872: "If our kind hearted judge can only be kept from destroying the effect produced by the convictions of these midnight assassins, I can within six months rid this entire district of Ku Klux." Such was not to be the case, however, as Judge Hill *reduced* his penalties for terrorists over the next four years. A total of 307 Mississippi whites faced charges of violating the Enforcement Acts in 1874–75, with only 63 convicted and none imprisoned. No convictions resulted from the ten indictments filed in 1876–77.[83]

Ballots and Bullets (1871–83)

Federal indictments produced mixed results during Mississippi's election campaigns of 1871. While Klansmen in some counties kept a low profile, similar groups (or Ku Klux fronts) proliferated, organized to carry the election for "Democracy" by fair means or foul. One such group, Native Sons of the South, advertised itself as a "negative copy of the Loyal League." Organized in Lowndes and Pontotoc counties, the Native Sons traded hoods and robes for "a glazed cap and a medal," staging barbecues to win black votes for the Democratic Party. One acknowledged member, attorney William Humphries Jr. of Columbus, called the Native Sons "a silly, ridiculous, fool thing," but detective Henry Clark compared it to the sinister Jack Robinsons. Another member told congressional investigators, "You all know what it was. We wanted to vote the freedmen; we were honest in it."[84]

A similar group, the Seventy-Six Society, surfaced in Kemper, Lowndes and Monroe counties. Inveterate joiner William Humphries forgot the society's oath when questioned by Congress, but called it "purely a political matter, in the interest of the democratic party." Kemper County sheriff William Chisolm claimed that the Seventy-Sixers organized after federal troops began arresting local Klansmen. Ku Klux defector John Taliaferro described the society as "entirely different" from the KKK, designed "not for anything except to have the democratic party thoroughly organized to carry the election." Taliaferro also joined the White Rose Society, created in Noxubee County "for the purpose of bringing thieves to justice." Six months later, at a meeting in the woods, he joined masked members in compiling lists of "radicals" and freedmen to be terrorized.[85]

Historian Irby Nichols ranked 1871's election as "the most exciting that had yet taken place" in DeSoto County, and the campaign featured enough statewide violence to prompt a fruitless federal investigation. Klansman Asa Doggett lost his race for county supervisor in DeSoto, but Grand Cyclops E.H. Crump won election to the state legislature from Marshall County. That victory was soon reversed, however, when Crump and his colleague J.H. Tucker were denied their seats on grounds of having won election by illegal means. Overall, of 115 members elected to the state's lower house, 66 were Republicans, 38 of them freedmen. On 30 November, Governor Alcorn resigned to join Adelbert Ames in the U.S. Senate, thereby promoting Ohio native Ridgeley Powers to command the state.[86]

The new governor's first public address was a masterpiece of wishful thinking, describing Mississippi as "an example of reconstruction based upon reconciliation" in which a "new era of good feeling has sprung up." On 18 April 1872 Wiley Wells cabled Attorney General Williams a warning that only U.S. troops could prevent the KKK from overrunning the Magnolia State entirely. "The removal of these troops," Wells repeated on 18 July, "would be the worst disaster that could be done." Violence heated up as Mississippians prepared to vote in their first presidential election since 1860, with Ulysses Grant seeking a second term against Democratic contender Horace Greeley. Klansmen rode freely throughout the campaign, aided in Oktibbeah County by a group called the "Square Robinsons," whose founders included Starkville Klansmen George Gillespie, Murray Maxwell and Hub Sanders. Members sported red shirts, which "proclaimed to the world the fact that a Democratic heart beat beneath" them. Armed men patrolled the polls on election day, harassing and assaulting black voters, with mixed results. L.Q.C. Lamar won election to the U.S. House of Representatives, but Republicans secured Mississippi's eight electoral votes for President Grant.[87]

The next year's state elections spawned more violence, encouraged by Judge Hill's leniency in Oxford and by the Supreme Court's *Slaughterhouse* ruling, which undermined application of the Fourteenth Amendment to black civil rights. On 2 January 1873 Wiley Wells reported the murder of "numerous" grand jury witnesses. Klansman J.E. Gillenwater, indicted for multiple felonies, escaped from custody after his first arrest and placed a bounty on the heads of Wells and Marshal James Pierce. During a subsequent arrest attempt, Gillenwater shot Pierce's horse, then led a flogging squad to whip the Corinth freedman who betrayed him to authorities. Pierce sent Deputy R.T. Dunn to investigate that case, but Klansmen killed him with a shotgun blast to the head. Republicans bypassed Governor Powers, nominating Adelbert Ames for a second gubernatorial term with a promise of fully integrated schools, whereupon James Alcorn launched his own competing race. "New Departure" Democrats declined to nominate a candidate and threw their weight behind Alcorn as the lesser of two evils, but they failed to carry the day. Ames won election with a black lieutenant governor, secretary of state and superintendent of education, while "radicals" dominated both houses of the state legislature.[88] Clearly, it was time for Democrats and Klansmen to adopt a more aggressive strategy.

The "Mississippi Plan"

On 18 January 1874, four days before Ames began his second term as governor, President Grant told the *New York Herald*, "I begin to think that it is time for the republican party to unload. There has been too much dead weight carried by it.... [A]ll the disaffection in the Gulf States [has been imposed] on the administration. I am tired of this nonsense.... I don't want any quarrel about Mississippi State matters referred to me. This nursing of monstrosities has nearly exhausted the party. I am done with them, and they will have to take care of themselves." The first such quarrel arose in February, when Ames tried in vain to cancel a federal land grant for the Vicksburg & Nashville Railroad, pitting his influence against that of Grand Wizard Forrest. Most Americans ignored the ironic spectacle of a "carpetbag" governor's fight for economy, opposed by the nation's top Klansman pleading for alms from Washington.[89]

With Grant's blank check in hand, supported by an open letter from southern congressional leaders urging whites to moderation and reliance on the good will of northern conservatives, Mississippi's incipient revolutionaries laid plans for August's election. James George paved the way, writing L.Q.C. Lamar on 15 April to ask if "there is a great reaction going on in the Northern mind against negro government in the South? I have concluded that our African friends have so misused the privileges that they have that the Northern people are dying to see the end of all this misrule.... Let me know ... what the North thinks of these things and whether the animosities of the war are dying out." Lamar's response is lost to history, but he quickly donned the moderate cloak, delivering a surprise eulogy for "radical" icon Charles Sumner in March 1874. Governor Ames observed that "Lamar makes very different speeches in Mississippi from those he delivers for the Northern market."[90]

Ames spoke no more of integrated schools in 1874, applying himself instead to the punishment of Alcorn's dissident Republicans. Encouraged by that rift and the increasing disaffection over taxes, Mississippi's Bourbons planned a full-scale racist assault on black suffrage. Their scheme to carry the election by any means necessary was variously dubbed the "Mississippi Plan," the "straight-out policy"—or, more bluntly, the "Shotgun Plan." Its spearhead consisted of "irregular militia companies" such as Vicksburg's White Leagues, heavily armed and commonly clad in "the red-shirt badge of southern manhood." Drilling in daylight, marching incessantly through black communities and recording the names of prospective targets in "dead books," the new militias intimidated Republican voters and candidates alike. Traditional Ku Klux dens also remained active in parts of Mississippi, despite claims that the order had dissolved entirely during 1873.[91]

With his wife and children safe in Massachusetts, Governor Ames appealed to the White House for aid on 29 July and again on 1 August, warning that without a military presence "Republicanism must go down in the South." Instead of troops, President Grant dispatched a lone investigator, whose report from troubled Vicksburg deemed violence unlikely. In refusing help, Grant warned Ames that most Americans "are ready now to condemn any interference on the part of government." Election day saw L.Q.C. Lamar named as a marshal in Lafayette County, while Vicksburg's White Man's Party secured the polls at gunpoint. Ames afterward wrote to his wife that "[t]he election at Vicksburg passed off quietly because the Democrats, or white man's party, had both intimidated the blacks and perpetrated frauds of registration, so, of course, they had no cause to commit murder. The whites are organized to carry the state as they have carried V."[92]

In the wake of that victory, Vicksburg's planters turned the White Leagues toward eradicating "all bad and leading negroes ... and controlling more strictly our tenants and other hands." Their primary target was Sheriff Peter Crosby, a freedman whom they soon indicted for embezzlement. Compelled to resign after five hundred armed whites besieged the courthouse, Crosby fled to Jackson and conferred with Ames, who urged Crosby to form a posse and retake his office, pending disposition of his case in court. Crosby complied—and the result was Reconstruction's bloodiest pogrom. Armed whites met Crosby's posse outside town on 7 December 1874, capturing the sheriff and killing some of his deputies, rolling on from there to murder an estimated three hundred blacks countywide (against two white men slain). Conservative spokesmen minimized the slaughter, claiming only twenty-five "insurgents" killed, but even white participants in the initial "battle" granted that their victory "didn't require any valor," since they carried long-range rifles against Crosby's handful of shotguns and pistols. State legislators appealed to Washington for troops, and Grant reluctantly complied on 5 January 1875, restoring Crosby to his tenuous authority.[93]

For L.Q.C. Lamar, the Vicksburg massacre revealed an "absence of all the elements of real authority" behind the Ames administration. Four days after the pogrom, Washington's *National Republican* declared that "Northern people have lost all interest in the welfare of colored Southern Republicans." As interpreted by one Democratic spokesman, "In 1874, the tidal wave, as it was called, of the North, satisfied us that if we succeeded in winning the control of the government of Mississippi we would be permitted to enjoy it." State lawmakers sought to forestall that coup with passage of a "Gatling Gun Bill," authorizing Ames to raise militia companies and arm them with rapid-fire weapons. Lamar, mildly concerned, warned his wife that if Ames formed militia units "[h]e will get them killed up, and then Grant will take possession for him." Architects of the Mississippi Plan, by contrast, envisioned killing freedmen without interference from the federal government. As the *Meridian Mercury* opined on 11 March 1875, "The negroes are our enemies.... [W]e must accept them as our enemies and beat them as enemies."[94]

"A Peaceful Revolution"

Despite such admonitions in the Democratic press and constant drilling in the countryside by terrorist "militia companies," Mississippi Conservatives clung to a façade of innocence. By recruiting a militia, Jackson's *Clarion* accused, Governor Ames "is organizing murder, civil war, rapine, a war of races, in our otherwise peaceful State." By contrast, the *Clarion* asserted, Democrats had "inaugurated a peaceful revolution" that was both "deep-seated and wide-spread.... Such revolutions never go backwards." Klansman James Glanville, meanwhile, emblazoned his *Forest Register* with the masthead slogan "A white man in a white man's place. A black man in a black man's place. Each according to the eternal fitness of things." As for the peaceful tone of Mississippi's revolution, the *Clarion* abandoned all pretense on 11 February 1875, with an editorial proclaiming "The time has come when companies that have been organized for protection and defensive purposes should come to the front.... Let every citizen hold himself in readiness to join one of these companies. The shameless, heartless, vile, grasping, deceitful, creeping, crawling, wallowing, slimy, slippery, hideous loathsome political pirates must be wiped out!"[95]

That call evoked a series of riotous demonstrations throughout the state, continuing from early spring until election day. L.Q.C. Lamar, Edward Walthall and other Democratic stalwarts toured Mississippi calling for whites "to throw off the ruin and dishonor that threatened them." Panola County whites used "[i]ntelligent negro speakers employed from a distance" to plead the Democratic case, while threatening to murder top Republicans. Red-shirted cavalry patrolled by day and night, staging parades that wound for miles through towns and over country roads, the participants displaying arms and warning former slaves that "they might kill a buck today." In Jackson and elsewhere, gunmen followed Republican activists through the streets, firing "accidental" shots to keep their nerves on edge. Armed Democrats invaded Republican meetings, demanding "equal time" and forcing captive audiences to endure racist harangues at gunpoint. At one such meeting in Monroe County, Confederate general Reuben Davis seized the podium to say, "My colored friends, you are ruining the white people of the South. If it goes much further, I am for war and blood, war to the knife, and the knife to the hilt." Countless tales of "whippings and worse" emerged from all parts of the state.[96]

Concerted violence began in June, with "a mysterious negro lynching and burning" at Forest. On 4 July, Vicksburg whites mobbed a black Independence Day party and killed two freedmen. A few days later, rumors of a black insurrection at Water Valley prompted whites to execute "a number" of former slaves. At Macon, in August, white rioters including an estimated one hundred Alabama horsemen fired on a black church, killing thirteen parishioners. The same month saw two black Republicans shot in Macon. On 1 September rioters in Yazoo City stormed a Republican meeting and killed four persons, then scoured the county and lynched "leading negroes" in each supervisor's district. A report dated 3 September told Governor Ames that terrorists had "taken military control of [Yazoo] County." One day later, whites fired on a black gathering in Clinton, killing four and wounding several others. The freedmen fought back, slaying two gunmen and touching off a pogrom that claimed thirty more lives by 6 September. (One witness described blacks gunned down "just the same as birds.") With Mississippi slipping into anarchy, Governor Ames appealed once more to the White House for aid on 8 September. President Grant consulted Attorney General Edward Pierrepont, then refused to send troops on grounds that "the whole public are tired of these annual autumnal outbreaks in the South." With that "flippant utterance," Ames declared, "the executive branch of the National government announced that it had decided that the reconstruction acts of congress were a failure."[97]

Thus encouraged, terrorists expanded their campaign. Aberdeen Democrats wrote to Grand Wizard Forrest in Memphis, seeking his help to obtain a cannon, then brought a field gun from Mobile when he failed to provide one. A "minor skirmish" at Satartia (in Yazoo County) claimed one freedman's life. Macon Democrats fired pistols and artillery on the main street, killing the black candidate for county treasurer. When Governor Ames ordered disbandment of white vigilante groups, the *Jackson Clarion* openly mocked him: "'Now, therefore, I, A.A., do hereby command all persons belonging to such organizations to disband.' Ha! ha!! ha!!! 'Command.' 'Disband.' That's good." Embittered James Alcorn, now denying that he was or ever had been a "negro republican," led the Coahoma County mob that deposed black sheriff John Brown, killing nine persons in the process. Members of Forest's Democratic Club killed the Rev. Sam West on a plantation near Homewood, while local planter Oliver Eastwood warned freedmen to vote Democratic or stay home on election day. On 29 October a Democratic torchlight procession ended with the Carrollton courthouse in flames and a Republican scapegoat killed while "trying to escape." Traditional Klan units also joined in the melee: Yalobusha County's den drove carpetbagger William Price and his son from the district, while DeSoto's ghouls "rode all night long, scaring negroes and warning them to stay away from the polls."[98]

By the time James George met with Governor Ames in October, promising a "fair and peaceful election," the damage was done. Ominous silence cloaked the polls in many areas, where red-shirted gunmen tended cannons loaded with buckshot and scrap iron. After a final spate of murders in Lowndes County, on election eve, the voting in Columbus proceeded "as quietly as a funeral." Observers in Jackson found it "fearfully quiet," while "hardly anybody spoke" in Yazoo City. The results were preordained. In the only contest for state office, Democrat William Hemingway won election as treasurer. Klansman Henry Myers was elected as sheriff in Marshall County, and Oktibbeah County voters sent Ku Klux leader Henry Muldrow to the state legislature "as a check upon the ignorant negroes in that body."

Statewide, Democrats carried Mississippi by some 50,000 votes, compared to the GOP's 20,000-vote margin of victory in 1873. They captured control of 62 counties, elected 4 of the state's 6 congressmen, claimed 26 out of 36 seats in the state senate, and 95 out of 115 in the lower house. Mississippi's white "scalawag" vote, estimated at some six thousand, was virtually eradicated. Republicans lost 800 votes in Coahoma County, 1,100 in Hinds, 1,600 in Holmes, and 1,300 in Jefferson. They won only 4 votes in Kemper County, 12 in Tishomingo, and 7 in Yazoo (where the victorious tally of 4,044 Democratic ballots exceeded the county's number of registered voters).[99]

Having guaranteed those results by his inaction, President Grant now struck a pose of outrage. "As to the state election of 1875," he told reporters, "Mississippi is governed by officials chosen through fraud and violence, such as would scarcely be accredited to savages." Justice Department officials investigated the results and indicted 187 terrorists, but only 6 were finally convicted. In Oxford, Judge Hill reduced his standard twenty-five-dollar fines to ten dollars, while charging three of those convicted a mere one dollar each. South Carolina's Wade Hampton visited his Mississippi holdings that autumn and took the lesson home with him, founding his own Redshirt brigades in the Palmetto State.[100]

Dixie "Redeemed"

By January 1876 only three southern states—Florida, Louisiana and South Carolina—remained under effective "radical" control. November's presidential election could change that, but Mississippi Democrats still had work to do at home before their state was finally "redeemed." Soon after New Year's Day, the new state legislature voted to impeach Governor Ames and black Lieutenant Governor Alexander Davis. Ames wrote from Jackson that "the crack of the pistol or gun is as frequent as the barking of dogs," with some shots aimed at the governor's mansion. L.Q.C. Lamar pretended to oppose impeachment, but Blanche Ames observed that "[t]he warmest friends of Lamar here are the most violent for impeachment—and Mr. Lamar is a double dealer on whom no dependence can be placed, as it is well known that in all matters political he does not hesitate to be false." Governor Ames resigned on 29 March, thus elevating John Marshal Stone—president pro tempore of the state senate—to fill his place.[101]

With that obstacle removed, Democrats focused once more on "straight-out" politics. L.Q.C. Lamar sought a U.S. Senate seat in 1876, while Grand Cyclops Henry Muldrow campaigned for a seat in Congress, but November's real prize was the White House. Ohio Governor Rutherford Hayes secured the Republican presidential nomination, opposing New Yorker Samuel Tilden. The summer election campaign was a replay of 1875's, complete with displays of small arms and artillery. Kemper County terrorists, identified in some accounts as Klansmen, fired their cannon at the home of former sheriff William Chisolm after he announced his race for Congress. In Hernando, the "DeSoto Blues" peppered black Republicans with rifle fire. Yalobusha County red-shirts paraded with banners reading "We are going to control or die" and "White man's county, white man's rule." A signed "Ku Klux" notice warned one Washington County freedman to depart within twenty-four hours. L.Q.C. Lamar addressed a Water Valley gathering where Klansman M.D.L. Stephens was hanged in effigy for switching his allegiance to the upstart Greenback Party. Sometime Klan attorney Edward Walthall led the cannoneers who drove black voters from Grenada on election day.[102]

The net results were gratifying. Lamar and Muldrow won their respective races, while William Chisolm lost his contest to Democrat Hernando Money. (Chisolm subsequently charged thirty Klansmen with violating the Enforcement Acts, thus triggering a chain of tragic circumstances in the new year.) Samuel Tilden polled 4,300,590 ballots nationwide, against 4,036,298 for Hayes, but the apparent Democratic victory hit a snag in the electoral college. There, while Tilden claimed 184 votes (including 8 from Mississippi) against Hayes' 165, twenty critical votes from Florida, Louisiana and South Carolina remained in dispute. While debate raged in Congress and the press, a correspondent known only as "P." sent a timely warning from Oxford, Mississippi, to the *New York Times*. The nameless scribe portrayed "a more defiant spirit manifesting itself than I ever knew during the war.... [C]ould the people who saved the Union and put down treason but know the actual facts, they would never permit Tilden to become President" by means of southern votes.[103]

Attorney General Akerman shared that view, declaring on 7 February 1877 that the "science of fraud in elections is better understood by the Democrats of the South than by any other politicians in the country ... and they put their learning in practice with unbounded audacity. The North will not fully comprehend the Southern question until it learns that where the negro, Northerners, or the United States government is concerned, very many men of character and influence of the South are governed by a ... code wholly different from that which they observe in ordinary life. The stratagems of war are deemed legitimate."[104]

The issue was finally decided behind closed doors, on 26 February, at Washington's Wormsley House hotel. Neither candidate attended the secret meeting, but those present included future president James Garfield, Georgia senator (and ex–Grand Dragon) John Gordon, and Senator-elect L.Q.C. Lamar. Together, they forged a bargain whereby Hayes received the presidency in return for ending Reconstruction in the states still subject to "radical" rule. Lamar, already planning out his next campaign, told friends, "We have no enemy in our front. But the negroes are almost as well disciplined in their silence and inactivity as they were before in their aggressiveness."[105] Eradication of that threat would be his next priority.

The KKK Assessed

Historians today almost unanimously recognize the Ku Klux Klan of Reconstruction as an insurgent terrorist movement whose propaganda was wholly without merit. "Negro rule" was the first shibboleth — a predictable fear, given Mississippi's tally of 86,973 black voters versus 68,587 registered whites in 1868 — but one never realized in fact. The Magnolia State never had a black governor or a black majority in its state legislature, and the three freedmen dispatched to Capitol Hill had little or no impact on daily life at home.[106]

Likewise, the Klan's pretense of helping to enforce the law was a transparent sham. Klansmen committed hundreds of violent crimes for each one they punished, and none of the victims they lynched for supposed violations were ever proved guilty at trial. Nor was "carpetbag corruption" a valid excuse for the order's existence, since Mississippi's "redeemer" government proved more graft-ridden than its "radical" predecessors. Democrats began by grossly exaggerating the Republican state debt (proclaimed as $2 million, rather than the actual $300,000), then proceeded to steal the state blind. Treasurer William Hemingway alone absconded with $315,612, a total surpassing all the money stolen by Republicans officials during Reconstruction.[107]

Those facts were known to Mississippi's "best people," yet they supported Ku Klux terrorism for a decade, either turning blind eyes to the order's crimes or blaming victims as the instigators of their own misfortune. The Democratic press, as elsewhere in the South, provided key support for Mississippi's Klan. Between calls to arms in 1868 and 1876, the *Jackson Clarion* alternately denied any knowledge of "Ku Klux combinations," then declared, "If they really exist we could not recommend their disbandment so long as the Loyal League conspiracies, whose operations they must have been designed to circumvent, are in full blast." The *Aberdeen Examiner* pretended to believe that all Klansmen were black, while the *Yazoo Banner* ran songs saluting the order. Some newspapers, like Dr. William Compton's in Holly Springs, James Glanville's in Forest, and Scott County's *Ku Klux Klan*, were little more than Ku Klux propaganda sheets.[108]

Those papers and others, combined with the public oratory of George, Lamar, Muldrow, Walthall and company, persuaded most white Democrats that Klansmen were their champions in a life-or-death struggle to preserve southern society. Any excess was legitimate, as during wartime, to eradicate the enemy. Fort Pillow was a prime example, hailed without embarrassment by those who saw Grand Wizard Forrest as a hero rather than as a murderer. It comes as no surprise, then, that the Klan was led by former generals and colonels, while a younger generation — wealthy planters' sons and "poor white trash" alike — assumed the rigorous pursuits of night riding. In southern eyes, the early Klan's technique was vindicated by its triumph over "Negro rule."

Such movements have a tendency to backfire, though. Georgia Senator Benjamin Hill had an opportunity to observe white terror firsthand while serving as a partner with Nathan Forrest, Grand Dragon John Gordon, and South Carolina's Wade Hampton in the Southern Life Insurance Company. In Hill's belated view, "This Ku Klux business ... is the greatest blunder our people ever committed."[109]

CHAPTER 2

Hiatus and Revival
(1877–1921)

Removal of federal troops was only the first step in Mississippi's "redemption." In their bid to restore a semblance of the antebellum status quo, Democrats slashed the state budget by 50 percent, restored millions of acres forfeited by antebellum planters for non-payment of taxes, and abolished the statewide school tax. Freedmen who opposed such measures were neutralized by various means. Their votes were gerrymandered into "shoe-string" congressional districts along the Mississippi River, while five new districts were created with white majorities. A new "pig law" elevated livestock pilferage to the status of grand theft, stripping convicted felons of their right to vote and leaving them subject to peonage under the state's convict-lease system. One former slave observed, "It looks to me that the white people are putting in prison all that they can get their hand on." When all else failed, bribery, fraud, and intimidation remained as standard techniques in election campaigns.[1]

Settlement of Reconstruction-era grudges was another top priority for Mississippi's white redeemers. Ex-sheriff William Chisolm failed to convict the Klansmen who fired cannon at his Kemper County home in 1876, but he continued feuding with local Democratic leader John Gully. A sniper killed Gully near Chisolm's home in April 1877, and Sheriff Fletcher Sinclair jailed Chisolm on 30 April, permitting Chisolm's family and friends to join him in protective custody. A mob of 300 then stormed the jail and set it afire, killing Chisolm, his two children, and his friend Angus McLellan. Democratic newspapers including the *Jackson Clarion, Meridian Mercury* and *Vicksburg Herald*—praised the lynchers, and Governor Stone declined to investigate, perhaps (as stated in the *Brookhaven Comet*) because "a vigorous effort to prosecute the Kemper County murderers would insure his certain defeat." Eight months later, freedman Walter Riley confessed to Gully's murder and was hanged, insisting to the end that Chisolm had no part in the crime.[2]

President Hayes maintained stoic silence on the Chisolm massacre, as on the violent raids conducted against freedmen in September 1877 by white "bulldozers" or "protective clubs" in Amite, Franklin, Pike, and Wilkinson counties. Some locals claimed the terrorists were Farmers' Alliance members, punishing white merchants who rented land to black tenants, but Governor Stone and the state legislature reserved their attention for crimes blamed on "radicals."[3]

Racism Ascendant

Encouraged by signals from Washington, where Congress banned use of federal troops to protect black voters, Mississippi Democrats proceeded with redemption at the ballot box in 1878. Former Klansmen and their allies did well in that year's elections. James Chalmers, of Fort Pillow infamy, secured reelection to Congress by intimidating black voters, while Samuel Gholson won election to the state house of representatives, Henry Myers became secretary of state (serving until 1886), and Thomas Keith launched a thirty-year career in the state legislature. Greene Chandler, a Confederate war veteran and lawmaker, replaced Thomas Walton as Mississippi's federal prosecutor. Before year's end, the state enacted its first "Jim Crow" legislation, mandating separate schools for white and black students.[4]

Those events sparked concern among Republicans in Congress. Senator James Blaine organized a committee to investigate charges of fraud and violence during the 1878 election campaign. Its final report concluded that officials in Mississippi, Louisiana and South Carolina had breached their vows to uphold the U.S. Constitution and safeguard equal rights, resulting in unpunished murder and intimidation of black citizens. The committee recommended new legislation to protect voters in federal elections, but the proposal languished until 1890. Meanwhile, New York Senator Roscoe Conkling complained that President Hayes took advice on southern matters chiefly from L.Q.C. Lamar and Georgia's John Gordon, "while the cold shoulder is given to the oldest and best of our Republican leaders."[5]

Discrimination and violence prompted a black exodus from Mississippi, beginning in 1877 and accelerating through 1878 under the added impetus of drought, crop failures, and a yellow fever epidemic. In May 1879, Congressman Chalmers led a band of terrorists who closed the Mississippi River to black migrants, threatened boat captains and stranded some 1,500 evacuees in the Magnolia State. On 17 May, a band of Lincoln County's "law-abiding citizens" convened to denounce "the continued outrages of the bull-dozers" spanning the past two years. Those assembled granted that the night riders "may have had some cause for [their] acts ... by being deprived of their homes by a system of extortion under the lien laws of this State," but condemned them for "punishing and assassinating unoffending colored citizens." Soon afterward, spokesmen for a local "regulating association" threatened participants in that meeting for "interfering in the business that does not concern you, by taking steps to uphold the negroes in their rascality, and to shield them from punishment." The terrorists vowed to "hold each and every man to a strict accountability for all measures taken against this association."[6]

Elsewhere, members of a "Democratic club" donned masks and "rode about the country, firing off their guns as they halted at the plantations to frighten the negroes." In Washington County, masked gunmen killed freedman Joseph Richards in July 1879, apparently because he pressed for an investigation of his brother's slaying two years earlier. The *Vicksburg Herald* blamed that slaying on "an organized ring of outlaws," warning that if the terror continued, "not a colored laborer will remain to gather the crops." Governor Stone urged state legislators "to personally investigate the condition of affairs" in several southwestern counties, but nothing came of the plea. Meanwhile, Stone named James Z. George to the state supreme court, where he soon became chief justice. In Washington, L.Q.C. Lamar opposed a resolution authored by Vermont senator George Edmunds, reaffirming the legality of the Thirteenth, Fourteenth, and Fifteenth amendments. Lamar, later praised by John F. Kennedy for his "courage" in healing the wounds of Reconstruction, sided with Alabama's Senator John Morgan, insisting that all three amendments were forced unjustly upon the South.[7]

Mississippi held no statewide elections in 1879, but local races sparked excitement in all seventy-five counties. Ironically, the target of white-supremacist wrath in Yazoo City was Henry Dixon, former chief of Dixon's Scouts, who led the Democratic Party's "committee on hanging" in 1875. Running for sheriff on the Independent ticket, Dixon found himself at odds with his former terrorist cronies. Five hundred of them besieged his home, retreating after a six-hour negotiation with Mayor J.H. Holt. Jackson's *Weekly Clarion* praised the mob for its "prompt and decisive" action to ensure "no race conflict in Yazoo," while the *Washington* (Mississippi) *Post* declared: "In sheer self-defense, just as they would have united against an insane man with a torch in his hand, or a wild animal, the citizens of Yazoo County, without distinction of politics, of color, came together and informed Dixon that he would not be allowed to turn their peaceful community into another hell." Still, Dixon refused to abandon the race, and he was slain on 19 August, shot in the back by prominent Democrat James Barksdale. The *Weekly Clarion* defended Barksdale, who faced no criminal charges.[8]

President Hayes declined to seek a second term in 1880, whereupon Republicans chose James Garfield as their standard-bearer. It was a close contest, with Garfield and Democrat Winfield Hancock each carrying nineteen states, Garfield emerging victorious by a margin of 9,464 popular votes among some 8.9 million ballots cast. The entire South followed Hancock, but Garfield mustered 214 electoral votes to Hancock's 155. On 29 December, Hayes confided to his diary that, while James Blaine and other GOP leaders had "reviled" his southern strategy in 1877, "Now, all are silenced by the results. Their president mutters not a word against it."[9]

In Mississippi, where state legislators had recently banned interracial marriage, James Chalmers won election to a third congressional term but faced a challenge from Rep. John Lynch on grounds of fraud. Forced to vacate his seat in April 1882, Chalmers held a lasting grudge against L.Q.C. Lamar for failing to support him. James Z. George, meanwhile, won election to the U.S. Senate, where he served until his death in August 1897. The year's great excitement came not from Washington County, where planters had imported fifty-one Chinese as experimental replacements for black field hands, but from Yalobusha, where Democrats clashed violently with dissident Greenbackers.

A.T. Wimberly, chairman of the Greenback Party's state committee, lived in Coffeeville, where party member R.V. Pearson sought the sheriff's office. At a public "joint discussion" on 21 August 1880, black Democrat Tom Spearman led a gang that fired a dozen shots at Pearson, wounding him. "General shooting" then erupted, much of it by Democratic snipers posted in second-story windows. On 23 August, a well-armed mob gathered in Coffeeville "to keep the peace," marching on Pearson's home to "demand that [he] cease advocating the National Greenback cause or [he] would be a dead man before midnight." Pearson refused, and the mob eventually dispersed, leaving Pearson to win the election despite false rumors of his impending death. Several Democratic gunmen were belatedly arrested and fined one dollar each by Judge Watson of Holly Springs, on charges of "public shooting on the highway."[10]

Overall, the November 1880 election produced less mayhem than normal in Missis-

sippi postwar contests. Interviewed by the *St. Louis Globe-Democrat*, Republican presidential elector J.M. Bynum "confirm[ed] the previous reports concerning Democratic bull-
dozing in his State, and [said] it consist[ed] not in physical demonstrations of shot guns
and kuklux as much as it does in indirect intimidation and the manipulation of the ballot
box." Magnolia Democrats were furthermore distracted by a power struggle between L.Q.C.
Lamar and Ethelbert Barksdale, both seeking control of the party. Barksdale and James
Chalmers vied to fill the U.S. Senate seat of Blanche Bruce when his term expired in 1881.
Lamar snubbed Chalmers once again, promoting colleague Edward Walthall, whereupon
Barksdale withdrew to support James Z. George and secured his swift endorsement at the
state caucus in January 1880.[11]

President Garfield's assassination in September 1881 elevated Chester Arthur to the
presidency, but it brought Mississippi's "Bourbon" Democrats no closer to federal patronage in Washington. At home, they faced a new challenge from the Fusion movement, combining Independents and Republicans. Ethelbert Barksdale sought the governorship,
opposed by ex–Governor Stone and his primary sponsor, L.Q.C. Lamar. James Chalmers
attacked Lamar in the pages of his *Vicksburg Commercial*, whereupon Lamar blasted the
"unscrupulous" Fusionists who "made a shameless partnership with the negroes of Mississippi to capture the government of the State, and to run it in the interest of their own ambitious schemes and selfish designs." Fusionism, said Lamar, "is simply *negro government*, to
be reestablished by carpetbaggers and a few ambitious natives, taking the role of the
scalawags under the names of Greenbackers and Independents." Their victory would mean
"domination [by] the negro vote," with untold "aggravation and degradation," making life
"unbearable in Mississippi."[12]

Lamar subsequently tempered his remarks by claiming that "I make no attack upon
the negro race," and claiming "I insist upon the observance of all his rights, even that of
participating in government." Still, he maintained, "the white race should use all the methods which the intelligent classes in every free society employ to control the ignorant and
the incompetent." In short, they "should combine and unite to prevent ... the negro from
grasping the power of the State as his own exclusive possession."[13]

That rallying cry produced only one classic incident of election-day violence. In Marion, after a drunken white man shredded a black voter's ballot, shoving and gunfire erupted,
leaving four whites and one freedman dead in the street and two other whites wounded.
Rumors spread that "the niggers were rising," whereupon sheriff R.L. Henderson led a mob
of "ugly-looking men with guns" to arrest white Republican Edward Vance. Vance tried to
flee and the mob opened fire, killing Vance's son, a black servant, and one of their own by
mistake. Subsequent posses failed to capture the original black gunmen.[14]

While loyal Democrat Robert Lowry won the 1881 gubernatorial race, his victory did
not suppress the Independent movement. James Chalmers moved from Vicksburg to Holly
Springs in 1882, launching his latest congressional race from Lamar's home district, supported by ex-governor Alcorn and others whom Democratic spokesmen branded "degen-
erates," "moral lepers," and "traitors to their race." Chalmers won the surprise endorsement
of President Arthur, despite articles in the *Philadelphia Press* that labeled him "the butcher
of Fort Pillow." Arthur also endorsed Col. E.B.C. Cash in South Carolina, described by the
New York Tribune as a rebel "guilty of murders so atrocious that they shocked a community accustomed to scenes of blood."[15] The *Tribune* wrote:

Arthur's attempt to place the negro vote under the control of the desperadoes of the South is ominous of evil. There is no moral strength to such a movement. It is inherently and inevitably bad — bad for the Republican party in the South, bad for it in the North, bad for the negro, bad for the country.... To take a new departure and accept for Republican leaders in the South men so bad that they were forced out of the Democratic party is a blunder so deplorable and withal so stupid that no previous Republican Administration would ever possibly commit it. Should not a halt be called?[16]

Protests notwithstanding, Chalmers won his race for Congress, survived another challenge (this one from Rep. Van Manning in the Second District), and was seated in June 1884 — five months before losing his next bid for reelection. Charges of fraud prompted another congressional investigation of the 1882 Mississippi elections, and when three Clay County whites were convicted of stuffing ballot boxes, a hometown crowd cheered their return, complete with a poem reading: "Our welcome gallant trio/Clay County's free-born sons!/Convicted of true manhood/Thrice welcome honored ones." Deputy U.S. Marshal J.L. Morphis opined that community support was geared to "hold these young men and others steady for the work at the next election."[17]

Those elections fell in 1883, soon after the U.S. Supreme Court ruled that the Fourteenth Amendment barred racial discrimination by states, not by individuals. In Copiah County, a gang of 150 night riders with cannon in tow began terrorizing Republicans and Independents ten days before the 6 November election. They flogged three white Republicans at Handy Fortner's house, then rode on to seize GOP ballots from other homes. On election eve, Ethelbert Barksdale told a Hazelhurst audience that Democrats would sweep the state if it took shotguns to do so. "Captain" E.B. Wheeler emphasized the point by leading 150 members of his Democratic militia through town, escorted by the county sheriff and Democratic Party chairman. On 6 November, terrorists murdered J.P. Matthews, chairman of Copiah's Republican Executive Committee. A U.S. Senate committee, created to investigate "alleged election outrages" in Mississippi, reported that Matthews was "slain solely because he was an eminent and influential Republican, that his death might strike terror into opponents of the Democratic party and enable that party, being in a minority of legal votes, to take possession of Copiah County."[18]

Democrats celebrated their victory with another spasm of bloodshed in Yazoo City. On 24 December, merchant John Posey — locally known as a "high-toned honorable gentleman" — led a mob to "whip a nigger" named John James for his participation in a barroom brawl. En route to capture James, the whites met William Foote, a Republican freedman who served as Yazoo's deputy collector of internal revenue. Posey assaulted Foote, then someone started shooting. When the smoke cleared, Posey, his son, and another white man lay dead. Authorities jailed Foote and five other freedmen, killed another one who was "defying arrest," then arrested white Republican A.S. Lynch for good measure. On Christmas Day, a mob of 200 lynchers took Foote and three other freedmen from jail, lynching all four despite intercession from state legislator James Barksdale (who murdered Henry Dixon in 1879).[19]

Federal investigation of the 1883 elections was hamstrung in October 1884 when burglars invaded the U.S. marshal's office in Jackson, stealing "every letter, telegram, and printed circular pertaining to elections." Rep. Lynch warned Republican presidential nominee James Blaine against expecting any votes from the Magnolia State, but Blaine insisted that "Mr. Lamar will see that I get a fair count in Mississippi." In fact, as Lynch observed, Lamar "not only made an aggressive speech against Mr. Blaine, but it was chiefly through his influence and efforts that the state was returned against Mr. Blaine by a very large majority." Democrat Grover Cleveland counted all eleven ex–Confederate states among those that propelled him into office on 3 November. The *New York Tribune* called 1884's election "the most quiet and peaceable that [Mississippi] has known in twenty years," noting that "the negroes generally did not vote."[20]

Cleveland displayed his gratitude in March 1885, when he appointed L.Q.C. Lamar as Secretary of the Interior, with former Oktibbeah County grand cyclops Henry Muldrow as his First Assistant Secretary. Edward Walthall won appointment to fill Lamar's Senate seat, serving until poor health forced his resignation in January 1894. Lamar's appointment raised the greatest outcry and was branded a "calamity" by the *New York Tribune*. "That Lamar was a rebel is not the argument," the *Tribune* declared. "That he still advocates the doctrine of secession as right; and is a bull dozer is a potent argument." In debates over his confirmation, Ohio governor Charles Foster recalled a conversation with Lamar, wherein Lamar "deprecated murder and Ku-Klux methods," but proclaimed that "Negro government was necessarily ignorant, and ignorant government was necessarily vicious and bad; that the white people of the South would continue to govern their states." The Senate finally confirmed Lamar by a vote of thirty-two to twenty-eight, three Republicans joining ranks with Democrats to support him.[21]

One of Secretary Lamar's first official acts was the settlement of an old score with Albert Morgan, Yazoo County's top Republican during Reconstruction. Morgan was elected sheriff of Yazoo in 1873, then hounded from his office and his home by terrorists in 1875. Employed since then as a second-class clerk in the federal Pension Office, Morgan published a memoir to promote the Republican cause in 1884, then found himself working for L.Q.C. Lamar in March 1885. His summary dismissal made the point that nothing was forgiven or forgotten.[22]

Scores were settled more directly in Mississippi, as with the Carrollton massacre of March 1886. The trouble began on 13 February with a visit from James Liddell Jr., an attorney and editor of the *Greenwood Valley Flag*. A drunken friend of Liddell's suffered "a difficulty" with freedman Ed Brown, who struck the white man with a jug of molasses. Later that day, Lidell met Brown and several other freedmen on the street, asked what they were doing, and received "an insulting reply." Drawing a pistol and firing at Brown, Lidell provoked a shootout that left him and several freedmen wounded. Ed Brown and his brother Charles charged Lidell and six other whites with attempted murder. All seven were arrested and their trial set for 17 March. At noon on that day, a mob of 100 armed men invaded the courthouse, riddling black spectators with an estimated 1,000 bullets. A report in the *New Orleans Picayune* described corpses piled "four or five [deep] on top of each other." Officially, thirteen freedmen died (including the Browns), while seven more were wounded.[23]

Jackson produced more reports of racist terrorism in 1887, but an investigation by the House Judiciary Committee failed to offer any remedies. More significant, in terms of later Ku Klux history, was that year's foundation of the American Protective Association in Clinton, Iowa. The APA picked up where the earlier Know-Nothing movement left off, warning against "the Papal army in the United States" subverting government and society at large. Its literature asked, "Can a good Romanist be at the same time a loyal American citizen?"

The reply: "*No ballot for a man who takes his politics from the Vatican.*" The APA had chapters in every state by 1895, with estimates of peak membership running as high as 2.5 million. It dominated politics in at least nine states, ranging from California to Massachusetts and southward to Tennessee, and elected twenty known members to Congress. An ill-advised rift with the GOP sapped the association's strength after 1896, but fierce nativist passions remained. In New York, the Rev. John Holmes wrote: "The Ku-Klux Klan agitation of the last few years was kindergarten play compared to that furious scourge that swept the hearts of men."[24]

President Cleveland promoted L.Q.C. Lamar again in January 1888, appointing him to a seat on the U.S. Supreme Court. Lamar was thus on hand to defend Mississippi's adoption of Jim Crow railroad cars (also in 1888), when the court upheld a state's right to mandate segregation in the case of *Louisville, New Orleans & Texas Railway v. Mississippi* (1890). Lamar served five years on the court, then died in January 1893. Grateful whites in Mississippi, Alabama and Georgia named counties in his honor. Cleveland, meanwhile, repeated his sweep of Dixie in 1884's presidential election, claiming some 91,000 popular votes more than rival Benjamin Harrison, but Harrison trumped Cleveland in the electoral college, with 233 votes to 168. Harrison's nod to the South, shortly before election day, was a conversation with Indiana superintendent of public education Harvey La Follette, wherein Harrison vowed that he would name no "ignorant Negroes" to office "simply because they were Republicans." Harrison seemed "confident that his policy would completely solve the Southern social problem," but it failed to sway Dixie voters.[25]

Political violence sputtered around Mississippi throughout 1888, beginning with Jackson's municipal elections on 2 January. Historian Clark Miller reports that federal officers appointed by President Cleveland "led the movement" to unseat Republican Mayor John McGill (in office since 1874), while black voters were frightened away from the polls by a militant Young Men's White League. McGill was unopposed until one week before the election, when Democrats threatened to "force a row" if blacks voted. John Martin, editor of the *Jackson Mississippian*, printed and distributed 500 circulars for the White League headlined "A Blast From the Youth—the Young Men of Jackson Utter Their Ultimatum." Its text vowed "in solemn and awful earnestness, that the corrupt, radical, negro government of our city should, must, and shall be wiped out, cost what it may." The flier cautioned blacks that "if any one of their race attempts to run for office in the approaching municipal election he does so at his extreme peril, and we further warn any and all of the negroes of this city against attempting, at their utmost hazard, by vote or influence, to foist on us again this black and damnable machine miscalled a government of our city."[26]

Threats served their purpose in Jackson, but serious mayhem erupted at Wahalak, in Kemper County, near year's end. Details of the initial incident remain vague today, compounded by the fact that key players on both sides apparently had the same surname. An interracial brawl of some sort brought a white "posse" into Wahalak's black community on 16 December 1888, where "fifty well-armed negroes" repelled them with gunfire, allegedly killing five white men and wounding six more. Within twenty-four hours of the initial shooting, some 100 whites returned and killed at least eight unarmed blacks. Reporters left Wahalak on 20 December, declaring the "riot" finished; but Shaqulak resident S.D. Chamberlin wrote to Governor Lowry and the *Mississippian* on 14 January 1889, declaring that lynchers were "still burning and robbing the negroes." By Chamberlin's count, terrorists had driven forty-odd families from their homes in Kemper County and southern Noxubee. Noxubee's sheriff saw "no mob law in this county," but acknowledged "some clandestine acts" along the county line. Governor Lowry ordered Kemper's sheriff to "arrest every man in your county that has been engaged in such violations of law," but no prosecutions resulted.[27]

Worse lay in store for 1889, as white Mississippi abandoned the last vestige of Fusionism in favor or "straightout" racism. In June, ex-congressman John Lynch called for federal intervention in his state, where "an election ... is a travesty indeed" and the black majority could not vote because "they fear murder," but his plea fell on deaf ears in Washington. Meanwhile, in Leflore County, the stage was set for what Clark Miller calls "the worst outbreak of politically and racially motivated murder in the State's history."[28]

Leflore, in the Yazoo Delta, was 85 percent black. Ninety-five percent of its farmers were sharecroppers, and Greenwood was the only town with more than 100 residents. There, in summer 1889, black organizer Oliver Cromwell established chapters of the Colored Farmers' Alliance, prompting panic among white landlords and tenants alike. Whites shadowed Cromwell, accused him of using the CFA for personal profit, and hounded him with Klan-type threats, including letters decorated with skulls and crossed bones. The CFA responded in August with letters to whites at Shell Mound, warning "that they proposed to stand by Cromwell and that if any efforts were made to disturb him, that they would kill, burn, and destroy Shell Mound." Sheriff L.T. Basket wired Governor Lowry a false report of 500 blacks parading with weapons, whereupon Lowry dispatched three militia companies to avert a "race war." Visiting Greenwood himself, Lowry worried that white "citizen volunteers" in Leflore "seemed determined to have it their own way." Addressing the mob, Lowry condemned "mob law" as "being wicked and disrespectable and unworthy of Mississippians," then assured his audience that "he was from the crown of his head to the soles of his feet a white man's man, and should always uphold the superiority of the Anglo-Saxon man."[29]

Lowry returned to Jackson on 3 September, and his troops and white vigilantes arrested forty CFA leaders (minus Cromwell, who escaped to Jackson) and killed at least twenty-five others who "refused to surrender and were shot." A report in the *Indianapolis World* described "thirty to sixty killed, after they were disarmed." Leflore's sheriff then sent the militia home, insisting that they were no longer needed. Soon after they left, four victims were lynched at Shell Mound, allegedly for burning a store whose white owner refused to sell the black "rebels" ammunition. A dispatch from Greenwood to the *Chicago Tribune* reported that "the alleged 'negro uprising' in Mississippi, which threw the whites into great terror, has ended as usual in a furious 'nigger hunt' by self-appointed 'regulators,' who slaughtered the blacks like sheep." The correspondent opined that "the state troops were withdrawn for the reason that the posse did not want them there because they would restrain and restrict them from carrying out their determination to kill every negro who had anything to do with the mob."[30]

J.C. Engle, a New Yorker traveling through Leflore on business when the trouble started, told reporters that "the number of negroes [murdered] will never be known." Victims, he said, "were shot down like dogs," while "in the dooryards, and even in houses men, women and children were murdered." In Engle's opinion, "If the whites of the North knew of the atrocities practiced in Mississippi, they would feel like sweeping the State from the face of the globe." The *Chicago Tribune* was more sanguine, regarding the slaughter as "only a repetition of the old kuklux outrages." Historian William Holmes places the final body count at around twenty-five, while the *Leavenworth Advocate* and the *New York Age* guessed that 100-plus were slain.[31]

With that mayhem still fresh in mind, James Chalmers launched his gubernatorial race as a Republican in autumn 1889. He planned his first campaign speech in Columbus, for the first week of October, but received a warning that if he appeared "he would find an armed mob waiting for him at the depot; that he would be killed in the broad open daylight, or assassinated in the night, if he attempted to speak." Chalmers moved on to West Point, where armed Democrats "thronged the streets, acting as pickets, [and] refused to let him speak there." He faced a similar scene in Okolona, barred from the courthouse while a white militia company "went parading and yelling over the street." Next morning, still in Okolona, friends warned Chalmers that if he delivered his speech "the killing of negroes would commence and they [Democrats] would charge it to me." Chalmers then abandoned the race, leaving a campaign devoid of Republicans candidates. The GOP State Executive Committee told reporters, "Mississippi is governed by a minority despotism, and we appeal to our country for redress.... Ever since the famous Mississippi plan was adopted, our path has been marked by the blood of our slain.... We refer not only to such well-known slaughters as Kemper and Copiah, Clinton, Carrollton, Wahalak and Vicksburg, Yazoo City and Leflore, but to the nameless killing by creek and bayou, on highway and byway. These are the Democratic arguments which crush us. We can do no more. We dare no longer to carry our tattered and bloodstained Republican flag." Those who tried in 1890, like Henry Fans in Aberdeen and Marsh Cook in Jasper County, were commonly whipped or murdered.[32]

White supremacy would not be fully guaranteed, of course, as long as blacks could vote. Pervasive violence had stained the state's honor, a point acknowledged by Judge J.B. Chrisman when he told reporters that it was "no secret that there has not been a full vote and a fair count in Mississippi since 1875 — that we have been preserving the ascendancy of the white people by revolutionary methods." Chrisman was among the delegates who gathered on 12 August 1890 to draft a new state constitution. Its drift was foretold by the convention's makeup, including 130 Democrats, one "National Republican," one "Conservative," and one Greenbacker. The sole black delegate was Isaiah Montgomery, a prosperous merchant who publicly favored black disfranchisement. Other well-known delegates included ex-governor James Alcorn, Henry Muldrow, and James Z. George — widely acknowledged as the "formulator" of the new constitution's provisions on suffrage.[33]

The convention's final product, imposed on Mississippi without a popular vote, established a two-dollar poll tax, mandated two years' residency in the state and one year in the would-be voter's district, and denied ballots to convicted felons or tax-defaulters. Section 244 further required that any voter must "be able to read any section of the constitution of this State; or he shall be able to understand the same when read to him, or give a reasonable interpretation thereof." The net effect, by 1892, was to remove 138,400 blacks and 52,000 whites from the state's electoral rolls.[34]

The new constitution had problems—future Governor Theodore Bilbo described it as a document "that damn few white men and no niggers at all can explain"— but James Alcorn hoped it would "accomplish the desired result" of preserving white supremacy "without any lawlessness," which in his view had the effect of "demoralizing the young men of our State by breeding in them a contempt for the law." Jackson's *Clarion-Ledger* dismissed the new literacy requirements on 23 October 1890, declaring that convention delegates "do not object to negroes voting on account of ignorance, but on account of color." A decade later, racist spokesman James Vardaman confirmed that judgment in the *Greenwood Commonwealth*. "There is no use to equivocate or lie about the matter," he wrote on 17 August 1900. "Mississippi's constitutional convention of 1890 was held for no other purpose than to eliminate the nigger from politics; not the 'ignorant and vicious,' as some apologists would have you believe, but the nigger.... Let the world know it just as it is."[35]

Populism Fails

Following "redemption," southern propagandists led by *Atlanta Constitution* editor Henry Grady trumpeted the concept of a "New South" to northern investors, seeking infusions of fresh capital. White farmers saw the Democratic Bourbons—led in Mississippi by corporate attorneys George, Lamar and Walthall—tighten their alliance with northern industrial interests, while sharecroppers of all races struggled in virtual peonage. Those impoverished farmers initially sought to gain control of the Democratic Party through candidates such as Ethelbert Barksdale and Putnam Darden (head of Mississippi's Grange), but their hopes were dashed in the Senate campaign of 1880 and the gubernatorial race of 1885.[36]

Two years later, in 1887, organizers of the Farmers' Alliance penetrated Mississippi, recruiting an estimated 50,000 members by autumn 1888, increased to some 75,000 in 1890. The Mississippi People's (or Populist) Party held its first convention in Jackson, in June 1891, where delegates from twenty-two counties chose Panola's G.W. Dyer as their chairman. The convention nominated Frank Burkitt, former Democratic agrarian leader and editor of the *Chickasaw Messenger*, to challenge incumbent Senator George that fall, but the recent disfranchisement of blacks and poor whites doomed that effort. Burkitt tried again in 1895, entering the gubernatorial race against Anselm McLaurin, but voters once again rejected him. Statewide voter registration increased between 1892 and 1896—by 68 percent for blacks and 43 percent for whites—but Populist candidates lost all of their congressional races during 1892–98. On the national scene, Grover Cleveland carried the South to unseat incumbent Benjamin Harrison in 1892. Two years later, he named Louisiana ex-Klansman Edward White to serve on the U.S. Supreme Court.[37]

Part of the problem, as always in Dixie, was race. Georgia's Thomas Watson and other Populist candidates stressed the common interests of farmers, regardless of color, and freely appealed for black votes. Watson toured his state with a black minister, the Rev. H.S. Doyle, and when whites threatened Doyle, Watson declared, "We are determined in this free country that the humblest white or black man that wants to talk our doctrine shall do it, and the man doesn't live who shall touch a hair of his head, without fighting every man in the People's party!" The *Natchez Democrat* replied, "If any White man ... can encourage such doctrines, he is unworthy of recognition despite his color." Political murders resumed with Mississippi's 1894 congressional race, while the *Bolivar County Democrat* declared, "We cannot believe that many [voters] will turn their backs on the white Democrats of the county and join the black brigade in the struggle for negro supremacy in our county.... The white people have determined to rule Bolivar county and no combination of Republicans, populites and soreheads can defeat them."[38]

So it was, as well, in national politics. William Jennings Bryan was a double loser in 1896, running for the White House both as a Democrat *and* a Populist (with Tom Watson as his running mate on the third-party ticket). William McKinley's 602,000 votes nearly tripled the Populist tally that year, and he crushed Bryan's Democratic slate again in 1900, while Populist candidate Wharton Barker received only 50,373 votes out of some 14 million cast. Theodore Roosevelt proved unstoppable in 1904, defeating the GOP by a margin of 2.6 million ballots, while Populist standard-bearer Tom Watson received only 117,183. Watson tried again in 1908, running sixth in a field of eight parties with 29,100 votes nationwide. By 1912, when Woodrow Wilson carried the South to restore Democratic control of the White House, the Populist Party had ceased to exist as a national force.[39]

Tom Watson analyzed his failure, deciding that "[t]he argument against the independent political movement in the South may be boiled down to one word — nigger." Comparing his effort to Bryan's, Watson wrote: "His field was the plastic, restless, growing West; mine was the hidebound, rock-ribbed Bourbon South. Besides, Bryan had *no everlasting and overshadowing Negro Question to hamper and handicap his progress*: I HAD." Watson's situation in Georgia differed from that of Mississippi. "In Georgia," he wrote, "they do not dare disfranchise the Negro because the men who control the Democratic machine in Georgia know that a majority of the whites are against them. They need the Negro to beat us with. The white people dare not revolt so long as they can be intimidated by the fear of the Negro vote." After 1904, Watson offered Populist support to any Democrat who would support "a change in our constitution which will perpetuate white supremacy in Georgia." Failing in that, he lapsed into overt racism, riding a wave of hatred to achieve the success that had so far eluded him.[40] And in the process, he would lay the groundwork for the rebirth of the Ku Klux Klan.

In October 1906, Watson purchased the weekly *Jeffersonian*, later supplemented by a monthly *Watson's Magazine*. In 1908 he shifted from Populist broadsides to unadulterated bigotry, compiling a personal fortune of some $250,000 over the next half-decade. Watson began with warnings against the "Hideous, Ominous, National Menace of negro domination," declaring that "there is no equality of sexes or races." In an editorial titled "The Ungrateful Negro," Watson asked his readers, "What does Civilization owe the negro? Nothing! *Nothing*! NOTHING!"[41]

In 1910, Watson rediscovered the "Catholic menace" formerly touted by Know-Nothings and the APA. A year later, he organized the Guardians of Liberty, soliciting one hundred dollars each from "American Americans" to support his crusade and pay the team of bodyguards allegedly required to forestall Watson's assassination by the Knights of Columbus. "I stand for the ideals of the Old South," Watson wrote. "The men behind the guns must be American-born; for the time is surely coming when he who is in command must give the order, 'Put none but Americans on guard tonight.'" In *Foreign Missions Exposed* (1912), Watson called upon Protestant pastors throughout the U.S. to join him and "save America from the wolves of Rome."[42]

While some of Watson's diatribes were simply childish — he labeled Pope Benedict XV, formerly Giacomo della Chiesa, "Jimmy Cheezy" — others revealed an increasing obsession with sex. In March 1911, Watson warned against "secret confessions to unmarried Lotharios, parading as priests and enjoying themselves carnally with the choicest women of the earth. At the confessional, the priest finds out what girls and married women he can seduce.

Having discovered the trail, he wouldn't be human, if he did not take advantage of the opportunity."

A month later, he turned on black priests: "*Heavens above! Think of a negro priest taking the vow of chastity and then being turned loose among women who have been taught that a priest cannot sin. It is a thing to make one shudder.*" That July, he asked, "Is there none among them [priests] to point out the absurdity and ludicrousness of their wearing a garment emblematic of sexual intercourse?" Federal authorities twice charged Watson with sending obscene material through the U.S. mail, but one indictment was dismissed, while the second led to acquittal at trial. By 1915, the *Jeffersonian* boasted 40,000 subscribers nationwide, while *Watson's Magazine* claimed 18,000.[43]

Whitecaps

Nineteen years after General Forrest disbanded the Klan, twelve years after the order's last reported outing in Mississippi, a new band of masked night riders arose in the land. Known as Whitecaps, the terrorists first appeared in 1888, among Tennessee migrants settled in Indiana. The movement quickly spread, adopting various causes in different locations: as vigilante "regulators" in the Midwest and Texas, scourging Republicans in New Mexico, protecting moonshine stills in Georgia — and pursuing a campaign of agrarian violence in southwestern Mississippi. Black farmers who rented land from white merchants in Amite, Franklin, Pike and Wilkinson counties had suffered sporadic raids by "bulldozers" or "protective clubs" since September 1877, with some observers blaming the Farmer's Alliance. During 1892–93, the targets were primarily black tenants and their Jewish landlords who obtained land from white farmers through foreclosure.[44]

Mississippi's Whitecaps organized in late 1891, founding paramilitary "clubs" with designated officers in Amite, Copiah, Franklin, Lawrence, Lincoln and Marion counties.Their dual purpose was to halt foreclosures and control black labor, to which end they adopted Klan-like disguises and swiftly turned to nocturnal terrorism. Smithdale's club demanded white supervision of black sharecroppers and declared it "illegal" for merchants to hire black workers away from their present white employers.[45] Lawrence County's Whitecaps explained themselves in more detail, with a manifesto published in the *Magnolia Gazette*:

> The conditions which surround us justify our cooperation. We meet in a state brought to the verge of ruin by European and Wall Street gold-bugs, backed by a corrupt class who dominate the ballot box, the legislature and congress and even touch the ermine of the bench. This demoralizes the white farmer and laborer. Most of the states have been compelled to isolate the voting places to prevent universal intimidation and bribery. Our homes are covered with mortgages and our lands are fast concentrating in the hands of syndicates, Wall Street and European gold-bugs.
>
> Pauperized Jews are imported here who use every damnable idea conceivable to obtain possession of our lands. The farmers are denied the right to organization for self-protection; consequently the earnings of millions are boldly stolen to build up colossal fortunes for a few, which is unprecedented in the history of mankind and the possessors of these fortunes in turn despise the Republic and endanger liberty.
>
> From the same prolific source of wrongs of governmental injustice come the two great classes, tramps and millionaires, and farmers, you will be the tramps and some one else the millionaires, unless you join hands to deter them.

The accursed Jews and others own two thirds of our land. They control and half bind the negro laborers who partly subsist by thefts from the white farmers; thereby controlling prices of Southern produce.

We therefore pray the white farmers to combine forces and gain control of the negro labor, which is by right ours, that we may tend the soil under white supremacy, and under no circumstances will the negro be allowed to cultivate a Jew's or syndicate's land, unless such lands are bought and will shortly be paid for. Our first object is to control negro laborers by mild means, if possible; by coercion if necessary.

Second, to control Jews and Gentile land speculators, and, if necessary, force them to abandon our country and confiscate their lands for the benefit of the white farmers.[46]

Like Reconstruction-era Klansmen, the Whitecaps swore secret oaths to obey their captains and other officers, forestalled by "nothing short of death." And like the KKK, Whitecap dens enlisted some members by fraud. Dr. Joel Goss, a physician and self-ordained preacher who led the Whitecaps in Marion County, portrayed the order to some recruits as "only a kind of Masonry," designed "to help each other in sickness and distress." By the time some new members received their first night riding assignments, they were pledged to loyalty and silence under threat of death.[47]

The *Pearl River News* first reported Whitecap violence on 17 February 1892, declaring that "negroes are nightly whipped and run off and so common have these occurrences become that the negroes now are afraid to tell when they have been visited." Whitecaps posted warnings to black tenants and Jewish landlords, like one in Natchez reading "The Jew place is not for sale or rent, but will be used hereafter as pasture." Blacks who bought their own land likewise became targets. Those who ignored the warnings were often whipped or shot and their houses burned. Hiller & Company, a Jewish firm that owned 400 houses in three counties, reported 27 burned within two months, amounting to some $50,000 damage. Governor Stone ignored complaints from Whitecap victims through October 1892, prompting 400 blacks at Liberty to "apply for colonization" outside Mississippi.

Around the same time, Marion County raiders murdered black tenant Jesse Pittman in his bed. In November, after fifty Whitecaps ordered Cicero and Henry McGehee to abandon their Zion Hill cotton gin, an interracial committee organized "to see if an adjustment could be reached." They failed, and white concern deepened in December, as Whitecaps turned their attention to Gentile landlords. On 17 December, the *Woodville Republican* said, "We are reliably informed that the Whitecaps have issued an order that no man in [Amite] county shall be a farmer and a store keeper at the same time."[48]

Simultaneously, Whitecaps also targeted black employees of Mississippi's two largest lumber companies, Keystone Lumber and Norwood and Butterfield. Those firms hired private investigators, while bankers threatened to withhold loans in Whitecap-infested counties. Thus motivated, prominent whites organized "Law and Order Leagues" to combat terrorism, while Governor Stone belatedly condemned whitecapping in January 1893, offering a 100-dollar reward for each night rider convicted. Within a week of Stone's pronouncement, Whitecaps flogged septuagenarian farmer Denny Watt in Adams County and ordered Jewish merchant Simon Simon to leave Jefferson County. Black farmer Flowers Wilson and his son were whipped in Pike County for smoking cigars and riding "in a top buggy." Soon afterward, the raiders returned to burn Flowers's home and steal fifty bushels of corn. Flowers filed charges against ten assailants, but jurors acquitted them in autumn 1893.[49]

While that drama played out in court, terrorism escalated. Copiah Whitecaps killed

Doc Thompson in March 1893, while those in Amite County whipped another black farmer, Bow Bell. Grand jurors indicted several suspects in Bell's case, but charges were dropped in July, after Bell was murdered and two other witnesses declined to testify. Copiah County authorities took belated action after Whitecaps subjected a black victim to "unusual, indeed revolting brutality. Some of the details are unfit to be put in print." Witnesses in that case identified nine raiders, but only ringleaders George Shields and James Tyson faced charges. Both were convicted in April, receiving one-year prison terms after Judge J.B. Chrisman yielded to the "tears and entreaties" of their families.

April 1893 also saw nine Lincoln County Whitecaps indicted for arson and attempted murder, held without bond by Judge Chrisman. A mob of seventy-five armed men disrupted the trial on 4 May, but Governor Stone was present four days later, when six defendants pled guilty and received two-year terms. Soon afterward, another forty-seven Whitecaps (including three part-time ministers) threw themselves on Chrisman's mercy and posted $500 peace bonds. The *New Orleans Times-Democrat* observed that "there was not a single man in the crowd who was of any note or established character for intelligence and high standing in the position of the county from which they came."[50]

Lincoln County's Whitecaps made a bold demonstration at Osyka on 13 May 1893, posting notices that ordered all unemployed blacks to leave town. That same night, raiders flogged black tenant Tom Brown in Pike County, telling him that "no Judge Chrisman could scare them and that they might visit Summit before long and clean up some of [its] negroes." In July, Marion County jurors convicted three Whitecaps for the April flogging of Sam Waller, whereupon Judge S.H. Terrell sentenced them to ten-year prison terms. Their comrades swore vengeance against white prosecution witnesses Jim and Will Buckley, subsequently murdering the latter. Jim Buckley named the triggerman as one Will Purvis, who was duly convicted in August and sentenced to hang. The rope broke on his execution date, in February 1894, prompting commutation of his penalty to life imprisonment. Purvis turned state's evidence, naming Dan and Elbert Watts as Jesse Pittman's slayers. They, in turn, named nine accomplices who fled the county and were never found. Governor McLaurin pardoned Purvis in 1898, but another quarter-century passed before ex–Whitecap Joe Beard named Lewis Thornhill as the actual killer. The Waller flogging produced other trials, sending three Whitecaps to prison for ten years, while a fifth got one year and jurors deadlocked on a sixth.[51]

Lawrence County violence escalated in June 1893 with the murder of white farmer W.D. Morris. Governor Stone matched the 200-dollar reward posted by local authorities in that case, while Judge William Cassedy offered leniency to any Whitecaps who would sign a pledge of good behavior and share the order's secrets with a grand jury. A total of 112 accepted the deal, effectively ending the order in Lawrence County. Cassedy next extended his offer to Pike and Amite, but got no response. Pike County's Whitecaps had disbanded by autumn 1893, but Amite's raiders remained defiant. In December, local lawyers received letters signed "Liberty or Death," warning that Amite's farmers would die before submitting to "our families being thrown out of their homes, and the proceeds of their honest labor being sucked into the voracious jaws of the leeches, commonly known as the Jew." Peril awaited any lawyer who represented "a Jew against a farmer." While business leaders rallied in opposition to whitecapping, night riders posted arson threats at several cotton gins. No fires resulted, and investigators from a Jackson insurance firm "failed to find the existence of any organization styling themselves White Caps."[52]

Whitecapping reared its shrouded head again in 1902, when a group "composed of the leading farmers" in Amite County declared it "bad policy to sell land to negroes." Threats followed, coupled with offers of protection for blacks who sought to "elevate themselves morally." By autumn, full-scale raiding had resumed in Amite, Franklin and Lincoln counties. Amite County Whitecaps called themselves the Farmers' Protective Association, while Franklin boasted a Farmers' Industrial League and Lincoln harbored the Farmers' Progressive League. All swore oaths to "assist in every way directed by the organization to compel negroes to vacate any and all property owned by merchants, and to assist to put out of the way any and all obnoxious negroes within the jurisdiction of the club." Members also vowed, if called for jury duty, never to convict a fellow Whitecap, under penalty of death. As with the first Whitecap societies, no merchants were admitted, though rural physicians, mechanics and preachers were welcome.[53]

Franklin County Whitecaps launched their campaign on the night of 11 December 1902, posting notices at more than fifty homes, warning black tenants to leave their lands and find work with white farmers. Threats quickly followed in Amite and Lawrence and were succeeded by arson, floggings, and shootings. On 15 December, white leaders from Amite and Lincoln called upon Governor Andrew Longino, voicing fears of an incipient "labor famine" if whitecapping ran unchecked. Longino responded with a proclamation condemning night riders and offered fifty dollars for each raider convicted. In Liberty, on 18 December, bankers and merchants sought to placate Whitecaps with a promise to hire white supervisors for their black workers, but the nocturnal raids continued. As in 1892–93, the violence sparked a new black exodus, while worried bankers threatened termination of all loans in the affected areas.[54]

In Franklin County, Whitecap leader and former Populist state legislator A.M. Newman seemed confused about the future of his Farmers' Industrial League. He wrote to Meadville's *Franklin Advocate* on 16 December 1902, announcing his resignation as FIL president and warning against the dangers of secret societies. Six days later, a second letter from Newman declared that the League would be a force for law and order after "expurgation and reorganization." Great plans notwithstanding, the group disbanded in January 1903, after Mississippi's attorney general advised Newman not to seek a state charter.[55]

Lincoln County officers jailed three Whitecaps in February 1903, for threatening black tenant Steward Fairman two months earlier. The trio pled guilty in May and convinced sixty more to do likewise, all released by Judge Robert Powell after paying five-dollar fines and signing peace bonds. Amite County's unit suffered its deathblow in April 1903 with the indictment of ringleaders J.W. Huff, Levi Green, and M.V.B. Newman. Defense attorneys brokered a deal whereby the Farmers' Progressive League disbanded and the three defendants accepted suspended jail terms without admitting guilt. On 15 April, Franklin County's grand jury indicted fourteen Whitecaps (including one black man, Tip Shell), but all were acquitted at trial despite testimony from their latest victim and two white witnesses. That victory prompted A.M. Newman to run for sheriff; he won the race despite opposition from local merchants. At least six other FPL members won elective office in Franklin County during 1903.[56]

James Vardaman's 1903 gubernatorial campaign inflamed racial hatred while downplaying Whitecap terrorism. On 2 January, Vardaman declared, "This outside play, this gubernatorial stage thunder, is worth nothing. It only serves to magnify and give wider publicity to the unfortunate condition which prevails in a small subdivision of the sate. If the sheriff of the 'whitecap' infested counties would summons [sic] twenty-five brave and determined men and make them deputies, they could bag every 'whitecapper' in that county within sixty days. No trouble about it." A local farmer, writing to the *Lincoln County Times*, reported that his neighbors supported Vardaman in the belief that Vardaman would pardon any white man convicted of killing blacks.[57]

More mayhem followed the election. In late November 1903, Lincoln County raiders killed black farmers Henry List and Eli Hilson, flogging and shooting several others who survived. Most officials in Franklin and Lincoln counties ignored the problem, though Sheriff Newman attached himself to one "committee of resolution" as a Whitecap spy. In February 1904, Governor Vardaman reluctantly hired Pinkerton detective A.J. Hoyt to investigate matters in Lincoln County, resulting in formation of a civilian Law and Order Executive Committee. Suspects W.P. Adams and Jeff Wills cracked in July, revealing Whitecap oaths and naming members from county tax rolls. Three of Henry List's killers were jailed in September, while five more fled into hiding. At trial in December, after Judge M.H. Wilkinson purged six Whitecaps from the juror's list, all three defendants pled guilty and four more surrendered, receiving sentences that ranged from ten years to life. Another 300 Whitecaps then responded to Judge Wilkinson's call for surrender, including a state legislator, the chancery clerk, and two county supervisors.[58]

Franklin County was the last Whitecap stronghold. In November 1904, a federal grand jury indicted seventeen suspects on charges of driving black farmers from federal homesteads. Detective Hoyt organized a new merchant's committee in January 1905, denounced by Sheriff Newman as a gang of "crap shooters, gamblers and crooks." Hoyt soon collected 198 signed confessions, producing another 309 federal indictments, with Newman first on the list. Others charged included a state lawmaker, the county assessor, treasurer, coroner, circuit clerk, and one supervisor. Defendant John Nettles shot informant W.P. Adams in November 1905, escaping murder charges with a plea of self-defense. At trial, in May 1906, all 309 defendants pled guilty as charged. Judge Henry Niles fined each of them twenty-five dollars, then suspended their thirty-day jail terms, effectively ending the Whitecap movement.[59]

Rewriting History

While Whitecaps terrorized southwestern Mississippi and state legislators pondered fresh Jim Crow statutes in Jackson, a new generation of historians prepared to rewrite the history of Reconstruction, adopting Dixie's Democratic formula wherein freedmen were witless "children" or lecherous fiends, "radical" Republicans personified evil, and Klansmen were heroic (if sometimes overzealous) saviors of civilization. Columbia University professors William Dunning and John Burgess were the movement's chief spokesmen. Their writings and their students dominated white America's view of Reconstruction and "Redemption" for the first half of the twentieth century.[60]

Dunning himself believed that Congress did "a monstrous thing" by granting black suffrage, since "a black skin means membership in a race of men which has never of itself succeeded in subjecting passion to reason, has never, therefore, created any civilization of any kind." Southern historical societies, including Mississippi's, filled their journals with articles praising the Klan and condemning any move to challenge white supremacy. Thus, F.Z. Browne described "hordes of carpetbag vultures" looting Mississippi, while Hattie Magee denounced "scalawags [who] were so despicable that their course arouses indignation and merits the severest condemnation." Black schools were invariably taught by "Northern people of questionable character." Those schools were well attended, Ruth Watkins declared, because "old and young alike sought education rather than work," while learning "had a bad influence over the negroes." John Kyle described the Black Codes as "efforts to properly regulate the relations between the freedmen and the whites"; without them, "[s]ocial turmoil and strife, verging at times on a war between the races, left their demoralizing effects, and it was not until the whites regained control in 1875 that order was restored." It was "the policy of the administration at Washington [that] forced the Southern leaders to adopt extraordinary measures for protecting the lives and fortunes of their people, and for preserving Anglo-Saxon civilization." Julia Kendel found Mississippi plagued by the "blighting curse of the carpetbagger, scalawag, and negro rule" until whites organized to "throw off the ruin and dishonor that threatened them."[61]

The vehicle of their salvation was the KKK, which "exercised great power for good ... in keeping down the vicious negroes" and "brought comfort and peace to the trembling women and terrified children of the South." Ruth Watkins praised Klansmen for "intimidating the negroes through their superstitions, as well as through bodily correction." Legal efforts to suppress Klan violence "marked extreme fever heat in the reconstruction rabies." J.S. McNeilly claimed "[i]rrefutable and conclusive proof" that Klan prosecutions "originated in a conspiracy of radical leaders to serve the purpose of perpetuating Republican negro rule in the Southern States." Fred Witty thanked Mississippi's redeemers for "disfranchising the negro in the State indefinitely, at least: forever, we hope." Historian James Garner declared "that much of the responsibility for these so-called Kuklux disorders must rest ultimately upon the authors of reconstruction." Incredibly, he also proclaimed that the pogroms of 1875 were "really the last race conflict in the state of Mississippi."[62]

While that skewed version of history filled textbooks and scholarly journals, it reached an even wider audience through the popular novels of Thomas Dixon Jr. A native of North Carolina born in 1864, Dixon shared classes with "Dunning School" historian and future president Woodrow Wilson at Johns Hopkins University. Elected to North Carolina's legislature before he attained voting age, Dixon soon abandoned politics in favor of the Baptist pulpit, where he preached the imperative of white Christian supremacy over "creeping negroidism." His best sellers, described by Wyn Wade as "racist sermons in the guise of fiction," included *The Leopard's Spots* (1902), *The Clansman* (1905), and *The Traitor* (1907). Collectively, they made him rich and reinforced the image of the KKK as a heroic order, rather than a band of terrorists.[63]

"Progressive" Mississippi

The Progressive Era (1900–1920) was marked in Mississippi and America at large by reform of ills and abuses arising from the nation's increasing urbanization and industrialization. Those reforms included child labor laws, women's suffrage, a graduated income tax, antitrust legislation, and various consumer-protection measures such as the Pure Food and Drug Act. Ironically, on both the state and national scene, so-called progressivism also included more blatant calls for white supremacy (via Jim Crow statutes or lynch-mob terrorism) and a reversion to "old-time religion" (embodied in the prohibition of liquor and Darwinist teachings).[64]

Mississippi's first "progressive" governor was James Vardaman, an unabashed racist whose appeals to bigotry earned him renown as the "Great White Chief." Born in 1861 and admitted to the Mississippi bar at age twenty, Vardaman edited a series of newspapers, including the *Advance* (in Winona), the *Commonwealth* and the *Issue* (both in Greenwood). He served first in the state legislature (1890–1896), then lost two gubernatorial bids (1895 and 1899) before finally winning the post in 1903.

A self-styled "friend of the people" and "scholar of George," Vardaman coupled support for progressive causes with unalloyed hatred of blacks. In his opinion, "[t]he good [Negroes] are few, the bad are many, and it is impossible to tell what ones are ... dangerous to the honor of the dominant race until the damage is done." In 1897 Vardaman declared that black votes "will be either cast aside or Sambo will vote as directed by the white folks.... There is no use multiplying words about it. The negro ... will not be permitted to rise above the station which he now fills." Black disfranchisement was not a matter of qualification, "but rather a matter of race prejudice — as deep-seated and ineradicable as the Anglo-Saxon genius for self-government." Furthermore, it did not trouble Vardaman if lynch mobs sometimes claimed innocent victims. "We would he justified in slaughtering every Ethiop on the earth," he wrote, "to preserve unsullied the honor of one Caucasian home. If it is necessary every negro in the State will be lynched; it will be done to maintain white supremacy."[65]

Lynching, indeed, was a constant threat to people of color in progressive Mississippi. While statistics are disputed, Terrence Finnegan reports that Mississippi lynchings nearly doubled in white-majority districts during the decade after black disfranchisement, from forty-two cases during the period of 1882–1890, to seventy-five from 1891 to 1900. Overall statistics for the nation's "lynching era" vary widely, ranging from a low of 3,786 to a high of 5,000 between 1882 and 1951. Mississippi contributed at least 476 of those lynchings, perhaps as many as 591, leading the nation with a per capita rate of 53 lynchings per 100,000 residents. Between 1900 and 1944, at least fifteen victims were burned alive in spectacles which the *Jackson Daily News* dubbed "negro barbecues."[66]

One such case with unexpected ramifications occurred in February 1904, when Doddsville planter James Eastland interrupted a quarrel between two of his black tenants. Shooting resulted, leaving Eastland and tenant John Carr dead, while suspect Luther Holbert and his wife fled the plantation. Mobs led by Eastland's brothers scoured the district, killing three blacks who "resembled" Holbert before the fugitive couple was captured. Their deaths were horrific, torture with knives and corkscrews preceding live immolation. James Eastland's nephew and namesake, born at Doddsville nine months later, would grow into Mississippi's most hard-bitten racist senator of the civil rights era.[67]

Before his election, Governor Vardaman praised lynch law. After a gruesome case at Corinth in September 1902, he editorialized: "I think they did right to kill the brute, but it would have been better had the crowd been denied admission. It does not help a man morally to look upon a thing of that kind. It is rather hardening. But I sometimes think that one could look upon a scene of that kind and suffer no more moral deterioration than he would by looking upon the burning of an orangoutang [*sic*] that had stolen a baby or a viper that had stung an unsuspecting child to death." Ten months later, he wrote, "If I were the sheriff and a negro fiend fell into my hands, I would run him out of the county. If I were governor and were asked for troops to protect him I would send them. But if I were a private citizen I would head the mob to string the brute up." The *Vicksburg Herald* praised his "courage" for that statement, challenging Vardaman's opponents to disagree. None did.[68]

As governor, Vardaman made no drastic moves against blacks, but neither was he eager to defend them. He ignored the letter from a tenant farmer in Neshoba County who complained that "[a] crowd of lawless rough brutal men has beaten and run off all the Negroes in this community without cause. All we know as reason that it was done is because they are Negroes. It was done in the night and we could not help it. We are expecting someone to be killed any time. The sheriff cannot do much or has not. He seems to be afraid or careless." Likewise, Vardaman declined to investigate when five black families were hounded from West Point, or when threats dissuaded a black physician from buying one of the "handsomest and finest" homes in Jackson. When Indianola's white residents protested appointment of a black postmistress in 1904, Vardaman declared that Mississippi whites "are not going to let niggers hold office." He *did* send troops to Wahalak in 1906, forestalling a Christmas pogrom, but Vardaman voiced no concern for a victim lynched before they arrived, by whites intent on "strik[ing] terror into the negroes, who have been getting defiant of late."[69]

In 1907, Vardaman challenged Rep. John Sharp Williams for a seat in the U.S. Senate. Georgia's Tom Watson wrote letters to various Mississippi newspapers on Vardaman's behalf, branding Williams "one more doodle-bug" owned by big business, while Vardaman ran his usual racist campaign. Greenville's LeRoy Percy branded Vardaman "infamous" for his willingness "to inflame the passions and hatred of his audience, hoping out of it to gain a few paltry votes." Williams followed a similar course, condemning Vardaman's "ceaseless agitation" and "indiscriminate cursing of the whole negro race." Vardaman lost that race, but only by 648 votes out of 118,344 ballots cast. Theodore Bilbo—a Vardaman protégé and future Klansman from Poplarville, fired as a teacher in Wiggins for bedding one of his students—had better luck that autumn, winning election to the state senate.[70]

Racist violence persisted for the remainder of Vardaman's tenure, with twenty blacks lynched in his last year as governor (sixty-eight overall during his four-year term). In 1908, a young white Mississippian told historian Albert Hart, "You don't understand how we feel down here. When there is a row, we feel like killing a nigger whether he has done anything wrong or not." The same year found Mississippi's congressmen complaining that federal peonage investigations damaged their state's prospects for immigration and northern investment. The latest case in point, from Vicksburg, saw a white planter charged with enslaving Italians. That case prompted rulers of Italy and Austria-Hungary to warn their citizens against visiting Mississippi.[71]

Senator A.J. McLaurin died suddenly in December 1909, giving Vardaman new hope for a seat in Congress. Eugene Bryant, the black editor of the *Brookhaven People's Relief*, opposed Vardaman and paid the price: mobs led by police burned his home, his press, and five of Bryant's rental homes. LeRoy Percy won the appointment in 1910, but not before Theodore Bilbo muddied the water with bribery charges against Percy's camp. Senate investigators found Bilbo's story riddled with "unexplained inconsistencies and inherent improbabilities," condemning it as a "trumped-up falsehood, utterly unworthy of belief." The senate censured Bilbo, branding him "unfit to sit with honest, upright men in a respectable legislative body," and urged him to resign. When he refused, the *Macon Beacon* pronounced him "attractive in the same way that freaks of nature are regarded." As for Vardaman, the Mississippi press widely condemned his association with a "pimp," a "frequenter of lewd houses," "a thorough rascal," and "a self-confessed bribe-taker."[72]

Despite that scandal, both Vardaman and Bilbo were ready for more tough campaigning in 1911. Bilbo struck a wounded martyr's pose and won election as lieutenant governor, spouting rhetoric which the *Memphis Commercial-Appeal* deemed "horribly repulsive, disgusting and shocking." Vardaman faced Percy in another senate challenge. Percy branded Vardaman's supporters "cattle" and "rednecks," the latter insult prompting many to don red ties. Percy's son William described a typical Vardaman crowd as an "ill-dressed, surly audience, unintelligent and slinking.... They were the sort of people who lynched Negroes, that mistake hoodlumism for wit, and cunning for intelligence, that attend revivals and fight and fornicate in the bushes afterwards." That disdain failed Percy on election day, as Vardaman secured 79,369 votes to Percy's 21,521.[73]

In the Senate, Vardaman maintained his reputation for vitriolic bigotry. He called for repeal of the Fourteenth and Fifteenth Amendments, painting blacks as "veneered savages." Pressed on the subject of black education, Vardaman declared that the average African American was a "lazy, lying, lustful animal which no conceivable amount of training can transform into a tolerable citizen. Why squander money on his education, when the only effect is to spoil a good field hand and make an insolent cook?... [T]he way to control the nigger is to whip him when he does not obey without it." His supporters at home agreed, prompting one black Mississippian to tell the *Progressive Farmer*, "If we own a good farm or horse, or cow, or bird-dog, or yoke of oxen, we are harassed until we are bound to sell, give away, or run away, before we can have any peace in our lives."[74]

The Klan Reborn

In 1914, director D.W. Griffith purchased film rights to Thomas Dixon's trilogy of Ku Klux novels. Dixon initially asked for ten thousand dollars, but settled for 25 percent of the movie's eventual profits. After viewing the final production, complete with sweeping Civil War battles, Dixon deemed his original title too tame. Instead of *The Clansman*, he suggested, Griffith should call their epic *The Birth of a Nation*.[75]

The film premiered to sold-out crowds in Los Angeles, on 18 January 1915. Despite some rave reviews, however, its portrayal of heroic Klansmen lynching bestial black rapists inspired criticism from black activists and white liberals alike. On 3 February, Dixon met with former classmate Woodrow Wilson at the White House and invited him to view the film. Wilson agreed, and emerged from the 18 February screening visibly moved. "It is like writing history with lightning," he declared, "and my only regret is that it is all so terribly true." Hedging his bets, Dixon also sought endorsement from Edward White, a Reconstruction-era Klansman turned Chief Justice of the U.S. Supreme Court. White watched and praised the film, but after violence marred screenings in New York and elsewhere, he warned producers to desist from spreading "rumors" that he had endorsed the movie. Dixon banked his profits from the film, but declined suggestions that he revive the KKK as the White Heart League or the Aryan League of America.[76]

In Georgia, meanwhile, a sordid murder case helped pave the way for a Klan revival. On 27 April 1913, young Mary Phagan was found dead and presumably raped at the Atlanta pencil factory where she worked. Police initially detained Jim Conley, the plant's black janitor, then switched their focus to manager Leo Frank, a New York Jew. Conley accused Frank of killing Phagan, then forcing him (Conley) to hide her corpse in the factory basement. Jurors convicted Frank on 25 August 1913 and he received a death sentence, while Conoley escaped with one year at hard labor. Governor John Slaton created a firestorm of controversy by commuting Frank's sentence to life imprisonment on 21 June 1915.[77]

The case was tailor-made for racist demagogues, and Tom Watson led the charge with a two-year campaign of anti–Semitic editorials. He branded Frank "a typical young Jewish man of business who lives for pleasure *and runs after Gentile girls. Every student of soci-*ology knows that the black man's lust for the white woman *is not much fiercer than the lust of the licentious Jew for the Gentile.*" According to Watson, "Jews of this type have an utter contempt for law and a ravenous appetite for the forbidden fruit — a lustful eagerness enhanced by the racial novelty of the girls of the uncircumcised." To Watson, commutation of Frank's sentence smacked of conspiracy. Frank belonged to "Jewish aristocracy," he wrote, and that shadowy clique had decreed that "no aristocrat of their race should die for the death of a working-class Gentile." Watson closed that editorial with a clarion call: "Rise! People of Georgia!"[78]

Heeding the call, a lynch mob organized, calling itself the Knights of Mary Phagan. Ringleaders included an ex-governor, a local prosecutor, the son of a U.S. Senator, a Methodist preacher, a judge and a state legislator (both of the latter themselves suspected in separate murder cases). On 17 August 1915, hand-picked killers kidnapped Frank from a state prison farm and hanged him, posing unmasked with the corpse for photographs. Watson hailed the lynching, his *Jeffersonian* announcing that "a Vigilance Committee redeem[ed] Georgia and carrie[ed] out the sentence of the law on the Jew who raped and murdered the little Gentile girl, Mary Phagan.... Let Jew libertines take notice." On 2 September, Watson called for "another Ku Klux Klan ... to restore HOME RULE" in Dixie. Six weeks later, on 16 October, the Knights of Mary Phagan took a leaf from Thomas Dixon's novels and burned a giant cross atop Stone Mountain, visible throughout Atlanta.[79]

While Watson called for the Klan's revival, that task fell to other hands. William Joseph Simmons was an Alabama native, born in 1880, who claimed that his father rode with the original KKK. After serving in the Spanish-American War, Simmons became a Methodist preacher, but the Alabama Conference defrocked him in 1912, on grounds of "inefficiency and moral impairment." Thus rebuffed, he turned to the world of fraternal recruiting and prospered, earning $15,000 in 1914 as a district manager for the Woodmen of the World. Along the way, he joined at least a dozen other lodges and two different churches, adopting a self-imposed rank of "colonel." "They call me 'Colonel,' largely out of respect," Simmons explained. "Every lawyer in Georgia is called 'Colonel,' so they thought I was as good as a lawyer; so they called me that." Somewhere along the way, Simmons experienced an alcoholic vision of hooded riders galloping across the sky, and "as the picture faded out, I got down on my knees and swore that I would found a fraternal organization that would be a memorial to the Ku Klux Klan."[80]

An auto accident gave Simmons the time to realize his dream. While convalescing for three months, he plagiarized and expanded the first Klan's prescript as *The Kloran*, adding elaborate rituals, ranks, and titles. Most began with the letters *kl*, so that Klansmen met in "klaverns," communicated via "klonversation," rallied at "klonvocations," and so on. "It was rather difficult, sometimes to make the two letters fit in," Simmons admitted, "but I did it somehow." Galvanized by America's first cross-burning, Simmons applied for a state charter in October 1915. His initial recruits included two members of the original Klan and the speaker of Georgia's state legislature. On Thanksgiving night, timed to coincide with *The Birth of a Nation*'s premier in Atlanta, Simmons scaled Stone Mountain with sixteen Klansmen and lit the country's second fiery cross.[81]

Ex-Populist Tom Watson's virulent bigotry paved the way for the modern Klan's revival (**Library of Congress**).

Within two weeks, ninety-two recruits joined the KKK. Newspaper advertisements billed the Klan as "A Classy Order of the Highest Class ... No 'Rough Necks,' 'Rowdies,' nor 'Yellow Streaks' admitted." *The Kloran*, Simmons said, offered rituals "altogether original, weird, mystical, and of a high class." While Simmons, as Imperial Wizard, claimed dominion over a global "Invisible Empire," membership in the order was restricted to "white male persons, native-born gentile citizens of the United States of America, who owe no allegiance of any nature or degree to any foreign Government, nation, institution, sect, ruler, person or people; whose morals are good; whose reputations and vocations are respectable; whose habits are exemplary; who are of sound minds and at or above the age of eighteen years." The Knights of the Ku Klux Klan, Inc., received its permanent state charter on 1 July 1916.[82]

World War I

While the Klan grew in Georgia and planted outposts in neighboring Alabama, most Americans were preoccupied by news of the Great War overseas. Public opinion was deeply divided throughout Mississippi, as elsewhere, on the question of U.S. intervention in Europe. Senator John Williams supported President Wilson's call to arms, while James Vardaman stood firm for isolationism, branding the conflict "a rich man's war and a poor man's fight." Worse yet, he warned, conscription of black servicemen would plague Dixie with "arrogant

Lynchers executed Leo Frank in 1915 and joined the reborn KKK soon afterward (National Archives).

strutting representatives of the black soldiery in every community." In April 1917, Vardaman joined five other senators in voting against declaration of war, a move that ultimately doomed his reelection bid in 1918. Tom Watson joined Vardaman in denouncing the war, whereupon postmaster general Albert Burleson banned his magazines from the U.S. mail.[83]

On the home front, some critics accused Governor Theodore Bilbo (elected in 1915) of dragging his feet on conscription. Eight thousand Mississippians either dodged the draft or deserted after induction, and armed resistance emerged in some districts. In spring 1918, federal troops scoured Lauderdale, Neshoba, and Tippah counties for deserters harbored by friends and relatives. Most surrendered peacefully, but two Tippah County deserters died in a skirmish with soldiers. The KKK despised such traitors, and they worked with the American Protective League and the Citizens' Bureau of Investigation to nab suspected "slackers," marched in patriotic parades, harassed prostitutes near military bases, and broke up a shipyard strike in Mobile, Alabama. President Wilson encouraged xenophobic vigilantism, declaring that "[a]ny man who carries a hyphen about with him carries a dagger that he is ready to plunge into the vitals of this Republic whenever he gets ready." Engrossed by war work, Wizard Simmons ordered the "submerging [of] membership in the Klan." As he later explained, "Our secret service work made this imperative. Membership in the Klan was *always* a secret thereafter."[84]

Race remained a life-and-death issue in wartime Mississippi. In December 1917, rumors spread that agents of northern industry were "stealthily at work" statewide, luring "otherwise contented" blacks away from the cotton patch. Cleveland's affluent whites pledged any action "as may be necessary" to halt the black exodus, while police in Greenville, Hattiesburg and Jackson jailed would-be emigrants. At Brookhaven and Meridian, white railroad employees sidetracked cars filled with blacks fleeing the state. In Vicksburg, during 1918, a "vigilance committee" organized to rout the state's first NAACP chapter. Encouraged by police and the local War Savings Committee, whites tarred-and-feathered Dr. J.A. Miller, charged him with "sedition," and ordered him to leave or die. Three other NAACP members—another physician, a lawyer, and a dentist—fled under threat of similar treatment. In Tupelo, future congressman John Rankin warned black leaders to avoid any "action which might prompt racial consciousness." For those who missed the point, nine lynchings during 1917–18 drove home the message.[85]

Barred by law from succeeding himself, Governor Bilbo ran for Congress in 1918, while backing lieutenant governor Lee Russell as his handpicked successor. William Percy labeled Bilbo "a pert little monster, glib and shameless, with that sort of cunning common to criminals which passes for intelligence. The people loved him. They loved him not because they were deceived by him, but because they understood him thoroughly; they said of him proudly, 'He's a slick little bastard.' He was one of them and he had risen from obscurity to the fame of glittering infamy—it was as if they themselves had crashed the headlines." That pride notwithstanding, Bilbo carried only one of eighteen counties in his district on election day.[86]

Red Scare, Red Summer

The Russian revolutions of 1917–18 alarmed conservative Americans, aggravating wartime paranoia over anarchists, "Reds," and radical unions typified by the Industrial

Workers of the World. In 1919, some 3,600 strikes nationwide sparked fears of incipient rebellion, while a spate of unsolved bombings spawned FBI raids and mass deportations of "enemy aliens." White city dwellers, alarmed by the wartime migration of 750,000 rural blacks to urban industrial centers, rioted during that "red summer" in twenty-six cities across the U.S., including Omaha, Chicago, and the nation's capital. Lynch mobs claimed seventy-four victims before year's end, the highest number in a decade. Several of the victims were black veterans still in uniform.[87]

Governor Bilbo warned against the return of black Mississippi soldiers "contaminated with Northern social and political dreams of equality. We have all the room in the world for what we know as n-i-g-g-e-r-s, but none whatsoever for 'colored ladies and gentlemen.'" In June 1919, after the *Jackson Daily News* announced the public burning of rape suspect John Hartfield and 3,000 spectators rallied for the event, Bilbo told reporters, "I am utterly powerless. The State has no troops, and if the civil authorities at Ellisville are helpless, the State is equally so. Furthermore, excitement is at such a high pitch throughout south Mississippi that any armed attempt to interfere with the mob would doubtless result in the death of hundreds of persons. The negro has confessed, says he is ready to die, and nobody can keep the inevitable from happening."

Five days later, Bilbo told the *Daily News*, "This is strictly a white man's country ... and any dream on the part of the negro race to share social and political equality will be shattered in the end. If the northern negro lover wants to stop negro lynching in the South, he must first get the right conception of the proper relation that must necessarily exist between the races and teach and train the negro race along these lines and in this way remove the cause of lynching." The *Clarion-Ledger* concurred that blacks who "demand or seek social equality ... will get it in the neck."[88]

James Vardaman, though out of office, could not resist comment. After another rape suspect was "roasted" in Vicksburg, *Vardaman's Weekly* declared:

> O, it is horrible! Deplorable! Regrettable! But, as I have often said, it is going to happen as often as rapes happen, and I do not know but that the mob is the only protection to the white man's home. Every community in Mississippi ought to organize and the organization should be led by the bravest and best white men in the community. And they should pick out these suspicious characters—those military, French-women-ruined negro soldiers and let them understand that they are under surveillance, and that when crimes similar to this one are committed, take care of the individual who commits the crime.[89]

The presidential election of 1920 featured two candidates from Ohio. Republican Warren Harding promised a return to "normalcy" after the World War and its subsequent upheavals, presumably sobered by ratification of the Eighteenth Amendment banning alcoholic beverages in the United States. Democrat James Cox fared badly on election day, winning only the South (minus Tennessee) and Kentucky. He trailed Harding by 7 million popular votes, losing in the electoral college by a margin of 404 votes to 127. In Mississippi, Lee Russell occupied the governor's mansion, while ultra-racist John Rankin won his first term in Congress. Labor organizer Palmer Weber later told author Neal Peirce, "If a black man got on the elevator with Rankin, the blood would come up in his face. I saw it actually happen myself in the House Office Building elevator. He couldn't stand the sight."[90]

Building an Empire

Prohibition was old news in Mississippi, where voters had opted for a "dry" state in 1908. Nonetheless, it would become a major issue for the reborn Ku Klux Klan — along with staples such as white supremacy, nativism, anti–Semitism, and suppression of "radicals." There were issues aplenty for Klansmen in Warren Harding's America, yet the order failed to prosper in the early postwar years. Most accounts peg total Ku Klux membership between two and three thousand in early 1920, with chartered klaverns confined to Georgia and Alabama. Despite his bumbling best efforts, Wizard Simmons clearly needed help.[91]

He found it in the persons of Edward Young Clarke and Elizabeth Tyler, partners in the Atlanta-based Southern Publicity Association. Together, Clarke and Tyler represented clients including the American Relief Fund, the Anti-Saloon League, the Salvation Army, the Red Cross, the YMCA, and the Theodore Roosevelt Memorial Association (which sued Clarke for embezzling $5,000). In late October 1919, Atlanta police had found Tyler and Clarke — a married man — drunk and half-naked at a "notorious underworld resort." They gave false names to the arresting officers, paid five-dollar fines for disorderly conduct, and the records subsequently disappeared. As Tyler later told reporters, she and Clarke "came into contact with Colonel Simmons and the Ku Klux Klan through the fact that my son-in-law joined it. We found Colonel Simmons was having a hard time [getting] along. He couldn't pay his rent. The receipts were not sufficient to take care of his personal needs.... After we had investigated it from every angle, we decided to get into it with Colonel Simmons and give it the impetus that it could best get from publicity."[92]

To that end, on 7 June 1920, Simmons contracted with Clarke and Tyler to create a new KKK Propagation Department. Under terms of their contract, each new recruit's ten-dollar "klectoken" (initiation fee) was divided as follows: four dollars for the local "kleagle" (recruiter), one dollar to the state's "king kleagle," fifty cents to a district "goblin," $2.50 to Clarke and Tyler, and two dollars to the Imperial Treasury. By early 1921, 1,100 kleagles were energetically seeking recruits in nine "domains," reporting to goblins based in Atlanta, Boston, Chicago, Houston, Los Angeles, New York City, Philadelphia, St. Louis, and Washington, D.C. Each kleagle catered his recruiting pitch to local appetites, stressing "hot button" issues that ranged from crime control to fear of immigrants or radicals. Protestant ministers were prime Ku Klux targets, and thousands from coast to coast were lured by offers of free membership and employment as "kludds" (pastors) or traveling orators. Fraternal lodges were another fertile breeding ground of "klannishness," mined avidly by kleagles who were often high-level Masons.[93]

Klan membership exploded under Clarke and Tyler. Within fifteen months of meeting Simmons, the duo had inflated Ku Klux ranks from 3,000 members to 100,000. An estimated $1.5 million filled Klan coffers from klectokens and sales of robes, literature, and other paraphernalia. Gate City Manufacturing emerged as sole producer of Klan regalia, while Searchlight Publishing printed the order's literature. Simmons received $170,000 in "commissions," a $40,000 home (dubbed Klan Krest), a salary of $1,000 per month, and a bonus of $25,000 for his first five years of solitary toil. Builders broke ground for a $65,000 Imperial Palace on Peachtree Street in Atlanta. Despite those huge strides, Simmons told reporters in September 1921, "The Ku Klux Klan has not yet started to work and may not do so for a year. We are merely organizing at the present time and we do not

William Simmons (in skull mask) revived the Klan in 1915 (SPLC).

William Simmons waits to testify before Congress in 1921 (Library of Congress).

intend to start any definite activity until we have sufficiently organized to make sure [of] success."[94]

Even as Simmons spoke those words, two rival newspapers were gunning for the Klan. Joseph Pulitzer's *New York World* focused primarily on local activities, documenting acts of violence, while William Randolph Hearst's *New York Journal-American* served up inside gossip on chicanery at Klan headquarters. Together, the papers raised enough questions to prompt calls for a congressional investigation. The House Rules Committee convened hearings on the KKK in October 1921, including three days of testimony from Simmons. Georgia senator Tom Watson, elected in 1920, dropped by to congratulate Simmons on his performance, capped by a prayer and theatrical swoon. Thousands of new recruits joined up by year's end, many using facsimile applications clipped from the *New York World*. In retrospect, Simmons gloated, "Congress made us."[95]

CHAPTER 3

Invisible Empire
(1921–1944)

Atlanta's eager kleagles had high hopes for the Magnolia State. The qualities that prompted social satirist H.L. Mencken to dub Mississippi "the worst American state" in the 1920s made it fertile ground for klannishness and "100-percent Americanism."[1]

No documents exist to date the modern Klan's debut in Mississippi, but the *Hattiesburg American* of 26 January 1921 reported "a movement on foot" to revive the order locally and quoted at length from the *Kloran* and elevated Imperial Wizard Simmons to "professor of History of Lanier University, of Atlanta, Ga." Two weeks later, the *American* noted "whispers and rumors" that "an off-shoot of the Klan is to be organized here." No names were mentioned, since "the utmost secrecy is being observed," but the paper predicted that Simmons "will have some fellow club members in this city." On 1 September 1921 kleagle J.Q. Nolan delivered a Hattiesburg sales pitch with "ladies especially invited." He symbolized the Klan's goals with a square, its four sides including "advancement of pure white, native born Anglo-Saxon Protestants; white supremacy; separation of Church and State; and the upholding of womanhood."[2]

Elsewhere in Mississippi, Vicksburg's exalted cyclops claimed a "keen" response to his recruiting efforts in May 1921, while Jackson's knights delayed their first public appearance until 4 July 1922. That night, an estimated 450 to 600 Klansmen bearing fiery crosses marched four abreast along Capitol Street, from the old statehouse to Union Station. Masked marchers carried signs reading "America for Americans," "Separation of Church and State," "Sanctity of the Home," and "We Stand for Free Speech, Free Schools, Free Press." Reporters for the *Jackson Clarion-Ledger* were impressed by the "stately cadence of the march," declaring it "an impressive spectacle." That demonstration, followed by a similar march through Hattiesburg, hailed Mississippi's emergence as the Klan's fifth sovereign realm, with Grand Dragon T.S. Ward of Canton presiding.[3]

While trading freely on the gilded image of its Reconstruction-era ancestor, the modern Klan offered recruits a mixture of fraternalism, bedrock Protestant moralism, nativism a lá Tom Watson, and traditional white-supremacist dogma. Baptist minister Norris Roberts—whose father helped launch the 1860s Klan in Leake County, and who proclaimed himself "no bigot"—joined the new order based on its promise "to control the government by crooked politicians, money-hungry Jews, the control of Negro votes by evil politicians, and immoderate demands upon government by Roman Catholics."[4] Another minister, H.E. Carter of Senatobia, described his own initiation to researcher Laura Bradley, forty years after the fact:

The oath or obligation taken was as far from doing any wrong as the obligation taken by people joining the church. No night riding or doing any harm to anyone or damage to property. It was clean and honest. We were urged to be loyal to the Klan, also to our church. They did not go under cover of night.... The members were to be loyal and of course if they were church members the better. Our lodge were [*sic*] practically all members of my church.[5]

Published estimates of the Klan's success in Mississippi, as nationwide, vary widely. National tallies of peak membership range from historian Kenneth Jackson's low of 2,028,000 to the *Washington Post*'s improbable (and suspiciously precise) 8,904,887. Jackson claims a peak membership of 15,000 for Mississippi, while author Arnold Rice puts the number "between 50,000 and 200,000," and the *Post* cites a statewide membership of 93,040. Bishop Duncan Gray, speaking for the Episcopal Diocese of Mississippi, offered no statistics but claimed that in Bolivar County, at least, the Klan's *Tri-State American* had a larger circulation than the *Memphis Commercial-Appeal*.[6]

The Fraternal Klan

The Klan's primary appeal to many recruits, in Mississippi and elsewhere, was the same fraternalism that entranced Wizard William Simmons. In his *Kloran*, Simmons described the Klan as "a standard fraternal order enforcing fraternal conduct, and not merely a 'social organization.'"[7] More specifically:

Its ritualism is vastly different from anything in the whole universe of fraternal ritualism. It is altogether original, weird, mystical, and of a high class, leading up through four degrees. Dignity and decency are its marked features. It unfolds a spiritual philosophy that has to do with the very fundamentals of life and living, here and hereafter. He who explores the dismal depths of the mystic cave and from thence attains the lofty heights of superior knighthood may sit among the gods in the empire invisible.[8]

Fraternal lodges flourished in postwar Mississippi, appealing to members described by Laura Bradley as "almost professional joiners." Itinerant kleagles found their first prospects among Masons, Elks, Odd Fellows and Orangemen, characterized by Reverend F.L. Applewhite of Tylertown as "some of the old fellows who wanted to get into something."[9] Baptist minister and Klansman F.V. McFatridge, of Morton, told Bradley:

I suppose it would be difficult today for one to realize how impressive its appeal [was] to a young man. The secrecy regarding membership, the care exercised in admitting members, the secret meetings in remote places, where guards were posted at least half a mile in each direction, the big barbecue suppers, the patriotic speeches, etc.[10]

Another Mississippi minister and Klansman, J.H. Moore of Forest, came to the KKK with a grudge from World War I, complaining that "the Masons were not allowed to minister to our boys overseas, and all Masonic money was channeled through the Salvation Army." Elsewhere, the *Lexington Advertiser* featured a regular "Klan Kolum," while Kligrapp Cully McKinney turned the *Aberdeen Weekly* into a virtual Ku Klux newsletter with his front-page bulletins headed "Notice! Klansmen!" A typical offering from August 1926 announced a Klan barbecue and "mammoth street parade of Klansmen in robes," advising all members, "If you are looking for a good time both spiritually and morally, then I say to you don't fail to be at the meeting."[11]

Greenville's klavern sprang from the local Masonic lodge, where the state's top Mason — dubbed "a well-meaning old simpleton" by author William Percy—first joined the KKK, then persuaded his brethren to follow. "These composed the Klan leadership in our county," Percy wrote, "though they were aided by a few politicians who knew better but who craved the Klan vote. It was a pretty leadership—fanatics and scalawag politicians."[12]

While full-fledged Klan membership was restricted to white, native-born Protestant men, imperial headquarters soon grasped the profit potential of recruiting women and minors. Various women's auxiliary movements sprang up in 1921–22, dominated by the Ladies of the Invisible Empire, but none enjoyed official sanction from Atlanta. William Simmons, ousted as imperial wizard by dentist Hiram Evans in November 1922, retaliated the following year by creating Kamelia, a Klanlike women's order divorced from Atlanta's control. Evans countered by founding the Women of the Ku Klux Klan (WKKK) in June 1923, paying Simmons $145,000 to disband Kamelia and retire from Klan affairs. A list of active WKKK chapters in the Klan's September 1925 *Fellowship Forum* failed to mention Mississippi, but all states were represented when the WKKK held its first national klonvokation in St. Louis, during 1927.[13]

Hiram Evans (left, pictured here with a member of the original 1860s KKK) seized control of the Klan from William Simmons in 1922 (Georgia Department of Archives and History).

While preempting Kamelia with the WKKK in 1923, Evans also created a Junior KKK for boys and a Tri-K Klub for girls. Milton Elrod, editor of the *Fiery Cross*, published the *Junior Klansmen Weekly* for the "leaders of tomorrow," branding adolescence "the most dangerous period of a young man's life." The Junior KKK, Elrod claimed, would "inculcate into the members a desire to live clean and wholesome lives, keep the laws of our land, and honor the flag." The Tri-K Klub, meanwhile, operated under auspices of the WKKK, with Major Kleagle Leah Bell proclaiming that "[m]oral education is the need of America today, and that is the reason for the Tri-K Klub. It is our purpose to bring the young women of today who will become the mothers of tomorrow into a sense of responsibility of their duties. These are the vital things that they should know if the womanhood of America is to be kept clean."[14]

Keeping their women and the nation "clean" would prove to be a full-time job for members of the KKK.

The Moral Klan

Ku Klux morality in the 1920s was narrowly defined in terms of Protestant fundamentalist "old-time religion." In the *Kloran*, William Simmons proclaimed that "each Klansman by the process of thought and conduct determines his own destiny, good or bad: May he forsake the bad and strive for the good, remembering always that the living Christ is a Klansman's criterion of character."[15] In real-world terms, the order's stated principles included the following:

> Suppression of graft by public officeholders; preventing the causes of mob violence and lynchings; preventing unwarranted strikes by foreign agitators; sensible and patriotic immigration laws; sovereignty of State rights under the Constitution; separation of church and state; and freedom of speech and press, a freedom that does not strike at or imperil our Government or the cherished institutions of our people.[16]

Note that Simmons proposed to attack the "causes" of lynching, not lynching itself—a distinction that allowed Klansmen to rail against black crime and "insolence," while ignoring (or participating in) mob violence. Likewise, when seen through Ku Klux eyes, *all* strikes were "unwarranted," *all* union organizers "foreign agitators." "State rights under the Constitution" comprised segregation and disfranchisement of blacks, while "separation of church and state" applied chiefly to Catholics and Jews. Supporting free speech only when it praised "the cherished institutions of our people" was, in fact, a call for censorship.

A Mississippi kleagle spoke more pointedly to local issues when he said the Klan "is going to drive the bootleggers forever out of this land. It is going to bring clean motion pictures ... clean literature ... protect homes. It means the return of old-time Southern chivalry and deference to womanhood; it means that 'the married man with an affinity' has no place in our midst."[17]

While Hiram Evans labeled the KKK "a recruiting agency" for Protestant churches, his kleagles avidly proselytized clergymen. The order's first appearance in many towns was a "surprise" invasion of Sunday services by masked knights who handed the parson a cash donation and a written list of Ku Klux principles. Depending on the warmth of their reception, the Klansmen might fill pews to hear the sermon or depart as they arrived, marching

Klansmen pack a rural church during the 1920s (Florida State Archives).

in silent ranks. The *Laurel Daily Leader* described a typical Klan visit to the West Laurel Methodist Church in May 1926, where knights bestowed a donation on the Rev. B.L. Sutherland "as an expression of their appreciation of his strong stand during the meeting, for civic righteousness." Five months later, Klansmen called at Laurel's First Baptist Church, leaving a note that read: "We want all our Christian brethren to know that it is our purpose to stand with and back up with our work and our money at all times the Gospel program as it is in Christ." Similar visits occurred at churches in Brookhaven, Lexington, Maben, Morton, Poplarville, Quitman, West Point, and Woodville. In Moselle, Baptist minister C.F. Austin seated his masked visitors in the front row and "delivered a dramatic eulogy on the historical record of the Klan from the days after war strife until the present day."[18]

Most, if not all, church visits were prearranged between Klan leaders and clergy who welcomed the cash and attention. Those who rebuffed the order's private overtures, like the Rev. Frank Purser in Oxford, received no visit and no money. Evangelist Billy Sunday, by contrast, abstained from any criticism of the Klansmen who followed his tent revivals, pocketing donations like the 200 dollars delivered by masked knights during a 1925 sermon at Jackson's Municipal Auditorium. While Sunday never joined the KKK, he thrilled its members with his declaration that "Christianity and Patriotism are synonymous terms, and hell and traitors are synonymous."[19]

Members of Aberdeen Klan No. 70 were well received at Greenwood Springs, on 26 August 1926, when they visited the Dan Kelley Revival. As described by kligrapp Cully McKinney in the *Aberdeen Weekly*, "The good people of that community gave us a most hearty welcome among them[,] but what pleased us most was the convincing evidence that the prejudice heretofore prevailing in some communities ... was not in evidence.... Indeed we are assured that people generally are becoming [*sic*] to know the principles for which we stand, and, of course, where this is true the animosity and opposition to our organization will more and more die away." The Klan's monetary donation was "very thankfully and heartily received and the accompanying expression of our hearty co-operation of the work [which] had been done was read to the congregation who seemed to be thoroughly in sympathy with our purpose which all understood to come from our humble hearts."[20]

Nationwide, hundreds of Protestant ministers joined the Klan, many serving as chaplains for their local klaverns, while others embarked on careers as traveling orators. The Rev. J.H. Moore signed up in Forest, "as most of our preachers were doing." Methodist minister J.E.J. Ferguson joined Wesson's Beauregard Klan after leaders agreed to waive the usual initiation fee, but Atlanta still billed Ferguson ten dollars for regalia. Other recruits included the Rev. Victor Clifford of Centreville, and at least four other members of the Mississippi Methodist Conference. Presbyterian ministers in Bolivar and Warren counties also joined the KKK. Dr. Oscar Haywood left his pulpit in West Point to preach the Klan creed, nearly enduring martyrdom when he was mobbed by angry Catholics and Jews in Perth Amboy, New Jersey, on 4 June 1923. Things were safer at home, where the *Aberdeen Weekly* ran a front-page obituary for Klansman George Greely, "whom the Supreme Imperial Wizard of the Universe saw fit to take." When Greenville opponents barred a kleagle from the county courthouse, the pastor of Leland Baptist Church led protests against that decision.[21]

In daily practice, Klan moralism ran the full gamut from warnings and boycotts to vigilantism, all lumped together by Greenville's LeRoy Percy as a "recrudescence of Puritan meddlesomeness." In March 1922 Greenville Klansmen sent a letter to the *Leland Enterprise*, vowing to clean up Washington County. The letter warned bootleggers: "We have our eyes on you, and we are many; we are everywhere, and you will not escape." Adulterers were told to mend their ways, while young men fond of parking with their dates were asked, "Had you ever thought that what you do, some other boy is entitled to do to your sister?" The real problem, as William Percy saw it, was a wartime influx of "an alien breed of Anglo-Saxons," unaccustomed to Greenville's "laxity in church matters."[22]

Prohibition, with its nationwide deluge of bootleg liquor and corruption, offered Klansmen a perfect excuse for vigilantism. The Rev. J.H. Holder, of Iuka, told Laura Bradley that reputable men joined the Klan to "frighten Negroes and the lawles [*sic*] and prevent crime." The Rev. W.L. Meadows, in Quitman, claimed that the KKK "simply appealed for good, clean government, observance of laws, and order." F.V. McFatridge called the Klan "just a band of higher class citizens helping to enforce the law and working against all forms of evil," including liquor, prostitution, and pornography. The Rev. H. Jack Moore found bootlegging prevalent in Long Beach, until Klansmen teamed with "a good set of officers ... [and] there was quite a cleaning up of the situation."[23] Methodist clergyman W.C. McCay furnished Laura Bradley with a specific example from Baldwyn:

> I remember one time during a revival out in the country the rough boys were on the ground disturbing the buggies, cuting [*sic*] harness and taking wheels off of the wagons. [T]he Klan came out one night and annouce [*sic*] what was happening on the outside [and] said they wanted it stopped. He [*sic*] laid Fifty Dollars on the table and left, and from then on there was no more trouble.[24]

Vicksburg's exalted cyclops, writing for the Klan's *Weekly News Letter* of 13 May 1921, explained: "The reason why everybody here has taken so keenly to the Klan is due to the fact that years ago the Jews and Roman Catholics formed a liaison with the liquor interests and have had politics in this city throttled, and it is our intention to whip and rout them at the polls when the next election comes around in 1922. We intend to put these un–American elements out of office precisely as other communities have done."[25]

Few tales of full-dress raiding have emerged from Mississippi, though the *Jackson Clarion-Ledger* reported a Klan visit to the Blue Goose, a "notorious dive" in Columbus, on 18 February 1927, noting that the knights seized "only a small quantity of liquor." Kligrapp Cully McKinney led the Aberdeen and Monroe County Law and Order League, backed by clergymen C.E. Freeman and L.P. Wasson, but no accounts of night riding survive. C.Y. Higginbotham, a Methodist preacher and Klansman in Sharon, told Laura Bradley that "cases to which the Klan gave attention" were debated at open meetings, insisting that Klansmen "conducted themselves as good citizens, and not as mobsters, or racial Biggots [sic] ... and no violent conduct was indulged in, *that could be condemned as un–American and un–Christian.*"[26] (Emphasis added)

Indeed, most former Klansmen interviewed by Bradley in the early 1960s denied any violence whatever, maintaining that the Klan achieved good works by peaceful means. Gulfport's klavern was a primary donor of funds to purchase a car for Harrison County's probation officer, in recognition of her services. Summit's the Rev. J.E.J. Ferguson offered two cases of nonviolent Klan intervention. One involved the widow of a murdered philanderer, defended by Klan lawyers (including a future circuit judge and Copiah County's future district attorney) when relatives of her late husband's mistress sued to seize the widow's farm. The second case involved abuse of a twelve-year-old girl by her father, stepmother, and a hired man, abuse terminated when Klansmen bypassed apathetic police and hired an outside marshal to arrest the miscreants. An unnamed minister in Washington County told Bradley that a prominent attorney–Klansman used the courts "to put many bootleggers and gambling dives and highway joints out of business," then added, "He could have done this without a night shirt."[27]

The moralist impulse survived a decline of Klan prestige and membership in the late 1920s. On 24 February 1928, the *Aberdeen Weekly* ran a front-page story detailing Grand Dragon Fred Wankan's offer of a $200 scholarship — equivalent to one year's tuition at any state or Protestant college in Mississippi — to the graduating student from a secular high school or Protestant "prep" school who produced the best essay on "The History and Influence of Protestantism upon American Ideals and Institutions." Wankan told the newspaper, "Two prominent Protestant ministers and three prominent laymen will constitute the judges to judge the manuscript. Every branch of leading Protestant Churches will be represented."[28]

Nativism Resurgent

Imperial headquarters pledged the Klan to defend "100-percent Americanism," a phrase widely attributed (sans sources) to Theodore Roosevelt. The *Kloran* restricted Ku Klux membership to "native born American citizens who believe in the tenets of the Christian religion and owe no allegiance of any degree or nature to any foreign Government, nation, political institution, sect, people, or person." Simmons described the Klan's patriotism as "[a]n uncompromising standard of pure Americanism untrammeled by alien influences and free from the entanglements of foreign alliances."[29]

In fact, Klan patriotism was a regurgitation of Know-Nothing nativism leavened with the dubious wisdom of Tom Watson, whom Mississippi Klansmen hailed as "the most active proponent of true Americanism" for his defense of "liberty and freedom" against "papists." Wizard Hiram Evans blamed Catholicism for the submissive "mental nature" of Celts, Southern Europeans and Latin Americans, which he claimed produced widespread poverty in their respective homelands and disqualified them as would-be citizens of the United States. Black Catholics were even worse, Tom Watson maintained. In April 1922 the Klan's *Searchlight* magazine declared that Roman clergymen were "after the negro as one of its major steps in dominating the American republic." Four months later, a Mississippi Klanswoman wrote to the *Searchlight* predicting that Catholic conversion of southern blacks would spark revolution recalling the nineteenth-century "horrors of Hayti and San Domingo," with black men "yearning for the fertile fields and fair women of their masters."[30]

Wherever kleagles plied their trade, the Pope and his minions were primary targets. Greenville's William Percy was "astonished" to learn "that of all the things hated in the South, more hated than the Jew or the Negro or sin itself, is Rome." Greenville Klansmen boycotted Catholic merchants and dismissed Catholic employees, while Klan spokesmen railed against the Pope as "that old dago on the Tiber." The Rev. Norris Roberts listed "immoderate demands upon the government by Roman Catholics" among his chief reasons for joining the Klan, and the Rev. Tyrone Williams of Tunica told Laura Bradley that the Klan's "main purpose ... was to keep the Roman Catholics and the Jews from taking over this country as they saw it." For Bishop Duncan Gray, the message of the Klan's *Tri-State American* "was not a package deal, but anti–Catholic. Jews and Negroes were forgotten; it all became a Protestant-Roman fight." During the 1920 presidential election campaign, Forest's the Rev. J.H. Moore recalled, "we were told that [President Woodrow] Wilson was bitterly anti–Mason and that 70% of his appointments were Catholic."[31]

Contrary to Bishop Gray's observation, however, the Klan did not ignore Jews. Fueled by the writings of Henry Ford and the long-discredited *Protocols of the Learned Elders of Zion*, Klan leaders pushed anti–Semitism as another facet of "100-percent Americanism." A Klan publication, the *Imperial Night Hawk*, declared in August 1923 that "Bolshevism is a Jewish-controlled and Jewish-financed movement in its entirety." In February 1925 the *Kourier* reported that Germany's *Hammer Magazine* welcomed the KKK as an ally "to shatter the bonds in which the Jewish offender has smitten all honorable nations." Seven months later, the *Kourier* reprinted an article from Germany's Nazi press, lambasting the "terrible misdeeds" of "the Jew" and declaring, "The people's Germany knows only one task—the warding off and the annihilation of the blood-enemy of the Aryan peoples—the Jew." Hiram Evans deemed Jews inassimilable "by deliberate election," bent on corrupting America through the "Jew-produced motion picture industry and the Jew-monopolized jazz music [and] sex publications." Tunica's Tyrone Williams found the local Klan organized to prevent "Jewish encroachment." The Rev. J.B. Cain of Bolton recalled hearing a Moselle Klansmen announce that he was "going to Meridian 'to show those Jews how to live.'"[32]

While Catholics and Jews received special attention from Klan orators, the KKK despised *all* immigrants who broke the Anglo-Saxon or Teutonic mold. In October 1920 the *American Mercury* published a roster of Ku Klux pet peeves, including the "menaces of [Joseph] Tumulty [Catholic private secretary to President Wilson] and the Pope, foreign entanglement, the hyphenated American, the German spy at Odd Fellows, the uppity nigger in khaki, and the Knights of Columbus giving away free coffee and cigarettes to soldiers." The *Hattiesburg American* of 3 September 1921 quoted remarks from kleagle J.Q. Nolan denouncing alien "cuckoo birds who are trying to kick me out of my mother's nest." Robert Henry, a farmer in Delat and former missionary to China, noted "the determination of certain individuals in the community to exclude both the Chinese and Jewish businessman." In Oxford, the Rev. Roland Leavell attended a Klan courthouse rally from which "a large majority went away convinced that these minority groups were about to take over the way of life in America — thus destroying '100% Americanism.'"[33]

Defending White Supremacy

Given Mississippi's history and black majority, it is not surprising that Magnolia State Klansmen devoted much of their attention to "the Negro problem." In his *Kloran*, defining the "Ku-Klux Kreed," William Simmons wrote: "We avow the distinction between the races of mankind as same has been decreed by the Creator, and we shall ever be true to the faithful maintenance of White Supremacy and will strenuously oppose any compromise thereof in any and all things."[34] Furthermore, Simmons declared:

> [I]f the Anglo-Saxon race is to maintain its prestige, if it is to continue as the leader in the affairs of the world and to fulfill its sacred mission it must maintain and jealously guard its purity, its power, and its dignity; and while it should aid and encourage to the limit of its ability all men of whatever race or creed, it must forever maintain its own peculiar identity as the Anglo-Saxon race and preserve the integrity of its civilization, for the shores of time hold the shipwreck of all the mongrel civilization of the past which is evidence that in keeping the laws of creative justice nature has decreed that mixed civilizations, together with governments of mixed races, are doomed to destruction and oblivion.[35]

On the subject of lynching, whose "causes" concerned him, Simmons told one hooded audience, "It's all rot about the K.K. swinging [hanging] niggers. Niggers were loafing and the K.K. made 'em go to work." In another speech, Simmons predicted a full-scale race war, saying, "An inevitable conflict between the white race and the colored race is indicated by the present unrest. This conflict will be Armageddon, unless the Anglo-Saxon, in unity with the Latin and Teutonic nations, takes the leadership of the world and shows to all that it has and will hold the world mastery forever!" Simmons spoke more bluntly in private, sometimes brandishing pistols and knives at Klan meetings while shouting, "Bring on your niggers!"[36]

Successor wizard Hiram Evans maintained the Klan line on racial orthodoxy. "We believe," he told one Ku Klux audience, "that the races of men are as distinct as breeds of animals." In 1937 Evans wrote, "The negro, so far in the future as human vision can pierce, must always remain a group *unable* to be a part of the American people. His racial inferiority has nothing to do with this fact; the unfitness applies equally to *all alien races* and

Theodore Bilbo made no secret of his Klan membership (Library of Congress).

justifies our attitude toward Chinese, Japanese, and Hindus. No amount of education can ever make a white man out of a man of any other color. It is a law on this earth that races can never exist together in complete peace and friendship and certainly never in a state of equality."[37]

Ex-governor Theodore Bilbo, himself an admitted Klansman, acknowledged that white men had "poured a broad stream of white blood into black veins," but nonetheless insisted that "Southern white women have preserved the integrity of their race, and there is no one who can today point the finger of suspicion in any manner at the blood which flows in the veins of the white sons and daughters of the South." Lynching and other forms of violence were fully justified, in Bilbo's view, to safeguard the reputed purity of Anglo-Saxon blood. Jones County resident Hulon Myers, interviewed in 1979, recalled that Mississippi lawmen, when confronted with lynch mobs, "just kept hands off most of the time."[38]

That said, a Mississippi Klansman still felt qualified to tell blacks, in a letter to the *Leland Enterprise*, "We are your best friend, but we wish you to do right." To Klansmen, "doing right" meant strict adherence to the color line established at "Redemption." Hulon Myers deemed the Klan "all right" because it was "the only thing that kept the raping down and all like that." A Presbyterian minister in the Delta told Laura Bradley that Klansmen sought "control of the upstart Negro who had been put in uniform and given some authority." Grand Dragon T.S. Ward played to memories of Reconstruction-era vigilantism with a large advertisement in the *Clarion-Ledger* of 10 August 1924, for a screening of *The Birth of a Nation*. Ward's personal note declared, "I feel sure that all good Americans in our city and surrounding territory, both men and women[,] will come to see this wonderful picture."[39]

African Americans, by contrast, had no rights that Klansmen were bound to respect. In August 1921 Herman Mason, a black resident of Gunnison in Bolivar County, publicly "resented the treatment shown his wife by a band of [white] rowdies." On 26 August planter J.E. Walters led a gang of Klansmen from Clarksdale and Shelby to Mason's home, where they kidnapped and flogged him, then delivered him for trial on fabricated charges, resulting in a $100 fine and six months on the county work farm.[40]

In particular, as the Rev. Frank Purser of Oxford told Laura Bradley, Mississippi whites dreaded a return to the supposed horrors of Reconstruction and harbored "great fear of economic deprivation by the Negro." Klansmen opposed that menace by classic means. On 23 October 1922, twenty-five hooded knights called on "Mr. Letow," a black restaurateur in Hattiesburg, demanding removal of his café from the town's white district. S.D. Redmond, a black attorney who also owned a drugstore and "considerable property" in Jackson, received a typical warning in November 1922.[41] It read:

> This is to warn you that unless you and a few other niggers leave town at once you are going to be tarred and feathered. Now we mean business, and you are certainly going to get a good dose. This is a fair warning and you had better take heed and leave.
>
> You niggers are getting too much of a foothold in Jackson and we propose to put a stop to it.
>
> You have entirely too many niggers hanging around your store and they are a regular nuisance. You are too near Capitol street for your own good. Now you had better leave at once for we intend to tar and feather you and if you do not leave then we will give you a dose of a stone around your neck and some Pearl river bottom.
>
> K.K.K[42]

While Redmond blamed the letter on "some crank" and suffered no violence, a full-scale reign of terror engulfed black employees on Mississippi's railroads. Since the early 1900s, blacks had been driven from most railroad jobs, leaving only black brakemen, firemen, and switchmen in posts deemed too dirty or too dangerous for whites. After World

War I new equipment made those jobs more desirable, thus prompting a new purge of blacks. When railroad management ignored demands for whites-only employment, the Klan's vigilantes stepped in.[43] Burton Blanks, a fireman from West Point, Mississippi, on the Mobile & Ohio Railroad, received the following warning in August 1921:

> This is to advise you that we will give you until the 1st of September to hunt you another job. We have organized for the purpose of removing the Negro from the railroad jobs, and we expect to do it if we have to get on your train at some water tank or another place and shoot you down like rabbits. We understand that you are the leader of the Negro firemen, so we want you to tell the rest of the Negro firemen and porters that we intend to kill every one that goes out on a train after September 1, and we expect to kill you and Doc Allen and Porter Silas first.
>   K.K.K[44]

By the time Blanks received his warning, violence was already rampant throughout Mississippi. Klan floggings of black railroad workers on the Memphis-Clarksdale run began in January 1921. Masked gunmen snatched Howard Hurd from his Yazoo & Mississippi Valley Railroad train at Clayton on 16 March 1921 and riddled him with bullets, leaving a note with his corpse that read "Take this as a warning to all nigger railroad men." Snipers killed a black fireman on the Illinois Central line, south of West Point, in August 1921, and two other slayings followed on that line before year's end. Two whites arrested for shooting trainmen in the Water Valley district told federal agents that they were paid $500 to kill black railroad employees.[45]

Klan violence was not confined to Mississippi's railroad lines, by any means. In January 1922 a Klan-allied group dubbed "Run, Africans, Run" tried in vain to drive all blacks from Ellisville. Five years later, blacks in Scott County blamed the Klan for terrorism that crushed their chapter of the National Association for the Advancement of Colored People (NAACP). "Stirred up as never before" by disfranchisement and white rapes of black women, the small NAACP chapter saw its leaders flee under threat of death. "The Klan is very powerful in here," one survivor complained to national headquarters. "They term the NAACP High Class Meddlers."[46]

Lynching continued apace through the 1920s, but no reliable statistics exist for the decade, and Mississippi newspaper reports of mob violence were haphazard at best. A case in point is the August 1922 lynching of victim Parks Banks, near Yazoo City, who was killed after ignoring several warnings to leave town. Banks' death was reported in the *Memphis Commercial-Appeal* but was universally ignored by Magnolia State newspapers. Other lynchings no doubt were suppressed, and we may surmise that Klansmen joined in some of the era's mob slayings. (In a parallel case from Georgia, where three black victims were lynched by "persons unknown" in 1926, private NAACP investigators identified twenty-four lynchers—including fourteen law enforcement officers—and named all twenty-four as Klansmen.) In the reported Mississippi cases, five black men were publicly burned at the stake between 1923 and 1929; black brothel owner Alex Smith was lynched in March 1922 for hiring white prostitutes; and elderly Mose Taylor died at Georgetown for an "altercation with whites." After Taylor's lynching, a Simpson County newspaper warned that "Negroes must learn — and most of them do know — that they occupy a peculiar place in this land and must keep it." Black residents of Yazoo City heard that message and fled en masse after the public burning of Willie Minnifield in August 1923.[47]

Lynching opponents noted that such crimes declined sharply whenever federal anti–lynching bills surfaced in Congress. The first such lynching moratorium occurred in 1922, followed by lulls when new laws were introduced in 1934, 1935, and 1938. Each of those bills in turn was "talked to death" in southern filibusters, but even the prospect of passage deterred mob violence. In Mississippi, jurists who dispatched militia to restrain lynch mobs frankly admitted that their actions were inspired by fear of federal intervention, rather than any opposition to mob violence.[48]

William Percy claimed that the Mississippi River flood of April 1927 taught "mutual helpfulness instead of the tenets of the Klan," but other observers dispute that judgment. Throughout the flood's range, damage to cotton crops sparked new guerrilla warfare against labor contractors who lured black farmhands to other locales, and persistent claims of peonage emerged from the disaster. Several accounts described whites saving livestock while black tenant farmers were left to drown, including 400 in one case at Scott, Mississippi. Other black tenants were held incommunicado in refugee camps, watched by National Guardsmen who barred relatives and Red Cross workers from visiting. General Curtis Green, commanding the Mississippi Guard, told reporters, "It is our duty to return these people to their homes, and every camp under our control will handle the situation in this manner." Green changed his tune after the story broke, insisting that "refugees come and go at will," but Walter White of the NAACP still found black laborers "closely guarded, especially from Negroes who might help them go somewhere else." Unmoved by that report and echoes from the Red Cross, secretary of commerce Herbert Hoover denounced White's statement as "without foundation."[49]

Growth and Opposition

Most authors agree that Mississippi's Ku Klux realm reached its peak strength in 1923, but accounts of its decline vary dramatically. Researcher Laura Bradley found the Klan "dying" statewide in 1925 and 1926, maintaining that "by 1928, though there was still a scattered semblance of organization, the group was quite unpopular and hardly vital." Nonetheless, as we shall see, Klansmen dominated Mississippi's delegation to the Democratic National Convention in 1924, elected one of their own as governor in 1927, and committed acts of terrorism through the Great Depression.[50]

Klan estimates of total membership are even less reliable. In 1926, for instance, Aberdeen kligrapp Cully McKinney claimed that "over a half million of your patriotic Brothers" had participated in the Klan's second march through Washington, D.C.— an estimate vastly inflated from the actual fifteen to twenty thousand marchers present. Most sources agree that early Klan converts included "prominent and respectable citizens," among them "some very fine people" and "some of the best citizens of the community." One such was Clarksdale planter J.E. Walters, who led the flogging of Herman Mason in August 1921. The Rev. H.E. Carter of Senatobia quit the Klan after "some hoodlums got in," and the Rev. J.H. Moore agreed that "as time went on, the Klan became anti–Jew and Negro, and anti–most everything else. Beside the reports of violence by the Klan, it got to where any bootlegger could join if he had ten dollars, and for these anti–appeals, and the low moral standard evident, I withdrew from the Klan." Bootleggers aside, however, there is no doubt

The Klan parades on Pennsylvania Avenue in Washington, D.C. (Georgia Department of Archives and History).

that "hoodlums" joined the Klan from day one, drawn by recruiting appeals that were *always* anti–black, anti–Catholic, and anti–Semitic. The problem for many "respectable" Klansmen was clearly a matter of public embarrassment linked to notorious cases, rather than any private revulsion against Ku Klux bigotry.[51]

Mississippi's press and clergy waffled in their handling of the Klan. Some local newspapers, such as the *Aberdeen Weekly* and the *Lexington Advertiser*, supported the order through publication of regular "Klan Kolums." The Mississippi *Baptist Record* of 21 October 1921 declared, "We are no advocates of the KKK and see no necessity for them," but the paper never actively condemned Klan racism or violence. Most Mississippi newspapers maintained cautious neutrality toward the Klan, leaving Memphis editor Charles Mooney's *Commercial Appeal* as the main voice of statewide media opposition.[52]

While some Protestant clergymen flocked to the Klan, others opposed it. Dr. W.B. Selah, a Methodist pastor in Jackson, preached a sermon in 1924 calling the Klan "unnecessary, un–American, and certainly un–Christian." Warren County's Presbyterian ministers split on the issue, one joining the Klan while the other denounced it. Indianola's Presbyterian pastor praised certain Klan principles from the pulpit, then told his congregation he was "operating as a Minister of Jesus Christ and not as a police officer in disguise." The Rev. A.Y. Brown of West Point used Acts 5:38 against Klansmen: "Refrain from these men, and let them alone." Statewide, the Rev. J.B. Cain told Laura Bradley, "Ten percent of the Methodist ministers were active [Klan] members. Fifteen percent were members under social pressure. Twenty-five percent while not members gave mild approval. Twenty-five percent offered vigorous opposition." Deacon Sam Neill of Indianola's Presbyterian church told the kleagle who approached him, "If Indianola is as bad as you say and there are people who need to be run out of town, just give me their names with the evidence and I will take five men ... and see each one personally and guarantee that they leave town. When I put on a nightshirt you can be sure I am going to bed and not downtown."[53]

The prime movers of Mississippi's anti–Klan movement were Greenville's LeRoy Percy and his son William. Both shared the Dunning School's distorted view of the original Klan, claiming that it "played so desperate but on the whole so helpful a part in keeping the peace and preventing mob violence" during Reconstruction. The new Klan suffered gravely by comparison, William Percy branding Imperial Wizard Simmons a "fraud," his brainchild a "monstrosity ... not even a bastard of the old organization." LeRoy Percy, wed to a Louisiana Catholic, framed his opposition to the KKK in terms of its divisive impact on communities and its aggressive bigotry, "a venomous intolerance, abhorrent alike to Luther and Christ." (In fact, Martin Luther paraded his hatred of Jews, whom he described as "nothing but thieves and robbers.") On a more practical note, Bishop Duncan Gray surmised that LeRoy's dim view of the modern Klan arose from its attempt to wrest political control of Greenville from his hands.[54]

Washington County's first klavern surfaced in 1921, a year after masked vigilantes kidnapped black attorney Nathan Taylor, the newly elected president of the National Equal Rights League, and compelled him to leave Greenville under threat of death. In March 1922 itinerant kleagle Joseph Camp scheduled a rally at the county courthouse, while LeRoy Percy's friends — including local Jewish banker Joe Weinberg — invited Percy to attend and answer "Colonel" Camp's recruiting pitch. Percy, still smarting from his U.S. Senate defeat by James Vardaman in 1912, agreed to the plan.[55]

On 18 March Camp delivered a patented tirade in which he blamed Catholics for assassinating Presidents Garfield and McKinley, accused them of stockpiling weapons in churches, and hinted at a Roman plot to seize the U.S. Military Academy at West Point, New York. LeRoy Percy followed with an hour-long speech that buried Camp in ridicule, branding Klansmen a "gang of spies and inquisitors."[56] In conclusion, he said:

> Any Southern man standing out and proclaiming himself as a champion of Southern womanhood and white supremacy should do it in the broad light of day, in the noonday sun, thanking his God that he can stand on his feet and battle for the right. You don't need a masked face for that kind of declaration.... I do not care anything about this war on Catholics and war on Jews. It would not have brought me out here tonight. They can take care of themselves, but I know the terror this organization embodies for our negro population and I am here to plead against it. There is no need of it.... Friends, let this Klan go somewhere else where it will not do the harm that it will in this community. Let them sow dissension in some community less united than is ours. Let this order go somewhere else if there is any place it can do any good. It can do no good here."[57]

As Percy took his seat, banker J.D. Smythe offered the courthouse audience a resolution stating that Washington County "condemn[s] that organization called by itself the Ku Klux

Klan, but having no connection with the real Ku Klux Klan, which having served its usefulness, was dissolved many years ago.... Its impertinent assumption of the right to judge the private lives of American citizens ... is against the spirit of free institutions and the traditions and laws of our country, and is un–American." That resolution passed by acclamation, while Greenville's Catholic constable escorted Camp to his hotel.[58]

Battered but unbowed, Camp spoke in Bolivar County the following night, telling a more receptive audience that the Catholic Knights of Columbus had paid LeRoy Percy $1,000 to insult him. Back in Greenville, despite Percy's influence, a klavern led by county prosecutor Ray Toombs embarked on what William Percy called "a bloodless, cruel warfare, more bitter and unforgiving than anything I encountered at the front [in World War I]." Boycotts and whispering campaigns were the Klan's local weapons of choice, and while the Greenville klavern shunned full-dress parades, the threat of violence lingered.[59]

The Percys faced their greatest danger not from Mississippi Klansmen but from Morehouse Parish, Louisiana, where Exalted Cyclops J.K. Skipworth's klavern whipped and murdered two white men outside Mer Rouge on 24 August 1922. That episode resulted in a federal investigation, and the crime — although officially unsolved — drove many of the order's "better" members to resign. Soon after the Mer Rouge bodies were found, a scruffy-looking stranger called at LeRoy Percy's home one rainy night, claiming his car had broken down nearby and stranded him and his sister. Percy offered to help, but the arrival of three friends prompted the stranger to excuse himself, saying he had to "take a leak." When he did not return, neighbors told Percy that his caller had departed in a car driven by a second unidentified man. Two years later, William Percy saw the same man jailed for robbery and spoke to him in custody, the inmate telling him, "Old Skip[worth] nearly put that one over." Enraged by the apparent kidnapping attempt, William Percy called on Ray Toombs at Greenville's Masonic Temple, warning him, "I want to let you know one thing: if anything happens to my father or to any of our friends you will be killed. We won't hunt for the guilty party. So far as we are concerned the guilty party will be you." Uncle LeRoy Pratt Percy seconded that sentiment from Alabama, writing to LeRoy: "If they should kill you nothing could stop the wholesale massacre of the Ku Klux's [sic]."[60]

In February 1923 LeRoy Percy joined Louisiana governor John Parker to address a rally in Chicago, sponsored by an anti–Klan organization called the American Unity League. His speech stressed local efforts to uproot the Klan, noting that since the KKK appealed to Protestants, "whether there shall be a Klan does not depend upon what Jew, Catholic, nor negro thinks." Protestantism, Percy said, must lead the fight by refusing to "enter as its champion in the lists a simpleton astride a hobby-horse, clothed not in shining armor, but in a sheet, with a mask for a vizer [sic] and armed not with a flaming sword, but with a bucket of tar and feathers." Greenville's Klansmen, he declared, "have already done what I anticipated and predicted they would do — absolutely destroy the feeling of community harmony which had always prevailed in this county more than in any place I have ever known." His audience, perhaps expecting something more dramatic, responded with lukewarm applause. Discouraged, Percy never spoke publicly again outside of Washington County.[61]

Percy's message proved more popular at home, where a crowd of 1,500 rallied to hear him lambaste the Klan on 23 April 1923. Addressing Klansmen directly, Percy asked, "Can't you come back and take part with us in the life of the community? Come back to your father's house." Failing that, he declared, "We are going to clean you up from top to bottom," noting that "a spy in time of war is shot like a dog." Percy sarcastically thanked J.K. Skipworth for restraining the Morehouse Parish Klan, saying a monument should be erected to Old Skip, built "of white marble and smeared with blood."[62]

Skipworth, hoping to trap Percy in a libel suit, penned a letter quoting excerpts from the speech and asking Percy if they were correctly quoted in the press, adding his hope that Percy would "not be branded before the public as a willful malicious character assassin of your fellow man." Percy replied that, while the Mer Rouge murders were unsolved, he personally held the Klan responsible and felt that Skipworth, as the order's local chief, shared moral guilt for the crimes. In closing, Percy wrote, "I had no intention of slandering you: I did not know that it could be done." Greenville's newspaper printed both letters, leaving the Klan's *Tri-State American* to respond with an editorial headlined "Percy's Puny Propaganda Plays Political Pranks Pervertly [*sic*]."[63]

By that time, while his national debut had failed, Percy was recognized statewide as the Klan's primary opponent. His next contest with the Invisible Empire would be waged at the ballot box.

The Political Klan

Wherever Klansmen rallied in the 1920s, they eventually tried their hands at politics. Across the nation, countless incumbent or would-be officeholders joined the KKK, either because they shared its principles or hoped Klan votes would make the difference in their next campaigns. The Klan's prize recruit, according to William Simmons and others at imperial headquarters, was President Warren Harding himself. Klan leaders claimed that Harding took his Ku Klux oath in the White House Green Room, rewarding Simmons and other members of the induction team with War Department license plates that exempted them from speeding tickets. True or not, the Klan held mourning ceremonies after Harding's death in 1923, blamed Catholics for his sudden demise, and posted armed guards at his grave.[64]

Mississippi Klansmen made their first political overtures in the year of Harding's death. Their bids for state and national office in 1923 all failed: Theodore Bilbo lost his second gubernatorial race to Henry Whitfield, incumbent U.S. Senator John Sharp Williams defeated a Klan-backed challenge from James Vardaman, and Vicksburg congressman John Collier vanquished another Klan contender. On the local front, however, evidence does not support the claim of Arnold Rice that Mississippi's Klan was a "negligible force" in politics.[65]

LeRoy Percy's Greenville was a case in point, where Klansmen fielded George Archer as a candidate for Washington County sheriff. Percy's forces nominated George Alexander, while three independent candidates also tried their luck in the primary. Percy soon learned — and publicized the fact — that in addition to prosecutor Ray Toombs, Greenville's elected knights included the chancery clerk, circuit court clerk, county health officer, school superintendent, roads supervisor, and two out of five county supervisors. The Klan's electoral campaign officially launched in March 1923, when a local Ku Klux minister attacked

Percy from the pulpit, saying, "No man in the county ought to have a boss, especially one who hasn't opened the Bible in ten years." Ray Toombs echoed that theme at a rally in Leland, branding Percy "the Big Cheese" and assuring Klansmen, "The day of kings has passed."[66]

Percy responded by creating an anti–Klan group, named in various accounts as the Protestant Anti-Ku Klux Klan Committee, Protestant Organization Opposed to the Ku Klux Klan, or the Washington County Protestant Committee of Fifty Opposed to the Ku Klux Klan. By any name, the group excluded Catholics and claimed independence from LeRoy Percy, though William Percy and others named LeRoy as the committee's leader. On 23 March the group ran a large ad in the *Greenville Daily Democrat*, explaining its goals and debunking Klan rumors. One month later, on 23 April, LeRoy Percy took the forefront in a meeting at the People's Theater, telling his audience, "The day of kings may have passed, but the day when wizards will rule Washington County will never come!"[67]

Ray Toombs seemed to repudiate the Klan himself, in his final preelection speech, appealing for votes from his "friends among the Jews [and] Catholics." That bid for reconciliation was too little and too late. Alexander carried the sheriff's race with 1,181 votes to Archer's 1,094, while other contenders divided 748 additional ballots. The Klan's defeat sparked a riotous celebration at Percy's home, while "[o]ur Ku Klux neighbors stood on their porch watching—justified and prophesying Judgment Day." The Greenville Klan endured, but without real power. In 1925 local voters elected a Catholic mayor.[68]

Still, Greenville's experience was not typical of Mississippi Ku Klux politics. Bishop Duncan Gray told Laura Bradley that "every man running for state office in 1923 was a Klan member, with two exceptions." He added, "If you ran for office, you were running for fun, unless you were a member of the Klan in Mississippi." An Episcopal rector in Natchez confirmed that "any parishioner holding [local] public office would have been a Klansman, as the group was involved in a local religio-political fight."[69]

By all accounts, the Klan dominated Mississippi's state Democratic convention in May 1924, described by the *Clarion-Ledger* as "the stormiest on record in the annals of the Magnolia state." Dissatisfied with the composition of Washington County's delegation, LeRoy Percy took his own group to Jackson, but the assembled delegates jeered him until he surrendered the podium without delivering his speech. At least three hundred delegates were Klansmen, giving the KKK a ninety-vote majority. Fred Sullens, editor of the *Jackson Daily News*, condemned the state convention's "spirit of intolerance. A proceeding of this character cannot be viewed by thoughtful men with anything save a feeling of alarm." Senator Pat Harrison avoided the convention and was chosen to lead Mississippi's delegation at the national convention in New York City. LeRoy Percy, while granting that neither Harrison nor Senator Hubert Stephens were Klansmen, still branded Harrison "the head of and spokesman for a Ku Klux Klan delegation."[70]

In that, he was not unique. While reporters estimated that 75 percent of Mississippi's delegates were Klansmen, Georgia boasted 85 percent; Arkansas, Kansas, and Texas claimed 80 percent; delegations from Iowa, Kentucky, Michigan, Ohio, Tennessee and West Virginia were all at least half Klan. Senator Harrison delivered his keynote speech on 24 June 1924 to a convention whose Ku Klux members shared two overriding goals: defeating the presidential nomination of New York governor Alfred Smith, and blocking adoption of a campaign plank damning the Klan by name. They succeeded on both counts, nominating West Virginia's John Davis after 103 ballots and narrowly beating the anti–Klan plank by a vote of 546.15 to 542.85. Even so, the chaotic proceedings ensured Democratic defeat in November, when Republican Calvin Coolidge led Davis by 7.3 million votes, crushing him in the electoral college with 72 percent of the total. Mississippi and the rest of the Solid South stood with Davis, all in vain.[71]

Theodore Bilbo, meanwhile, had taken his 1923 defeat in stride, launching a weekly newspaper, the *Mississippi Free Lance*, with the motto "Nothing But the Truth." Within a year Bilbo claimed "the largest circulation of any paper published in the State of Mississippi," using the *Free Lance* as his springboard to the governor's mansion. In the 1927 gubernatorial campaign ex-senator John Williams branded Bilbo an "insidious demagogue," while opponent Dennis Murphree linked Bilbo to Al Smith and "wet" enemies of Prohibition. Neither tactic worked with Mississippi voters, although Bilbo's margin of triumph was only 9,385 votes, far below the 75,000 he predicted. Historian David Chalmers calls Bilbo "a one-time Klansmen" in 1927, but Bilbo himself declared lifelong Klan membership two decades later.[72]

Exit the Dragon

One of the strangest incidents in Ku Klux history began in Coahoma County on 15 October 1925. Sometime that night, thieves entered the store owned by planter J.T. Traynham at Count's Spur, south of Clarksdale, and bludgeoned clerk Grover Nicholas, leaving him bound with corset strings and plow lines while they fled with thirty dollars from the till. Traynham found Nicholas at eight o'clock the next morning and summoned authorities. Nicholas died eight hours later, at Clarksdale's hospital, without regaining consciousness.[73]

Bloodhounds imported from Crystal Springs reached the Traynham store at 9:00 P.M. on 16 October and followed a scent to the home of John Fisher, a black man "small in statute and dull of comprehension" who lived a half-mile from the store. Surrounded by lawmen and a posse of would-be lynchers, Fisher denied any part in the crime, saying he spent the previous day repairing an old car with neighbor George Banks and a teenage "strange negro." The stranger slept at Fisher's home overnight, but was gone when Fisher woke in the morning. If the dogs had followed anyone from Traynham's store, he said, it must have been the nameless youth.[74]

Deputies jailed Fisher and Banks, then set off in search of more culprits. Their dogs led them first to a home south of Clarksdale, where "the strange negro" was seen, then to a burglarized store in Riverton, and finally to railroad tracks where their elusive quarry hopped a passing train. Soon, manhunters jailed four more suspects, all black, including Lindsey Coleman, Albert Hobbs, "giant" Raeford Leonard, and teenager Smith Bunns. A mob from Quitman County did its part, kidnapping a black telephone company worker named Burns who was later released to Clarksdale police and cleared of any part in the murder. George Banks was also released after preliminary questioning.[75]

Over the next three weeks, masked men employed "the third degree with rope and the water cure" to extort confessions from the remaining prisoners. John Fisher cracked on 5 November, followed shortly by Leonard and Hobbs (who claimed the others forced him to join in the holdup at gunpoint). Smith Bunns died in jail, purportedly during "an epileptic fit." Lindsey Coleman alone stood firm in proclaiming his innocence.[76]

As if to prolong agitation among local whites, prosecutors scheduled separate trials for each of the four surviving defendants, beginning with John Fisher on 1 December 1925. When defense counsel challenged the validity of Fisher's confession, prosecutors produced two black prisoners—a swindler and a convicted killer awaiting appeal of his capital sentence—who swore that Fisher had confessed to them before he was tortured. Persuaded by that evidence, jurors convicted Fisher on 4 December, and he was sentenced to hang.[77]

Raeford Leonard was next, his trial commencing on 7 December. Codefendant Albert Hobbs "made a splendid witness" for the prosecution, telling jurors "how he fasted and prayed to God for guidance and help and finally decided that God would not help nor hear him with a lie upon his lips." Accordingly, he turned state's evidence and accepted a life prison term in lieu of hanging, for testimony against his alleged accomplices. The all-white jury spent forty-five minutes in deliberation, then convicted Leonard. The court proved lenient, granting Leonard the same life sentence negotiated for Hobbs.[78]

Lindsey Coleman was the last in line for Clarksdale "justice," distinguished by his silence under torture and by the appearance of septuagenarian Grand Dragon T.S. Ward as his chief defense counsel. Imperial headquarters offered no opinion on Ward's selection to defend a black alleged killer, but fireworks marked the first day of trial, on 16 December 1925. Appearing for the prosecution, J.T. Traynham accused Ward during cross-examination of "seeking to force him to give false testimony." As described in the *Clarksdale Register*, "Col. Ward asked the witness if he thought he was that kind of man and Mr. Traynham ... replied that any man who would come from south Mississippi to defend a negro who had killed a white man, might be guilty of most any offense." When Traynham refused to apologize, Judge W.A. Alcorn fined him twenty-five dollars for contempt of court.[79]

After that rocky start, the case proceeded with "rapidity and ease." Albert Hobbs repeated his performance for the prosecution, joined by George Banks and "Willie Coleman, negress," who supplied incriminating testimony. Defense attorneys challenged the confessions wrung from Fisher, Hobbs, and Leonard, stressing that the bloodhounds used to catch John Fisher showed no interest in the other three defendants. White spectators in court expected no surprise, until jurors returned after eight hours of deliberation to pronounce Coleman innocent.[80]

Confusion surrounds the next half-hour's events. All sources agree that the courtroom was nearly empty when the jury returned. Various accounts claim that T.S. Ward demanded a force of 100 men to see his client safely out of town, or told Judge Alcorn that "with two guns and twenty men, he could handle the situation." Alcorn later testified that he was willing to rouse the militia if need be, but Ward left the courthouse with Coleman alone. Sheriff Glass and several deputies apparently followed Ward and Coleman at a distance. Outside, Ward and J.T. Traynham "went together" in a scuffle, while an uncertain number of white men seized Coleman, fleeing in one or two cars. Coleman's corpse, shot twenty-six times, was found on DeSoto Avenue.[81]

Public outcry was immediate and intense. The *Memphis Commercial-Appeal* deemed Coleman's lynching "unique in its violation of the law of the land, contempt of juries, contempt of court and in the weakness of the sheriff's office." Governor Henry Whitfield called the lynching a "wanton murder" and a "horrible crime." Condemnatory resolutions issued from the Clarksdale Rotary Club, the Coahoma County Federation of Men and Women's

Clubs, and Coahoma's League of Women Voters. Governor Whitfield repeatedly urged Sheriff Glass to recuse himself for the duration, but Glass demurred, insisting that Ward's public denunciation of his office "absolutely misrepresented the facts." Far from standing idle, Glass maintained, he and his deputies did their best until overcome by superior numbers and firepower. If anything, Glass said, Ward "owed his life" to sheriff's deputies.[82]

Conflicting versions of the crime drew battle lines in Clarksdale. T.S. Ward described the lynchers as a gang of four, with J.T. Traynham in command. Sheriff Glass claimed he was overwhelmed by "a body of men" armed with guns, Deputy Hunter Scott placing their number at forty or fifty. The *Neshoba Democrat* published an editorial questioning whether Coleman's death even qualified as a lynching. In fact, the editors declared, "The unfavorable advertising that has come to Mississippi in recent years is largely due to the carelessness of the state press in the dissemination of news." Glass made things worse for himself, first granting that the killers were unmasked, then snapping at reporters, "I refuse to tell you whether I recognized any of them."[83]

On 22 December Sheriff Glass arrested four suspects on charges of conspiracy to murder Lindsey Coleman, swearing out the warrants "on his own information." Those arrested — and instantly released on bond by Judge R.E. Stratton, without spending a minute in jail — were J.T. Traynham, Gold Cane (or Cain), Tom Nicholas (brother of Grover Nicholas), and H.S. Blockley (married to the late storekeeper's niece). Attorney W.F. McGee and Claremont planter J.R. Adams posted bond for the accused, while Governor Whitfield and the local bar association challenged Judge Stratton's right to set bail without a preliminary hearing. Whitfield's expression of concern was typical: "If the citizens do not act in such matters as these, we may expect federal legislation. If we don't handle this matter satisfactorily, the United States will pass laws regarding lynching."[84]

Concurrent with the revolving-door arrests, Judge Alcock reconvened the county's grand jury, charging its members to identify Coleman's killers and furthermore to "[i]nvestigate this third degree business that is rumored. No man can be made to testify against himself: that law is as old as the hills. Methods to extort confessions are despicable, heartless and cruel. Most any man will tell anything to save his life, when a rope is around his neck, his head is in a rack and his fingers being bent back. If you find that third degree methods have been used have the courage and the manhood to bring those responsible to justice."[85]

Sheriff Glass told the grand jury that "a number of men" seized Coleman while his deputies were separating combatants Ward and Traynham. "I tried to rescue him at the risk of personal violence to myself," Glass said, "and continued my efforts until I was overpowered by the mob." At that point, he "went for help," then led a futile search for Coleman and his kidnappers, culminating in discovery of Coleman's corpse. Publicly condemned by the Coahoma County Bar Association, Glass defended himself by noting that 489 executions had occurred during his nineteen months as sheriff, versus a mere 210 during his predecessor's four-year term.[86]

On Christmas Eve the grand jury returned indictments against eight defendants. Suspects Traynham, Blockley, Cane and Nicholas were charged with murder. Sheriff Glass faced charges of "failure to return offenders" (the unnamed men who tortured John Fisher in jail), plus "misdemeanor and crime in office." Deputies R.A. Frazier, Lee Mathews, and Hunter Scott were also charged with failure to return offenders. Glass finally recused himself when local lawyers threatened to impeach him, and was replaced by wealthy planter H.H. Hopson as sheriff pro tem. Judge Alcorn overruled defendant Traynham's ironic motion to nullify his murder charge on grounds of mob hysteria and prejudice.[87]

Sheriff Glass was first to face Judge Alcorn, pleading guilty on 2 January 1926 to one count of failure to return offenders. Alcorn fined him the maximum $500 but declined to remove Glass from office, telling the world "he would be given a second chance." Soon afterward, prosecutors dropped the charges filed against Deputies Frazier, Mathews and Scott.[88]

On 6 January 1926 Judge Alcorn empanelled jurors for Gold Cane's murder trial. Reporters hailed the twelve white men as being "far above the intelligence of the average jury in every way." Cane's lawyer, W.W. Venable, had spent five years in Congress and would later serve as president of Mississippi's bar association. T.S. Ward appeared first for the state, declaring that four men kidnapped Lindsey Coleman; of the four, he recognized only J.T. Traynham. Sheriff Glass named Cane as one of the kidnappers, but contradicted Ward in other respects, describing a much larger mob. Deputy Hunter Scott named Tom Nicholas as the kidnap car's driver, while repeating his estimate that the mob included forty to fifty men. Black mortician Mack Adams described Coleman's body, torn by twenty-six gunshots.[89]

The defense used a two-pronged strategy, calling character witnesses from Clarksdale and Memphis to defend Cane's "reputation for peace and quietude," simultaneously chipping away at the state's key testimony. Deputy Joel Adams Jr. testified to seeing all four murder defendants at Clarksdale's courthouse after Coleman was kidnapped by twenty-five strangers. Deputy R.A. Frazier saw only ten or twelve lynchers, yet remained "positive" that none of the four defendants was among them. L.V. Ruth told jurors that he drove Tom Nicholas home to Quitman County while the lynching was in progress. Frazier, bailiff Tom Austin, Garner Johnson, and Joel Adams Sr. (J.T. Traynham's bondsman) all testified that Sheriff Glass had told them he could not identify the kidnappers. On 10 January, all four murder defendants took the witness stand, denying any part in Coleman's death. Newspapers described their testimony as a clear-cut challenge to the state for any future trials.[90]

Cane's jury voted for acquittal on 13 January, after deliberating for twenty-six hours. Sheriff Glass and his three briefly indicted deputies resumed their posts that afternoon, while District Attorney J.T. Smith requested a delay of any further trials until the court's next term, beginning on 22 February. Six days before that deadline, Smith dismissed the charges filed against Traynham, Blockley, and Nicholas.[91]

Grand Dragon Ward's performance in the Coleman case undoubtedly confused and angered many Klansmen, but one member—G.E. Jarman of Aberdeen—penned a letter to the *Memphis Commercial-Appeal* chastising that paper for ignoring Ward's Klan affiliation while it criticized knights who broke the law. "In other words," Jarman wrote, "give the devil his dues, and quit being so unfair to us Ku Klux." The editors replied: "We did not know that Colonel Ward is the grand dragon.... In view of the trouble that most of the grand dragons get in it is refreshing to see at least one of them do something worth while." The case had been too much for Ward, however. Citing poor health, he announced his resignation as grand dragon on 21 March 1926. Imperial Wizard Evans visited Jackson in April, installing Texas attorney Fred Wankan as the new grand dragon. Speaking from his headquarters suite at the Henry Memorial Building, Wankan ordered all local klaverns "to drop out the undesirable material from the mass mobilization days."[92]

Al Smith Redux

While Wankan's housecleaning hastened the Mississippi Klan's decline in membership, the dragon focused on 1928's presidential campaign. Still anti–Catholic and anti-"wet" to the core, in September 1927 Wankan published an open letter to Senator Pat Harrison, asking if Harrison favored a state delegation pledged to nominate Al Smith. Harrison replied through the press that he preferred an uninstructed delegation. Rumors spread that Smith had offered Harrison a cabinet post, if elected.[93]

A month before the state Democratic convention, in May 1928, the *Jackson Clarion-Ledger* branded Smith "a soaking wet Tammanyite and a nullifier of the constitution," calling for a delegation pledged to support "Prohibition — Bone Dry." Governor Bilbo echoed the call for a dry delegation, without citing names. Fred Sullens and his *Jackson Daily Press* thought it obvious that Smith would win nomination on the national convention's first ballot. "In light of this plain state of affairs," Sullens wrote, "which even the radical religionists, the Anti-Saloon League, and the Ku Klux Klan must recognize[,] it would be worse than folly for Mississippi to instruct its delegation to vote against the New York Governor." Pat Harrison concurred in his speech to the state convention in June, saying, "This year we cannot be tripped at the door of bigotry, prejudice, or intolerance." The delegates finally rejected both an instruction for Smith *and* a pledge to vote dry. While the *Clarion-Ledger* called the result a defeat for Al Smith, Sullens declared that "The plain fact is that the [D]emocratic state convention, in no uncertain manner, repudiated the Ku Klux Klan and the various religious bodies who have been attempting to tell the Democratic party in Mississippi what it must do, and administered to them the most complete drubbing that has been given to a political clique or faction in this state in a long time."[94]

Governor Bilbo missed the national convention in Houston, sending in his place a Baptist minister who doubled as secretary of Mississippi's Anti-Saloon League. The other delegates refused to seat him, and without Bilbo's tie-breaking vote the delegation split with 9.5 votes for Smith and 9.5 against. After Smith's first-ballot nomination, Mississippi delegates brawled in their front-row seats over whether or not to join in Smith's victory march. Reporters described "a regular knock-down scuffle," quelled by police, before delegate James Eastland seized the state's banner and joined the parade.[95]

Klan headquarters threw its political weight behind Republican candidate Herbert Hoover, a typical broadside from the Mississippi realm's *Official Monthly Bulletin* warning that Smith, if elected, would "no doubt fill every key position in the Republic with Roman Catholics ... [and] no doubt leave the Army and the Navy in the hands of Rome." Pat Harrison told the *New York Times* in August 1928, "I never saw anything approximating in bitterness and in its character the campaign that is now being waged against Governor Smith in the South." At the Neshoba County Fair, he reminded a sullen audience that Jefferson Davis and several Confederate generals attended Catholic schools, while Daniel Emmett — the author of "Dixie"— was himself a Catholic.[96]

Failing to sell religious tolerance in the Magnolia State, Smith's advocates fell back on race. On 2 November Pat Harrison assured the state's newspapers that "Governor Smith does not believe in the marriage of whites and blacks." The next day, Fred Sullens told subscribers of the *Jackson Daily News* that "A vote for the Democratic ticket next Tuesday will be a vote for preservation of white supremacy in Mississippi." In case they missed the point,

Sullens wrote on 4 November: "A vote for Hoover and [running mate Charles] Curtis will be a vote to bring the negro back into politics." That same day, the *Clarion-Ledger* ran a large ad purchased by the Mississippi Democratic Party, urging racial loyalists to "Vote the White Man's Ticket." Even Governor Bilbo did his part for the cause, claiming that Hoover had danced with a black woman named "Mary Booze" in Mound Bayou. Challenged to defend the lie, Bilbo replied, "It was like asking old High Collar Herbert if he had stopped beating his wife. I did not say that as a direct statement from me. What I did say was that that statement was made at a public rally in Jackson some time ago."[97]

The Solid South voted for Smith, against the Klan's advice, but it was not enough. On 7 November Smith trailed Hoover by 6 million popular votes, while Hoover won a crushing 84 percent majority in the electoral college. A sideshow to the main event involved Bilbo and Grand Dragon Wankan in a patronage scandal concerning the alleged sale of low-level post office jobs to black candidates by GOP activist Perry Howard. A federal grand jury indicted Howard, but he won acquittal at trial with public support from Governor Bilbo and the Klan. On balance, it was felt by white supremacists that Howard's "Black and Tan" Republicans maintained the color line by keeping blacks in jobs that fit "their place."[98]

Although Hiram Evans claimed full credit for Al Smith's defeat, the Klan gained no prestige from 1928's election. When Fred Wankan launched a new recruiting drive that year, Fred Sullens warned his fellow Mississippians: "Don't kick the corpse."[99]

Depression Days

The Wall Street crash of 1929 and the ensuing Great Depression further thinned Klan ranks, but the order persisted in Mississippi, as elsewhere. On 1 January 1930 the state was blanketed with Klan notices printed in Alabama soliciting funds for relocation of American blacks to Africa.[100] In February 1934 another flyer stated the Klan's case for white supremacy:

> If blacks do not wish to live under the rule of whites, let them return to their native land.... [H]is position as a slave was better than anything he had ever known at home.... We owe the Negro nothing, we found him a naked, snake-worshiping savage and conferred upon him all the polish of civilization that he is competent to receive ... and supplanted his serpent fetish with the Christian faith. Having lifted him out of savagery, we are under no obligation to bear him over our shoulders.... [R]eading, writing and arithmetic ... is [*sic*] as much as they can absorb to advantage. A Negro crammed on Latin [or] Greek ... is a ruined Nigger!... [N]o matter how many books you rub into his head, Nature created him Inferior ... and if ever the white man lowers his level to that of the Negro ... The Crime Against Civilization Will Be Punished.... Negroes with a suggestion of intellect are usually ... mongrels in whose veins flow the blood of some depraved white man. The pure blood blacks who have exhibited intellectual and moral qualities superior to those of the monkey are few and far between and yet the pure-blooded Ethiop is generally much safer ... than the "yaller Nigger" who appears to inherit the vices of both races and the virtues of neither. I am not an advocate of "lynch law" but I have red blood in my veins and I believe it is no more contemptible to string up a Negro in the face of high heaven than it is to pounce upon an unprotected white woman and defile her.... [T]he proper thing to do is to crack their necks with the least possible delay.... [W]e must see to it that the Negro makes no Haitian hell of the United States.[101]

Such calls to action sometimes brought results. On 8 May 1930 Lauderdale County authorities jailed five Meehan Klansmen for whipping black victim "Boss" Williams and leaving him chained to a tree overnight. All were released on $2,000 bond, but no further record of their case survives. In the mid–1930s Jones County Klansmen harassed members of the light-skinned mulatto Knight family, whipping one white man "because he had dated a Knight girl."[102]

Lynching remained a chronic threat for Mississippi blacks in the Great Depression, but reliable statistics remain elusive. Author Terrence Finnegan lists seven lynchings during the period 1930 to 1932, with thirteen more aborted by authorities. Jesse Ames reports ten lynchings with thirteen victims from 1931 to 1935, including one victim killed for "being smart" and another fatally whipped for speaking disrespectfully to a white man. Charles Payne logs twenty-seven lynchings from 1931 to 1939, including a Columbus victim killed for failure to pay the last ten dollars on his wife's funeral bill. Authorities publicly condoned some lynchings, as in June 1934, when District Attorney Greek Rice ordered two victims hanged outside Lambert to be left dangling from a railroad trestle overnight. Ten months later, after prosperous black farmer R.J. Tyrone was "shot to pieces" by his white neighbors, Lawrence County's coroner ruled the death a suicide. Mount Pleasant's prosecutor echoed that verdict in 1935, after a lynching announced in advance by the *Memphis Press-Scimitar*. Bolivar County residents criticized their sheriff for jailing four whites who murdered an elderly tenant farmer for "insolence," and grand jurors refused to indict them.[103]

Mississippi's newspapers waffled on the morality of lynching. In July 1935 the *Clarion-Ledger* deemed a double lynching at Columbus "more than regrettable," yet found it "to the credit of the Lowndes County citizens forming the mob that they did not indulge in the barbarism of torture but inflicted the death penalty with as much mercy as the state itself allows." Two years later, after another mob used blowtorches on two black victims at Duck Hill, the *Sunflower Tocsin* editorialized that "the two brutes ... richly deserved what they got," further predicting that "nothing will ever come of any investigation." That proved true, although Winona's former mayor said, "There are a thousand people in Montgomery County who can name the lynchers." Ironically, while the Duck Hill murders were in progress on 12 April, Governor Hugh White delivered a speech declaring, "We are justly proud of the fact that Mississippi has not had a lynching in 15 months." (He was wrong: another victim had been lynched at Laurel in December 1936.) Overall, an NAACP investigator reported, "The citizens of Duck Hill seemed rather well pleased with themselves. The only feature of the incident displeasing to them was the pictures taken of [the victims] and widely circulated through the press."[104]

Lynch law did not go unopposed, however. Two members of the Methodist missionary society, Bessie Alford of McComb and Ethel Stevens of Jackson, launched a statewide campaign in January 1931 to secure anti-lynching pledges from sheriffs and women in each of Mississippi's eighty-two county seats. Some seven hundred women signed by November 1931, their names indexed for rapid contact if mob action threatened their communities. In one case where a sheriff proved elusive, Alford rallied local relatives to guard the jail until a highway patrolman arrived from Jackson. In 1936 Mississippi's Conference of the Methodist Church passed its first antilynching resolution under pressure from Alford, though it refused to let her speak.[105]

In November 1933 the Southern Commission on the Study of Lynching blamed mob violence on Dixie's "consuming fear of Communism," an attitude fostered by Klansmen and white politicians alike. The worst threat came from Washington, D.C., where anti-lynching bills became a cause célèbre. In 1934 Judge Kuykendall of DeSoto County summoned troops to prevent a triple lynching, then apologized to the mob, saying, "[T]here are now several anti-lynching bills pending in Congress. The effect of these bills would be to destroy one of the South's most cherished possessions—the supremacy of the white race—and I believe a lynching in this case would have effect inevitably in the passage of one of these laws by congress." After Duck Hill, a Mississippi congressman asked one of his New York colleagues if proposed antilynching legislation would apply to the "gang murder for which your state is known." The *New York Daily News* replied: "This Southern attitude is markedly different from the Northern attitude toward gangster killings.... Up North, we deplore gang killings and hire men like [special prosecutor] Thomas E. Dewey to try to break up rackets; we don't defend them with flowery speeches about Northern womanhood or insults to our dignity."[106]

Mississippi's senators stood firm against a federal ban on lynching. In 1922 John Sharp Williams had proclaimed that "[r]ace is greater than law now and then, and protection of women transcends all law, human and divine." Theodore Bilbo, elected to the Senate without opposition in 1934, deemed lynching the only "immediate and proper and suitable punishment" for black violence against whites. In 1938's filibuster against the Gavagan Anti-Lynching Bill, Bilbo ignored four decades of congressional debate to ask, "Why is it now, after three-quarters of a century ... that an attempt is made to cram down the throat of the South this insulting, undemocratic, un–American piece of legislation?" His predictable answer: a conspiracy by "Negro lovers, Negro leaders, and Negro voters."[107]

Bilbo's election to the Senate was a triumph for Mississippi racism, if not for the state's KKK. His campaign was typically crass. One reporter wrote that Bilbo "promised everything but a guaranteed entry to Heaven, and this wasn't necessary because his election would bring Heaven to earth." Above all else, he promised white supremacy, vowing to "raise more hell than Huey Long" in Washington. While speaking in Decatur, Bilbo singled out two black youths near the stage and told his audience, "If we fail to hold high the wall of separation between the races, we will live to see the day when those two nigger boys right there will be asking for everything that is ours by right." In that, he was prophetic: the boys were brothers Charles and Medgar Evers, future leaders of the Mississippi civil rights movement.[108]

In 1938 Bilbo offered an amendment to a Senate work-relief bill, aimed at cutting unemployment by sending 12 million American blacks to Africa. His four-hour tirade promoting the plan echoed the Klan's support for European fascism: "Race consciousness is developing in all parts of the world. Consider Italy, consider Germany. It is beginning to be recognized by the thoughtful minds of our age that the conservation of racial values is the only hope for future civilization. It will be recalled that Hitler ... gave as the basis of his program to unite Germany and Austria 'German blood ties.' The Germans appreciate the importance of race values." Bilbo revived his scheme in 1939, seeking to establish "Greater Liberia" on 400,000 square miles of land seized from Britain and France as partial payment of their World War debts to the United States. The plan failed, with northern critics branding him "the Bilbonic Plague" and "the Mussolini of Mississippi," but it secured Bilbo's reelection without opposition in 1940.[109]

Another Klan ally in Congress, though never an admitted member, was Tupelo's John Rankin. Elected to the House of Representatives in 1920, Rankin surpassed even Bilbo in racist histrionics. Southern journalist James Cobb labeled Rankin "Negro hating, Jew hating, hydrophobically demagogic, and hammily emotional." Union organizer Palmer Weber told author Neal Peirce, "If a black man got on the elevator with Rankin, the blood would come up in his face. I saw it actually happen myself, in the House Office Building elevator. He couldn't stand the sight." When Tennessee congressman Estes Kefauver called for abolition of the poll tax, Rankin physically attacked him, shouting, "Traitor!"[110]

Ku Klux headquarters initially supported Franklin Roosevelt's presidential candidacy, with Klan lawyer Paul Etheridge leading the Roosevelt Southern Clubs from Atlanta; but a rift occurred in June 1932, when Democratic Party leaders reminded Klansmen that the clubs were supposed to raise money for FDR, not spend the cash themselves. Overnight, Atlanta "discovered" that Roosevelt campaign manager James Farley was Catholic.[111] Unable to prevent FDR's nomination, the Klan cautioned its members:

> Don't be fooled. Farley is Roosevelt; Tammany Hall, Catholic controlled, is Roosevelt.... Every Prominent Roman Catholic You Can Find Is For Roosevelt.... The Underworld is a unit for Roosevelt. The gangsters of Chicago, St. Louis ... and New York are for Roosevelt.... Roosevelt, their subservient tool, will turn our country over to Tammany and thus we will have Catholic Control of American Government and Life, if he is elected.... Beware the 8th of November![112]

Mississippi voters ignored that warning in 1932, and in Roosevelt's three successive campaigns, but Klansmen saw their fears realized in FDR's appointment of Farley as postmaster general, while Jews Harold Ickes III and Henry Morgenthau led the Departments of the Interior and Treasury, respectively. Klan orators complained that FDR had "honeycombed Washington with Communists," praising Adolf Hitler while they lambasted the "communism of FDR and the Jews."[113]

Senator Bilbo proved more flexible, supporting New Deal measures when they benefited whites, opposing any aid to African Americans. Distribution of relief in Mississippi followed color lines: despite their majority, only 8 percent of impoverished blacks received state or federal relief, versus 14 percent of poor whites. In 1936 the state legislature launched its first industrial recruitment program, dubbed Balance Agriculture with Industry, which proved a resounding success. The program owed its triumph to cheap labor, guaranteed by a collaboration of police and vigilantes to suppress collective bargaining.[114]

Klan terrorism against Mississippi's black railroad workers resumed in 1931, the *New Republic* reporting that "[d]ust had been blown from the shotgun, the whip, and the noose, and Ku Klux practices were being resumed in the certainty that dead men not only tell no tales but create vacancies." Terrorists killed at least six victims and wounded a dozen more. The *Vicksburg Evening Post* wrote on behalf of those slain: "Their only offense was that they sought to earn their bread by the sweat of their brows." Two white killers received prison terms in 1932, but the terror was relentless, leaving fewer than 100 black railroad employees statewide by 1940. Labor historian Charles Johnson observed, "They used to have Negroes braking and firing on the roads. The only reason they are not there now is that they will be shot off like dogs."[115]

A new target for violence, from 1934 onward, was the Southern Tenant Farmers Union (STFU). Founded in Arkansas, the union reached Mississippi by early 1935. In March vigilantes shot the Rev. T.A. Allen, a black STFU organizer, and dumped his chain-weighted corpse in the Coldwater River near Hernando. Still, the union claimed five locals by 1936, when violence stalled the movement. Recruiting resumed in 1938, prompting claims of 500 members in five counties by mid–1939. A year later, Mississippi's STFU was broken by terror including arrests, beatings, and at least one castration. An organizer in Lowndes County wrote to headquarters: "This is a Bad place Down hear. I will hafta goe sloe to get By[;] they no me." Union cofounder Harry Mitchell said, "When a Mississippi sharecropper stuck his head up, he got it shot off." Union supporters in the North declared that "Hitler stalks the cotton fields of the South."[116]

While Klansmen and police were busy eradicating the SFTU, another threat arose in the form of John L. Lewis' Congress of Industrial Organizations (CIO), founded in 1938. Lewis and company sought equal treatment for blue-collar workers regardless of race and, at least briefly, welcomed communists into the union. From Atlanta, the *Fiery Cross* headlined "CIO Wants Whites and Blacks on Same Level." Scattered violence followed, but the Klan's real war against the CIO would wait until a greater conflict was decided on the battlefields of Europe, Asia, and the South Pacific.[117]

Hiram Evans resigned as imperial wizard on 10 June 1939, succeeded by Indiana veterinarian James Colescott. Colescott dedicated his Klan to "mopping up the cesspools of Communism in the United States," but told reporters, "I am against floggings, lynchings and intimidations. Anyone who flogs, lynches or intimidates ought to be in the penitentiary." As an incentive to recruiting, Colescott shaved four dollars off the Klan's initiation fee and nearly halved the cost of robes, predicting that "[t]he fiery cross will again blaze on the hilltops of America." Embarrassment soon followed, as New Jersey Klansmen held a joint rally with the pro–Hitler German American Bund, applauding a brown-shirted Nazi who proclaimed, "The principles of the Bund and the principles of the Klan are the same." Mississippi, meanwhile, dropped out of the "regular" lynching states, with no mob slayings officially recorded during 1940 and 1941.[118]

World War II and Disbandment

When Pat Harrison died in June 1941, Governor Paul Johnson Sr. chose James Eastland — a Sunflower County attorney, planter, and namesake of an uncle whose murder sparked mob violence in 1904 — to replace Harrison pending a special election to name his successor. Eastland served for ninety days but declined to seek election in September, ceding the post to congressman Wall Doxey. It was a different story in 1942, however, when Eastland sought and won his first of six Senate terms. An unabashed racist who said that "[t]he mental level of [blacks] renders them incapable of suffrage," Eastland would hold the color line in Washington for thirty-six years, scuttling 127 civil rights bills and offering tacit encouragement to Klansmen, even as he denied the order's existence in Mississippi.[119]

Senator Bilbo, meanwhile, remained as flamboyant as ever, leading filibusters against the Geyer Anti-Poll Tax Bill (1940) and new antilynching legislation (1942). In July 1945, when the head of the National Committee to Combat Anti-Semitism complained of Bilbo's slurs against Jews, Bilbo replied on Senate stationery with a letter headed "My dear Kike."[120]

After Pearl Harbor, Mississippi whites divided in their views of black conscription. Some believed that African Americans in uniform became too worldly-wise and "biggity," while others complained that the draft left too many black men adrift on the unguarded home front. Rumors of clandestine "Eleanor Clubs," named for First Lady Eleanor Roosevelt, described a black maids' conspiracy to desert white homes for war industry jobs and "put a white woman in every kitchen." Those tensions sparked violence, and while Mississippi officials acknowledged no lynchings between 1939 and 1945, the NAACP counted six. A black leader in Meridian placed the true total "nearer twenty," noting that outside major cities "such news is hardly ever published." Local editors admitted ignoring mob violence, since "such things always result in hard feelings" and "publicity on such matters merely results in a lot of adverse criticism by outside papers."[121]

Despite such fertile ground for agitation, Wizard Colescott's Klan fell on hard times in World War II. The draft sapped membership, while Klan flirtation with the Bund earned Colescott an appointment with the House Committee on Un-American Activities in January 1942. Chairman Martin Dies scolded Colescott for the Klan's anti–Catholicism, but committee member Joe Starnes of Alabama deemed the KKK "just as American as the Baptist or Methodist Church, as the Lions Club or the Rotary Club." Colleague John Rankin agreed, hailing the Klan as "an American institution. Our job is to investigate foreign 'isms' and alien organizations."[122]

The Internal Revenue Service proved less charitable to the invisible empire. In April 1944 the IRS slapped Colescott with a bill for $685,305, representing unpaid taxes, penalties, and interest from the 1920s. Unable to pay, Colescott convened a special klonvocation on 23 April, where he "repealed all decrees, vacated all offices, voided all charters, and relieved every Klansman of any obligation whatever." Subsequent statements muddied the disbandment issue, but Colescott soon retired to Florida, telling reporters, "Maybe the government can make something out of the Klan. I never could."[123]

CHAPTER 4

A Closed Society
(1944–1962)

Even as he formally disbanded the national Klan in April 1944, James Colescott established a five-man governing board to manage the order's affairs. Colescott remained nominally in charge, but his retirement to Florida placed effective control in the hands of Dr. Samuel Green, an Atlanta obstetrician who had joined the KKK in 1922. Green organized an unchartered Association of Georgia Klans (AGK) on 21 May 1944, and went public in October 1945 with a rally billed as the first cross-burning since Pearl Harbor. On 22 March 1946, Atlanta lawyer Morgan Belser filed new incorporation papers for the Klan, paying back fees for the years 1940–46.[1]

Invisible Empire Reborn

The Klan's reappearance prompted national concern. In summer 1946 Attorney General Tom Clark announced FBI investigations of the order's activities in Mississippi and five other states. The House Un-American Activities Committee (HUAC) debated investigating the Klan, then decided against it, prompting panel member John Rankin to remark, "After all, the KKK is an old American institution." Senator Bilbo appeared on *Meet the Press* on 9 August 1946, and was asked if he had ever joined the Klan. He replied, "I have. I am a member of the Ku Klux Klan No. 40, called Bilbo Klan No. 40, Mississippi. I attended one meeting and have not attended it since, because I was not in sympathy with some of the things in it." Asked why he simply had not quit the order, Bilbo explained, "No man can ever leave the Klan. He takes an oath not to do that. Once a Ku Klux, always a Ku Klux." And Bilbo *sounded* like a Klansman, telling the Senate, "There are a few Catholic priests in this country, who, along with some Jewish rabbis, are trying to line up with the Negroes teaching social equality.... [S]ome of them are rotten.... We, the people of the South, must draw the color line tighter and tighter, and the white man or woman who dares to cross that color line should be promptly and forever ostracized."[2]

The Klan's resurgence coincided with the birth of America's first postwar Nazi group, the Columbians Inc., in Atlanta. The Columbians borrowed their uniforms and insignia from Hitler's Third Reich, compiled "lynch lists," and plotted to bomb homes of blacks who moved into white neighborhoods. One member, Maynard Nelson, penned a fan letter to Mississippi congressman John Rankin, supporting Rankin's call for concentration

Dr. Samuel Green (with sword) initiates new Klansmen in 1946 (National Archives).

camps to hold "disloyal minorities" and Rankin's observation that Jews "have been run out of every civilized country on earth except this one, and they are headed for the same treatment here." Rankin replied, "I cannot tell you how grateful I am for your expressions of confidence; and I need not tell you that I agree thoroughly with every statement you make of your own views on these matters. I assure you that I will stand by my guns and continue to do my best to save America for Americans." In early 1947 Maynard and several other Columbians drew jail terms for stockpiling weapons and terrorizing Atlanta minorities. At year's end, both the Columbians and Klan were added to the attorney general's list of "subversive" organizations.[3]

Senator Bilbo, meanwhile, was engaged in the political fight of his life. Spring 1946 found him campaigning for his third Senate term in a Mississippi shaken by the aftermath of World War II. Returning black servicemen had tasted freedom in the outside world. Some — like Medgar Evers, while in France — had dated white women, a racist's nightmare reported stateside by national news magazines. Worse yet, some of the soldiers who had risked their lives for democracy came home to demand their reward at the polls. The U.S. Supreme Court encouraged those hopes in 1944, banning "white primary" elections in the case of *Smith v. Allwright*.[4]

Bilbo's reaction was predictable. On 23 June 1946, broadcasting statewide from a Jackson radio station, he declared, "The white people of Mississippi are sleeping on a volcano, and it is left up to red-blooded men to do something about it. I call for every red-blooded white man to use any means to keep the nigger away from the polls. Do not let a single nigger vote. If you let a handful go to the polls in July there will be two handfuls in 1947, and from there on it will grow into a mighty surge. You and I know what's the best way to keep the nigger from voting. You do it the night before the election. I don't have to tell you any more than that. Red-blooded men know what I mean. If you don't understand what that means, you are just plain dumb." The *Jackson Daily News* echoed Bilbo's sentiment with a headline reading "Don't Try It!" The front-page editorial warned blacks: "Don't attempt to participate in the Democratic primaries anywhere in Mississippi on July 2nd. Staying away from the polls on that date will be the best way to prevent unhealthy and unhappy results."[5]

Vigilantes answered the call to arms. Black veteran Etoy Fletcher was kidnapped and flogged in Rankin County after he tried to register. Amzie Moore, a black activist in Bolivar County, claimed that whites killed an average of one black victim per week between January and July 1946, ceasing only when FBI agents arrived to investigate. Civil rights historian Charles Payne deems that tally improbable, citing the only documented fatality as a prisoner killed by the county sheriff; but as we have seen, reports of racist murders in the press were haphazard at best. If history proved anything, it verified that some white Mississippians were ready — even eager — to kill in defense of white supremacy.[6]

Despite the public threats, despite actual mayhem or rumors of bloodshed, thousands of blacks *did* try to vote on 2 July 1946. And they were met with the tactics that Bilbo encouraged. Charles and Medgar Evers registered in Decatur, ignored the subsequent threats, and led a group of friends to cast their ballots on primary day. When an armed mob blocked them at the polls, they went home for guns of their own, but stopped short of initiating a bloodbath. Police with drawn guns prevented Tougaloo College chaplain William Bender from voting in Hinds County. The Rev. T.C. Carter was barred from the Louisville polls by armed whites. In Pass Christian, fifteen "poor-looking white men" beat Gulfport NAACP president Vernado Collier and his wife while police stood by watching. Statewide, roughly half of Mississippi's 2,500 registered blacks were allowed to cast ballots, and reprisals continued for weeks afterwards. On 22 July 1946 white vigilantes from Lexington whipped Leon McTatie to death for allegedly stealing a saddle.[7]

It seemed that Bilbo had finally gone too far. Already beset by financial scandals, he now confronted a "National Committee to Oust Bilbo," organized by the Civil Rights Congress. Petitions from fifty Mississippians, including several whites, prompted creation of a Senate Campaign Investigation Committee, which convened public hearings in Jackson on 2 December 1946. Bilbo entrusted his fate to friend and panel chairman Allen Ellender of Louisiana, while claiming that liberal reporters had edited his plea for whites to block black votes by "any *lawful* means." Few blacks were expected to attend the Jackson hearings, but nearly two hundred appeared to testify, some with the bloody clothes they had worn on primary day. Ellender's Democratic majority exonerated Bilbo of inciting violence, but the Senate still refused to seat him. Diagnosed with terminal cancer of the mouth, Bilbo left Washington on 4 July 1947, declaring, "If I live, the people of Mississippi will send me back. If I don't live, it doesn't matter either way." He died on 21 August, in a New Orleans hospital.[8]

Some expected John Rankin to win the special election held in November 1947 to fill

Bilbo's Senate seat. Greenville editor Hodding Carter sent Rankin a copy of *Mein Kampf* to help him hone his campaign rhetoric, but on 4 November Rankin ran fifth in a field of six candidates. Victor John Stennis later said, "Some of my advisers thought if I didn't make an anti–Negro statement I might not be elected. But I wouldn't do it, and I never have." He would, however, follow Bilbo's lead by opposing every civil rights bill proposed during his four decades in Washington.[9]

Holding the Color Line

Black suffrage was not the only postwar threat to white supremacy. In Washington, President Harry Truman proposed a Fair Employment Practices Commission (killed by southern filibuster in February 1946) and desegregated the U.S. armed forces. The Supreme Court banned segregation in interstate bus travel and forbade restrictive housing covenants. The Congress of Industrial Organizations launched "Operation Dixie" in 1946, recruiting workers of all races. From Atlanta, Dr. Green declared, "No CIO or AFL carpetbagging organizers, or any other damned Yankees are going to come into the South and tell southerners how to run either their businesses or their niggers." The CIO enjoyed some success in Mississippi between 1946 and 1948, winning fifty-seven union elections affecting 11,000 workers, then dropped the campaign as too expensive for the results achieved.[10]

Southern racists faced new crises in 1948. On 2 February, Truman urged Congress to pass civil rights legislation, including his FEPC, revocation of poll taxes, and an antilynching bill (branded "a bill to encourage rape" by John Rankin). In Philadelphia, on 14 July, delegates at the Democratic National Convention adopted Truman's program as a plank in the party's national platform. Mississippi governor Fielding Wright immediately led his delegation from the hall, followed by thirteen Alabama delegates (including Birmingham's Klan-allied police commissioner, Eugene "Bull" Connor). Three days later, white supremacists convened in Birmingham to form the States' Rights Democratic Party (Dixiecrats), nominating South Carolina governor Strom Thurmond for president, with Wright as his running mate. Klansmen and their allies, including Georgia's Jesse Stoner and veteran anti–Semite Gerald L.K. Smith, joined in the festivities. Democrats suffered another wound on 25 July, when breakaway Progressive Party members nominated ex-vice president Henry Wallace as the left's presidential candidate.[11]

Mississippi's mood was ugly as election day drew near. Governor Wright warned blacks who sought equality to "make your home in some state other than Mississippi." *Natchez Democrat* editor Elliott Trimble opined that African Americans "are not fit, mentally, morally, or physically, for this new kind of emancipation." On 2 November, Harry Truman amazed his detractors, defeating Republican rival Thomas Dewey by 2.1 million votes. The Dixiecrats claimed 83 percent of Mississippi's votes, but polled only 1,169,021 nationwide. Henry Wallace trailed Thurmond by some 13,000 votes, to take fourth place.[12]

Mississippi's Klan left no records for 1946 through 1949, but it still had friends in public office. Theodore Bilbo's death was a loss, but John Rankin stood firm in the House of Representatives, and Senator James Eastland made no secret of his unabashed racism. Sheriff Julius Harper, of Copiah County (1948–52), later served as one of Mississippi's two grand dragons in the 1960s. When asked by HUAC counsel whether "you as a sheriff [would] tolerate the existence of a Ku Klux Klan organization in your jurisdiction," Harper sought refuge in the Fifth Amendment's ban on self-incrimination.[13]

The AGK suffered a major blow with Dr. Green's death, on 18 August 1949. Atlanta policeman Sam Roper replaced Green as grand dragon, but his honeymoon in office was short-lived. On 24 August the IRS filed a tax lien against the AGK for $9,322.40 in unpaid taxes from 1946, 1947, and 1948. Roper settled that bill on 12 September, then faced another lien one week later, this time for $8,383.72. While Roper scrimped to make ends meet at headquarters, rival Klans surged to the fore in Georgia, Alabama, and the Carolinas.[14]

The most flamboyant contender was "Doctor" Lycurgus Spinks, an aging ex-minister, self-styled "sexology" expert, and all-around flimflam man who once billed himself as the reincarnation of George Washington. Around 1930, Spinks fled South Carolina one jump ahead of embezzlement charges and landed in Mississippi, where Governor Bilbo refused extradition.

Turning to politics in the Magnolia State, Spinks lost one gubernatorial race and two bids to become tax collector. He also sued Governor Wright for $50,000, after Wright "threw a slanderous dagger into [his] back," then he dropped the case prior to trial. On 23 August 1949, after a meeting in Montgomery, Alabama, that included representatives from splinter Klans in Mississippi and five other states, Spinks crowned himself "Imperial Emperor" of the Knights of the Ku Klux Klan of America.[15]

Spinks scored a publicity coup on 9 September 1949 when he appeared on *Meet the Press* before a panel that included Drew Pearson, Lawrence Spivak, and Edward Folliard of the *Washington Post*. Spinks claimed to represent "every Klansman in America," whether they knew it or not, adding that "[a]ll the niggers down South know that the best friend they've got on earth is the Knights of the Ku Klux Klan." Asked to name one black group that supported the Klan, Spinks hedged: "I don't keep up with Negro organizations except what the Baptist Church is doing among the niggers. That's the only one I've preached in." On the subject of violence, he claimed, "There has never been a Klan in this United States that ever endorsed flogging or in any way violating the law"; then he backpedaled to admit, "I would not say that no Klansman ever flogged anybody." Confronted with denials of his claim that he once served as Mississippi's grand dragon, Spinks snapped, "I don't care what they claim. They're just like you. They claim anything on earth that pays off politically and financially."[16]

On balance, it was not the order's finest hour. Mocked by rival wizards for his grandiose claims, Spinks pulled up stakes on 25 March 1950, announcing relocation of his headquarters from Montgomery to Jackson, Mississippi. What happened next is anyone's guess. The only record of the Mississippi Klan from 1950 is a rare commemorative plate, offered for sale on the Internet in 2005, inscribed with the message "Ku Klux Klan, 1950, Realm of Mississippi." Its reverse side bore the legend "Yazoo City, Mississippi, 1950."[17]

While the Magnolia Klan idled, Mississippi's civil rights movement slowly gained momentum. Dr. T.R.M. Howard, a black physician and entrepreneur in Mound Bayou, founded the Regional Council of Negro Leadership in 1951, pursuing full citizenship for African Americans via the ballot box. Medgar Evers, lately graduated from Alcorn College and resettled in Mound Bayou with his new bride, worked for Howard's Magnolia Mutual Insurance Company and joined the RCNL, before moving on to the NAACP in 1952. Soon, he began to organize new NAACP chapters throughout the Delta.[18]

White supremacists took note, encouraged by Governor Wright's vow that "[w]e shall insist upon segregation regardless of consequences," but the Korean War and presidential politics distracted them. By 1952, antipathy toward Republicanism was so ingrained with southern whites that even Dwight Eisenhower's war-hero status could not lure most away from the party of their fathers. Governor Hugh White launched his second administration with a reminder that Mississippi stood "where she stood in 1948," but no Dixiecrats emerged to champion the Southern Way of Life. Instead, loyal Dixie Democrats were forced to cast their votes for Adlai Stevenson of Illinois, branded a liberal "egghead" by Eisenhower running mate Richard Nixon. On election day, Mississippi gave 60 percent of its votes to Stevenson, but Eisenhower surprised hard-line Democrats, winning 40 percent of the popular vote — a huge increase over the former twenty-five-year high of 6.4 percent.[19]

"Black Monday"

A year before the presidential vote, NAACP attorneys launched a multipronged attack on segregated schools across the nation. They began in Kansas, where segregation was allowed but not required, and moved on from there to file lawsuits in Delaware, South Carolina, Virginia, and Washington, D.C. Combining all five cases under *Brown v. Board of Education*, a unanimous Supreme Court ruled on 17 May 1954 that segregated schools were inherently unequal, and thus unconstitutional. A year later, seeing no progress in Dixie, the court ordered classroom integration to commence with "all deliberate speed."[20]

The reaction was immediate and true to form. Governor White proclaimed himself "shocked and stunned" by the ruling. On the day *Brown* was announced, Senator Eastland vowed that Dixie "will not abide by nor obey this legislative decision by a political court. Any attempt to integrate our schools would cause great strife and turmoil." Eight days later, he declared, "Mr. President, let me make this very clear: The South will retain segregation." Fred Sullens, at the *Jackson Daily News*, predicted that "Mississippi will not obey the decision. If an effort is made to send Negroes to school with white children, there will be bloodshed."

Brookhaven judge Tom Brady delivered a fiery speech to Greenwood's Sons of the American Revolution in late May 1954, later published as a pamphlet titled *Black Monday*. In it, he spoke of "Negroid blood like the jungle, steadily and completely swallowing up everything." Violence would follow any effort to enforce the *Brown* decision, Brady warned: "We have, through our forefathers, died before for our sacred principles. We can, if necessary, die again. You shall not show us how a white man 'may go through the guts' of a negro! You shall not mongrelize our children and grandchildren!"[21]

William Faulkner, Mississippi's Nobel laureate, understood the depth of his native state's passion for white supremacy. He told London's *Sunday Times*, "The South is armed for revolt. After the Supreme Court decision you couldn't get as much as a few rounds for a deer rifle in Mississippi. The gunsmiths were sold out. These white people will accept another civil war knowing they're going to lose." Judge John Minor Wisdom, on the Fifth Circuit Court of Appeals, marveled at Mississippi's "eerie atmosphere of Never-Never Land."[22] And "Never" soon became the slogan of the organized resistance to desegregation in the South.

Councils and Klans

In James Eastland's Sunflower County, planter Robert "Tut" Patterson grasped *Brown*'s threat to segregation a year before the ruling was announced. The menace was particularly fearsome in the Delta, where black majorities ranged from 51 percent in Warren County to 82 percent in Tunica. On 11 July 1954 Patterson and thirteen other residents of Indianola organized the first Citizens' Council, pledged to "stop desegregation before it begins." On 12 October 1954 delegates from thirty chapters met to organize a statewide Association of Citizens' Councils (ACC), with Patterson in charge. Jackson's Council was a late-bloomer, founded in March 1955 by William J. Simmons (no relation to the Klan's wizard of 1915–1922). Eight months later, the ACC claimed 65,000 active members, led from headquarters in Greenwood. April 1956 saw the Citizens' Councils of America founded in New Orleans as a national organization.[23]

The Councils championed "respectable" defiance, taking their cue from Tom Brady's threat of economic boycotts in *Black Monday*. Dallas County chairman Alton Keith vowed to "make it difficult, if not impossible, for any Negro who advocates desegregation to find and hold a job, get credit, or renew a mortgage." On 5 June 1954 the Mississippi NAACP advised its various chapters to petition for integration of local schools. Petitions were soon filed in Jackson, Natchez, Vicksburg, Yazoo City, and Clarksdale — where the announcement prompted organization of a new Citizens' Council with 3,000 members. Yazoo City's Council ran a full-page newspaper ad, including "an authentic list of the purported signers to an NAACP communication to the school board," and other chapters followed suit. Many petitioners were subsequently fired from jobs and otherwise harassed by "lawful" means until they quit the fight. Throughout the process, Council efforts bore a flavor of Judge Wisdom's Never-Never Land, as when Tut Patterson told a reporter from the *New York Herald Tribune*, "Sir, this is not the United States. This is Sunflower County, Mississippi."[24]

The early Citizens' Councils took pains to distance themselves from the Klan, although Indianola's founders initially debated calling themselves "Sons of the White Camellia." Spokesmen condemned the "nefarious Ku Klux Klans" and claimed to screen out applicants "with the Ku Klux Klan mentality." As one Council member explained, "We want the people assured that there is responsible leadership organized which will and can handle local segregation problems. If that is recognized, there will be no need for any 'hot-headed' bunch to start a Ku Klux Klan. If we fail, though, the temper of the public may produce something like the Klan."[25]

Still, there were problems with the Council's wholesome image. Tut Patterson's recommended reading list, compiled in August 1954, included blatantly anti–Semitic sources such as Conde McGinley's *Common Sense*, Gerald Winrod's *Defender*, Frank Britton's *American Nationalist*, Gerald L.K. Smith's Christian Nationalist Crusade, and John Hamilton's National Citizens Protective Association of St. Louis. Another recommended author, Bryant Bowles, had preached at Klan rallies before founding his own National Association for the Advancement of White People.

When Mississippi Council members rallied on 9 September 1954, Associated Press dispatches noted that one spokesman "predicted violence"; another opined that "a few killings" would help Mississippi "save a lot of bloodshed later on." Outside of Mississippi, Council members rioted against school integration in Alabama and Tennessee and bombed schools in Little Rock, Arkansas.[26]

It came as no surprise, then, when some journalists compared the councils to the KKK. Atlanta's Ralph McGill and Greenville's Hodding Carter dubbed the Citizens' Council "a hoodless Klan," "an uptown Klan," "a button-down Klan," "a scrubbed up cousin of the Klan," and "a country club Klan." P.D. East, owner-operator of the *Petal Paper*, ran a mock ad exhorting racists to "Join the Glorious Citizens Clan," thereby attaining "freedom to be superior without brain, character, or principle!"[27]

Various sources remark on the "possible" overlap of Klan and Council membership. That was certainly the case in Birmingham, where Asa Carter's North Alabama Citizens' Council morphed overnight into the Original KKK of the Confederacy, and in Little Rock, where Council leader E.A. Lauderdale planned his school bombings in concert with Klansmen. In Mississippi, author Reed Massengill claims, "It was common knowledge that [Medgar] Evers, along with a number of other civil rights leaders in the state, was on a Ku Klux Klan hit list, even though the Klan had not yet formally organized in Mississippi."[28]

Or had it?

Atlanta resident Eldon Edwards organized the U.S. Klans in 1953, then chartered the group as a "social and charitable" organization on 24 October 1955. Between those events, in August 1954, liberal Pascagoula newsman Ira Harkey received a visit from one Tommy Harper, whom Harkey named as a local Klan leader. Harper warned Harkey: "If any niggers try to register at white schools, we're not gonna bother them. The one we'll get is the white man that's behind them, and we know who he is." On the night of 1 September, six-foot crosses blazed at local schools, at Pascagoula's largest black church, and outside Harkey's home — the latter with a note reading "We do not appreciate niggerlovers. We are watching you. KKKK."[29]

Reign of Terror

While officially decrying violence, Mississippi officials continued to preach and practice defiance at every turn. Governor White resurrected the antebellum doctrines of "interposition" and "nullification," while state legislators passed a new statute banning integrated education at "high school level or below." On 12 August 1955, James Eastland told a Senatobia Citizens' Council rally, "You are not required to obey any court which passes out such a ruling. In fact, you are obligated to defy it."

Six months later, Mississippi repealed its compulsory education law as a first step toward closing integrated schools. On 12 March 1956, a total of 101 Dixie congressmen endorsed the "Southern Manifesto," a call for resistance coauthored by Eastland. Another new law (reluctantly vetoed by Governor James Coleman) imposed six-month jail terms and a $1,000 fine on anyone who "breached the peace" through "disobedience to any law of the State of Mississippi, and nonconformance with the established traditions, customs, and usages of the State of Mississippi."[30]

On 29 March 1956 Mississippi created a State Sovereignty Commission, described by state legislator Philip Bryant of Oxford as a "private Gestapo" created to conduct "cloak-and-dagger investigations that develop into character assassinations." For seventeen years,

Eldon Edwards led the dominant Klan faction of the 1950s (Florida State Archives).

the commission spied on civil rights workers, disseminated far-right propaganda, and channeled state funds to private racist groups. The Citizens' Council received an initial donation of $20,000, followed by monthly $5,000 payments that ultimately topped $200,000.[31]

Nor were Mississippi's leaders shy about hinting that violence might follow if their peaceful efforts to preserve white supremacy failed. After the South's first school riots, Governor Coleman warned, "What happened in Clinton, Tennessee, will be like a boil on the side of Mt. Everest compared to what could happen in Mississippi." John Satterfield, president of Greenville's bar association, listed "the gun and the torch" among various means of preserving segregation, though he claimed to find violence personally "abhorrent." William Simmons stirred his council members to the boiling point with declarations that "an all-out war is being waged against the white race."[32]

One crucible of tension was Belzoni, the "Heart of the Delta" and seat of Humphreys County. There, in February 1953, a group of African American businessmen filed federal complaints against sheriff Ike Shelton for obstructing voter registration. When no action followed, the Rev. George Lee and grocer Gus Courts founded a local NAACP chapter on 8 February 1954, with Courts as president. Both registered to vote, then persuaded ninety-two more to do likewise. The Citizens' Council struck back in March 1955, circulating a list of registered blacks to local banks and merchants. Courts was soon evicted from his store but found new quarters in a building owned by a fellow NAACP member. In mid–April, Dr. T.R.M. Howard hosted a rally at Mound Bayou, where ten thousand would-be voters gathered to cheer speeches by the Rev. Lee and others.[33]

Two weeks after that rally, on the night of 7 May 1955, night riders shot the Rev. Lee as he drove home from work at his Belzoni printing shop. The *Clarion-Ledger* reported his murder beneath the headline "Negro Leader Dies in Odd Accident." Sheriff Shelton initially claimed that the shotgun pellets extracted from Lee's face were "fillings from his teeth." After three independent physicians insisted that lead was not used in dental fillings, Shelton changed his story. "This is one of the most puzzling cases I have ever had," he declared. "If Lee was shot, it was probably by some jealous nigger. He was quite a ladies' man." Witnesses scattered, one pursued by FBI agents to Illinois, but the killers remain unidentified. A coroner's jury composed of Citizens' Council members first ruled Lee's death accidental, then changed its verdict to murder by persons unknown.[34]

The next to die was Lamar Smith, a black farmer and veteran of World War II who organized voter-registration drives and campaigned against a Lincoln County supervisor known for his outspoken racism. On 13 August 1955, nine days before a runoff election that threatened the supervisor's job, three white men accosted Smith at the Brookhaven courthouse. One drew a pistol and shot Smith at point-blank range, killing him instantly. Sheriff Robert Case was close enough to hear the shot and see the suspects flee, one spattered with blood, but he stalled for eight days before making arrests. By then, no witnesses were found to testify against the suspects (all of whom are now deceased). The case remains officially unsolved.[35]

Mississippi's next and most notorious race murder of 1955 was unrelated to the civil rights movement. Fourteen-year-old Emmett Till's mother sent him from Chicago to stay with relatives and sample rural life, but the experiment went disastrously wrong on 24 August 1955, when Till allegedly whistled at or made suggestive remarks to white store-keeper Carolyn Bryant, in Money. Armed men snatched Till from his great-uncle's home

Mourners throng the memorial service for the Rev. George Lee (Library of Congress).

at 2:30 A.M. on 27 August, and he was not seen again until his mutilated corpse surfaced in the Tallahatchie River four days later. Relatives identified the body from its clothing and a ring engraved with Till's father's initials. Sheriff H.C. Strider challenged the identification, while an anonymous local told *The Nation*, "The river's full of niggers." Finally, with visible reluctance, Strider booked Carolyn Bryant's husband and his half-brother on murder charges. Five lawyers volunteered to represent the suspects, while local whites raised $10,000 to fund their defense. Governor White assured the country, "This is not a lynching. It is straight-out murder."[36]

At trial, an all-white jury would not grant even that much. Moses Wright identified defendants Roy Bryant and J.W. Milam as the men who abducted his nephew. Bryant himself admitted snatching Till, but claimed he left the boy alive. Witness Willis Reed saw Milam drag Till into a barn, followed by screams within. Two of Milam's employees described hosing blood from the bed of his pickup, on Milam's orders. In their summations, defense attorneys accused the NAACP of planting "a rotting, stinking body in the river" to discredit Mississippi; they called on the jurors, as "custodians of American civilization," to "turn these boys loose" or "your forefathers will turn over in their graves." The panel acquitted both defendants on 24 September, after which Bryant and Milam confessed the murder to *Look* magazine for $4,000. Black boycotts and white embarrassment ultimately ruined both killers, but Sheriff Strider remained adamant, warning one television crew, "I just want to tell all of those people who've been sending me those threatening letters that if they ever come down here the same thing's gonna happen to them that happened to Emmett Till."[37]

By the time Till died in Tallahatchie County, economic coercion and "personal visits" had reduced Belzoni's list of registered black voters from a high of 126 to 35. Gus Courts, one of the stubborn holdouts, was wounded in a drive-by shooting at his store on 25 November 1955. Friends rushed him to Mound Bayou for treatment, where his surgeon offered the recovered shotgun pellets to a pair of FBI men and was told "to keep them." Sheriff Shelton, flexible as ever in his theories, first blamed customers for shooting Courts, claiming that there were "three or four niggers in the store and nobody outside." When reminded that the shots came through a window from the street, Shelton replied, "There was bound to be one outside because that's where he got shot from." In Shelton's view, witnesses who described a carload of white gunmen "don't know whether they were white men or light-skinned niggers." Finally, Shelton told reporters, "I honestly think some damn nigger just drove there and shot him." As for questioning Courts, Shelton said, "I'm not going to chase him down. Let the 'Naps' [NAACP] investigate. They won't believe anything I say anyway." Upon recovering, Courts fled to Chicago, describing himself as an "American refugee from Mississippi terror."[38]

Courts was not alone in Chicago, as the spate of murders prompted other activists to seek refuge in the Windy City. Dr. T.R.M. Howard—whose name appeared on the "Ku Klux" death list with those of George Lee, Medgar Evers, and Greenwood NAACP leader Richard West—first hired bodyguards, then fled the state when they could not prevent a cross-burning in his front yard. Charles Evers endured boycotts and threats in Neshoba County, but left after a staged car accident and lawsuit drained his savings. The NAACP's Natchez chapter collapsed when menacing incidents forced leader Audley Mackel and his family to leave the state "secretly and swiftly."[39]

Those who remained behind were still at risk. Author Anne Moody describes an incident from Wilkinson County, where Sheriff Ed Cassidy allegedly delivered a black youth named Jerry to white vigilantes. The gang accused Jerry of making obscene calls to a white telephone operator, then tied him to a tree and whipped him "nearly to death" with a leather strap and hose pipe. The boy survived, but Clinton Melton was less fortunate. On 3 December 1955, at the Glendora filling station where he worked, Melton apparently put more gasoline than requested into a customer's tank. The white motorist shot Melton where he stood, escaping prosecution with a plea of self-defense. On 24 December, authorities pulled black schoolteacher James Evanston's corpse from Long Lake, in Tallahatchie County. His murder remains unsolved.[40]

White Mississippians were outraged when the NAACP published a pamphlet titled *M is for Mississippi and Murder*, but they reserved their greatest wrath for those whom the Citizens' Council called "scalawag Southerners." One such, Hodding Carter, condemned the Council's "police state maneuverings" in his *Delta Democrat Times*, and compared the Council's members to "a pack of baboons yelling, grinning, and making faces." Next, Carter wrote a piece for *Look* titled "A Wave of Terror Threatens the South." State legislators promptly censured him for "selling out the state for Yankee gold," whereupon Carter branded the resolution's signatories "89 angry jackasses." Editor Hazel Brannon Smith suf-

NAACP official Medgar Evers (right) consoles the widow and children of Clinton Melton (Library of Congress).

fered similar travails in Holmes County, convicted of libel after she criticized the sheriff's shooting of an unarmed prisoner, then challenged by a rival Citizens' Council newspaper that cut her advertising revenue by 50 percent.[41]

Despite their racism and florid defiance of Washington, Mississippi's white leaders still cringed with embarrassment at each new violent incident. At his January 1956 inauguration, Governor Coleman vowed that "Mississippi will be a state of law and not of violence.... [D]espite all the propaganda which has been fired at us, the country can be assured that the white people of Mississippi are not a race of Negro killers." A year later, Coleman proudly said, "We did not have a single racial incident in the state in 1956." In fact, however, three racial killings occurred within days of Coleman's inaugural speech. On 20 January 1956 a Yazoo City policeman shot unarmed African American Jessie Shelby for "resisting arrest." One day later, Milton Russell died in an arson fire at his Belzoni home. The month ended with Edward Duckworth's murder in Raleigh, shot by another white gunman who claimed self-defense.[42]

Anne Moody describes another fatal arson incident, from Centreville that allegedly occurred in June 1956. According to Moody, white terrorists mistakenly killed eight or nine members of the Taplin family while trying to murder a neighbor suspected of dating white women. Correspondence with local journalists failed to corroborate Moody's account. Andy

Lewis, publisher of Wilkinson County's weekly *Woodville Republican*, found no reports of house-fire fatalities in 1955 or 1956, adding, "If a fire had happened then which killed eight or nine persons, I am positive that it would have been reported." Peter Rinaldi, with the *Natchez Sun*, interviewed Wilkinson County's sheriff from the period in question and was told, "I don't know anything about what the Klan was doing." Rinaldi dismissed that statement as "a bold face lie," adding that "sheriffs at that time were either Klan endorsed or Klan members, and sheriffs and deputies in Wilkinson were all white and Klan supporters, so I thought he was lying." That said, no coverage of the Taplin fire appeared in the *Sun*, a fact that proves nothing.[43]

What was the Klan's role, if any, in the violence of 1955 and 1956? Most published accounts deny any Ku Klux activity in Mississippi during those years, but such claims are challenged by Ira Harkey's Pascagoula observations, and by reports from three other authors. William McCord reports that Carthage "revamped its KKK" after the *Brown* rulings. Maryanne Vollers describes the 1955 expansion of a Louisiana Klan, the Original Knights, which recruited "scattered members of old, traditional outfits like the Knights of the White Camellia in southern Mississippi." According to Vollers, "People joined out of family tradition more than anything else. It was a racist's low-rent fraternity with costumes and funny titles." Journalist Jack Nelson's report is more specific. He claims that future Mississippi Klan leader Samuel Bowers joined the Original Knights in Natchez, around the time of his 1955 arrest for liquor violations. Conversely, the FBI and HUAC claim that the Original Knights did not exist before 1960, expanding to Mississippi in autumn 1963. No account specifically blames Klansmen for any crimes in 1955 and 1956, but stories persist of a "Ku Klux death list."[44]

Girding for War

White Mississippi's alienation from the national Democratic Party increased in 1956. Adlai Stevenson carried the state with 58 percent of the popular vote, while 17 percent endorsed the Independent States' Rights team of Harry Byrd and Mississippi's John Bell Williams. A statewide purge of 1,300 blacks from voter registration rolls assisted that result — and prompted Congress to raise the ante in 1957 with passage of America's first civil rights act since 1875. The new statute created a Civil Rights Division within the Justice Department, empowered to seek federal injunctions against counties that obstructed black registration and voting.[45]

Less than four weeks after Congress passed the 1957 Civil Rights Act, on 24 September, President Eisenhower sent federal troops to enforce desegregation at Central High School in Little Rock, Arkansas. The two events combined to spur recruiting among racist groups. By year's end, the Citizens' Councils claimed 300,000 members in 500 chapters, while 19 different Klans competed for members in Dixie. The U.S. Klans had klaverns in at least eight states, while Alabama and South Carolina boasted six competing factions each, Florida claimed four independent Klans, and Georgia harbored two. Mississippi's death toll was relatively light for 1957: Charles Brown, the state's only acknowledged race-murder victim that year, was shot in Yazoo City on 25 June, while "visiting a white man's sister." Police made no arrests.[46]

The year 1958 started badly for black Mississippians. On 8 January, a sheriff's posse killed murder suspect George Love near Ruleville. Further investigation cleared Love of all charges. On 27 April, white gunman L.D. Clark killed Edward Smith at his home in State Line; despite Clark's boasts of the slaying, grand jurors refused to indict him. Yalobusha County Sheriff Buck Treolar beat prisoner Woodrow Daniels to death on 1 July; following Treolar's acquittal on manslaughter charges, he retrieved his blackjack from the prosecutor's table and declared, "Now I can go back to rounding up moonshiners and niggers." Before year's end, Walter Bailey established the Mississippi Knights of the KKK, with headquarters in Gulfport.[47]

While violence flared in the hinterlands, the State Sovereignty Commission opened a file on "Medgar Evers, Race Agitator." Lead investigator Zak Van Landingham, a former FBI agent, ordered that "spot checks be made of the activities of Medgar Evers, both day and night, to determine whether he is violating any laws." Evers had moved his family to Jackson in 1955, with his promotion to serve as state secretary of the NAACP, and continued to aggravate white officials with his demands for racial parity. In 1958 he was beaten while trying to integrate Jackson's Trailways bus terminal. Soon afterward, Evers supported Alcorn College professor Clennon King's attempt to pursue doctoral studies at the state university in Oxford, but the effort ended badly. Authorities committed King to a psychiatric hospital, with Governor Coleman remarking that if King "were not a lunatic," he would not have tried to enroll at Ole Miss.[48]

Mississippi's most sensational case of the late 1950s began on 23 February 1959, when Jimmy Walters's car stalled on Highway 11, between Lumberton and Poplarville. He went for help, leaving his family in the vehicle, and returned to find wife June hysterical, saying she had been raped by one of four black men who stopped at the car during Jimmy's absence. Sheriff Osborne Moody arranged a lineup, from which June Walters chose Lumberton truck driver Mack Parker as her attacker. By the time a grand jury indicted Parker in mid–April, Pearl River County was a racial tinderbox. On 22 April a self-described 1920s Klansman from Hattiesburg invited Jimmy Walters to a secret meeting at the Masonic Hall in Gumpond, east of Poplarville. Walters declined to attend, but others on hand included ex-deputy sheriff J.P. Walker, farmer L.C. Davis, self-ordained minister James Lee, and his son. Walker—a candidate for sheriff in August's primary, two-time army deserter, and one of the "toughest and least law-abiding men in the county"—quickly emerged as the leader of a lynch mob in the making.[49]

At 12:30 A.M. on 25 April, jailer Jewel Alford admitted Walker's gang to the county lockup. Mack Parker fought for his life but was soon overpowered. The mob planned to hang him from a bridge, but shot him instead when he leaped from their car at the scene. Authorities found his body near Bogalusa, Louisiana, on 4 May. A coroner's jury deliberated for twelve minutes, then pronounced the mystery unsolvable. According to the *Poplarville Democrat*, "the general consensus ... is that the abductors were from outside Pearl River County," yet the *New York Times* asserted that "details of the lynching and the names of those involved are common knowledge." A North Carolina Klan spokesman assured reporters that "The Ku Klux Klan does not advocate violence. Mob action is ugly."[50]

Governor Coleman, fearful that Mississippi would be "punished by civil rights legislation," invited FBI agents to investigate the lynching. Under federal grilling, one of the lynchers suffered a fatal stroke, while two others were hospitalized for nervous breakdowns.

G-men delivered a massive report to Coleman in November 1959, naming twenty-three participants in Parker's murder, but Poplarville's prosecutor withheld the file from his grand jury, ensuring that no indictments resulted. A federal grand jury convened in Biloxi on 4 January 1960, with Judge Sidney Mize presiding, but its conduct was irregular at best.

Ignoring FBI testimony, the panel focused instead on June and Jimmy Walters. One juror asked June, "You mean you let that nigger fuck you?" then demanded of Jimmy, "You mean to tell me that after that nigger fucked your wife you still live with her?" Judge Mize declined to call more than a dozen crucial witnesses (including J.P. Walker), then advised the jury that indictments required participation in the murder by "a sheriff or other law officer." Apparently deciding that a jailer did not qualify, the panel dissolved on 14 January without charging anyone. Judge Mize declared himself unable to identify the lynchers "on the basis of the evidence presented" by the FBI.[51]

J.P. Walker lost his sheriff's race in 1959, but won on his next attempt, in 1963. During his four-year term, Pearl River County's Klan staged regular parades through Poplarville. Meanwhile, the State Sovereignty Commission sent Poplarville judge Selby Dale off to speak at Brandeis University, in Massachusetts. When a member of the audience inquired whether Parker's lynchers would ever be caught, Dale embarrassed Mississippi further by replying, "Three of them are already dead."[52]

The big winner in August's primary was Ross Barnett, successful at last in his third gubernatorial campaign. Born in 1898, Barnett earned $100,000 yearly as Jackson's top personal-injury lawyer, occasionally deviating from his area of expertise to defend racist agitators like Klan ally John Kasper against riot charges. Despite his commercial success, some critics questioned Barnett's intelligence. In one campaign press conference, asked for his opinion on the disputed Chinese islands of Quemoy and Matsu, Barnett replied, "They're good men, and I'm sure I can find a place for them in Fish and Game."

Still, he stood firm for segregation—*Time* magazine called him "as bitter a racist as inhabits the nation"—and that was his key to success. "I believe that the Good Lord was the original segregationist," Barnett declared. "Mixing the races leads inevitably to the production of an inferior mongrel…. The Negro is different because God made him different. His forehead slants back. His nose is different. His lips are different, and his color sure is different…. We will not drink from the cup of genocide." In another speech, he said, "Hitler offered the people of Germany a short cut to human progress. He gained power by advocating rights for minority groups." Nonetheless, Barnett claimed that he never met "a single Negro who has been discriminated against," adding that many received "better treatment than whites."[53]

Both candidates for governor in 1959 were Citizens' Council members, but Barnett proved more extreme than rival and lieutenant governor Carroll Gartin. He thus secured the hard-core racist vote; and he also won support from Senator Eastland, who furnished campaign posters reading "Don't forget that it was the Coleman-Gartin regime that called the FBI into Pearl River County. Vote for Ross Barnett and Preserve our Southern Way of Life." Barnett's campaign song, "Roll with Ross," assured listeners that "He's for segregation one hundred percent. He's not a mod'rate like some other gent."

With victory in hand, Barnett told the media, "I am proud that I have been a Citizens' Council member since the Council's early days. I hope that every white Mississippian will join with me in becoming a member of this fine organization." The Council soon moved

its headquarters from Greenwood to Jackson, across the street from the governor's mansion, while *The Nation* tagged Barnett as the group's "unabashed front man."[54]

Violence continued during and beyond the primary campaign. On 14 August 1959
nocturnal gunmen killed Samuel O'Quinn near his Centreville home. Anne Moody, a friend
of O'Quinn from high school, reports that he had recently returned from the North, where
he joined the NAACP. The crime remains unsolved, but Moody blamed Centreville Klansmen, some of whom she says employed her as a maid in 1959.[55]

October 1959 was worse. On the twenty-third, a motorist found Booker T. Mixon
naked and dead on a road outside Clarksdale. Police called the incident a hit-and-run,
while critics questioned Mixon's nudity and the chunks of flesh seemingly carved from his
body. One week later, Philadelphia patrolman Lawrence Rainey — a future Klansman and
defendant in Mississippi's most sensational trial of the 1960s — found Luther Jackson and
Hettie Thomas chatting in a parked car. Rainey ordered Jackson from the vehicle, shot him
twice without apparent cause, then used his radio to summon chief of police Bill Richardson. Arriving with Philadelphia's mayor, Richardson pistol-whipped Hettie Thomas and
booked her on various trumped-up charges, resulting in a $40 fine. A coroner's jury ruled
Jackson's death justified, on 27 October, while the FBI found "no basis for any action" under
federal law. Finally, on 1 November, eight white youths in Corinth killed fifteen-year-old
William Prather in a belated "Halloween prank." Prosecutors charged one suspect with
manslaughter, but later dismissed the case.[56]

Invasions

Both sides in Mississippi's racial crisis were primed for action by 1 February 1960, when
black college students in Greensboro, North Carolina, staged the first sit-in protest at a
whites-only lunch counter. "Direct action" appealed to impetuous youth, and to some older
African Americans discouraged by the sluggish progress of civil rights litigation in court.
The movement swiftly spread, accompanied in many cities by white violence and a surge
in Klan recruiting. By the end of 1960, observers from the Anti-Defamation League pegged
nationwide Klan membership as between 35,000 and 50,000. The U.S. Klans remained dominant, with an estimated 20,000 members.[57]

Mississippi's first public demonstration, on 14 April 1960, was a "wade-in" at Biloxi's
restricted beach. Police dispersed the protesters, but made themselves scarce ten days later,
when the NAACP's Dr. Gilbert Mason returned with more would-be swimmers. Forty
whites armed with chains, pipes, and baseball bats mobbed the invaders, leaving them
bloody and bruised. Around the same time, students from Jackson's three black colleges
launched a boycott of white shops on Capitol Street. Evaluations of the campaign's impact
varied widely, but the color bar remained firmly in place.[58]

On 6 May 1960 President Eisenhower signed a new civil rights act, whose provisions
permitted (but did not require) the FBI to investigate racial bombings if explosives were
transported interstate. A rash of blasts had plagued southern and border states since 1956 —
and long before, in troubled Alabama — but Mississippi was thus far unscathed. Another
presidential race gave white supremacists a chance to air their discontent with Washington
and offered a potential replay of the 1928 campaign as Catholic John Kennedy prepared to

Lawrence Rainey personified the collusion between Mississippi lawmen and the KKK (National Archives).

claim the Democratic nomination. When the party gathered in Los Angeles, Tom Brady nominated Ross Barnett and carried Mississippi's votes, but Kennedy secured first-ballot nomination without aid from the Magnolia State. The neo–Nazi National States Rights Party (NSRP), formed from remnants of the Columbians by Georgia Klansman Jesse Stoner and chiropractor Edward Fields, countered by nominating Arkansas governor Orval Faubus, with veteran Jew-baiter John Crommelin as his running mate.[59]

While Klansmen recycled their stock anti–Catholic pamphlets, and a Florida Klan leader embarrassed GOP contender Richard Nixon by endorsing him during Nixon's televised debates with Kennedy, Mississippi Democrats went shopping for a candidate who met their needs. The ultimate solution for 116,248 voters was a slate of unpledged electors who cast their ballots for Virginia Senator Harry Byrd. Six Alabama electors and one from Oklahoma followed suit, helpless to prevent JFK's narrow win over Nixon. The NSRP, campaigning on frankly racist lines, ran a distant third, with 214,195 votes nationwide.[60]

The campaign season's only Klan-type violence occurred in Union, where a white minister, the Rev. J.H. German, lent a hand in constructing a black seminary. On 26 August 1960 a mob of twenty whites dispersed black workers at the school, then beat the Rev. German unconscious. German identified several of his assailants as local Citizens' Council members, but police made no arrests. On 1 January 1961 white gunmen on a motorcycle wounded two black victims in Greenville.[61]

Tension mounted as white Mississippi braced itself for the onset of JFK's liberal "New Frontier." On 5 December 1960 the U.S. Supreme Court extended its ban on segregation in interstate bus travel to include depot restrooms and other facilities. Eight weeks later, James Meredith of Kosciusko applied for admission to Ole Miss and informed the registrar that he was black; his application was rejected on 4 February 1961. On 27 March, nine Tougaloo College students staged a "read-in" at Jackson's whites-only public library. Two days later, at their first court hearing, Medgar Evers was beaten by racist bootlegger G.W. Hydrick and two white policemen.[62]

Meanwhile, the Congress of Racial Equality (CORE) prepared to test the Supreme Court's latest desegregation ruling with a wave of "freedom rides" through Dixie. The first busload of thirteen integrated passengers left Washington on 4 May 1961, soon followed by a second. Ten days later, they were mobbed by Alabama Klansmen, lost one bus to arson, and required 600 U.S. marshals to defend their lives from Klan-led rioters.

When the first bus left Montgomery for Mississippi on 24 May, ex-governor Coleman warned assistant attorney general Burke Marshal that the freedom riders would be killed before they reached Jackson. Bomb threats delayed the bus near Meridian, but authorities found no explosives. Police in Jackson peacefully arrested twenty-eight demonstrators on 24 May. Seventeen more went to jail on 28 May, with the total rising to 100 by mid–June and 328 at summer's end.[63]

Mississippi's relative passivity seemed anticlimactic, after Alabama's chaotic violence in spring 1961, but CORE was not finished with the Magnolia State. Field secretary Tom Gaither expanded CORE's mission to include voter registration, while Bob Moses pursued the same goal for the Student Nonviolent Coordinating Committee (SNCC). The Klan was also in transition following the August 1960 death of Eldon Edwards in Atlanta. Robert "Wild Bill" Davidson succeeded Edwards as imperial wizard of the U.S. Klans, while rival E.E. George schemed to unseat him. Dissension split the order on 18 February 1961, with Davidson and Grand Dragon Calvin Craig defecting to form a new Invisible Empire, United Klans, Knights of the KKK of America three days later. Wearied by the struggle, Davidson resigned as wizard on 1 April, leaving Craig in charge. On 8 July 1961 Craig merged his group with Robert Shelton's Alabama Knights, creating the United Klans of America (UKA). Shelton assumed the wizard's mantle and moved imperial headquarters to Tuscaloosa, Alabama.[64]

At this point we encounter yet another version of the Klan's "return" to Mississippi. Natchez historian Jack Davis reports that the Louisiana-based Original Knights spilled across Mississippi's border in 1961, not 1955 or 1963, as claimed by others. His source is Natchez native and former Grand Dragon Edward McDaniel, whose brother served on the local police force, and whose grandfather had told him, "Son, if you ever have a chance to join the Klan, join the Klan." Journalist Paul Hendrickson confirms Klan infiltration of the Natchez Police Department in 1961, but provides no specific details. Confirmation of sorts comes from another McDaniel interview, in which he told *Clarion-Ledger* reporter Jerry Mitchell that the Original Knights reached Mississippi "in 1960 or so."[65]

Registration of black voters remained a perilous pastime in Mississippi during summer 1961. On 15 August police jailed Bob Moses for leading three applicants to the courthouse in Liberty. Two weeks later, while repeating the attempt, Moses was beaten by Billy Jack Caston, a cousin of Amite County's sheriff. Moses pressed assault charges, whereupon six white witnesses testified that Moses started the "fight." On 5 September Moses suffered another beating, with SNCC worker Travis Britt, at the Liberty courthouse. Two days later, Walthall County's registrar pistol-whipped SNCC activist John Hardy in Tylertown. Sheriff Edd Craft jailed Hardy for assault. On 24 September, Justice Department attorney John Doar toured Amite County with Moses. They interviewed NAACP member E.W. Steptoe, who reported frequent threats against himself and comrade Herbert Lee from state legislator Eugene Hurst. As a result, Steptoe refused to leave his home unarmed.[66]

The next morning, Hurst and Billy Jack Caston confronted Herbert Lee at a local cotton gin. Lee had infuriated local racists by driving Bob Moses around Amite County to meet potential voters. On 25 September, after an exchange of heated words, Hurst drew a gun and shot Lee dead in front of witnesses. Hurst claimed that Lee owed him $500 and refused to pay, pulling a tire iron when Hurst asked him for the money. Black witness Louis Allen confirmed that story for the coroner's jury that ruled Hurst's action justified, then recanted to Moses and FBI agents, insisting that whites had coerced him into perjury. Soon after Allen filed that statement, a deputy sheriff called at his farm and assaulted him, breaking his jaw with a flashlight.[67]

White violence continued through the last three months of 1961. In McComb, on 11 October, thugs beat two newsmen covering a black protest march. On 29 November, when five New Orleans freedom riders tested the latest court order requiring integrated bus depots, McComb racists turned out to maul them in force. The mob scene was repeated on 1 December, when another busload of protesters arrived, and again on 2 December, when thugs attacked Tom Gaither in his car. On 3 December racists pummeled a local newspaper editor deemed "moderate" on racial matters. For the year overall, CORE and the Southern Regional Council logged twenty-four beatings and shootings statewide.[68]

The new year brought no respite from terror. In March 1962 reports from the Delta depicted voter-registration workers "catching hell" from police and white vigilantes. On 9 April a Taylorsville patrolman killed Corporal Roman Duckworth Jr. when Duckworth — on leave to attend the birth of his sixth child — refused to vacate his bus seat for a white passenger. In May, Neshoba County Sheriff Ethel "Hop" Barnett and Deputy Lawrence Rainey (both named as Klansmen in FBI reports) killed black prisoner Willie Nash while transporting him to a state hospital. Nash was handcuffed in the backseat of Barnett's car at the time, his death fulfilling Barnett's prior threat that "If I ever get that son of a bitch in my car again, I am going to kill him." On 20 June police stopped and beat a black journalist who was en route from Jackson to Forest pursuing unconfirmed reports of another racial murder in Scott County.[69]

In 1962, members of CORE, SNCC, and the NAACP combined to form a Council of Federated Organizations (COFO), pressing for wholesale registration of black voters statewide. Activists met the stiffest organized resistance in neighboring Leflore and Sunflower counties, where black majorities threatened the power base of white politicians including James Eastland. Sam Block ran Greenwood's COFO office, at risk to his life. In July 1962 he was beaten by whites on the street, then he was nearly killed by a hit-and-run driver in a separate incident. Greenwood police were little better, flogging fourteen-year-old Welton McSwine with a bullwhip for allegedly "peeping" at a white girl. On 15 August night riders armed with guns and chains stormed Greenwood's COFO headquarters and smashed its furnishings. On 31 August, Ruleville tenant farmer Fannie Lou Hamer joined a registration pilgrimage to Indianola. Her landlord evicted her on 8 September; she complained of harassment from the Klan and Citizens' Council. One night later, drive-by gunmen blasted three Ruleville homes housing SNCC activists. Two registration workers suffered wounds and one was hospitalized in critical condition.[70]

Rebellion at Ole Miss

By summer 1962, seven years after the Supreme Court's order for desegregation "with all deliberate speed," no Mississippi classroom had been integrated. Across the South, observers calculated that the glacial speed of integration seen in other states should bring full compliance by the year 9256.[71] James Meredith intended to accelerate that pace with his assault upon the University of Mississippi at Oxford.

On 10 September 1962 the Fifth Circuit Court of Appeals ordered Meredith's admission to Ole Miss "effective immediately." Three days later, Governor Barnett assured his white constituents that "No school will be integrated in Mississippi while I am your governor!" Barnett personally blocked Meredith's admission on 20 and 25 September, gave Lieutenant Governor Paul Johnson a chance to do likewise on 26 September, and then returned with William Simmons and a mob of 2,500 jeering racists to bar Meredith once more on 27 September. In separate hearings on 28 and 29 September, the court of appeals found both Barnett and Johnson guilty of contempt. Barnett celebrated his contempt citation on 29 September at a football game in Jackson, where he told a cheering throng, "I love Mississippi! I love her people! I love her customs!"[72]

Militant racists mobilized to help Barnett defend those customs, spurred by a radio broadcast from Texas, where ex-general Edwin Walker called for volunteers to defend white supremacy at Oxford. Wizard Robert Shelton prophesied "another War Between the States," but reports of a forty-two-car Ku Klux caravan leaving Tuscaloosa on 16 September proved unfounded. Ed Fields of the NSRP wired Barnett from Birmingham, promising storm troopers to "place our lives and fortunes at the disposal of your supreme authority as the governor of the sovereign state of Mississippi." Anniston's Klan sent a similar wire, announcing hundreds of knights "on a stand-by alert." Georgia's Calvin Craig vowed that when orders were issued, "a volunteer force of several thousand men would be on its way to Mississippi straight off." Birmingham's Eastview Klavern No. 13, later implicated in a fatal 1963 church bombing, ordered members to assemble and be ready to march on 29 September. That same night, 3,000 racists gathered in Shreveport, Louisiana, announcing plans for a 210-car procession to Oxford. Melvin Bruce, a sometime member of the American Nazi Party in Georgia, packed his rifle and hit the road after wiring Barnett his pledge of service "as a combat infantryman." A ham radio broadcast from Kansas City summoned "all Minutemen organizations, all ranger units, Illinois civilian control units [and] Washington militia" to stand by for marching orders. Even the "law-abiding" Citizens' Council was ready to fight, pledging 20,000 volunteers from Louisiana and 1,500 from Florida.[73]

The actual number of Klansmen who answered Walker's call is anyone's guess. Author William Doyle reports UKA "observers" in mufti at Ole Miss, while FBI memos placed 600 Alabama knights in Jackson, lodging at the Robert E. Lee and King Edward hotels. Oxford attorney William Goodman described numerous "scary people who had come to town to see the show, armed with hunting rifles, shotguns, hatchets and bricks." FBI sources confirmed the departure of a twelve-car caravan from Prichard, Alabama, bearing three dozen self-styled "Citizens for the Preservation of Democracy" to Ole Miss.

Before battle was finally joined on 30 September, Oxford airport administrators barred Robert Shelton's private plane from landing, but combatants had no difficulty reaching the campus by car, truck, or bus. Highway patrolmen stationed around Ole Miss admitted scores of vehicles with license plates from Alabama, Arkansas, Florida, Georgia, Louisiana, and Texas. One procession of twenty or thirty cars was briefly halted outside Oxford, then allowed to proceed without searches for weapons. At least one chartered bus slipped through, with fifty armed men aboard and loudspeakers blaring the UKA anthem, "Cajun Ku Klux Klan." One who failed to pass was Greenwood's Byron De La Beckwith, who was stopped outside town with a truckload of weapons and warned to go home. According to author Maryanne Vollers, police "said they expected he would be coming, and with some difficulty, they convinced him to turn back."[74]

Against that tide, Governor Barnett mobilized the highway patrol and 250 game wardens of the Mississippi Fish and Game Commission under H.C. Strider. Lafayette County judge Russell Moore used the patrol's radio network to summon Mississippi's sheriffs, along with all the deputies they could muster on short notice. State senator John McLauren ordered fire engines deployed on campus, while seven Mississippi congressmen wired the White House, warning President Kennedy that "the highest state of heat and tension prevails in Mississippi.... A holocaust is in the making." Alabama governor-elect George Wallace sent soon-to-be public safety director Albert Lingo (recently introduced at a UKA rally as "a good friend of ours") to observe the action at Ole Miss with an eye toward Wallace's forthcoming challenge at the University of Alabama. Another controversial Alabama lawman, Klan-allied sheriff James Clark of Dallas County, announced that he and Chilton County sheriff Hugh Champion would bring their "special posses" to Oxford, but neither appeared. Meredith himself arrived at Ole Miss with a bodyguard of some 300 U.S. marshals and Border Patrolmen.[75]

Rioting erupted at Ole Miss around 8:30 P.M. on 30 September, soon after Meredith's arrival on campus. Besieged in the Lyceum, federal officers armed only with tear gas and revolvers ducked sniper fire and repelled waves of attackers lobbing bricks, pipes, and Molotov cocktails. Edwin Walker led one charge, with an estimated one thousand rioters behind him. Racists commandeered a bulldozer and fire engine, but failed to breach the federal line. "That's not a riot out there anymore," deputy marshal Al Butler advised Assistant Attorney General Nicholas Katzenbach. "It's an armed insurrection."

FBI Agent Robert Cotton saw dozens of outsiders leaping from cars and pickups, brandishing rifles and shotguns. Based on those observations and others, riot historian William Doyle concludes that the Oxford melee was, in fact, "the beginnings of a Ku Klux Klan rebellion." Through it all, Mississippi lawmen stood idle for the most part, while some reportedly joined in the riot. Journalists heard one policeman on his radio, saying, "Better tell those people from Alabama to bring gas masks." A highway patrolman waved Georgia Nazi Melvin Bruce through the supposed blockade, telling him, "They need help in there." Robert Kennedy later charged that "approximately 150 of the police were observed sitting in their automobiles within one-half mile of the rioting and shooting."[76]

Twelve thousand soldiers quelled the rebellion at 5:30 A.M. on 1 October. Despite the high volume of gunfire on campus, the battle claimed only two lives. Oxford resident Ray Gunther, watching from the sidelines, died from a stray shot to the head, while some unknown gunman executed French reporter Paul Guihard between Ward women's dormitory and the fine arts center, 165 yards from the Lyceum. Both fatal shots came from .38-caliber pistols; and while FBI experts tested 450 federal sidearms, both deaths remain unsolved. Snipers shot 30 U.S. marshals, while another 136 marshals and 48 soldiers suffered wounds from objects hurled by rioters. (Klan leader Sam Bowers later claimed that six marshals died in the riot, their deaths concealed by Robert Kennedy.) Medics at the campus infirmary treated twenty-eight students and three highway patrolmen for minor injuries or tear-gas inhalation. Soldiers seized hundreds of weapons, ranging from clubs and knives to a submachine gun. On 1 October a tip led troops to a cache of firearms at the Sigma Nu fraternity house, where future senator Trent Lott presided. Sigma Nu's national headquarters later gave Lott its "Achievement of the Year" award as a campus peacemaker.[77]

Governor Barnett blamed the riot on "trigger-happy" marshals, whom he accused of "instability and unwarranted brutality against unarmed youths." Federal marshals arrested 300 rioters, barely one-third of them registered students. On Monday night, 1 October, soldiers nabbed two dozen armed intruders on campus; one father-son team carried two shotguns, a rifle, a saber, two hunting knives, and a large supply of ammunition. Of eighteen defendants initially charged, a grand jury indicted four: sniper Melvin Bruce and three men from Prichard, Alabama. Hugh Cunningham, senior partner of Ross Barnett's law firm, defended the Alabamians, while Georgia's Jesse Stoner represented Bruce. Prior to trial, Stoner told journalist Michael Dorman, "I'd pass out if any of these defendants was convicted. I was surprised as hell to find that any of them had been indicted. You noticed, didn't you, that not one of those indicted was from Mississippi?" As Stoner predicted, white jurors ignored a cache of confiscated weapons and acquitted all four defendants.[78]

State of Siege

For some racists, the "loss" of Ole Miss sounded a death knell for nonviolent resistance to segregation, tipping the balance away from the Citizens' Councils toward militant groups like the Klan and fledgling Americans for Preservation of the White Race. On the night of 2 October 1962 night riders firebombed Dr. Gilbert Mason's clinic in Biloxi and the office of Gulfport NAACP leader Dr. Felix Dunn. One night later, terrorists torched the residence of a Columbus NAACP leader and burned a cross at Hodding Carter's Greenville home. On 4 October drive-by gunmen peppered the homes of Leake County blacks who had signed school integration petitions.[79]

Was this the Klan at work? Author James Silver claims that Walter Bailey disbanded his Mississippi Knights after the Ole Miss riot "because nobody showed up for a council of war," yet HUAC found the group still marginally active five years later. As we have seen, several authors date the Mississippi invasion by Louisiana's Original Knights well before the official date in 1963, espoused by HUAC and the FBI. Reporter Jerry Mitchell contends that the White Knights of the KKK, an offshoot of the Original Knights, organized in 1962 rather than early 1964 as stated by most sources. His documentary evidence, a White Knights pamphlet titled "The Most Awful Disease of Our Time" unfortunately bears no date, but two employees of Laurel's Bee Hive Newsstand recall Sam Bowers and six or seven other Klansmen meeting in the shop's storeroom, initially disguising their klavern as a chapter of the John Birch Society. In any case, as Maryanne Vollers observes, "Although it is said that an organized, violent Klan was not present in Mississippi until early 1964, the retaliation that followed Meredith's admission to Ole Miss showed a pattern indicating that someone was directing a terror campaign in the state. Whoever it was knew the targets, what they owned, and where they lived."[80]

Pascagoula was a case in point. Jackson County Sheriff James Ira Grimsley answered Judge Russell Moore's call to action at Oxford, leading three sworn deputies and fifty-two assorted gunmen in a chartered bus, vowing to "show them goddamned niggers that they weren't going to take Mississippi." A press camera caught Grimsley lobbing a brick in the riot, and Ira Harkey says his posse members boasted that "they'd done more damage than any other outfit that went, burning cars, breaking windows, slugging people." Whatever the truth of their prowess in battle, FBI files paint a curious portrait of Grimsley. A premed student at Jackson's Millsaps College, Grimsley served as coroner from 1957 to 1960, while pursuing the more lucrative office of sheriff and tax collector (average yearly take, $300,000). Bureau reports highlight his alcoholism, along with penchants for bribery and "cutting" (sexually assaulting) black women in jail.[81]

Grimsley returned from Oxford to lead the Jackson County Citizens Emergency Unit, a civilian vigilante group that claimed 600 members by mid–October 1962. *Pascagoula Chronicle* editor Ira Harkey learned of the group's existence from an anonymous caller reporting a courthouse meeting of "people who want to see you get killed." For further details, said the caller, "Ask the sheriff." On 15 October, after Harkey ran an editorial counseling moderation, a sniper fired into the *Chronicle*'s office. At the Unit's next meeting, Grimsley branded Harkey "the state's leading nig-gerlover," complaining that the *Chronicle* "actually call[s] niggers 'Mr.' and 'Mrs.' and Harkey's all the time ridiculing our great governor." On 22 October, after Grimsley called for a boycott of all local merchants with black employees, Harkey blasted the unit as "a drift from reality, for drunks and loons." Gunfire shattered his windows again on 1 November.[82]

Declassified FBI files confirm that Grimsley's cohorts planned "to do away with" Harkey, whom unit members and G-men alike deemed "very liberal in the past with his racial viewpoint." Another memo claims that "the purpose of the

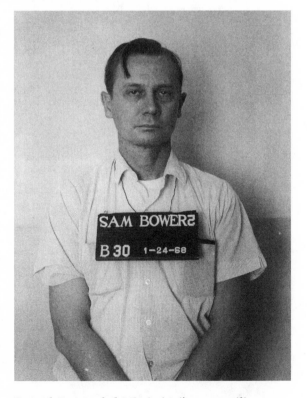

Samuel Bowers led Mississippi's most militant Klan faction in the 1960s (National Archives).

Unit was to secretly go to the University of Mississippi at Oxford, Mississippi, 'to get' or kidnap [Name Deleted], recent Negro enrollee at the University." In fact, the group accomplished neither goal, and apparently dissolved by year's end. Forbidden to succeed himself as sheriff, Grimsley sought a seat in Congress, running fourth in a field of five candidates.[83]

The year ended with violence and rumors of violence. On 23 December 1962 night riders fired shotgun blasts into James Meredith's Kosciusko home, narrowly missing his younger sister. Anne Moody claims that during the same week, an unknown black man's headless and emasculated corpse was found between Canton and Tougaloo "with K's cut into the flesh all over his body." My inquiries to various newspapers and libraries failed to document that case, but Jackson librarian Michele Hudson noted that "[i]t would not be surprising for the *Clarion-Ledger* not to print such a story."[84]

Whether or not the homicide in question actually occurred is now beside the point. Over the next five years, competing Klans in Mississippi would outstrip all others in the South for sheer ferocity, and in the process make headlines around the world.

CHAPTER 5

"A Ticket to the Eternal"
(1963–1969)

Official sources and the authors who rely on them insist that the Klan "returned" or was "revived" in Mississippi sometime during 1963. Author Don Whitehead, working from FBI files at J. Edgar Hoover's personal direction, dates the arrival of Louisiana's Original Knights from March 1963 and pegs defection of the dissident Mississippi White Knights (MWK) more precisely at 14 December 1963. HUAC dates the first Original Knights klavern's foundation from "autumn 1963," but agrees that the split occurred in December. Until reporters Jerry Mitchell and Jack Nelson challenged those reports, most authors accepted them without question, dating the MWK's "formal" creation from February 1964.[1]

Douglas Byrd served as Mississippi grand dragon of the Original Knights until December 1963, when kleagle J.D. Swenson expelled Byrd and Edward McDaniel for allegedly embezzling Klan funds. Both suspects replied with similar accusations against Swenson, but McDaniel's troubled history lent credibility to the charges. In 1959 he was fired from the Johns-Manville plant in Natchez for theft, and two years later filed bankruptcy to avoid payment of debts in California. Whichever Klan McDaniel served, disgruntled members ultimately branded him a leader prone to "hold a rally, burn a cross, and take the money."[2]

A power struggle ensued for control of the MWK, climaxed by the election of Imperial Wizard Samuel Holloway Bowers Jr., from Laurel. A New Orleans native, born in 1924, Bowers was the grandson of a four-term Mississippi congressman and a wealthy Louisiana planter. Despite such auspicious beginnings, his parents divorced and his father disowned him. After naval service during World War II, Bowers spent a year at Tulane University, then transferred to the University of Southern California as an engineering student. There, he met Robert Larson and they dropped out together before completing their sophomore year, returning as young business partners to Laurel, in Forrest County (named for the Klan's original grand wizard). Together, Bowers and Larson ran the Lincoln Theater and the Sambo Amusement Company, distributing vending machines and jukeboxes.[3]

Most sources credit Bowers with writing the MWK's distinctive and elaborate constitution, though HUAC named the document's authors as Douglas Byrd, Gordon Lackey, "and others." While cribbing from the *Kloran* and its predecessors, the MWK constitution also established a unique "legislative branch" within the Klan. Its lower house, the Klanburgesses, included all Klansmen in good standing, while the Klonvocation (analogous to the U.S. Senate) ostensibly elected officers, fixed dues, and so forth. The democratic façade was a sham.

Four years later, HUAC investigators found no evidence that the Klonvocation ever convened.[4]

Still, officers *were* elected and members recruited. Julius Harper served as grand dragon, supervising a full staff of kleagles, titans, and cyclopes. While FBI spokesmen claim that the MWK "numbered no more than a few hundred men," the group planted fifty-two klaverns in thirty-four counties. Even HUAC, always prone to understate the strength of right-wing groups while inflating leftist ranks, credits the MWK with 6,000 members. Other observers counted 10,000 Mississippi Klansmen by May 1964. Most of Laurel's knights worked at the local Masonite plant, while Pascagoula's klavern recruited from the Ingals shipyard. Jackson Klansman Thomas Gunter printed the MWK's *Klan Ledger* and other literature at his Capital Blueprint & Supply Company. Identified "front" groups included the Mississippi Constitutional Council, the Mississippi White Caps, and WASP Inc.[5]

As members, Bowers wrote, he wanted "ONLY: sober, intelligent, courageous, Christian, American white men who are consciously and fully aware of the basic fact that their physical life and earthly destiny are absolutely bound up with the survival of this nation, under god." In fact, while the MWK ostensibly accepted only men whose "habits are exemplary," the membership turned out to be a motley crew. Bowers himself had a liquor conviction on file, and Deavours Nix — grand director of the MWK's Klan Bureau of Investigation (KBI) — logged his first assault conviction in 1962. Edward Fuller, cyclops of the MWK's only "foreign" klavern (in Sligo, Louisiana), boasted nine arrests between 1947 and 1958 on charges ranging from drunk and disorderly conduct to fighting, carrying concealed weapons, and suspicion of rape.[6]

Sam Bowers ranked among the MWK's most volatile members. Acquaintances from 1963 recall him quoting at length from Adolf Hitler's *Mein Kampf* and snapping off stiff-arm Nazi salutes to his dog. One observer from the Bee Hive Newsstand later said that Hitler "was his hero." Upon receiving news of President Kennedy's assassination in November 1963, Klansmen report that Bowers "danced around" in glee. "He just thought it was wonderful," one told Jack Nelson. "He went into happy, crazy acting." Long convinced that the Original Knights were "too passive," Bowers espoused a "militant Christianity" strongly influenced by the sermons of California Klansman and Aryan Nations founder Wesley Swift. Don Whitehead notes that Bowers had "little interest in women," while another critic dubbed him "an unasylumed lunatic"; but he was clearly dedicated to the racist cause. "As Christians," Bowers wrote, "we are disposed to kindness, generosity, affection and humility in our dealings with others. As militants we are disposed to use physical force against our enemies."[7]

That said, Bowers did not intend to lead the charge himself. While readying his grand crusade, he told a friend, "The typical Mississippi redneck doesn't have sense enough to know what he's doing. I have to use him for my own cause and direct his every action to fit my plan."[8]

While Bowers whipped the MWK into shape, another racist group formed in Natchez. Most sources agree that the Americans for Preservation of the White Race (APWR) was launched on 15 May 1963 and received its state charter on 25 June, but Natchez historian Jack Davis names APWR leaders as the prime movers behind foundation and funding of the all-white Adams County Private School (ACPS) in 1962. According to Davis, the ACPS owed its existence to Rowland Scott, a Natchez accountant who served as state president of the APWR. The school's legal advisor doubled as attorney for the Natchez Citizens' Council, while its board president, Ernest Parks, was an MWK member implicated (but never charged) in a 1964 double murder.[9]

Persistent controversy dogged the APWR throughout its life, including accusations from FBI spokesmen that it served as a "shell organization" for the Klan. The group's charter proclaimed that it sought to "unite white men" in devotion to racial self-respect and "PRIDE." APWR president Arsene Dick, writing in July 1964, claimed that his group was "non-political, non-profit, and by all means non-violent." Nonetheless, one month later, the *Delta Democrat-Times* observed that "so many KKK members belong to the APWR in certain areas of southwest Mississippi, that it is impossible to tell where one stops and the other begins." The APWR's *White Patriot* newsletter published articles defending Klan terrorists, and one acknowledged member, Klansman Ernest Avants, died in prison while serving time for a racist murder committed in 1966.[10]

First Blood

In January 1963 twenty-eight of Mississippi's Methodist ministers signed a public statement titled "Born of Conviction," supporting free speech from the pulpit and maintenance of public education versus all-white private schools. Social reprisals were immediate, and fell most heavily on the Rev. Elton Brown in Morgantown, a tight community known to blacks in surrounding Oktibbeah County as "the Klux's Den."[11]

While ostracism was unsettling, black Mississippians faced the prospect of Klan-inspired violence. The first recorded death occurred on 17 January 1963, when Sylvester Maxwell's brother-in-law found his mutilated corpse outside Canton, four hundred yards from a white farmer's home. Canton blacks considered the murder a lynching. It remains officially unsolved today.[12]

One month later, on 20 February, fire leveled four buildings in Greenwood's black business district. Flames missed the local SNCC office, presumed to be the target, but destroyed the dry-cleaner's next-door. When SNCC activist Sam Block accused whites of setting the fire, Greenwood police jailed him for making "statements calculated to breach the peace." A local judge offered to drop the charge if Block quit SNCC, but Block refused, accepting a jail term and a $500 fine.[13]

On the night of 28 February 1963 whites ambushed a SNCC car seven miles outside of Greenwood. Eleven machine-gun bullets pierced the vehicle, critically wounding driver James Travis and narrowly missing Bob Moses and attorney Robert Blackwell. Mayor Charles Sampson, widely regarded as a Klansman, blamed the shooting on "individuals and organizations from other areas who, activated by motives other than the welfare of our people, are dedicated to creating disunity and discord between us." Under pressure from Washington, local police arrested MWK member Wesley Kersey and petroleum wholesaler William Greenlee, but neither was convicted. In response to the shooting, spokesmen for SNCC, CORE, the NAACP, and the Southern Christian Leadership Conference (SCLC) announced the launch of a full-sale voter registration drive in Greenwood.[14]

Local Klansmen responded as might be expected. On 6 March drive-by gunmen fired into a car parked outside SNCC headquarters, narrowly missing Sam Block and three other occupants. Police responding to the incident asked one activist, "Didn't you know that you didn't have any business being in the car with that nigger Sam Block?" Arsonists burned the SNCC office on 24 March. Two nights later, shotgun blasts ripped through the home of George Greene, an African American whose son had applied to Ole Miss. The shooters escaped in a car resembling one owned by self-styled "rabid" racist Byron De La Beckwith, a friend of Mayor Sampson and charter member of the local Citizens' Council. When ten SNCC members led 100 blacks to register in Greenwood on 27 March, police locked them up for "inciting a riot."[15]

Author Charles Payne suggests that Greenwood's modern terrorists "fell far short of their racist forefathers" in terms of courage, confined to night riding and sneak attacks in lieu of old-style spectacle lynchings. Following the shooting at his home, George Greene warned civic leaders that he planned to kill the next attackers. Others followed suit, black farmers packing "nonviolent Winchesters" to rural mass meetings, while SNCC members took turns on guard at their office and homes where they slept. Such tactics would not quell Klan violence indefinitely, but they stalled the next local outbreak until summer 1964.[16]

Meanwhile, arsonists firebombed the Clarksdale home of state NAACP president Aaron Henry on 12 April 1963. Police detained two whites, who escaped prosecution with claims that they were "just having fun." In Lexington, where fourteen blacks tried to register on 9 April 1963, the local *Advertiser* named would-be voter Hartman Turnbow as an "integration leader." A Klan informer warned SNCC worker John Ball that the MKW had plans for Turnbow, and his words proved prophetic on 9 May, when night riders firebombed Turnbow's home. The arsonists fled when Turnbow peppered them with gunfire, but Sheriff Andrew Smith jailed Turnbow for torching his own house, then arrested Bob Moses for "impeding an investigation" when he photographed the damage.[17]

On 27 May 1963 the U.S. Supreme Court clarified its 1955 *Brown* ruling, officially proclaiming that "all deliberate speed" meant cessation of any further delays in school integration. One day later, black students from Tougaloo College invaded the whites-only lunch counter at Woolworth's, on Jackson's Capitol Street. They left quietly when refused service, but CORE's John Salter led a more determined team back to the store on 31 May. A mob of some 200 whites met the protesters with blows, kicks, and showers of condiments. That night, a firebomb scorched the carport at Medgar Evers's home in Jackson. Police dismissed the bombing as a "prank." The next morning, *Clarion-Ledger* columnist Charles Hills told his readers that "Times have changed to the extent that most folks down South consider it an honor to be termed a bigot, a reactionary, and a race-baiter. These are terms invented by the mentally depressed Yankee who thinks his skin ought to be black ... a situation in which he is unwanted either by the true white people or the true Negro."[18]

The Mississippi Klan had found its audience.

Medgar Evers Assassinated

Four days after his carport was firebombed, Medgar Evers told journalist Michael Dorman that he was receiving "plenty of calls" from anonymous racists. One caller held a revolver next to his telephone's mouthpiece and spun the cylinder repeatedly. Evers responded by stocking his home with a half-dozen guns, chaining a German shepherd in the yard, and carrying a pistol in his car. None of it helped at 12:40 A.M. on 12 June, when a sniper shot Evers in his own driveway. A neighbor heard the shot and ran outside, firing a pistol in the air, but did not see the gunman. Evers died in surgery at 1:20 A.M. Strangely, while Evers had complained of round-the-clock police surveillance during recent months, no officers were present to observe his murder.[19]

Pressed for a comment on the slaying, Governor Barnett remarked, "Apparently, it was a dastardly act." Jackson's mayor and the chairman of Mississippi's Democratic Party echoed that lukewarm condemnation, while the NAACP offered $10,000 for the killer's capture and conviction. Perhaps embarrassed by their own racist rhetoric, the *Clarion-Ledger* and *Jackson Daily News* pooled their resources to offer an additional $1,000 reward.[20]

Eight hours after Evers died, police found the sniper's rifle concealed in shrubbery 150 feet from his home. Local newspapers ran photos of the weapon and detectives shipped it off to the FBI laboratory in Washington. Technicians there also received the fatal bullet, but they could not match it to the weapon. Neither were they able to identify a partial fingerprint found on the rifle's telescopic sight. Meanwhile, on 13 June, a resident of Itta Bena telephoned Jackson police, reporting that he had traded a similar rifle to Greenwood's Byron De La Beckwith in January 1960.[21] From there, reports of how the FBI identified the sniper radically diverge.

In one version, published by a former FBI undercover agent, the Bureau paid New York mobster Gregory Scarpa $1,500 to kidnap a member of the Mississippi Citizens' Council and drive him to a shack in the Louisiana bayou country, where Scarpa shoved a pistol in his captive's mouth and demanded the name of Evers's assassin. G-men crouched outside an open window, taking notes, and thus identified Beckwith. The official story has FBI agents tracing the rifle's telescopic sight from its Chicago manufacturer to a Grenada gun shop, where Beckwith traded two pistols for it in May 1963. With the suspect's name in hand, technicians then identified the rifle's partial fingerprint from Beckwith's military records.[22]

In either case, G-men arrested Beckwith on 22 June, on charges of plotting "with unknown persons" to deprive Evers of his civil rights. Federal prosecutors dropped that charge

Klansman Byron De La Beckwith murdered Medgar Evers in 1963 but avoided conviction for three decades (Library of Congress).

two days later when Jackson authorities charged him with murder. Formal indictment followed on 2 July, Medgar Evers' thirty-eighth birthday.[23]

Byron De La Beckwith was born in Sacramento, California, in November 1920, a circumstance that prompted a disingenuous *Clarion-Ledger* headline: "Californian is Charged with Murder of Medgar Evers." His parents, however, were Mississippi natives, and his mother returned to Greenwood with Byron in December 1926 after his father died from pneumonia and "contributory alcoholism." Beckwith lost his mother six years later, and thereafter lived with relatives whose neighbors often entertained ex-senator James Vardaman. Kinfolk recall that Beckwith "idolized" Vardaman and later "revered" Theodore Bilbo. His distant cousin, James Eastland, served with Bilbo in the Senate. Beckwith enrolled at Starkville's Mississippi State College in 1940, but flunked out at midterm. He then joined the Marine Corps, seeing action during World War II at Guadalcanal and Tarawa, where he was wounded. A buddy from the service recalled Beckwith collecting the skulls of slain Japanese.[24]

Discharged from the service in January 1946, Beckwith returned to Greenwood and found work as a fertilizer salesman. He married a woman whose alcoholic thirst matched his own, embarking on a relationship marked by violent arguments (including gunfire in the house), repeated divorce and remarriage. "Black Monday" unhinged him in 1954. "That's when De La really went crazy," his wife later said. "He just lost his damn mind." A charter member of Greenwood's Citizens' Council, Beckwith nurtured (in his ex-wife's words) "a kind of worship" for Council leader Tut Patterson. In May 1956 Beckwith wrote to Governor Coleman, requesting a job with the State Sovereignty Commission, billing himself as "Rabid on the Subject of Segregation." No appointment was forthcoming, so he penned a letter to President Eisenhower, entrusting it to Rep. Frank Smith for delivery. Smith described the letter as "abusive" and "illiterate" and refused to deliver it. "I knew that De La was a racial nut," Smith said. "He was an extremist, and he wasn't rational at all." Still, the *Greenwood Morning Star* ran his letter in full, complete with misspellings and a warning that desegregation would "inevitably lead to the loss of life itself."[25]

Beckwith became increasingly radical after his wife divorced him for the second time, in 1962. A lifelong Episcopalian, he denounced his own church as "the Devil's Workshop" when national leaders endorsed integration. In January 1963 he wrote to the National Rifle Association, observing that "for the next 15 years we here in Mississippi are going to have to do a lot of shooting to protect our wives, children and ourselves from bad niggers." Beckwith publicly threatened to kill Hodding Carter III for moderate editorials published in Carter's *Delta Democrat-Times*, and he also focused on Medgar Evers, telling friends, "He's a bad nigger. He's got to go."[26]

Following Beckwith's arrest, Citizens' Council state treasurer R.F. Parish and state finance chairman Ellett Lawrence created a White Citizens' Legal Fund to bankroll his defense. Author Reed Massengill reports that Governor Barnett personally delivered donations to the fund, while Barnett's law partner, Hugh Cunningham, joined Hardy Lott (past president of Greenwood's Citizens' Council) on Beckwith's defense team. Tut Patterson and other leading Council members visited Beckwith in jail, leaving Beckwith "virtually delirious" with pleasure. So did Oxford warrior Edwin Walker, who described Beckwith as "a fine southern gentleman." Authorities moved Beckwith to a psychiatric hospital for testing on 26 July 1963, but Judge O.H. Barnett — the governor's cousin, who in 1959 told the

Scott County Times, "There is no place for any moderation in the matter of segregation"—halted those tests six days later, condemning them as "evidence by compulsion." Back in the Hinds County jail, Beckwith wrote letters boasting of his "red-carpet treatment."[27]

Jury selection for Beckwith's murder trial began on 27 January 1964, with opening statements delivered four days later. FBI agents tied Beckwith to the presumed murder weapon, while other prosecution witnesses described him lurking at NAACP meetings, asking for his victim's home address. Defense attorneys produced two Greenwood policemen who belatedly "remembered" seeing Beckwith ninety miles from Jackson at the time Evers was shot. Beckwith testified on his own behalf, alternately boasting of his marksmanship and denying guilt, admitting ownership of the rifle and claiming it was stolen shortly before the murder. Jurors retired to deliberate on 6 February, moments before ex-governor Barnett entered the courtroom to shake Beckwith's hand. Judge Leon Hendrick declared a mistrial on 7 February, with the jury deadlocked seven-to-five for acquittal.[28]

Beckwith remained in jail pending retrial, which convened on 6 April 1964. The jury was empanelled on 8 April and included a cousin of a State Sovereignty Commission investigator. On 9 April night riders burned ten crosses in Jackson. Klansmen and Citizens' Council members also packed the court's white gallery, rising in unison when Beckwith entered, leaving him "deeply moved" by their support. Prosecutors repeated their case against Beckwith, while defense attorneys added one new witness to their roster: Jackson resident James Hobby testified that he had parked his car, the same model as Beckwith's, near a restaurant where prosecution witnesses saw Beckwith park on 12 June 1963. Jurors began deliberating on 15 April, and two days later declared themselves deadlocked eight-to-five for acquittal, resulting in a second mistrial.[29]

This time, Beckwith made bond with funds provided by the White Citizens' Legal Fund. Hinds County sheriff Fred Pickett drove Beckwith home on 17 April after lending him a .30-caliber carbine for self-defense en route. Pickett's cruiser led a raucous motorcade to Greenwood, where cheering crowds greeted Beckwith with a banner reading "Welcome Home De La." It was, observer Thatcher Walt declared, "a real circus." Beckwith's third murder trial was scheduled for 13 July, then pushed back to October, and finally forgotten entirely. Greenwood's police department recruited Beckwith as an auxiliary officer, assigned to patrol local ghettos.[30]

Overwhelming evidence identifies Beckwith as a Klansman, but confusion persists as to when and where he joined the hooded order. On 26 June 1963 Beckwith told police interrogators "that we definitely needed a Ku Klux Klan at this time, that it could do a lot of good." The same detectives noted that Beckwith also went "way overboard when Masonry is mentioned." In September 1963, writing from jail, Beckwith informed a correspondent that the Mississippi Klan had been revived and he was invited to join. Most sources agree that Greenwood neighbor Gordon Lackey, an MWK kleagle, initiated Beckwith into the White Knights, but different authors place that event in summer 1964 or 1965.

After his second trial, Beckwith's soon-to-be three-time ex-wife reported, Beckwith was out every night. "He was running with hoodlums and everything," she said. "But he would say, well, they had a cause." G-man Tom Van Riper told Reed Massengill that "Beckwith really looked up to [Sam] Bowers. Bowers was very big on having a covey of people like Beckwith that he could depend on. That was very important to him." Meridian Klansmen led by police sergeant Wallace Miller staged a celebratory cross-burning after Beckwith's second mistrial, and Miller posed with the cross in a photo for the local *Star*, flashing a Klan recognition sign with one hand. "Every Klansman who saw that picture recognized the sign and got a big laugh out of it," Miller said. "I was a big man around town for several days."[31]

Suspicion of a Klan conspiracy behind the Evers murder persists to the present. Early on 12 June 1963, before news of the slaying was broadcast, a man phoned the Greenwood NAACP office saying, "We have just killed Medgar, and you are next." The Rev. Delmar Dennis joined the MWK after Evers was killed, but came to believe that the murder "may have been sanctioned" by Bowers. Prosecution witnesses at Beckwith's trials described Beckwith attending a Jackson NAACP meeting with two unknown white men on 7 June 1963, where Beckwith tried to purchase an NAACP membership card. G-men questioned Gordon Lackey as a suspect before arresting Beckwith, then accepted testimony from two witnesses who placed him at Camp Shelby, a National Guard base near Hattiesburg, on the night Evers died. That solution seemed hasty three years later, when a "reliable" informant relayed Lackey's boasts of killing Evers himself. "They got the wrong man," Lackey allegedly proclaimed. "Beckwith did not do the shooting." Another informant reportedly eavesdropped on Beckwith's conversation with two Citizens' Council members in a Greenwood café, listening while they planned the assassination. An FBI memo from the period describes Evers' slaying as a Klan plot, "with the Citizens' Council implicated as well." Beckwith himself bragged of the murder at various Klan rallies, claiming that he also took "a Shriner's oath" to kill Charles Evers.[32]

Violence Escalates

The death of Medgar Evers did not satisfy white terrorists. On 18 June, while approaching Tougaloo College, CORE's John Salter and the Rev. Ed King were rammed in their car by the son of a prominent Citizens' Council leader. Although Salter was hospitalized, police failed to charge his assailant. That same night, in Itta Bena, a smoke bomb hurled into a rural church sent several voter registration workers to the hospital. On 26 June bombers struck the Gulfport office of Dr. Felix Dunn for the second time in eight months. Four days later, another bomb demolished a two-family home in Jackson's ghetto.[33]

Paul Johnson seized upon the overheated climate to launch his fourth gubernatorial race. Himself the son of a former governor, Johnson had waged unsuccessful campaigns in 1947, 1951, and 1955 (with the plaintive slogan "It's Paul's turn"). In 1963 he urged Mississippians to "Stand Tall with Paul" and ran a frankly racist campaign, branding the NAACP a collection of "Niggers, Apes, Alligators, Coons, and Possums." Campaign posters featured photographs of Johnson blocking James Meredith and his federal escorts, and his federal contempt citation helped Johnson sweep the field on primary day. SNCC's Bob Moses predicted that Johnson's election meant "the entire white population will continue to be with the Klan." Some Johnson backers were surprised, therefore, when his inaugural address included a promise that "hate, or prejudice, or ignorance, will not lead Mississippi while I sit in the governor's chair." White critics soon branded Johnson "ambivalent Paul," but Hodding Carter III took a more pragmatic view, opining that Johnson's version of moderation was "to keep his mouth shut."[34]

On 31 October 1963 four klansmen trailed SNCC workers George Greene and Bruce Payne from Natchez to Port Gibson, than attacked and beat them when they stopped for gas. Two nights later, terrorists pursued Greene and Payne in the same neighborhood, flattening one of their tires with gunshots before the intended victims escaped. Eleven months passed before Mississippi highway patrolmen arrested White Knights Ernest Avants, James Greer Jr., and Myron "Jack" Seale on charges of assault with intent to kill. Arresting officers retrieved an arsenal of weapons from Seale's home, including automatic rifles. Avants and Greer were also members of the "nonviolent" APWR. Ex-governor Barnett defended the four klansmen and secured dismissal of the charges.[35]

The year closed with a flurry of racist propaganda and violence. October witnessed circulation of Klan posters bearing photographs of Medgar Evers, Ed King, James Meredith, Bob Moses, John Salter, Emmett Till, and others, with crosses drawn over those already dead. In November night riders tried to kidnap Leonard Russell, a black shop steward at the International Paper Company in Natchez, but he drove them from his Franklin County home with shotgun fire.

In December, Wilkinson County authorities found three African Americans—Lula Mae Anderson, Eli Jackson, and Dennis Jones—dead in a car on a rural highway. A local paper claimed the trio fell asleep with their motor running and died from inhaling carbon monoxide, but a black mortician contradicted that report, saying two of the victims were shot, while the third suffered a broken neck. In early January 1964, Pike County gunmen blasted six black-owned businesses and two homes in McComb, wounding a teenage boy in one attack. Police chief George Guy, doubling as head of the local APWR chapter, downplayed the victim's injury, reporting that the shots only "blistered his tail a little bit."[36]

Louis Allen was the next to die. Harassed incessantly since recanting his statement on the 1961 murder of Herbert Lee, Allen had watched his credit and his logging business dry up in the face of white boycotts. In 1963 deputy sheriff Daniel Jones assaulted Allen, breaking his jaw with a flashlight. When Jones was elected sheriff of Amite County, Allen decided to leave, but he waited too long. At 8:30 P.M. on 31 January 1964, gunmen ambushed Allen at his rural home. He crawled beneath his logging truck for sanctuary, but in vain; two close-range shotgun blasts

Myron Seale (in helmet, with a congressional investigator) was an active Klan terrorist in the 1960s (HCUA).

nearly beheaded him. Sheriff Jones blamed the murder on "voting agitation" and made no arrests. The same night, klansmen burned seven crosses in Vicksburg.[37]

Klansmen accelerated their campaign of terror in February 1964. In Charleston, two black youths were hospitalized after being pistol-whipped and beaten with axe handles in a white-owned grocery store. On 14 February armed whites kidnapped Alfred Whitley, a black employee at the Armstrong Rubber plant in Natchez, questioned him about his non-existent ties to the NAACP, then flogged him. The following night, three Natchez Klansmen wearing Halloween masks snatched janitor James Wilson from the International Paper Company, repeated their fruitless interrogation, then whipped him and poured a bottle of castor oil down his throat. That same night — 15 February — while Sam Bowers lectured 200 knights at Brookhaven on the desirability of "violent physical resistance," Klansmen lured black mortician Archie Curtis and his assistant to a deserted field outside Natchez, where they were stripped and flogged. Curtis was targeted because he led the Natchez Business and Civic League's drive to register black voters. On 18 February night riders stopped and whipped a black motorist whom they accused of "following" a white woman.[38]

And the mayhem continued. Natchez klansmen bombed the home of Leonard Russell, an International Paper employee active in the Negro Pulp and Sulfite Workers local. Woodville police failed to solve the murder of a still-unidentified black woman. On 28 February, while Laurel's knights burned two crosses "to prove that the Klan was not bluffing," terrorists killed Clifton Walker, another black worker at International Paper in Natchez. Ambushed on his drive home to Wilkinson County, Walker was riddled with rifle and shotgun fire in what some observers regard as the MWK's first "official" homicide. Local newspapers ignored the crime, but author Patsy Sims reports that Walker was suspected of seducing a white woman.[39]

Preparing for "Invasion"

In January 1964 the COFO began recruiting volunteers for its "Mississippi Summer Project," a frontal assault on the closed society that enlisted more than 1,000 northern clergymen and college volunteers. Announcement of the project galvanized Klansmen and worried Governor Johnson, who on 3 March warned state legislators to keep a tight rein on Klan-type "paramilitary or vigilante groups. Conditions which spawn the night-riders and the hushed attack will exist only if we fail to act now [and] only if we fail to justify the confidence of the people in the adequacy of their duly-authorized law enforcement agencies."[40]

In fact, the warning came too late. Klansmen and APWR members were already well organized and committed to a course of violent resistance. On 25 March, Hinds County vandals smashed the windows of a black-owned grocery and left Klan pamphlets in the wreckage. The same night, in Greenwood, crosses blazed outside SNCC headquarters and the Leflore County courthouse. Pike County Klansmen detonated their first firebomb on 1 April. Three nights later, while seven crosses burned in Philadelphia, Klansmen bombed a black-owned restaurant in Bude (Franklin County). On 5 April, more crosses flared in Brookhaven, McComb, and Natchez, and across Neshoba County. Sheriff Lawrence Rainey blamed the Neshoba incidents on "outsiders," saying that he "definitely felt that the burning was not done by local people and that it was an attempt by outside groups to disrupt the good relations enjoyed by all races in this county." Natchez Klansmen ambushed Richard Butler on 5 April and shot him several times but failed to kill him. On 6 April dynamite shattered another café in McNair.[41]

White officials and journalists either ignored the mayhem or seemed to condone it. On 9 April the *Neshoba Democrat* editorialized that "[o]utsiders who come in here and try to stir up trouble should be dealt with in a manner they won't forget." From Washington, James Eastland told the world, "If violence erupts, the blood will be on the hands of those who formed and led this invasion into a state where they were not welcome or invited." Mayor Jim Burt of McComb declared, "I don't care what the devil happens to these people who come down here to stir up trouble. If the monkey is on anyone's back, it is not on ours—it's on the people who come down here." Pike County Sheriff R.R. Warren told an APWR meeting that he would "recruit some of you" if his deputies could not cope with COFO's volunteers. "They say we are going to have a long hot summer," Warren said, "and I sort of believe that."[42]

Thus encouraged, Sam Bowers convened an April meeting "to discuss what we are going to do about the COFO's nigger-communist invasion of Mississippi." His decision: "Any personal attacks on the enemy should be carefully planned to include only the leaders and prime white collaborators of the enemy forces." Klan recruiting continued apace, with two cross-burnings in Laurel on 9 April, and sixty-one across southwestern Mississippi on 21 April. On 24 April, Highway Patrol spokesmen reported another seventy-one cross-burnings statewide. Throughout Mississippi, the MWK distributed a list of "Twenty Reasons WHY you should, if qualified, join, aid and support the White Knights of the KU KLUX KLAN of Mississippi."[43] Amidst much talk of "Christian-like brotherhood" and opposition to communism, two points stood out:

> 4. Because it is a working organization that not only talks but ACTS.
> 5. Because it is a very secret organization and no one will know that you are a member.[44]

In Panola County, terrorists broke into a church used for voter registration, smashing windows and furniture. Two black sharecroppers were beaten in Natchez, one by Klansmen and the other by police local historian Jack Davis deemed "possibly Klan members as well." On 28 April, two days after the Mississippi Freedom Democratic Party (MFDP) organized to challenge white officeholders, bombers struck the Bear Town barber shop owned by Curtis Bryant, leader of McComb's NAACP chapter. By early May 1964, when crosses burned in sixty-one counties on a single night, the APWR claimed 30,000 members and the MWK claimed 100,000. Even most skeptical observers granted Sam Bowers a head count of 10,000 knights.[45]

On 3 May 1964 Bowers issued an "Imperial Executive Order," warning his knights that "the events which will occur in Mississippi this summer may well determine the fate of Christian civilization for centuries to come." Sketching a two-pronged defensive plan, he wrote: "When the first waves of Blacks hit our streets this summer, we must avoid open daylight conflict with them, if at all possible, as private citizens or as members of this organization. We should join with and support local police and duly constituted law enforcement agencies with Volunteer, LEGALLY DEPUTIZED men from our own ranks.... IN ALL CASES, however, there must be a secondary group of our members, standing back away from the main area of conflict, armed and ready to move on very short notice who are not under the control of anyone but our own Christian officers.... The action of this Secondary group must be very swift and very forceful with no holds barred."[46]

While secrecy prevailed, the *Klan Ledger* warned Mississippi's invaders of their potential peril: "We are not going to sit back and permit our rights and the rights of our posterity to be negotiated away by a group composed of atheistic priests, brain-washed black savages, and mongrelized money-worshippers, meeting with some stupid or cowardly politician. Take heed, atheists and mongrels, we will not travel your path to Leninist Hell, but we will buy YOU a ticket to the Eternal if you insist." The National States Rights Party chimed in with a warning letter to SNCC that read as follows: "You are right about one thing — this is going to be a long hot summer — but the 'heat' will be applied to the race mixing TRASH by the DECENT people."[47]

By the time Bowers issued his call to arms, MWK members had already claimed two more victims. The murders sprang from baseless gossip that Black Muslims were smuggling weapons into Franklin County to support an insurrection against whites. On 2 May 1964 a Klan patrol found Henry Dee and Charles Moore, both African Americans, hitchhiking from Meadville to Natchez in search of jobs. The Klansmen grabbed them at gunpoint and drove them into the Homochitto National Forest for interrogation. While being whipped with sticks, one of the victims "confessed" that the Rev. Clyde Briggs stockpiled firearms at his church in Roxie, but the false lead came too late to save their lives. The Klansmen next beat their victims unconscious, then drove them across the Mississippi River to Tallulah, Louisiana, before weighting their bodies with Jeep engine blocks and dropping them alive into a backwater known as the Devil's Punchbowl.[48]

Moore's mother notified authorities when he did not return from Natchez by 4 May, but Franklin County's sheriff told her Charles and Henry were staying with relatives of Dee's in Louisiana. The truth surfaced, literally, on 12 July 1964, when a Tallulah fisherman snagged a decomposing human torso. More body parts surfaced the next day, and both victims were identified. Another four months passed before authorities arrested Klansmen Charles Edwards and James Seale for murder, on 6 November. Edwards signed a confession, while Seale charged highway patrol officers with false arrest. Both Klansmen posted bond on 7 November, and a local justice of the peace subsequently dismissed all charges. Further investigation by the KBI failed to resolve the case.[49]

The Franklin County insurrection rumors almost claimed a third victim in Burl Jones, a Roxie sawmill worker. Soon after the Dee-Moore slayings, a highway patrolman stopped Jones in Meadville for driving through a red light. Unable to pay his ten-dollar fine, Jones sat in jail for three days, until officers came to release him at dawn. Leaving the cell block, he met two men dressed in Klan regalia and armed with baseball bats. They beat him to the floor, shoved a hood over his head and forced him into the trunk of a car, then drove him to a wooded area where other Klansmen waited. Jones' clothes were sliced away with knives, then he was whipped while being questioned about guns and sinister "construction workers." Ordered to leave Mississippi or die, Jones told his captures (truthfully) that he already planned to seek work in Chicago. They dumped him beside U.S. Highway 84, and he fled the state two days later.[50]

Such individual actions were probably unsanctioned by MWK headquarters in Laurel, where Sam Bowers graded "projects" on a scale from 1 to 4. Number 1 was a cross-burning; Number 2 was whipping; Number 3 involved arson or bombing; and Number 4 was "elimination." Informants told the FBI that Bowers "was the only man who could order a No. 3 or No. 4 in the KKK of the State of Mississippi." If true, he kept busy that May. Bombers struck a black motel in Jackson on the sixth, and hit Laurel's *Leader-Call* four days later. A week later, Bob Moses wrote, "We are being deluged. There have been five killings in S.W. Miss. in the last 3 months, Klan activity — 3 whippings, scattered shootings, 180 cross burnings."[51]

By then, the Alabama-based United Klans had invaded Mississippi. On Friday and Saturday, 15–16 May, UKA leaders from various states convened in Natchez, at the Eola Hotel, to launch their new realm as the Mississippi Rescue Service. HUAC investigators later claimed that Natchez Klansman Edward McDaniel "secretly recruited" for the UKA while still an active member of the MWK, then split with Bowers in a dispute over McDaniel's "abnormally high expense accounts" as a province investigator. On 29 August 1964 a Natchez klavern of the MWK defected en masse to become UKA Unit No. 719, disguised as the Adams County Civic & Betterment Association. In September, at a klonvocation in Birmingham, Robert Shelton named McDaniel to serve as the UKA's Mississippi grand dragon.[52]

Both Klans maintained a public façade of legality, while preaching and practicing violence in private. On 2 June 1964, Neshoba County's Sheriff Rainey and Deputy Cecil Price (both active White Knights) arrested Chicago native Wilmer Jones for inviting a white girl to dinner. They held him in jail until midnight, then released him to a gang of Klansmen who drove him to an abandoned farmhouse. Surrounded by guns, Jones braced himself for death until a Klansman others called "Preacher" ordered his release. Jones swiftly returned to Chicago, but later helped FBI agents locate the farmhouse, five miles southwest of Philadelphia.[53]

The day after Jones' ordeal, on the evening of Canton's third Freedom Day celebration, police stopped black businessman Otha Williams outside of town and beat him severely before he escaped on foot into the woods. On 3 June two carloads of night riders riddled COFO's Jackson headquarters with bullets. The next day, black motorist Alvin Higgins and passenger Ethel Jordan stopped to help a stranded driver in Hinds County, then found themselves surrounded by Klansmen who beat them unconscious. On the same day, 4 June, black-hooded knights whipped Ivey Gutter outside Summit. On 6 June armed Klansmen snatched Roland Sleeper from his home, near Liberty, and whipped him while demanding details about local NAACP activity. Two nights later, bombers struck at Canton's Freedom House.[54]

In the midst of that violence, on 4 June, Governor Johnson addressed the Mississippi Economic Council in Jackson. His speech — stamped "Absolutely Restricted, Not For Publicity" — condemned "citizens who ally themselves with secret undercover groups ... [which] can do Mississippi great harm this summer." Two weeks later, the *Jackson Daily News* quoted Johnson's admonition to "steer clear of such groups as the Ku Klux Klan and Americans for Preservation of the White Race." That prompted a complaint from APWR spokesman Rowland Scott, and while the State Sovereignty Commission opened an investigation of the APWR, Johnson henceforth refrained from criticizing any right-wing group by name.[55]

On 7 June Sam Bowers addressed a Klan audience at an abandoned church, five miles west of Raleigh. He read once more his executive order from May, concerning "enemy attack and countermeasures to be used in meeting same." That done, Bowers yielded the pulpit to Louis DiSalvo, a firearms dealer from Bay St. Louis who instructed the assembled Klansmen on the use of venomous serpents as weapons. Two days later, in Hinds County, MWK grand giant Billy Buckles solicited funds for a project "that would make the murder of Medgar Evers look sick." An ex-convict had agreed to do the unspecified job for $1,200, and Buckles collected $100 toward that end before the Klansmen dispersed.[56]

Liquidating "Goatee"

Michael Schwerner personified every Klansman's nightmare: a bearded Jewish social activist from New York City, pledged to tamper with the Southern Way of Life. He had served CORE in New York's ghettos and gone to jail for demonstrating in Maryland. On 21 January 1964 he arrived in Meridian, with his wife, Rita, as scouts for COFO's Summer Project. Within a month, the Schwerners established COFO's Meridian Community Center, with a library of ten thousand volumes. Local Klansmen dubbed Michael "Goatee" and "Jew Boy," bombarding him with threats and obscene phone calls, while Sam Bowers plotted a "No. 4" to remove him permanently from the scene.[57]

Not satisfied to focus solely on Meridian, Schwerner and local CORE member James Chaney soon expanded their efforts into neighboring Neshoba County. In April 1964 Neshoba's only claim to fame was that its residents consumed more chewing tobacco per capita than those of any other American county. Local voters had elected Lawrence Rainey sheriff in August 1963, on his promise to "take care of things for you," with aid from deputy (and fellow Klansman) Cecil Price. FBI memos described Neshoba's MWK klavern as "one of the strongest Klan units ever gathered and one of the best disciplined groups." Agent Joseph Sullivan recalled that Neshoba Klansmen "owned the place. In spirit, everyone belonged to the Klan.... [T]here proved to be no difference between a real Klansman and someone who was not a member but whose friends and neighbors were. Even if they themselves had declined to join the klavern, they identified totally with those who had."[58]

The top Klansman in Lauderdale and Neshoba counties was kleagle Edgar Ray "Preacher" Killen, an ordained Baptist minister and sawmill operator whose order spared Wilmer Jones from execution on 2 June 1964. Killen boasted of traveling "very, very often" to visit Senator Eastland at home in Doddsville, a circumstance which, if true, cast a sinister light on Eastland's persistent claims that "[t]here's not a Ku Klux Klan chapter in the state of Mississippi." Schwerner's high visibility boosted Killen's recruiting, as did the enlistment of Killen's childhood friend Wallace Miller. Under Killen's leadership, Neshoba Klansmen infiltrated Philadelphia's auxiliary police force and thronged the Steak House Café, where a white sheet in the window proclaimed the owner's loyalty.[59]

On Memorial Day, 25 May, Schwerner and Chaney addressed the all-black congregation of Longdale's Mount Zion Church, hoping to secure facilities for a COFO Freedom School. Sheriff Rainey soon learned of the visit, and mounted surveillance beginning on 31 May. Around the same time, Sam Bowers met with Killen and other knights to discuss Schwerner's murder. Bowers told the group, "Goatee is like the queen bee in the beehive.

You eliminate the queen bee and all the workers go away." On 14 June, with Schwerner and Chaney at a COFO training session in Ohio, Deputy Price and ex-sheriff Ethel "Hop" Barnett trailed two Mount Zion parishioners from Philadelphia to a friend's rural home and searched their car, citing rumors that the couple was smuggling white passengers. Two nights later, Klansmen left a meeting at the Bloomo School gymnasium, four miles east of Philadelphia, and surrounded Mount Zion. They interrogated worshipers, severely beating several, then left the scene. At 1:00 A.M. a Ku Klux arson squad returned and burned the church.[60]

Schwerner and Chaney returned to Meridian on 20 June, accompanied by New York volunteer Andrew Goodman. Locals informed them of the Mount Zion raid, and they drove to Longdale on 21 June. Unknown to Schwerner, his movements were tracked by the Klan, by police in two counties, and by agents of the State Sovereignty Commission. At 3:00 P.M. Deputy Price stopped Chaney's car and arrested him for speeding; he booked Schwerner and Goodman into jail "for investigation." Preacher Killen rallied his Klansmen, directing members of the hand-picked murder team to purchase gloves and await further orders. "We have a place to bury them," he told the knights, "and a man to run the [bull]dozer to cover them up." Before Price freed the trio, Killen led his executioners to the jail and showed them where to park their cars to be ready for hot pursuit. He then went home to wait for word of their success.[61]

Price released his prisoners at 10:00 P.M., with orders to leave Neshoba County, and followed them as far as Highway 19 before turning back. Twenty-five minutes later, leading two carloads of Klansmen, he stopped them again and delivered the trio to their executioners. The Klansmen drove from there to lonely Rock Cut Road, then stopped and dragged the captives from their cars. Klansman Alton Roberts—one of three racist brothers whose neighbors deemed them "mean as yard dogs"—first shot Schwerner in the heart, then executed Goodman. Roberts and triggerman James Jordan both shot Chaney, after which the bodies were conveyed to Klansman Olen Burrage's "Old Jolly Farm" and planted in an earthen dam.[62]

Alarms spread quickly when the trio failed to return from Longdale. Attorney General Robert Kennedy ordered an FBI investigation on 22 June, and Meridian G-man John Proctor interviewed Deputy Price the same day. He accepted Price's denial of wrongdoing at face value and wound up drinking confiscated moonshine with Price from the trunk of Price's cruiser. Sheriff Rainey shrugged off the disappearances, telling reporters, "If they're missing, they just hid somewhere, trying to get a lot of publicity out of it, I figure." Senator Eastland took a similar line with President Lyndon Johnson, saying, "I don't think there's a damn thing to it. There's no organized white men in that area, so that's why I think it's a publicity stunt."[63]

Johnson called Eastland back on 23 June, after searchers found Cheney's burned-out car on a Neshoba Choctaw reservation. On that occasion, Eastland told LBJ that "The governor says if you'll send some impartial man down here, that you'll get the surprise of your life.... There's no violence, no friction of any kind." Johnson chose ex–CIA chief Allen Dulles, who departed for a tour of the Magnolia State. Meanwhile, on 24 June, Grand Giant Billy Buckles gave the lie to Eastland's confidence, telling his Klansmen, "Now they know what we will do. We have shown them what we will do and we will do it again if necessary." Johnson fielded 200 sailors to help with the search, while Dulles recommended

orders for an FBI campaign to "control and prosecute terroristic activity" by the Klan and APWR.[64]

Coordinating any FBI response was problematical. Aside from his personal hatred for Robert Kennedy, J. Edgar Hoover was an outspoken enemy of the civil rights movement who praised Governor Johnson as "a man I have long admired from a distance." Furthermore, the FBI had closed its Jackson field office in 1947, while maintaining only fifteen one-man "resident agencies" statewide. Those agents, like John Proctor in Meridian, were friendly with local police and thus viewed with utmost suspicion by civil rights activists. Reluctantly, prodded by LBJ, Hoover agreed to mount a three-pronged offensive in Mississippi. His agents would solve the Neshoba County mystery, expand recruitment of Klan informants, and pursue "a full check on Klan activities and plans, past, present, and future." To that end, Hoover approved expenditure of $25,000 or $30,000 (reports differ) to recover the three missing men.[65]

Robert Shelton arrived in Philadelphia to conduct his own "investigation," predictably concluding that the triple disappearance was a hoax. "These people," he announced, "like to dramatize situations in order to milk the public of more money for their causes. They hope to raise two hundred and fifty thousand dollars for their campaign in Mississippi, and I understand that these funds are slow coming in. So they create a hoax like this, put weeping mothers and wives on national television, and try to touch the hearts of the nation. Their whole purpose is just to get more money." On 25 June Shelton's political patron, Alabama governor George Wallace, joined Paul Johnson at Jackson's Mississippi State Coliseum for a rally launching Wallace's first presidential race. In his speech, Wallace referred to a "report by Col. Al Lingo ... that three persons resembling the group had been seen in Alabama Tuesday [23 June]." When pressed for details, Governor Johnson said, "Governor Wallace and I are the only two people who know where they are, and we're not telling."[66]

Preacher Killen's knights, meanwhile, were not content with their achievement. In the early hours of 26 June they tried to ambush Rita Schwerner, SNCC member Robert Zellner, and a COFO lawyer near Longdale. A logging truck blocked Zellner's path while several cars and pickups closed in behind, but Zellner escaped by swerving around the roadblock.[67]

Official accounts of the FBI's MIBURN investigation (short for "*Mississippi Burn*ing") are confused and contradictory. J. Edgar Hoover claimed that 258 G-men scoured the state for clues, while other sources place the number at 153. Headquarters calculated that agents questioned 1,000 Mississippi residents, including 480 Klansmen ("just to let them know who we are"), at a total cost of $815,000. Agents rushed to outfit a new field office in Jackson, and Hoover flew down for its grand opening on 10 July. Meeting with Governor Johnson, Hoover expressed his conviction that Schwerner, Chaney, and Goodman were dead. He also delivered a list of Mississippi lawmen who had joined the Klan, reportedly leaving Johnson both "speechless" and vowing to "take care of the matter immediately."[68]

Assistant FBI director Cartha DeLoach recalls that the list included two highway patrolmen and several other officers in "scattered localities," and insists that "[c]ontrary to popular myth, the Klan had little success recruiting members among state and local lawmen."

Opposite: Searchers drag a river for the corpses of Klan victims Michael Schwerner, James Chaney, and Andrew Goodman (Library of Congress).

Governor Paul Johnson (right) announced the opening of an FBI office in Jackson, in July 1964. Behind him are bureau director J. Edgar Hoover and aide Cartha de Loach (Library of Congress).

Conversely, HUAC reported that "several" highway patrolmen were also Klansmen, and historian David Chalmers claims that Mississippi's highway patrol supplied "a substantial increment of membership for the Klan."

Governor Johnson "took care" of the problem by giving state troopers a choice: quit the force or produce a letter from their klavern's exalted cyclops releasing the officers from their Ku Klux oaths. Whether those notes had any real validity remains a topic of debate. Charles Evers, for one, remained unconvinced. As late as 1970 he told reporters, "The highway patrolmen were no good. No good. A bunch of redneck murderers, most of them. Nigger-haters, let me call them, and long-haired-hippie-haters.... Most of them were ignorant, and most of them were avowed racists, and many of them were ex–Klansmen or present Klansmen who went from the sheet to the badge. They were the Segregationist Army."[69]

One lawman repulsed by the Neshoba murders was Meridian police sergeant Wallace Miller. FBI agents described him as "guilt-ridden and eager to unburden himself." Rather than quit the Klan, however, Miller grudgingly agreed to stay and file reports from the inside. A Neshoba rancher and bootlegger told G-men that he joined the MWK after being warned that the Klan "was going to control the county." And indeed, his liquor business prospered, as Sheriff Rainey turned a blind eye to whiskey-peddling Klansmen. Buford Posey, Mississippi's first white NAACP member, told G-men that Rainey and Deputy Price were involved in the Neshoba murders. Within hours of filing that statement, Posey found himself shadowed by "deputy sheriffs" in old pickup trucks and who lobbed bricks through his windows after nightfall. Notice of a Klan "death sentence" ultimately drove him from the state.[70]

Bribery paid off for the FBI on 31 July, when an informer told agents where the three missing victims were buried. On 4 August agents invaded the Old Jolly Farm with road-grading equipment and began dismantling Olen Burrage's new dam. At 2:05 P.M. they smelled decaying flesh, and the heavy equipment retired. Michael Schwerner's body was uncovered at 3:18, Andrew Goodman's at 5:07, and James Chaney's at 5:17. A Jackson pathologist, Dr. W.P. Featherston, conducted the initial autopsies, reporting that all three victims were shot with .38-caliber pistols. On 5 August state spokesmen announced that none of the victims were beaten. An independent medical examiner, Dr. David Spain of New York, contradicted that statement after conducting his own examination of Schwerner and Chaney at the request of their parents. According to Spain, Chaney received an "inhuman beating" before he was shot. "Under the circumstances," Spain declared, "these injuries could only be the result of an extremely severe beating with either a blunt instrument or chain. I have never witnessed bones so severely shattered, except in tremendously high-speed accidents such as airplane crashes."[71]

Mississippi's reaction to Dr. Spain's statement was swift and severe. Dr. Featherston teamed with agents of the State Sovereignty Commission to file an ethics complaint with the College of American Pathologists against Spain. A hearing was scheduled on that complain for October 1964, but no record survives of its results. The Sovereignty Commission also advised Governor Johnson that Spain had shared his Jackson hotel room with "a Negro doctor from New York"—Dr. Aaron Wells, chairman of the Medical Committee on Civil Rights, who arranged for Spain to perform the autopsies. Most published accounts of the case blame FBI agents for damaging Chaney's corpse with their heavy equipment. According to Dr. Featherston, "a lot of damage done to Chaney's body occurred when the scoop caught his body. He was the last one to be buried. He was the one who suffered most of the injury due to disinterment." Agent Joseph Sullivan refuted that assertion in an interview with Jerry Mitchell, saying, "There was never any damage to the bodies at all from the mechanical equipment on site." The bulldozers withdrew, he insisted, before Schwerner's corpse was unearthed. "Some of the digging was actually done by hand, and I'm not talking about shovels. I'm talking about hands. Then a boot showed up."[72]

Governor Johnson himself added a strange footnote to the controversy, insisting in an interview in 1970 that the Klansmen "did not actually intend to kill those people." He continued:

> What happened was that they had been taken from the jail and brought to that particular spot. There were a good many people in the group besides the sheriff and the deputy sheriff and that group. What they were going to do, they were going to hang those three persons up in a big cotton sack and leave them hanging in a tree for about a day and a half, then come out there at night and turn them loose. They thought that they'd more or less scare them off. While they were talking this Negro, the Negro boy from over at Meridian — he seemed to be the ringleader of the three — he was acting kind of smart-aleck, and talking pretty big, and one of the Klansmen walked up behind him and hit him over the head with a trace chain.... The chain came across his head and hit him just above the bridge of the nose and killed him as dead as a nit. After this boy had been killed, then is when they determined, "Well, we've got to dispose of the other two."[73]

Johnson's claim of inside knowledge is peculiar in several respects. First, the bizarre portrait of James Chaney sassing a lynch mob contradicts the confession secured from one of his killers. It fails to explain why Chaney, if already dead, was shot three times, and it disputes statements from various informants that Sam Bowers planned Schwerner's murder weeks in advance. Finally, Johnson's statement is the only one on record placing Sheriff Rainey at the murder scene.

Neshoba's county fair, a traditional venue for political speeches in presidential election years, opened on 10 August 1964 with fifty auxiliary policemen on hand to enforce segregation. On 12 August a low-flying airplane showered the fairgrounds with MWK fliers blaming communists for the recent murders. White House hopefuls George Wallace and Barry Goldwater both made excuses and kept their distance, leaving Governor Johnson to close the fair alone on 13 August. He was preceded to the dais by a spokesman for Jackson's John Birch Society chapter who was escorted by Deputy Price.[74]

Prosecuting the Neshoba County killers proved more difficult than finding their victims. Justice Department spokesmen declared that a federal grand jury would meet in Biloxi to consider the case on 21 September. Judge O.H. Barnett countered on 18 September with an announcement of a local grand jury meeting ten days later, widely regarded in FBI circles as a fishing expedition to expose the prosecution's case. When Barnett requested all G-men involved in the case to appear in his courtroom, J. Edgar Hoover refused to comply. As an FBI memo explained the decision, "A Klansman judge is unlikely to disqualify himself or to eliminate Klan members as an impediment to service on a grand jury or petit jury." Barnett forged ahead nonetheless, regaling his panel with attacks on the COFO, NAACP, and other "irresponsible organizations," introducing Lawrence Rainey as "the most courageous sheriff in all America."[75]

The Biloxi grand jury interviewed numerous witnesses, including Neshoba County rancher Florence Mars. En route to the hearing, a local Klan leader and ex-sheriff Hop Barnett followed Mars's car; Barnett later approached Mars outside the grand jury room with a cryptic warning: "Don't tell on us, and we won't tell on you." Within twenty-four hours of her testimony, neighbors warned Mars that the Klan planned to ruin her business with boycotts and harassment, a campaign that ultimately drove Mars from her local church. Observers may have been surprised when the first federal indictments, issued on 2 October, charged Sheriff Rainey, Deputy Price, Hop Barnett, and two Philadelphia policemen with beating various black prisoners. FBI agents arrested the defendants on 3 October. U.S. Commissioner Esther Carter set bond at $2,000 each and released all five.[76]

Klan triggerman James Jordan fled Meridian on 5 October, but G-men traced him to Gulfport eight days later and hounded him daily, until they procured a confession of sorts. Jordan admitted being present on 21 June but denied shooting Chaney. A second member of the lynching party, Horace Barnette, confessed to agents on 19 November, in Louisiana. His statement corroborated most of Jordan's, but named Jordan as one of the shooters (with Alton Roberts). While the John Birch Society's *American Opinion* dismissed the triple murder as "the work of *agents provocateur*," FBI agents announced on 25 November that they had identified the killers. Ten days later, with Barnette and Jordan already in custody, G-men arrested eighteen alleged conspirators. The next morning, 5 December, Cecil Price told *Life* magazine, "It took me an hour to get to work this morning, I had to shake so many hands."[77]

Federal prosecutors made their decision to proceed with conspiracy charges after Governor Johnson dismissed any hope of a state conviction. Any murder trial, Johnson noted, would involve Judge Barnett, who was "distantly related to some of the defendants" and branded a Klansman in FBI memos. The federal case, however, also had its problems—starting with Esther Carter, who branded Horace Barnette's confession "hearsay" and dismissed all charges on 10 December.

In early January 1965 the *Clarion-Ledger* announced formation of a White Christian Protective and Legal Defense Fund, ostensibly founded by "a group of patriots from all walks of life, and representative of no particular political viewpoint" to support "any White Christian Patriot who has or may be indicted and forced to stand trial for some real or imagined infraction of the Communist inspired Civil Rights Act." In fact, the fund was launched by MWK Grand Dragon Julius Harper on 23 November 1964 at a Meridian Klan meeting. The *Clarion-Ledger* article carried no byline, but its text was vintage Sam Bowers.[78]

"Freedom Summer"

The Neshoba County murders did not occur in a vacuum. Klan terror began far in advance of the COFO Summer Project's 15 June launch date and continued far beyond the campaign's official termination two months later. While certain hard-core pockets of resistance dominated media reports of violence, no town or county was immune.

On 15 June arsonists burned the auditorium of a Catholic church in Hattiesburg whose priest had complimented blacks for adopting nonviolent civil disobedience. Two days later, hooded Klansmen snatched a black man from the streets of Jackson and whipped him without apparent cause. On 18 June terrorists smoke-bombed an Itta Bena church during a memorial service for Medgar Evers. In McComb, where members of the UKA's Pike County Wolf Pack drew lots for "wrecking crew" assignments at their weekly klavern meetings, raiders flogged a black man on 19 June, then bombed four homes and a black-owned barbershop the following night. On 21 June, while Neshoba County Klansmen committed their triple murder, other night riders bombed a church in Branson and mobbed a carload of civil rights workers in Maben. McComb's bombers shattered two more homes on 22 June. The same day, a hit-and-run driver killed a black youth in Brandon. On 23 June, Jackson gunmen fired into a black-owned café and a white minister's home, while arsonists torched the Moss Point Knights of Pythias hall, used for voter registration. The next day, after a shooting in Canton, thieves stole forty rifles and 1,000 rounds of ammunition from a National Guard armory in Collins. On 25 June, dynamite damaged a church in Ruleville, while another in Longdale was firebombed. The next night, arsonists struck a Catholic church in Clinton whose pastor taught a black Bible class. On 27 June Klansmen hurled a Molotov cocktail at the *McComb Enterprise-Journal*'s office, complete with a note signed "KKK."[79]

FBI agents made their first arrests on 26 June, the day after Klansmen kidnapped two voter-registration workers from Itta Bena and held them at a local gas station, warning that they would "disappear" like the Neshoba County victims if they stayed in Mississippi. J. Edgar Hoover reaped national headlines from the arrests in "Teensy Weensy," as he called Itta Bena, but none of the three Klansmen ever faced trial. Perhaps as a result of those arrests, the State Sovereignty Commission furnished G-men with a copy of its file on UKA leader Robert Shelton.[80]

The MWK suffered more substantial damage on 25 June, with the resignation of early member and financial angel John Thornhill. A wealthy oilman named in the *Enterprise-Journal* as Pike County's "top Klan representative," Thornhill bankrolled several klaverns and, through his drilling operations, offered easy access to explosives. Still, the sudden rash of violence unnerved him and he quit the order, telling reporters that demolition of churches was "not in the true spirit of the Ku Klux Klan." In Thornhill's view, the Klan "apparently ha[d] lost control of its hoodlum rebels."[81]

The steady toll also influenced Congress, which passed a new Civil Rights Act on 29 June 1964. President Johnson signed the law into effect on 2 July, prompting new charges of treason from Klansmen. Soon afterward, a Ku Klux flier warned white Mississippians: "If we don't win in the next eight months, we're all destined for Communist slavery and our wives and daughters will be chattels in Mongolian and African brothels." The *Southern Review*, edited by Elmore Greaves and described by critics as the MWK's "unofficial organ," lumped LBJ, Senator Eastland, and Governor Johnson together as scheming "leftists." Baptist minister C.O. Stegall warned APWR members against violent action, predicting martial law "the day we kill three or four," but the Magnolia State's committed terrorists ignored such admonitions.[82]

In Greenwood, brothers Jake and Silas McGhee made the first of seven attempts to integrate the Leflore Theater on 5 July 1964 and were mauled by whites in the process. Thereafter, Byron De La Beckwith led Klan patrols through the theater's aisles armed with baseball bats and flashlights. On 16 July, after a Freedom Day rally in Greenwood, Klansmen grabbed Silas McGhee and drove him to an isolated shack for whipping, but he seized a shovel and fought his way clear. That assault produced the first arrests made under the 1964 Civil Rights Act, but no convictions resulted. Drive-by gunmen blasted a volunteer's car on 20 July and shot up the McGhee home five days later. On 21 July white vandals smashed windows of three black-owned cafés and another volunteer's car. On 25 July, as many as 200 whites mobbed the McGhee brothers outside the Leflore Theater, sending Silas to the hospital. After Thatcher Walt, editor of the *Greenwood Commonwealth*, published an editorial condemning violence, night riders shot out his windows and lobbed a bomb into his yard. Walt's publisher soon fired him, whereupon Walt moved his family to Florida.[83]

The FBI's return to Mississippi did not initially impress Magnolia State Klansmen. On 10 July, while Director Hoover met with Governor Johnson, terrorists killed black victim Jasper Greenwood outside Vicksburg and assaulted five civil rights workers (including Cleveland rabbi Arthur Lelyveld) in Hattiesburg. The latter incident produced three arrests, but the attackers were released without jail time after paying $500 fines. On 11 July, with Hoover en route back to Washington, Klansmen bombed a café in Vicksburg, lobbed Molotov cocktails at Canton's Freedom House, and burned a Browning church which black parishioners refused to sell on demand. That same day, five white men offered a resident of Shaw's ghetto $400 to bomb the local Freedom House, but he declined. In Natchez, on 12 July, night riders burned two churches and firebombed a black contractor's home. White witnesses recorded the license numbers of two suspect cars, but police made no arrests. Overall, Don Whitehead reports seven churches burned within a week of the Jackson FBI office's reopening.[84]

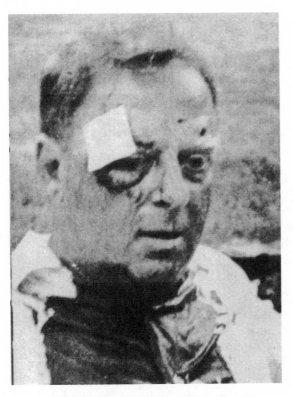

Rabbi Arthur Lelyveld after his beating by Hattiesburg Klansmen (Library of Congress).

McComb, in Pike County, witnessed the most concentrated violence and harassment. In addition to the Klan and APWR (led by police chief George Guy), a "community service organization" called Help, Inc., was founded on 29 June to police racial mores in the Carroll Oaks and Westview subdivisions. The group's introductory flier included a long list of tips on handling "outsiders," including a "[t]emporary alarm to be three blasts from a shotgun or car horn." Help, Inc.'s first target was Albert "Red" Heffner, an insurance salesman and former classmate of Byron De La Beckwith who entertained two SNCC volunteers at his home on 17 July. Two days later, Heffner's landlord evicted him from his office. White boycotters doomed his business, and Heffner's family received 350 obscene phone calls before they left town in early September.[85]

Most resistance in McComb was more direct. During a three week span, between 7 and 27 July, terrorists bombed or burned five churches and three homes, together with the local Freedom House (leveled by two successive bombings) and the local COFO office. Night riders also beat at least three victims, tried to kill a black former policeman, and fired shots into a black family's home. On 27 July the *Enterprise-Journal* headlined a Klan reward offer for information leading to conviction of the bombers, but since Klansmen themselves were responsible, the bid drew no takers.[86]

Elsewhere around the state, July was much the same. Arsonists burned churches in Brandon, Jackson, Meridian, Raleigh (two), and rural Madison County. Drive-by shootings occurred in Moss Point, Batesville, and Greenville. Police jailed blacks who pursued the Moss Point shooters, while Clarke County's sheriff brought a six-man "board of education" to warn against conversion of an abandoned school to voter-registration work. ("If they weren't Klan men," an observer opined, "they were at least Citizens' Council.") In Wesson, hooded raiders beat a white man who both refused to join the Klan and hired blacks at his service station. Kidnappers snatched a COFO volunteer from Gulfport and held him at gunpoint, offering cash for inside information on the movement. Vandals missed the office of Laurel's NAACP leader and lobbed a stone through his neighbor's window, warning Dr. T.J. Barnes, "If you don't want the same thing to happen to you that happened to the three civil rights workers in Neshoba County, then stop working with the NAACP. KKK."[87] An MWK "Hate Sheet" distributed in Leflore County cautioned:

To those of you *niggers* who gave or give aid and comfort to this civil rights scum, we advise you that your identities are in the proper hands and *you will be remembered*. We know that the nigger owner of Collins shoe shop on Johnson Street "entertained" Martin Luther King when the "big nigger" came to Greenwood. We know of others and we say to you—after the showing and the plate-passing and stupid street demonstrations are over and the imported agitators have all gone, one thing is sure and certain—you are still going to be *niggers* and we are still going to be white men. You have chosen your beds and now must lie in them.[88]

Some Mississippi blacks refused to passively accept the threats and violence. McComb NAACP leader Charles Bryant and his brother Ora both fired on Wolf Pack bombing parties in July 1964. In Harmony, blacks shot at Klansmen trying to put bombs in rural mailboxes. Covington County activist Griffin McLaurin mounted armed patrols after Klansmen "blew up a lot of cars" around the local Freedom House. "They'd come in late at night," he later said, "and try to get to the center, but we had our guards. We stood our ground, and whenever we heard something that we thought wasn't right, we had our firepower." Walter Bruce, Holmes County chairman of the MFDP, also advocated "fighting fire with fire." After one shootout with Klansmen near Durant, he says the night riders went home complaining: "We not going to go back out there no more. Them niggers got all kinds of machine guns."[89]

Such tactics may have granted some relief in isolated areas, but they did nothing to restrain the Klan statewide; if anything, violence intensified during the Summer Project's last three weeks. In Leflore County, terrorists riddled the Greenwood SNCC office with bullets on 2 August, critically wounded Silas McGhee on 15 August, burned a church at Itta Bena on 20 August, and finally torched the McGhee family's home. Silas McGhee suspected his assailant was a policeman who had threatened his life a few hours before the shooting. Itta Bena's all-white fire department deemed the church "outside its jurisdiction" and ignored the fire. Madison County's raiders strafed Canton's Freedom House on 2 August, burned the church serving as Gluckstadt's Freedom School on 11 August, and blasted Canton's Freedom House a second time on 14 August. Warren County knights in full regalia stormed two Oak Ridge homes on 12 August, shooting up one house and whipping three tenants who had welcomed COFO volunteers. A highway patrol spokesman told reporters that "Warren County prides itself on not having a White Citizens' Council, let alone a KKK," but HUAC investigators found two active klaverns, one each for the MWK and UKA.[90]

Elsewhere, Bolivar County Klansmen burned two crosses in Shaw, on 6–7 August. Three days later, at nearby Merigold, a white gas station attendant beat up an elderly black customer, then summoned police who shot and killed the unarmed victim "in self-defense." Lauderdale County Klansmen burned a church at Collinsville and circulated a list of "traitors," including Meridian police chief Roy Gunn and Jewish businessman Meyer Davidson. Another church went up in flames at Smithtown, in Wayne County. Chicago volunteer Wayne Yancey died in a car crash at Holly Springs, on 1 August, prompting officers to charge his critically injured SNCC driver with manslaughter. Laurel's Klansmen beat another black man on the street, but some drive-by terrorists were clumsy: they missed three human targets in Ocean Springs, and a bomb they hurled at Mileston's Freedom Center fell forty yards short of its target.[91]

Robert Shelton's United Klans competed for dominance in Mississippi during the 1960s (SPLC).

In Adams County the MWK and UKA competed for members, while the Mississippi White Caps published handbills designed to embarrass Klan opponents. Governor Johnson was derided as "one of the most treacherous white men we have ever come across," a Judas who allied himself with "northern agitators" in pursuit of "the almighty dollar." Another unexpected target was John Nosser, a Lebanese native who immigrated to Natchez in 1939 and opened the city's first supermarket, then expanded into other enterprises. Nosser's sons, including two active-duty Klansmen, ran most of the business after 1960, when Nosser was elected mayor. Although he was a segregationist and target of black boycotts that compelled him to fire nearly half of his 147 employees, Klansmen still pegged Nosser as a "compromiser," since he would not cast his lot with terrorists. Meanwhile, night riders fired into the Archie Curtis Funeral Home on 2 August, burned churches at Finwick on 5 August and in Brandon six days later, and bombed a tavern near SNCC organizer George Greene's home on 14 August. Although a mixed-race couple owned the bar, firemen at the scene told bystanders "the wrong place" had been bombed. On 18 August patrons at Jake Fisher's Blue Moon bar defused a gasoline bomb on the premises. Another bar, owned by Fisher's brother in Louisiana, had been bombed by Klansmen the previous weekend.[92]

McComb remained one of the state's most violent areas. In early August Klansmen burned crosses at the homes of two white men: a physician who contributed to reconstruction of burned churches, and a merchant who refused to fire black workers when they registered to vote. On 14 August they bombed McComb's Masonic lodge and a supermarket owned by COFO supporter Pete Lewis. When a SNCC staffer chased the bombers' car, police jailed him for "interfering with an officer." On 18 August Klansmen bungled the firebombing of a black family's home, then rebounded the next day with six fiery crosses and a stench-bombing at the local Woolworth's lunch counter.[93]

The Summer Project's final week witnessed an escalation of harassment and violence. Scores of crosses blazed across Mississippi and Louisiana on 15 August, lit by prearrangement at precisely 10:00 P.M. That same night, gunmen killed Charles Fuschens in Monticello and narrowly missed SNCC staffer Preston Ponder in Jasper County as he returned from investigating a double flogging. Jackson Klansmen ran amok on 15 August, burning

six crosses, shooting two black men, and beating a white volunteer with baseball bats outside COFO headquarters. Laurel witnessed more beatings, at the Kress department store's
integrated lunch counter on 15 August and at a gas station the following day. In McComb,
Chief Guy raided the local COFO office on 16 August, ostensibly seeking bootleg liquor,
then threatened to arrest its staff for illegal pamphleteering. (Protests from the Justice
Department changed Guy's mind.) On 17 August, Philadelphia officeholders met to plot
expulsion of all COFO backers from their town. A friend told Florence Mars the meeting
was initiated by "the bunch that was big in the Klan." Outside Laurel, on 22 August, fifteen
Klansmen raided a farewell picnic for three COFO volunteers, beating some of those present with clubs and chains and firing shots at the rest. One member of the raiding party,
R.V. Lee, already faced charges of beating COFO volunteer David Gelfand on 14 August.[94]

Gelfand later described the FBI's response: "The bottom line was the federal government never did anything.... [It] was another interesting fiasco with the FBI.... [W]e had
been assured by our local congressman ... that the local FBI in Jackson and Laurel would
be very cooperative.... [It] turned out [that] the head of the Laurel FBI was ... related to
the sheriff and this Klan guy.... I wound up totally disenchanted with the FBI and the Justice Department."[95]

Overall, the two-month Summer Project produced more concentrated Ku Klux violence than any other period since Reconstruction. The official COFO tally listed 450 incidents, including 3 murders, 4 persons wounded by gunfire in 35 shootings, 52 "serious"
beatings, 65 buildings bombed or burned (including 30 churches), 7 bungled bombings with
no damage, 10 cars damaged or destroyed, and at least 250 arrests (some accounts say 1,000).
Author Don Whitehead claims that Sam Bowers ordered much of the mayhem to distract
FBI agents from their Neshoba County investigation, though that effort ultimately failed.[96]

Chaos and "COINTELPRO"

While the FBI launched its Mississippi anti–Klan campaign in June 1964, and Assistant Director Cartha DeLoach claims G-men toured the Mount Zion fire scene two days
before Neshoba Klansmen slew three civil rights workers, the Bureau initially made little
progress. Klansmen and unaffiliated whites alike stonewalled the "Federal Bureau of Integration," confronting agents with silence, lies, and occasional threats. DeLoach himself
admits that the campaign proceeded "by inches" until headquarters espoused a more aggressive strategy.[97]

The new solution was a "counterintelligence program"—COINTELPRO, in FBI short-
hand—proposed by assistant director William Sullivan on 27 August 1964. Hoover's memo
to the field officially inaugurating "COINTELPRO—White Hate" on 2 September explained:

> The purpose of this program is to expose, disrupt and otherwise neutralize the activities
> of the various klans and hate organizations, their leadership and adherents. The devious
> maneuvers and duplicity of these groups must be exposed to public scrutiny through the
> cooperation of reliable news media, both locally and at the Seat of Government [Wash-
> ington, D.C.]. In every instance, consideration should be given to disrupting the organ-
> ized activity of these groups and no opportunity should be missed to capitalize upon
> organizational and personal conflicts in their leadership.

Mississippi Klansmen bombed scores of homes, churches, and other targets in the 1960s (HCUA).

> The Bureau considers it vital that we expose the identities and activities of such groups and where possible disrupt their efforts. No counterintelligence action may be initiated by the field without specific Bureau authorization. You are cautioned that the nature of this new endeavor is such that under no circumstances should the existence of the programs be made known outside the Bureau and appropriate within-office security should be afforded this sensitive operation.[98]

To drive that last point home, Hoover decreed that "[m]ature experienced agents should he utilized and any investigation conducted should be done in a most discreet manner in order to Avoid Any Possibility of Embarrassment to the Bureau."[99]

"White Hate" was the FBI's third COINTELPRO campaign. Earlier programs targeting the Communist Party (1956) and the Socialist Workers Party (1961) were still ongoing when Hoover set his sights on the Klans and affiliated groups. Aside from cultivating more informants— an estimated 1 percent of Mississippi Klansmen — tactics ranged from petty harassment (anonymous mailings and phone calls, circulating rumors of corruption or other impropriety) to clear violations of state and federal statutes. By 1971, when Hoover allegedly discontinued all COINTELPRO operations, the Bureau acknowledged 2,218 specific "actions," including 1,884 illegal wiretaps, 583 burglaries to plant illegal "bugs," and a staggering 55,804 illicit mail-openings.

Disruption of Klan marriages included FBI reports to Klansmen when their wives complained of domestic violence, and authorized adultery on the part of FBI informants. G-men "explained the facts of life" to Klansmen, which Jack Nelson says "meant threatening and frightening the prospective informant in every possible way." Miscegenation was a potent weapon, according to agent Roy Moore, who told Nelson that Klansmen "were always getting out of bed with their black paramour and then coming to talk with us— that's what bothered me." It also bothered agent Tom Webb, a Mississippi native who complained that "a lot of Klansmen used the Klan as an excuse to go off and screw some women and their wife wouldn't know where they were."[100]

Hoover also ordered his agents to meet Klan threats head-on, while leaving their parameters deliberately vague. In Natchez, agent Paul Cummings recruited G-men to raid the local Klan bar and shoot out its windows. "We were at war," Cummings later told Jack Nelson, "and we used some muscle." Hoover gloated over such cases, boasting that Klansmen were "yellow" and "afraid to 'mix' with our Agents." Still, some plans lay beyond the pale, as when Roy Moore vetoed William Sullivan's scheme to embarrass the Klan by ordering twelve cases of embalming fluid in the APWR's name.[101]

While Sullivan was drawing up his COINTELPRO plan in Washington, Klan violence continued apace in Mississippi. On 26 August, in Canton, voter registration worker George Jackson survived three separate drive-by shootings between his home and the local Freedom House. One day later, Jackson Klansmen bombed the weekly *Northside Reporter*, whose editor, Hazel Smith, had received a Pulitzer Prize for "adherence to her editorial duty in the face of great pressure and opposition." On 28 August the Pike County Wolf Pack bombed yet another home.[102]

September's COINTELPRO launch brought no respite from terrorism in the Magnolia State. On 6 September Klansmen bombed a white-owned grocery in Canton's ghetto. The following night, they turned out in force to detonate three bombs in Summit, one in Auburn, one in Bogue Chitto, and one in Magnolia. In Pickens, also on 7 September, fourteen-year-old Herbert Oarsby vanished from his all-black neighborhood. Searchers hauled him from the Big Black River two days later, in a case that Sheriff Andrew Smith described as accidental drowning with "no evidence of foul play." Smith denied the family's report that Oarsby wore a CORE T-shirt the day he disappeared, but some accounts claim that the garment was still on his body when searchers retrieved it. Klansmen also bombed a minister's home in Summit on 9 September and burned two Madison County churches eight days later. Gunshots peppered a black-owned store in Vicksburg, and KBI director Ernest Gilbert hatched a scheme to burn a Mennonite school for "wayward girls" that dabbled in civil rights work, but Bowers rejected the plan.[103]

Neshoba County knights maintained their violent standard in September 1964. On the fourteenth they mobbed and beat a group of would-be voters at the courthouse while Deputy Price stood by smiling. Five days later, they burned two more churches outside Philadelphia, thereby pushing the Rev. Delmar Dennis to the point of resignation from the Klan. FBI agents called at his home and persuaded Dennis to remain in the MWK as their spy, drawing a salary of $100 per week plus expenses. Already serving as kludd (chaplain) for the Lauderdale County klavern, Dennis would soon be in line for promotion. On 27 September he was one of several FBI informants who cast votes for "loudmouth" Billy Birdsong as a KBI investigator, thus insuring that each plot the local Klan devised would be revealed through klavern gossip. One such conspiracy involved demolition of the Evers Hotel, which housed Philadelphia's remaining COFO personnel. On 8 October 1964 that tip sent G-men to the home of Klansman James Russell, where they seized a cache of dynamite and foiled the mass-murder plan. Despite that setback, two months later Methodist minister Clay Lee told Philadelphia's Rotary Club, "For all practical purposes, the Klan has taken over the guidance of thought patterns in our town. It has controlled what was said and what was not said." [104]

Violence escalated in Adams County after the UKA staged its first public rally in Natchez, on 29 August 1964. Convinced that Mayor Nosser had struck a bargain with black boycotters, Klansmen bombed two of his Jitney Jungle stores in mid–September. On 25 September, after Nosser and his aldermen offered a reward for capture of the terrorists, Klansmen bombed the mayor's home and the residence of a local NAACP activist. Two nights later, bombers struck the home of black businessman I.S. Sanders. Charles Evers, back from Chicago, wired the White House a warning that if federal agents did not halt "this mounting reign of terror ... I cannot and will not be responsible for the action which the Negroes may take upon themselves."

Governor Johnson sent agents from the highway patrol's elite Cattle Theft Division to investigate, but they hit a stone wall of defiance in Natchez. On 29 September state patrolmen stopped a car carrying three suspected bombers, outside of town. Its occupants included former sheriff William Ferrell and two of his ex-deputies. The patrolmen searched Ferrell's car for explosives, but found none. Author Paul Hendrickson opines that Ferrell—who kept a portrait of Nathan Bedford Forrest on his office wall throughout his tenure as sheriff—was either en route to a UKA rally when stopped or that he and his men "were acting as sentries for a bombing about to take place." FBI files list Ferrell as a Klansman "said to handle propaganda and spread rumors." A childhood friend of Grand Dragon Edward McDaniel, Ferrell had also hired McDaniel's brother as a deputy.[105]

Bombings aside, Mayor Nosser did his best to hold the color line in Natchez. On 30

September 1964 he obtained injunctions against demonstrations by either the NAACP or the Klan. Charles Evers led marches in protest, and Judge Harold Cox removed the injunction on 6 October, creating more tension in town. Edward McDaniel fielded UKA security guards to monitor black protests; the guards were dressed in paramilitary uniforms and were armed with heavy "nigger-knocker" flashlights, while Klansman Lane Murray — senior class president at Natchez High School in 1958 — cruised the streets in a sound truck, blaring the UKA anthem "Move Them Niggers North." McDaniel also led robed counter-marches through Natchez, one featuring Imperial Wizard Robert Shelton in the vanguard.[106]

And still, the Pike County Wolf Pack outstripped all rival klaverns for sheer ferocity. On 23 August hooded Klansmen kidnapped and terrorized a white McComb resident who befriended blacks. Four days later, the Klan bombed the home of a local MFDP supporter. On 2 September thugs beat a civil rights worker in downtown McComb while police turned blind eyes to the assault. Five bombs exploded in McComb on 7 September and another two nights later. An SNCC staffer wrote to the Justice Department for help on 9 September, whereupon J. Edgar Hoover withdrew twelve of the sixteen G-men stationed in McComb. On 20 September Klansmen bombed a church and the home of black entrepreneur Aylene Quinn. Police called Quinn's bombing a hoax and jailed twenty-four black suspects under Mississippi's "criminal syndicalism" statute. Two thousand blacks turned

A Klan bomb wrecked the home of Ayleen Quinn in McComb on 20 September 1964 (HCUA).

out to stone police that night, one of their bricks striking Chief Guy. When terrorists struck twice more on 23 September, Sheriff R.R. Andrews called the bombings "staged." Governor Johnson belatedly ordered a state police investigation after telling reporters that some of McComb's explosions "were plants set by COFO people," while "some were bombings by white people." Rather than hunt the bombers, Chief Guy's police twice raided Aylene Quinn's café. When she announced its closure following the second raid, her landlord told her, "Good, now I can go tell the sheriff and police chief and you won't get bombed."[107]

Armed with statements from informants, FBI agents arrested three McComb Klansmen on 30 September, another on 3 October, and five more by 7 October. Several raids turned up caches of illegal arms and explosives. Three bombers signed confessions and named their accomplices, prompting Pike County's grand jury to indict four defendants on 9 October and five more eleven days later. Aside from bombing charges, G-men also identified defendant Sterling "Bubba" Gillis, brother of a prominent McComb attorney, as the gunman who stole $38,076 from a Monticello bank on 2 March 1964. A week after the last arrests, on 13 October, UKA grand dragon Calvin Craig penned a letter to his Georgia knights, soliciting donations for the bombers' legal defense. "As you know," he wrote, "we do not condone nor advocate such acts of violence, but we beleive [sic] these men are victims of circumstances [sic]."

Explosives seized by FBI agents from Pike County Klansmen in 1964 (HCUA).

Julius Harper, addressing MWK members, advised any Klansmen possessing explosives to bury them for future use. The *Enterprise-Journal* ran an editorial condemning Klan violence on 14 October, prompting a sneak squad to burn a cross outside editor Oliver Emmerich's home. Upon learning that Emmerich's mother had died the same day, an anonymous caller phoned to say, "We would not have burned that cross in front of your home had we known of your mother's death."[108]

At trial, before Judge W.H. Watkins in Magnolia on 23 October 1964, six defendants pled guilty to specific bombing charges, while all nine entered "no contest" pleas on conspiracy counts. Judge Watkins sentenced the Klansmen to prison terms ranging from six months to fifteen years, plus various fines, then suspended all jail time on curious grounds. After calling the bombers "young men" (five of the nine were over thirty-five) and members of good families "who were shocked at their involvement," Watkins explained his rationale:[109]

> I want you to understand to start with that the Court understands and appreciates what you have done and the crimes you have committed have to some extent at least been provoked and brought about by outside influences. There have been outsiders come into your community and they have been unwelcome, their presence here has been unnecessary and they have been unwanted and they have been, insofar as some of them are concerned at least, they have been people of low morality and unhygienic and their presence here has provoked a lot of people. That is evident from the report of the grand jury. The grand jury of your county stated to the public that they resented their presence here, and so the Court understands, not condoning you understand to any extent what you have done, but the Court is bound to appreciate the fact that the crimes to which you have pled guilty were to some extent provoked by these outside influences.... Some of you have young children, fine wives to think about, and you all have good records. None of you have ever been in any trouble before.... And then, of course, I am taking into consideration that you were unduly provoked, ill-advised, and so forth.[110]

Judge Watkins ignored the bank robbery charges pending against Sterling Gillis, but warned the defendants against owning arms or explosives. In the event of any further local violence, he declared, they would be forced to serve their jail time, whether or not they joined in any future crimes.[111]

The McComb arrests did not immediately quell Klan violence. Night riders bombed Vicksburg's Freedom House on 4 October, injuring two occupants, and fired into a Meridian home housing civil rights workers. On 11 October, referring to the Vicksburg blast, Sam Bowers told an MWK executive meeting "They will not find out who did that one as I sent someone in from the outside." Sunflower County Klansmen burned Indianola's Freedom School on 27 October and teargassed the home of a teenage COFO supporter the following night. On 29 October, addressing a group of Forrest County knights in Petal, Bowers warned against anymore bombings of churches or homes, but his order did not prevent the immolation of a Freedom School in Ripley on Halloween night.[112]

Bowers got serious about the threat of new arrests on 15 November, at a Klan meeting held midway between Brandon and Harrisville. There, he ordered a ninety-day moratorium on "serious Physical Action Projects, especially those of the 3rd and 4th Magnitude," between 1 December 1964 and 1 March 1965. Projects already planned and scheduled for completion prior to 1 December were permitted to proceed; beyond that, Bowers sanctioned only "mild and humorous harassments of the enemy." Delmar Dennis, recently promoted to titan of his province, relayed the order to FBI agents. On the night of Dennis's promotion, 12 November, Bowers told a gathering of Klansmen in Meridian "There is no one I trust more than Delmar Dennis." Laurel's Klansmen set the tone for "mild and humorous harassment" on 17 November, when they kidnapped black CIO officer Otis Mathews, flogged him with a leather strap, and poured hot liquid into his wounds.[113]

The Pike County arrests, followed by Bowers' moratorium on bombings and murders, prompted hard-core Klansmen to seek outlets elsewhere for their pent-up rage. According to the FBI, November 1964 witnessed formation of a new and unabashedly violent faction, drawing members from the UKA, MWK, and Original Knights in Adams County, Mississippi, and neighboring Catahoula Parish, Louisiana. The new group's founders, pleased to call themselves the "toughest Klansmen in Mississippi or Louisiana," met first at Vidalia's Shamrock Motel to discuss the "lack of guts" displayed by their respective Klans. Guerrilla warfare training followed, at family picnics where Klansmen practiced new demolition techniques. In lieu of membership cards, each recruit carried a silver dollar minted in the year of his birth — and so the "Silver Dollar Group" was born.[114]

The gang's first victim was Frank Morris, a black shoe repairman in Ferriday, Louisiana, whom Klansmen suspected of romancing white women. In the early hours of 10 December 1964 Klansmen torched Morris's shop and living quarters, keeping him inside the blazing structure at gunpoint until he suffered fatal burns. Still, he lived long enough to tell G-men that he had recognized his killers. "I think," he said, "they might work at Johns-Manville or something like that, over in Natchez." The Morris case remains officially unsolved today, but it would not be the last homicide tied to the Silver Dollar Group.[115]

Opposing the "Great Society"

Presidential politics distracted some Klansmen and FBI agents alike in 1964. President Johnson ordered FBI surveillance of MFDP delegates to the Democratic National Convention that August, while police and Klansmen did their best to stunt the party's growth in Mississippi. Officers throughout the state jailed campaign workers on various trumped-up charges, including "criminal syndicalism," auto theft, reckless driving, "disorderly conduct," and distributing leaflets without a permit.

In Holly Springs, on 16 October, night riders burned a cross at the home of a newly registered black voter. On 21 October Klansmen forced an MFDP organizer off the road near Marks, beat him unconscious, then urinated on his body. The following day, in Indianola, the one-plane Klan Air Force circled an MFDP rally, dropping flares and small explosive charges on 250 persons. Indianola Klansmen teargassed a party supporter's home on 28 October, but failed in their effort to torch SNCC's Freedom House the same night. In Ruleville, a black merchant who displayed Democratic campaign posters had his windows shattered by stones on 24 October and by bullets five nights later.[116]

With George Wallace out of the running by August 1964, UKA leaders threw their support to Republican Barry Goldwater, conveniently ignoring the fact that he was Jewish and his running mate was Catholic. Goldwater had secured far-right support in July, when he told the Republican National Convention that "extremism in the defense of liberty is no vice," while "moderation in pursuit of justice is no virtue." He finally rejected Klan support, after a meeting with ex-president Dwight Eisenhower, but Robert Shelton stood fast in support of the GOP. In fact, as Greenville's William Percy wrote, "It would not have mattered if Senator Goldwater had advocated the collectivization of the plantations and open saloons in Jackson; he voted against the [1964] Civil Rights Bill and that was that." On 3 November 1964 Goldwater carried Mississippi, four other southern states, and his native Arizona, losing out to LBJ by a margin of 15.6 million votes nationwide.[117]

The LBJ landslide and subsequent White House vows to build a color-blind "Great Society" had less import for Klansmen in Neshoba County than their ongoing campaign to avoid federal prison. Following Esther Carter's dismissal of charges against nineteen indicted defendants, prosecutors dropped their charges against informants Horace Barnette and James Jordan, regrouping for new indictments. In the interim, on 12 December 1964, Klansmen huddled with authorities in Philadelphia, hatching a plot to convict and execute Barnette and Jordan on state murder charges, thereby pacifying all concerned. Informants leaked the plan to G-men and it went no further, leaving Sheriff Rainey to complain that he had tried to solve the triple murder, but "the FBI wouldn't cooperate."[118]

Klan paranoia increased as the FBI's COINTELPRO operations escalated. One week after the Philadelphia strategy session, Wallace Miller, accused of spying for the feds, faced

Three unidentified participants at a Mississippi Klan rally (HCUA).

an inquisition in Meridian. Miller denied the charges and escaped physical punishment, but he was exiled from the MWK. Ironically, federal informant Delmar Dennis read Miller's decree of banishment, forbidding any further contact with the order or its members.[119]

On 1 January 1965 a federal grand jury convened in Jackson to consider the Neshoba murders. Two weeks later, the panel issued indictments against eighteen defendants, dropping four from the original group and adding Philadelphia policeman Richard Willis to the list. Arrest warrants were issued for sixteen defendants residing in Mississippi, while FBI agents retrieved Barnette and Jordan from Georgia and Louisiana. Commissioner Carter set bond for sixteen of the accused at $5,750, while Barnette and Jordan posted $5,000 each. Twelve defense attorneys, including all five of Philadelphia's white lawyers, appealed to U.S. District Judge Harold Cox with claims that the federal government lacked jurisdiction to prosecute the case.[120]

Judge Cox seemed heaven-sent for the accused. The son of a former Sunflower County sheriff and a childhood friend of James Eastland, he had shared an Ole Miss dormitory room with Eastland in the 1920s. In June 1961, when President Kennedy nominated former NAACP attorney Thurgood Marshall for a seat on the U.S. Court of Appeals, Eastland demanded a federal judgeship for Cox, advising Robert Kennedy to "[t]ell your brother if he'll give me Cox, I'll give him the nigger." Thus Cox became JFK's first judicial appointment, bearing the American Bar Association's highest endorsement as "exceptionally well-qualified." He was, nonetheless, a blatant racist who, in March 1964, described black plaintiffs in his court as "chimpanzees" and "a bunch of niggers" who "ought to be in the movies rather than being registered to vote."

It was no great surprise, therefore, when Cox dismissed all charges against fifteen Neshoba defendants on 24 February 1965, declaring that "private individuals" were immune to prosecution under federal conspiracy statutes. Three remaining defendants—Sheriff Rainey, Deputy Price, and Patrolman Willis—faced misdemeanor counts of violating civil rights "under color of law." On 15 March the U.S. Supreme Court declined to hear the case on accelerated appeal.[121]

While federal prosecutors sparred with MWK attorneys in court, Robert Shelton's UKA launched a new Magnolia State recruiting drive in January 1965. Edward McDaniel addressed unhappy White Knights at a fishing camp near Meridian, urging them to defect and join "a strong national Klan that knows how to operate." Delmar Dennis joined the UKA, encouraged by his FBI handlers, but still retained his titan's post with the MWK. Defector Billy Birdsong branded Sam Bowers a "communist," claiming that Bowers hung portraits of Lenin, the Pope, and LBJ in his home. Dissenters in Meridian considered flogging Bowers and looting the MWK treasury, but later scrapped the plan. Another group of dissidents, led by Klansman Mordaunt Hamilton in Petal, actually held Bowers at gunpoint, relieving him of cash and weapons, then dodged retaliatory raids in January 1965.[122]

Violence continued, meanwhile, against Mississippi blacks and civil rights supporters. On 13 January 1965 a white gunman killed Jessie Brown in Winona. NAACP members named the slayer, but police made no arrests. Five days later, Klansmen in Laurel assaulted a white civil rights worker. Members of the same klavern botched their attempt to burn a black family's home at Soso, on 29 January, but other raids were more successful. They shot up Laurel's COFO office on 9 February, then returned to burn it eight days later. On 4 March 1965 they torched another home in Ellisville.[123]

Such incidents prompted the U.S. Civil Rights Commission to conduct five days of open hearings in Jackson between 16 and 20 February 1965. Most of the subpoenaed witnesses were public officials, called to account for their abuse and obstruction of would-be black voters. One of those summoned, Adams County sheriff Odell Anders, was named in FBI files as a Klansman. His city counterpart, Natchez police chief L.C. Nix, was grilled concerning his arrest of a black man who entered a "white" coffee shop. Asked if he had heard of the 1964 Civil Rights Act, Nix replied, "I have no civil authorities—criminal—until it becomes criminal." Nix evoked laughter from the gallery when he described his visit to a local Klan rally, saying, "I couldn't see anything that night that would make you think they were anything but upstanding people."[124]

The hearings changed nothing for white Mississippi. On 22 February ex-governor Barnett trailed Martin Luther King to Selma, Alabama, where he warned a Citizens' Council crowd that whites faced "absolute extinction of all we hold dear unless we are victorious." Four racist murders followed in rapid succession over the next six days: Saleam Triggs, "mysteriously burned to death" in Hattiesburg; John and Willie Lee, fatally beaten near Goshen Springs, where Willie had attended civil rights meetings; and Donald Rasberry, shot by his plantation boss at Okolona. On 5 March Klansmen firebombed a black home in Greenwood and burned Indianola's Freedom School and library; Indianola police jailed eight COFO staff members for "interfering" with their investigation. On 14 March Vicksburg Klansmen beat an elderly black patron in a newly integrated café, then returned to firebomb the place a week later. Arsonists torched another Vicksburg restaurant on 18 March, and firebombed two black churches in Meridian on 29 March.[125]

Against that background, on 30 March 1965, the House Un-American Activities Committee announced plans to investigate the Ku Klux Klan. For HUAC chairman Edwin Willis of Louisiana, the investigation was an opportunity to draw a line between "respectable" segregationists of the Citizens' Council variety and violent "crackers" in the Klan. New panel member Charles Weltner of Georgia had a different motive: elected to the House in 1962 with support from Atlanta's black voters, he sought to purge the Klan from southern life via exposure of its secrets as well as new legislation banning its conspiratorial activities. Neither attempt would prove successful, but as always, HUAC guaranteed its audience a show.[126]

Public hearings began on 19 October 1965 and continued through 24 February 1966, including testimony from 187 witnesses. Most of the Klansmen called to testify sought refuge in the Fifth Amendment's ban on compulsory self-incrimination, though a few spoke freely and one UKA kludd from North Carolina resigned on the witness stand. HUAC investigators named hundreds of Klansmen, identified local klaverns and their "fronts," produced financial records indicating shoddy bookkeeping or worse, and detailed acts of brutal violence throughout the South.

A total of forty-two Mississippi Klansmen were summoned to testify, forty of whom revealed nothing beyond their names and birth dates. Attorney Lester Chalmers, from North Carolina, represented most UKA members before the committee, while Mississippi lawyers Charles Blackwell and Travis Buckley accompanied MWK loyalists. Back home in Vicksburg, on 29 November 1965, HUAC investigator John Sullivan narrowly escaped death when a car-bomb demolished a black-owned home and store near his residence. The blast hurled Sullivan's son out of bed and across his bedroom.[127]

While HUAC exposed many Klansmen by name, embarrassing some with details of their criminal records or shady finances, its impact in the South was minimal. Robert Shelton and three of his grand dragons earned contempt citations and jail time for withholding UKA records, but Edward McDaniel escaped prosecution on similar charges and the MWK emerged unscathed. Charles Weltner's new anti–Klan legislation died in committee, and evidence suggests that HUAC's "bad" publicity — like northern newspaper exposés in 1921 — aided Klan recruiting by enticing members with a taste for rough-and-ready action. HUAC's final report identified "approximately" 16,810 Klansmen nationwide, with 15,075 in the UKA and the remainder dispersed among thirteen competitors. The committee found 1,150 Klansmen in Mississippi, 750 in the UKA and 400 in the MWK. Walter Bailey's Mississippi Knights, reduced to five members in June 1966, apparently dissolved with his death six months later.[128]

Independent reports suggest that HUAC's estimates were too conservative. In 1966 the Anti-Defamation League surveyed two Klans, the UKA and James Venable's Georgia-based National Knights, reporting a combined membership of 33,000 to 42,000. Klan historian David Chalmers estimates peak membership in the mid–1960s at 50,000. Most media accounts grant Mississippi 10,000 Klansmen during 1964 and 1965, while Edward McDaniel placed the state's total "way over ten thousand." The Klan's obsessive secrecy prevents any more detailed census of the Invisible Empire, but critics suggest that HUAC's low-ball figures were designed to minimize Klan influence in Dixie.[129]

No Surrender

Neither the FBI's covert campaigns nor HUAC's public inquisition managed to suppress Klan violence during 1965. On 23 April Klansmen torched a black family's home in Ellisville. On 16 May Jones County raiders burned a grocery store in Mount Olive, along with Laurel's community recreation center and the Rahaim Baseball Park. One night later, arsonists leveled a gas station in Laurel and a motel in Meridian. Greenwood resident M.F. White offended Klansmen by hiring Dewey Greene, related to a black enrollee at Ole Miss, to paint his house. To protest that decision, Byron De La Beckwith and Gordon Lackey painted a black ring around White's home. On 16 June Laurel's raiders fired into a black nightclub and the home of Dr. B.E. Murph, state president of the NAACP. Three nights later, Klansmen torched another home in Jones County and firebombed the garage of Herman Vavra, personnel chief at Vicksburg's Westinghouse plant.[130]

Robert Shelton staged a UKA klonvocation in Natchez on 15–16 May, drawing Klansmen from seven states. Charles Evers chose the same month to lead protests outside "white" hotels and stores in Natchez, facing Ku Klux counterdemonstrations, while Delmar Dennis placed Byron De La Beckwith in Philadelphia, assigned to "check with Rainey, Price, and Co." concerning progress in their legal case. On 10 July, one day after Congress passed the 1965 Voting Rights Act, Sheriff Rainey appeared with Shelton at the Suqualena race track, near Meridian. With a twenty-foot cross flaming in the background, Rainey addressed his thousand-member audience: "I'm glad to be here and see these fine people here. I just thought I'd come down here and see what this was all about, and I can tell you I met some of the finest people anywhere in the Klan this afternoon and tonight." His comments triggered "thunderous applause."[131]

Rainey's appearance with Shelton signaled yet another defection from the White Knights to the UKA. On 17 July Deputy Price joined Rainey for a rally at Crossroads, greeting some five thousand Klansmen. Five days later, Robert Shelton returned for a rally in Greenwood, where Edward McDaniel introduced Rainey as "a great American." On 29 July Rainey addressed a UKA crowd in Montgomery, Alabama, then returned to host a rally in Philadelphia on 31 July, where Klansmen peddled literature on the courthouse steps. One of them, triple-killer Alton Roberts, had enraged Sam Bowers by deserting the MWK to serve Shelton as a kleagle. Even the APWR wavered in its support of Bowers, welcoming New Orleans UKA spokesman Jack Helms to a Natchez meeting on 5 June, then distributing UKA pamphlets at a July "Conservative Rally" in Brandon, where attendees watched *The Birth of a Nation*.[132]

Whichever group claimed their allegiance, Klansmen still behaved like Klansmen. In Jones County alone, on the busy night of 1 July 1965, they burned eight crosses, sixteen homes, a barn, a drive-in restaurant, and Laurel's Freedom House. Two days later, they bungled an arson attempt at a black civil rights worker's home, then rebounded by incinerating a white lawyer's house on 19 July.

Philadelphia hired its first black policeman, Willie "Tripp" Windham, in July, but he appeared to work for Sheriff Rainey, summoned frequently to beat black prisoners in jail. On 1 August, after Florence Mars attended a meeting where Klansmen were ridiculed,

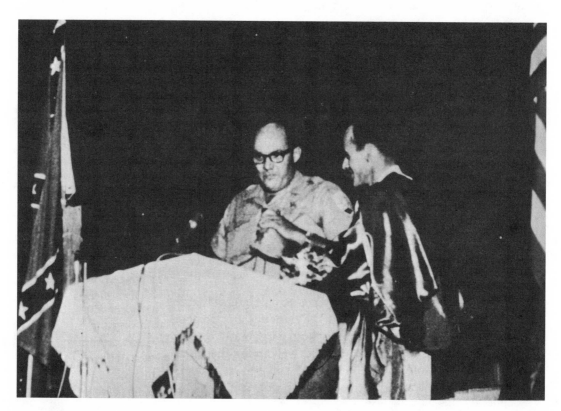

Sheriff Lawrence Rainey (left) addresses a 1965 Klan rally with Grand Dragon Edward McDaniel (Library of Congress).

Rainey arrested her and held her overnight. A friend warned Mars that Klansmen planned to kill her cattle, but the threat was never carried out.[133]

In July 1965 the State Sovereignty Commission assigned agent A.L. Hopkins to investigate Ku Klux activities in Adams, Claiborne, Hinds, Jefferson, Madison and Neshoba counties. Klansmen promptly branded Hopkins and his colleagues "Paul Johnson's niggers," and snipers fired at Hopkins' home in Jackson. Hopkins talked to the press: "If the Klan is of the opinion that they can change my mind about it by firing a few bullets into my home, they are likely to waste many bullets." His final report, a mere three pages long, focused primarily on what he called a "dangerous explosive" rivalry between the MWK and the UKA.[134]

On 8 August, two days after President Johnson signed the Voting Rights Act, Sam Bowers elevated Byron De La Beckwith to the rank of kleagle. Thus began a series of speeches in which Beckwith boasted of killing Medgar Evers and encouraged other knights to follow his example. "Killing that nigger," he informed one audience, "gave me no more inner discomfort than our wives endure when they give birth to our children. We ask them to do that for us. We should do just as much. So, let's get in there and kill those enemies, including the President, from the top down!"

At another rally, soliciting donations for the MWK's White Christian Protective and Legal Defense Fund, Beckwith declared, "The only time to be calm is when you pull the trigger." At Laurel's fairgrounds, Beckwith told 250 Klansmen that "Charles Evers has overdrawn his account in this world. He has bounced his check but it ain't caught up with him yet." Delmar Dennis and other informants reported those comments to FBI agents, but J. Edgar Hoover withheld Beckwith's confessions from the Justice Department, compromising with a memo to the U.S. Secret Service that labeled Beckwith a "subversive, ultraright, racist" with a "propensity for violence and antipathy toward good order and government."[135]

Meanwhile, Klan violence continued. Deavours Nix, elected grand director of the MWK's KBI on 27 June 1965, logged arrests for assault on 13 July and 14 August. At a meeting in Laurel, on 18 July, Sam Bowers boasted of sixteen recent arson raids. On 31 July gunmen shot up Columbia's COFO office. Night riders burned two homes in Sharon on 10 August, and apparently murdered one of their own near Meadville, six days later. Victim Earl Hodges quarreled with Clyde Seale, exalted cyclops of his Franklin County klavern, shortly before police found his corpse in the woods, on 16 August. A coroner blamed his death on "heart failure," but HUAC investigators reported: "There were welts from the bottom of the feet to the top of the head. There was a hole in the top of his head. A split from the left side of his nose to his left eye was so deep that the roof of the mouth was exposed." Unknown gunmen killed black teenager Freddie Thomas Jr. in Greenwood on 20 August; his family blamed Klansmen, but FBI agents never published the results of their brief investigation. Two days later, a shotgun ambush critically wounded the Rev. Donald Thompson, secretary of the Mississippi Council on Human Relations, outside his Jackson apartment. Police accused black members of Thompson's Unitarian congregation, advising Thompson that if Klansmen wished to kill him, he would certainly be dead. Thompson fled the state in November after receiving more death threats.[136]

Natchez also remained a racial tinderbox. The UKA drew local members from the Armstrong Rubber plant and the International Paper Company, where Klansmen often left their robes and leaflets plainly visible on the seats of their cars in the factory parking lots.

George Metcalfe, a black Armstrong employee who served as president of the Natchez NAACP, presented the city's school board with a new desegregation petition on 19 August 1965. The next day, both Natchez daily papers published rosters of the signatories' names. On 27 August, as he left the plant, a bomb wired to his car's ignition shattered Metcalfe's legs, mangled one arm, and blinded him in one eye. According to black witnesses, some whites who heard the blast inside the plant "decided it was a holiday, just like November 22, 1963." Don Whitehead blames the bombing, still officially unsolved, on members of the Silver Dollar Group.[137]

The *Natchez Democrat*, so quick to name Metcalfe's petitioners on 20 August, now charged anonymous "minority elements—hoodlums, renegades, and criminals"—with his near murder. Charles Evers convened a mass meeting and warned the press and white Natchez: "We're armed, every last one of us! And we're not going to take it!" While younger members of the audience chanted "We're going to kill for freedom!" Evers predicted new street demonstrations unless Mayor Nosser and his aldermen instantly conformed to terms of the 1964 Civil Rights Act. Nosser responded by banning liquor sales and nocturnal parades, imposing a 10:00 P.M. curfew. George Metcalfe, still hospitalized on 3 December, called off the black boycott of Nosser's stores, declaring a small-scale victory for the NAACP. On Christmas Eve Edward McDaniel swore out an arrest warrant for Natchez police chief J.T. Robinson, citing his "failure to enforce the law" against black protesters. Sheriff Anders made the arrest, then released Robinson on $100 bond. On New Year's Day 1966, Klan arsonists burned Mayor Nosser's Giant Discount Center to the ground.[138]

During September 1965 Jones County Klansmen bombed a COFO vehicle in Laurel, burned two homes in Sandersville and another in Ovett, torched a rural church, and made another strafing run at Dr. B.E. Murph's office. In October they burned an Ellisville farmhouse and shot up a black school in Laurel. Mayor Henry Bucklew publicly condemned the terrorists on 19 October, whereupon the *Klan Ledger* branded him a conspirator with "LBJ and [Attorney General] Katzenback [*sic*] and the source of all cash." In Sturgis, on 20 September, police blamed an unknown hit-and-run driver for killing black victim Jimmie Griffin; the coroner's report said Griffin was run over twice, at least. Neshoba County defendants Rainey, Price, and Alton Roberts graced a Philadelphia UKA rally on 25 October, introduced to the crowd as "great patriots of today." On 8 November, Klansmen lured white attorney Knox Walker to Gulfport's marina, there chastising him for representing black clients and ordering him to leave town. Black murder victim Lillie Powers died in Starkville on 10 November, slain by "persons unknown." On 29 November a Vicksburg car bomb wrecked civil rights activist James Chiplin's home and grocery store, overturned a passing taxi, and wounded three bystanders.[139]

As the 1965 Voting Rights Act brought federal examiners into Mississippi, so black registration increased. Klansmen responded by lighting crosses in nine Mississippi counties on 3 January 1966, from Adams in the far-southwest to Hinds, Rankin, and Lauderdale. Around Meridian, G-men arrested five night riders, including brothers Allen and Bobby Byrd, who fired shots at an FBI car. Hattiesburg merchant Vernon Dahmer, whose light skin (from a distant German ancestor) permitted him to pass for white outside of Forrest County, had served the local NAACP for decades and collaborated with SNCC's voter-registration workers since 1961, thereby earning the hatred of Klansmen statewide. FBI informants described Sam Bowers "pound[ing] on the table and say[ing] he was tired of fooling

$5000.00
REWARD

The Mayor And Board of Aldermen are vitally concerned about the many incidents of bombings, lawlessness and destruction of private property that have occurred in our fair city. Natchez is a tourist resort and an industrial area and depends heavily upon the income and patronage of tourists and industries that come into this area, and it is essential that we have an atmosphere in our city that is conducive to peace, trade, and business development. Many of our citizens have been threatened with bodily harm and property destruction. Under these circumstances we do not know when, where or whom the terrorists will strike next. Therefore, it behooves every law-abiding citizen to cooperate with the local authorities in assuring that these acts of violence will not be repeated.

FAILURE OF ANY CITIZEN TO ACT WOULD HAVE JUST AS DRASTIC A RESULT AS COOPER-ATING WITH THE PERSONS WHO ARE COMMITTING THE ACTS OF VIOLENCE.

Thus, the Mayor and Board of Aldermen do appeal to the citizens of Natchez and all of the civic organizations and clubs in the city for their full co-operation in reporting any unlawful incident and furnishing to the city authorities any information that would lead to the apprehension of those undesirable citizens who are determined to cause unrest and ill-feeling in our community by the destruction of private property and by threatening to do bodily violence to those who stand in their way.

The Mayor and Board feel that it is necessary that a reward be offered and do, therefore, offer for a period of 90 days from date the sum of $5,000.00 for evidence leading and substantially contributing to the arrest and conviction of the person or persons guilty of the unlawful acts of violence, bombing of buildings, homes or other establishments within the City Of Natchez.

Sincerely,
MAYOR
And
BOARD OF ALDERMEN

Advertisement, Natchez
Democrat, Sept. 16

Poster announcing rewards for the capture of Natchez bombers in 1965 brought no takers (Library of Congress).

around, something had to be done about that damn nigger down south." Bowers wanted Dahmer killed "if any way possible," and personally led hand-picked raiders on two dry runs past Dahmer's rural home and store in December 1965. Finally, after Dahmer broadcast a radio appeal to timid voter registrants on 9 January 1966, offering to collect their poll taxes at his store and deliver them to the sheriff himself, Bowers ordered the hit to proceed.[140]

At 2:30 A.M. on 10 January, eight White Knights in two vehicles struck at Dahmer's home and nearby store, where an elderly aunt occupied a back room. They shot out windows at both sites, then followed up with flaming plastic jugs of gasoline. Surprisingly, Dahmer slept through the gunfire but woke to the sound of roaring flames. Grabbing a shotgun, Dahmer fired on the raiders while his wife, children, and aunt escaped, all but one child unscathed. Outside, when raiders at the store turned on their headlights, nervous Klansmen at the Dahmer home cut loose on them, flattening a tire on the second getaway

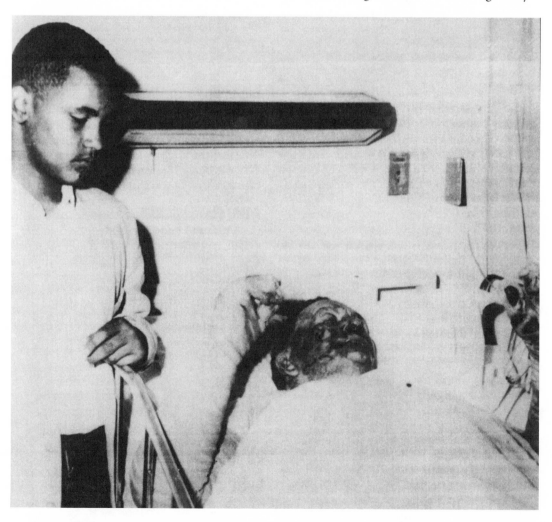

Vernon Dahmer lies dying from burns suffered during a Klan raid on his home. One of his sons stands at left (SPLC).

car. One raider dropped a pistol in his haste to flee, and the damaged car's driver abandoned his vehicle three miles outside Hattiesburg, rushing home to report it stolen. Vernon Dahmer lived to reach a hospital, but died at 3:45 A.M., his lungs ravaged by heat and smoke.[141]

FBI agents quickly traced the abandoned car to owner Howard Giles, a convicted car thief and employee at Laurel's Masonite plant, who also served as exalted cyclops of MWK Klavern No. 2 in Jones County. Giles claimed that his car disappeared after work, while he was dining at the Chow House restaurant, a Klan hangout owned by fellow White Knight Henry De Boxtel. On 11 January an FBI informant quoted Sam Bowers as saying, "The Laurel group scored a big one and the men involved were better than the Philadelphia group. The technical end was not as good as the Philadelphia job, but these men won't talk." Bowers also voiced hope that the White Knights "could pull one of these jobs every time the pressure begins to build against Klansmen in another part of the state so that we can keep the FBI and its men running." On 12 January another informant confirmed the MWK's involvement in Dahmer's murder, naming Jones County oilman, merchant, and White Knight's "senator" Lawrence Byrd as a prime suspect. Byrd confessed to G-men on 2 March 1966 and persuaded Cecil Sessum, cyclops of Jones County Klavern No. 4, to do likewise.[142]

Sessum soon recanted his statement, following a visit to John's Café in Laurel, owned by KBI director Deavours Nix, and signed a second affidavit claiming he was beaten by federal agents until he confessed. Sam Bowers presented a similar affidavit to Lawrence Byrd, but Byrd refused to sign. On 28 March FBI agents arrested thirteen suspects, including Giles, Nix, Sessum, and Billy Pitts, whose pistol was found at the murder scene. G-men missed Sam Bowers at home, but confiscated a "small arsenal" including thirteen guns and eight Halloween masks like those worn by Klansmen who tortured James Wilson in Natchez in February 1964. Bowers surrendered voluntarily with lawyers Charles Blackwell and Travis Buckley on 31 March, joining his codefendants as they were released on bonds ranging from $10,000 to $50,000. On 22 June 1966 a federal grand jury indicted Bowers and fourteen codefendants on charges of violating the 1965 Voting Rights Act. Klan attorneys subsequently challenged the indictments and secured their dismissal, ironically, on grounds that blacks and women were improperly excluded from the jury.[143]

Federal agents ignored another case, reported from Leflore County on 12 January 1966. Five Tallahatchie County voter-registration activists were homeward bound that Tuesday night after meeting with Senator Robert Kennedy in Jackson. According to police, they either struck or swerved to miss a second vehicle driven by a white man from Sidon. The resultant crash decapitated Birdia Keglar, one of Tallahatchie's first black voters and a long-time subject of state surveillance, and "cleanly" severed both arms of elderly Adeline Hamlet. Survivors noted the Klan's habit of running target vehicles off rural highways, and dismissed the local police investigation as a whitewash. Members of Keglar's family today regard the event as a "KKK lynching," but no hard evidence of a conspiracy exists.[144]

Marching Against Fear

Vernon Dahmer's sacrifice presumably was not an issue when the U.S. Supreme Court banned state poll taxes on 25 March 1966. His slaying prompted Forrest County law enforce-

Items seized by FBI agents from the home of Samuel Bowers following the Dahmer slaying (HCUA).

ment officers to collaborate with the FBI, rather than obstructing them, but little changed in the Magnolia State at large. On 2 February 1966 drive-by shooters wounded two civil rights workers lodging at a Natchez home. In April, Washington County sheriff Earl Fisher raided a black cemetery, opening various graves in a search of nonexistent arms caches, then blamed local Klansmen for spreading false alarms. On 26 May police in Fayette jailed a white man for shooting a black teenager outside his home.[145]

On 5 June 1966 James Meredith left Memphis, Tennessee, on the first leg of a one-man, 220-mile "March Against Fear." His destination was Jackson, Mississippi, but he never came close. On 6 June, two miles south of Hernando, Meredith was shot from ambush by Memphis resident Aubrey Norvell. Three shotgun blasts struck Meredith with nearly 100 lead pellets, but he survived his wounds without permanent injury. While Governor Johnson told reporters he was "particularly pleased that [Norvell] was not a Mississippian," police held Norvell on charges of assault with intent to kill. He later pled guilty and received a five-year sentence, with three years suspended. Authors David Chalmers and Christine Gibson later identified Aubrey Norvell as a Klansman.[146]

While Norvell sat in jail, Sam Bowers and the MWK schemed to take advantage of his crime. Learning that Martin Luther King planned to complete Meredith's march, Byron De La Beckwith addressed a White Knights rally: "Now is the time to start shooting, starting with Martin Luther King on down." Bowers himself met with aides to plot an ambush on Highway 19 between Meridian and Philadelphia, suggesting dynamite beneath a bridge, with snipers set at either end to fire on the procession. That plan went no further, but on 10 June FBI agents learned of another threat against King. The latest plot emerged from North Carolina, where a Klan leader told friends, "I'm going to Mississippi for the purpose of making sure Martin Luther King Jr. never reaches his destination. I've seen too many people bungle the job of killing King. I'm not going to bungle it. I'll kill him myself if no one beats me to it." G-men never found the would-be assassin, but while they were looking, more aggressive steps were taken by a group of Adams County Klansmen who styled themselves the Cottonmouth Moccasin Gang.[147]

The gang was Claude Fuller's brainchild, organized in May 1966, and its membership was strictly limited. The only other members named in subsequent reports were Natchez Klansmen James Lloyd Jones and Ernest Avants. Fellow knight James Greer heard rumors of the group, reporting that "[i]n order to get into this organization, you had to have killed a black." Their plan, on 10 June 1966, was to slay a victim picked at random, thereby luring Dr. King to Natchez and his death. They chose Ben Chester White, an elderly sharecropper, and requested that he help them find a missing dog. After driving White into the Homochitto National Forest, Fuller shot him with an automatic carbine, then Avants fired a shotgun point-blank at White's head. After tossing White's corpse from a bridge, they noticed that Jones's car was riddled with bullet holes and spattered with blood. They subsequently ditched the vehicle and torched it, certain they would never be identified.[148]

Police found White's body and the burned-out car on 12 June. They traced the vehicle to Jones, already named in HUAC hearings as a Klansman. Jones claimed his car was stolen while he worked at the International Paper factory, but police doubted his story and he failed a polygraph examination. Sitting in jail overnight, Jones experienced chest pains and feared for his life. Next morning, he confessed, naming his two accomplices. All three Klansmen were charged with murder, but justice took another strange detour. Jones was tried first, in December 1966, but jurors failed to reach a verdict despite his confession, resulting in a mistrial. Avants admitted the shooting to FBI agents in March 1967, but his statement was excluded at trial, nine months later. Lawyer Travis Buckley argued that White was dead before Avants shot him, already murdered by Fuller, and an all-white jury acquitted Avants. Fuller claimed illness, citing ulcers and arthritis, while his codefendants both refused to testify against him, leading to dismissal of all charges.[149]

Before White's killers went to court, the March Against Fear wound its way through Mississippi's countryside. Approaching Grenada on 14 June, marchers were greeted by a crude Klan message painted on the asphalt: "Red [sic] nigger and run. If you can't red run anyway." One week later, Dr. King led marchers into Philadelphia to celebrate the second anniversary of Neshoba's triple murder. While Cecil Price and town police stood idle, racists stoned the marchers in what King called "a complete breakdown of law and order." At the courthouse, King declared, "I believe in my heart that the murderers are somewhere around me at this moment." Flanking King, Cecil Price muttered, "You're damn right. They're behind you right now." That night, Klansmen roared through Philadelphia's ghetto, dubbed Independence Quarters, firing into homes. Blacks barricaded inside the local MFDP office returned fire, wounding one terrorist in the neck. The following night, blacks shot another raider as he hurled a firebomb at Canton's Freedom House. SNCC leader Stokeley

Carmichael brought more marchers to Philadelphia on 24 June, parading through another rain of bottles, stones, and eggs. Louisiana's well-armed Deacons for Defense and Justice drove to Jackson for the march's climax, on 26 June, but no further violence resulted.[150]

Mid-summer 1966 found Mississippi Klansmen torn between battling each other and their enemies outside the empire. Sam Bowers lost more members to the UKA, but Robert Shelton also had his problems. In late August, Edward McDaniel resigned or was fired (depending on who told the story), whereupon Shelton declared all state offices vacant and transferred control of the Magnolia realm back to his Tuscaloosa headquarters. Around the same time, dissident UKA members formed the Knights of the Green Forest, described by HUAC as "a small, militant group ... who left [the UKA] allegedly because of financial irregularities." Strangely, despite the conflict between Klans, Alabama attorney general Richmond Flowers told *Look* magazine that Shelton's group had asked the MWK "to rub me out as a fraternal favor." On other fronts, Neshoba County knights shot up the Nanih Wayia Mennonite Church, built near Coy in 1961 as a mission for Choctaws, and blasted the home of county school superintendent Jim Hurdle. Leake County raiders firebombed the home of a civil rights worker in Carthage. Obie Clark, chairman of Meridian's NAACP Education Committee, dodged bullets and received hate mail from various groups, including the Klan, the NSRP, and the National Socialist White People's Party.[151]

Grenada, home to a thriving UKA klavern, emerged as a hotbed of violence after the March Against Fear. Before the march, 697 local blacks were registered to vote, but that number nearly doubled in the two days demonstrators lingered. On 9 July two whites fired shots at an FBI agent and two civil rights workers outside a church. Police charged them with attempted murder on 10 July, but later reduced the charge to "pointing and aiming a weapon." Local jurors acquitted both defendants on 2 August, one week before 200 whites hurled bottles, bricks, and iron pipes at black demonstrators, injuring at least thirteen. On 12 September 1966, 400 racists armed with chains, pipes, and axe handles mobbed the first black students scheduled to attend Grenada's public schools. Police stood idle as three children were hospitalized, one with a broken leg. That night, 500 whites rallied at City Hall, one telling assembled councilmen, "You get the Highway Patrol out of here and in twenty-four hours there won't be a nigger left." On 13 September, after two more riots, Justice Department attorneys charged Grenada's mayor, city council, police chief, and Sheriff Suggs Ingram with "willful failure and refusal" to protect black students. A federal grand jury indicted eight defendants for conspiracy on 4 October, but white jurors acquitted them all at trial, in June 1967.[152]

Klansmen blamed Governor Johnson for enforcing integration of Grenada's schools. On 1 October 1966 a front-page article in the *Southern Review* declared: "To a white southerner, there can be no lower form of life than a scalawag.... [and] Paul B. Johnson ... is a scalawag.... Thirty years ago, Governor Johnson, the scalawag, would not have been allowed to sit in the Governor's chair in Jackson and perpetrate crime after crime against his State. The 'small bands' and 'toughs' and 'dividers' he vaguely and scornfully refers to were his supporters in 1963, only 3 years ago when he was elected as a 'segregationist.'" Jackson's APWR chapter circulated a petition seeking Johnson's impeachment for "high crimes and misdemeanors," but state legislators declined to oblige.[153]

Klan violence continued through year's end. In Philadelphia, on 1 September 1966, black patrolman Tripp Windham shot and killed a teenage boy, then fled town after he was fired. On 19 November, Natchez Klansmen firebombed a jewelry store and lobbed a grenade at a county supervisor's home. On 23 December bombers struck the Nanih Wayia Mennonite Church in Neshoba County. Congregants rebuilt the chapel, whereupon Klansmen bombed it again in February 1967.[154]

The Politics of Hate

News of the Mennonite bombing was lost amid international reports of the Klan's next sensational murder. Wharlest Jackson, a black father of six employed at Armstrong Rubber in Natchez, car-pooled with George Metcalfe after Metcalfe's near-murder in August 1965. As treasurer of the local NAACP, he also learned to check his pickup truck for bombs each day before he left the plant. On 25 February 1967 Jackson's employers promoted him to chemical-mixing, a previously "white" job that raised his pay by thirteen cents per hour. On 27 February Metcalfe worked a different shift and Jackson drove to work alone. Leaving the plant in pouring rain, he failed to check his truck and missed the time-delay bomb wedged beneath the driver's seat. Ten minutes later, it exploded, shattering his pickup, hurling Jackson's mangled body fifty yards away. FBI agents suspected the Silver Dollar Group but made no arrests. One G-man later told Don Whitehead, "Perhaps the perfect crime is one in which the killers are known, but you can't reach them for lack of substantive evidence."[155]

Charles Evers led protests at the Armstrong plant on 28 February, charging that the company had "harbored" Klansmen "for a long time." He called for a national boycott of

Wharlest Jackson's pickup truck, demolished by a fatal bomb in February 1967 (SPLC).

Armstrong tires and claimed that Mississippi racists had killed forty-one blacks since his brother was slain in June 1963. Armstrong executives offered $10,000 for the arrest of the bombers, topped by $25,000 from the city council. Following Jackson's funeral on 5 March, NAACP director Roy Wilkins told reporters, hopefully, "These killings are the tail end, we believe."[156]

A week before Jackson's murder, on 14 February 1967, Byron De La Beckwith announced his candidacy for lieutenant governor. He had lately moved to Jackson, earning $500 per month as a salesman for the Klan's *Southern Review*. Billing himself as "a candidate whose political position has already been established," Beckwith told voters, "I wish to express my heartfelt gratitude to the fine Christian people of Mississippi for the manner in which they have sustained and sheltered me in times past." Beckwith's campaign slogan—"He's a Straight-Shooter"—capitalized on his sole claim to fame, and Sam Bowers did his best to promote Beckwith's campaign, instructing Delmar Dennis to "take care of" Beckwith on his visits to Meridian. Beckwith himself denied Klan membership in public, but when asked about his murder case replied, "I don't think it will hurt me. Everybody knows how I feel about racial matters." In a typical campaign speech, he declared, "Everybody knows what my platform is. It's absolute white supremacy under Protestant Christian rule.... I'm not trying to please everybody; I don't want the nigger vote."[157]

Statewide, federal observers counted "slightly over 100 candidates" running for office with Ku Klux support in thirty-two counties. Jones County led the field with twenty-seven Klansmen seeking office, chief among them murder suspect Deavours Nix running for sheriff and Klan attorney Charles Blackwell seeking a seat in the state legislature. William Ferrell and Edward McDaniel vied for the sheriff's office in Adams County, while eleven other knights sought lesser posts. Informants embarrassed Ferrell by tipping G-men to his backwoods campaign meeting with fifteen hooded Klansmen. Rival knights Cecil Price (UKA) and Hop Barnett (MWK) found federal indictments no impediment to their bids for control of the Neshoba County sheriff's department. Grand Dragon Julius Harper ran for the state legislature from Copiah County, while Travis Buckley pursued a seat in Congress. Suspected murderer James Seale ran for sheriff in Franklin County.[158]

As usual, most pundits focused on the gubernatorial contest, where candidates included Ross Barnett, state treasurer William Winter, Rep. John Bell Williams (lately stripped of his seniority for scathing attacks on the national Democratic Party), ex-district attorney William Waller (who prosecuted Byron De La Beckwith), and radio disc jockey Jimmy Swan, running on a promise to establish "FREE, private, SEGREGATED SCHOOLS for every white child in the State of Mississippi." Swan's campaign bodyguard, Pat Massengale of Hattiesburg, served double duty with the Knights of the Green Forest. Paul Johnson, barred by law from succeeding himself, ran for lieutenant governor, ducking APWR broadsides that branded him "a turncoat from the day of his inauguration."[159]

The gubernatorial candidates adopted different strategies for dealing with the Ku Klux question. Jimmy Swan courted votes from the Klan and APWR, while Ross Barnett played coy: he welcomed invitations from the Citizens' Council and APWR, but when asked about the KKK, replied, "What Klan?" Bill Waller faced bomb threats and stench bombs when he spoke in Greenwood—coupled with pamphlets condemning his prosecution of Beckwith—and condemned Klan supporters in a speech before Laurel's Rotary Club. "The KKK is not alone to blame," he told that audience. "The work of these secret groups is protected by our silence. Their success is magnified by our fear. They speak for Mississippi only because brave men have been pressured into silence." A few weeks later, addressing the Citizens' Council in Jackson, Waller reassured nonviolent racists, saying, "I do endorse and support the ideals of state's rights and racial integrity as advocated by the Citizens' Council. I have been impressed by council literature in the past which emphasized peaceful means of resistance. I hope this will continue." Williams ignored the Klan entirely, running as a political martyr with fliers headlined "White Mississippi, Awake!"[160]

Black voters were a force to reckon with in 1967, their numbers inflated to 190,000 from a mere 28,500 in 1964. Conversely, white registration had also increased some 40 percent from 1960, when black ballots posed no challenge to the white supremacy. On primary day, Winter led Williams, while Swan, Barnett and Waller placed third, fourth, and fifth. Swan's 124,316 votes suggested the depth of hard-core racist sentiment in Mississippi, but Byron De La Beckwith's 34,675 ballots placed him fifth in a field of six candidates. Williams rebounded in the run-off, beating Winter by a margin of 61,288 votes, while twenty-one black candidates won various county-level offices statewide. Most Klansmen lost their races, although Hop Barnett and William Ferrell regained their sheriff's badges. In Adams County, where Ferrell held office until 1988 (then ceded power to his son), Grand Wizard Forrest's portrait remained on the sheriff's wall, while FBI reports noted wide-open gambling, bootlegging, and prostitution.[161]

Knights on Trial

On 28 March 1966 the U.S. Supreme Court unanimously reversed Judge Cox's dismissal of federal charges in the case of *U.S. v. Price, et al.* Cox stalled, telling reporters he had "no plans" for a trial. "This is just another lawsuit," he declared, "a common, ordinary, garden variety type lawsuit." Later, reluctantly, he scheduled trial to begin on 26 September, but defense attorneys recycled their motion from the Dahmer case, complaining that the grand jury which indicted their clients in January 1965 had illegally excluded blacks and women. On 6 October Cox dismissed both the conspiracy indictments *and* the charges filed against five Klan-affiliated lawmen for abusing prisoners.[162]

On 26 February 1967 a new federal grand jury indicted nineteen defendants in the Neshoba County case. The new charges omitted one teenager and one septuagenarian defendant from the first round, while adding three more: Sam Bowers, Hop Barnett, and Philadelphia patrolman Richard Willis. One day later, the same panel reindicted twelve of the original fifteen defendants charged in Vernon Dahmer's slaying. Judge Cox scheduled trial on the Neshoba charges for 26 May 1967, then pushed it back to 9 October.[163]

Before either case went to court, Klan lawyer Travis Buckley hatched a scheme to undermine the Dahmer prosecution. On 4 March 1967 he picked up ex-convict Jack Watkins and drove him into the wilds of Jackson County, where other Klansmen waited. Buckley then produced a tape recorder, demanding that Watkins confess to beating Lawrence Byrd and thus extracting his confession to the FBI. When Watkins refused to comply, Buckley held a knife to his throat while others aimed guns at his head and pretended to dig a grave. Finally, exasperated by his captive's defiance, Buckley drove Watkins home, telling the other knights, "He's an ex-con. He won't say anything."[164]

In fact, Watkins immediately called the state police and then the FBI. Based on his statements, Buckley and Dahmer defendant Billy Pitts were charged with conspiracy and obstructing justice. Federal jurors deadlocked at Buckley's trial, on 28 March 1967, whereupon Jackson County's grand jury indicted both Klansmen for kidnapping. Pitts, incensed that Sam Bowers supported Buckley while ignoring him, confessed participation in the kidnapping on 29 September. Aside from Buckley, Pitts named members of the kidnap team, including Bowers, Deavours Nix, and Cecil Sessum. At the same time, Pitts also gave a full confession to the Dahmer homicide.[165]

The Neshoba conspiracy trial convened before Judge Cox on 9 October 1967. Twelve attorneys, including Philadelphia mayor Clayton Lewis and a cousin of Klan victim Florence Mars, represented the defendants. James Jordan named members of the murder party; and prosecutor John Doar read Horace Barnette's confession aloud, after Cox ordered deletion of all names except Barnette's and Jordan's. Wallace Miller, already banished from the Klan, revealed himself as an FBI informant and named Preacher Killen as the murder plot's ringleader. The worst surprise for the defense was Delmar Dennis, breaking cover to describe the inner workings of the Klan in grim detail. He quoted Bowers, describing Michael Schwerner's slaying as "the first time that Christians planned and carried out the execution of a Jew." Dennis also embarrassed Mayor Lewis, describing a Klan rally held in his pasture, where Lewis greeted Klansmen "at the gate." Lewis called for a mistrial, but Judge Cox refused.[166]

The defense responded on two fronts. One tack assailed the FBI's informants for accepting money to violate the Klan's oath of secrecy. Wallace Miller admitted receiving $2,400 from FBI agents, while Dennis acknowledged banking $5,000 per year from the Bureau. The second angle of attack involved defaming Michael Schwerner, branding him a radical and worse. Judge Cox turned livid after lawyer Laurel Weir asked CORE activist Charles Johnson "if you and Mr. Schwerner didn't advocate and try to get young male Negroes to sign statements agreeing to rape a white woman a week during the hot summer of '64." Attorney Herman Alford named the question's source as "Brother Killen," whereupon Judge Cox declared, "I'm not going to allow a farce to be made of this trial and everybody might as well get that through your heads, including every one of the defendants, right now.... I'm surprised at a question like that coming from a preacher, too. I'm talking about Killen, or whatever his name is."[167]

Jurors retired on 18 October to consider their verdict. Behind closed doors, one member of the panel declared that she would never convict Preacher Killen, since her conscience forbade imprisoning a minister. On 19 October the jury reported a deadlock, but Judge Cox instructed them to try again. That order, sometimes called the "dynamite charge," prompted defendant Alton Roberts to threaten Cox. Outside the courtroom, Roberts told Cecil Price, "Judge Cox just gave that jury a 'dynamite charge.' We've got some dynamite for them ourselves." On 20 October the panel returned guilty verdicts on seven defendants (including Bowers, Price, and Roberts), acquitted eight, and deadlocked on three (Killen, Hop Barnett, and Jerry Sharpe). Following the verdicts, Judge Cox briefed those convicted on their options for appeal, then revoked bond for Roberts and Price.[168] Cox addressed the startled pair:

> If you think you can intimidate this court, you are as badly mistaken as you can be. I'm not going to let any wild man loose on a civilized society and I want you locked up. I don't think you have taken this thing very seriously, and I'm going to give you an oppor-

tunity to think very seriously about it. I very heartily endorse the verdict of this jury, particularly adjudging Mr. Roberts as guilty.[169]

At sentencing, on 29 December 1967, Bowers and Roberts received the maximum ten-year term, Price and Billy Posey each got six years, while Horace Barnette, Jimmy Snowden, and Jimmy Arledge received three-year terms. Martin Luther King called the Neshoba trial "a first step in a thousand-mile journey," while Judge Cox reverted to type. When a reporter asked about the sentences, Cox said, "They killed one nigger, one Jew, and a white man. I gave them all what I thought they deserved." Sam Bowers, confined to the Jones County jail on $10,000 bond pending appeal, issued new orders for another reign of terror.[170]

Confronting Terror

Three weeks before trial convened in Meridian, on 18 September 1967, night riders bombed Jackson's Temple Beth Israel, inflicting $25,000 damage. Unknown to law enforcement at the time, the bombers were a true Odd Couple of the ultra-right, Kathy Ainsworth and Thomas Albert Tarrants III. Ainsworth, née Capomachia, was a bride of one month who taught fifth grade at Jackson's Duling Elementary School. Raised in Miami by her anti–Semitic mother, who introduced her to the works of Gerald L.K. Smith, she attended Mississippi College in Clinton, where she roomed with the daughter of Sidney Barnes, a disciple of Klansman and neo-Nazi Wesley Swift. She often heard Swift's sermons played at Barnes' home, and met Tarrants on a visit to the Barnes family in 1964 after they moved to Mobile, Alabama.[171]

A Mobile native, born in 1947, Tarrants studied right-wing propaganda from the John Birch Society, then graduated to the Klan, NSRP, and the paramilitary Minutemen. He logged his first arrest in 1963 for leading violent protests against integration of his high school, then dropped out in February 1964 to work for Mobile's NSRP chapter, moonlighting with threatening phone calls to local blacks and Jews. As leader of his own Christian Military Defense League, Tarrants fantasized "distributing the dismembered body of a key black leader around the black community" and booby-trapping the body parts. August 1964 saw him arrested, in possession of a sawed-off shotgun, after assaulting a black gas station attendant.

In summer 1967 he visited Robert Shelton in Tuscaloosa, then moved to Laurel, Mississippi, in August, around the time Kathy Capomachia married Ralph Ainsworth and embarked on a honeymoon to Gerald Smith's Christ of the Ozarks compound in Arkansas. After spending his income from holdups in Mobile and Jackson, Tarrants found work as a janitor at the Masonite plant and offered his services to Sam Bowers as a "guerrilla for God." Kathy Ainsworth, already a member of the MWK and APWR, joined Tarrants to plan and carry out the Jackson synagogue bombing in September.[172]

Tarrants arrived in Laurel as the Masonite plant endured a bitter strike, sparked by automation and reduction of its labor force. Strikers and "scabs" fought hand to hand at the factory gates, killing one security guard, while bombers wrecked the plant's railroad tracks and water line. Masonite broke the strike by firing everyone involved, hiring college students on an interim basis, then luring black workers back to the plant with claims that

Klansmen directed the strike. If Tarrants joined in the mayhem, a subject he has not discussed, it would have served him as a training ground.[173]

Within two hours of the synagogue bombing, FBI agents approached the home of Joe Denver Hawkins, a militant Klansman who sat on the APWR's board of directors. They found him with son Joe Daniel "Danny Joe" Hawkins and MWK Grand Dragon Julius Harper. All three wound up in jail, charged with impeding and threatening G-men "by means and use of automobiles and a dangerous weapon, that is, a pistol." The charges were later dismissed without trial.[174]

Federal agents viewed the Hawkins clan, including its women, as "the meanest Klan family in Mississippi," natural suspects for any terrorist event. Sam Bowers ranked Danny Joe among his most trusted night riders and was duly impressed by his criminal record that ultimately listed thirteen arrests between 1963 and 1980. By 1967 Danny Joe faced charges of wounding a black man, beating one civil rights worker, and shooting at others—all without a conviction. Both father and son habitually carried firearms, while father Joe had access to dynamite through his construction work. Still, despite their records and the crimes they would commit thereafter, they were innocent in the synagogue case.[175]

On 6 October 1967 bombers struck the home of Dr. William Bush, a white professor at Tougaloo College whom Klansmen suspected of keeping a black mistress. On 15 November dynamite damaged the home of the Rev. Allen Johnson, an NAACP leader and pastor of St. Paul's Church in Laurel. Four nights later, night riders blasted the Jackson home of Robert Kochtitzky, another civil rights activist. On 21 November it was Rabbi Perry Nussbaum's turn, as bombers knocked his home off its foundation. The following day, fifty Jewish leaders met at a motel in Jackson to discuss the mounting reign of terror. Some advocated killing suspects Joe Denver and Danny Joe Hawkins, but a majority vetoed the plan in favor of raising rewards for the arrest of the bombers.[176]

On 20 December a constable in Collins found Sam Bowers and Thomas Tarrants sitting in a car, with Alabama license plates, parked at a gas station that had closed for the night. An illegal submachine gun lay in plain view on the backseat. The constable summoned state police and FBI agents, who arrested Tarrants on federal firearms charges. He posted bond, fled to Mobile and enrolled in community college, then dropped out and drove to California for "a fruitful week and a half" spent with Wesley Swift and West Coast Minutemen coordinator Dennis Mower. Tarrants bought a rifle from Swift in hopes of killing Martin Luther King, a project he called "my ambition." Back in Mobile on 23 March 1968, Tarrants found FBI agents watching his home, but he escaped unseen. His long flight from the law took him through North Carolina and Florida, sheltered en route by disciples of Swift. Back in Jackson, after robbing a supermarket of $4,279 at gunpoint, he penned a note reading: "Please be advised that since March 28, 1968 I Thomas A. Tarrants have been underground and operating guerrilla warfare."[177]

The Klan had not been idle in his absence. Meridian suffered its own localized reign of terror, beginning in March 1967, when drive-by shooters blasted the homes of a black dentist and a Project Head Start bus driver. Arsonists torched five black churches within as many weeks, prompting "shoot to kill" orders from police chief Roy Gunn. Born in 1904, Gunn served fifteen years with the Meridian Police Department before he was named chief in 1965, over the opposition of assistant chief Sam Keller. Keller was a Klan supporter and the brother of a Klansman, also a murder suspect who shot his mistress while "cleaning his gun." Gunn, already named on Klan blacklists, learned in 1967 that he was included on a list of targets marked for execution. He then required all of his officers to sign an oath denying membership in "subversive" organizations. Some resigned in protest, while others, in Gunn's words, "just lied and signed it." After Klansmen burned Wallace Miller's grocery story on 20 February 1968, Sergeant Lester Joyner formed a "blackshirt squad," nicknamed "Joyner's Guerrillas," to respond in kind. Lacking sufficient evidence to make arrests, the officers fired into Klansmen's homes and detonated small explosive charges on their lawns.[178]

While Meridian monopolized headlines, violence continued in Jackson. On 7 March 1968 Klansmen bombed the Blackwell Real Estate office, whose agents sold "white" homes to blacks. Senator Eastland, roused from his torpor by attacks on white constituents, pressured old friend J. Edgar Hoover to suppress the terror, but G-men could only do so much. A Klansman confessed to the Blackwell bombing, naming Danny Joe Hawkins as a participant, but white jurors acquitted Hawkins at trial.[179]

On 4 April 1968 a sniper killed Dr. Martin Luther King in Memphis, Tennessee. Two weeks elapsed before the FBI identified a suspect from his fingerprints, recovered near the crime scene. In the meantime, Klansmen everywhere were suspect because of the plots they had hatched against King since he first rose to prominence in 1955. Georgia lawyer, Klansman, and NSRP founder Jesse Stoner often called for King's assassination, but he had an airtight alibi on 4 April: being shadowed by FBI agents as he addressed Meridian's NSRP chapter at a Klansman's barbershop.

On 22 April G-men received information from Myrtis Hendricks, a waitress at John's Café in Laurel, suggesting that owner Deavours Nix and the MWK were involved in King's murder. According to Hendricks, Nix "had gotten a call on King" on 2 April. The following day, Hendricks saw two men remove a rifle from Nix's office and place it in car. On 4 April Nix allegedly received a call announcing King's murder, before the event was broadcast via normal news outlets. According to FBI files, unspecified statements from Sam Bowers on 5 April also "raised the possibility of his involvement in the assassination." Hendricks quit her job and fled to Texas, where she contacted FBI agents. The Bureau, already familiar with Nix and John's Café, "found no corroboration of the Hendricks rifle story" and dismissed her claims. A decade later, Hendricks recanted her statement in testimony before the House Select Committee on Assassinations.[180]

King's final legacy was the 1968 Civil Rights Act, passed by Congress on 10 April 1968 and signed by President Johnson the following day. One provision of the new law made it a federal crime to interfere with civil rights workers. That carried no weight in Meridian, where Alton Roberts divided his time between the Klan and the NSRP; his wife served as the NSRP's secretary, mailing its *Thunderbolt* newsletter to local Jews. On 2 May 1968 night riders machine-gunned the home of an NAACP member and Head Start employee, wounding her six-year-old niece. On 26 May, Tarrants and Danny Joe Hawkins bombed Meridian's Temple Beth Israel.[181]

The synagogue bombings produced cries of outrage from Mississippians who normally ignored Klan violence against blacks and "outsiders." As FBI agent Frank Watts told reporter Jack Nelson, "Once the Jews were attacked it was a different ball game. This wasn't just a local across-the-railroad-track case. It involved the whole United States." George Mitchell, Mississippi state president of B'nai B'rith, solicited donations to help G-men buy an informer close to the bombers. In Meridian, agent Jim Ingram branded local Klansmen "animals" and "murderers," telling his fellow agents to "just go out and pound on them until you get some results."[182]

G-men already had their sights on L.E. Matthews, a Jackson electrical contractor identified as the MWK's top bomb maker and heir apparent to the wizard's throne if Sam Bowers went to prison. A friend of Byron De La Beckwith and Danny Joe Hawkins, Matthews divided his free time between the Klan and the NSRP; but he proved immune to federal bribes. Not so the Roberts brothers, Alton and Raymond, who agreed to betray their fellow Klansmen for $30,000. On 19 June the brothers met Danny Joe Hawkins and arranged a raid on the home of Meridian Jewish leader Meyer Davidson. Hawkins and Thomas Tarrants failed to show on the first target date, eight days later, but Joyner's Guerrillas were ready and waiting when bombers approached Davidson's house on 29 June.[183]

The result was a chaotic running battle through the streets that climaxed when Tarrants crashed his car and tried to flee on foot, still firing at police. Joyner's Guerrillas admitted intent to kill Tarrants, but he survived critical wounds, as did one lawman and a neighborhood bystander. Kathy Ainsworth died in the ambush, pistol in hand, her handbag containing business cards from Sam Bowers, L.E. Matthews, the APWR, and Gerald Smith's Christian Nationalist Crusade. In his pocket, Tarrants carried a list of eighteen other targets, including Charles Evers, Aaron Henry, and two ministers in Selma, Alabama. Tarrants spent thirty-one days in the hospital, then transferred to Lauderdale County's jail, where police arrested his visiting father armed with a carbine and carrying a slip of paper with Danny Joe Hawkins' name and telephone number. At trial, in November 1968, Tarrants received a thirty-year prison term. Five more years were added in 1969, after Tarrants briefly escaped from prison with aid from Hawkins and other Klansmen. Tarrants "found Jesus" in prison the following year (around the time journalist Jack Nelson broke the story of the FBI's involvement in the Meridian ambush, thereby earning a place on J. Edgar Hoover's personal enemies list).[184]

State and federal authorities enjoyed more conventional, albeit mixed success against the Klan in early 1968, with prosecution of the Vernon Dahmer case. In January federal prosecutors charged a new defendant, Charles Clifford Wilson of Laurel, with conspiracy in Dahmer's death. A local businessman and Boy Scout leader who won the Laurel Jaycees' Distinguished Service Award the week before his indictment, Wilson had publicly denounced Dahmer's killers in 1966 as "vicious and morally bankrupt individuals." Now, he was named as one of the murder team and was soon indicted with Bowers and nine other Klansmen on state charges of murder and arson.[185]

Trials proceeded first in the state courts, for the Dahmer slaying and the Jack Watkins kidnapping. Defense attorneys challenged testimony from informants Billy Pitts and Delmar Dennis, further claiming that FBI agents poisoned Dahmer in his hospital bed on orders from President Johnson. Travis Buckley received a ten-year kidnapping sentence in February 1968, but Mississippi's supreme court overturned that conviction on appeal and Buckley served no time. Jurors convicted Cecil Sessum of murder on 15 March 1968, resulting in a life sentence. A second panel deadlocked at the murder trial of Henry De Boxtel, on 21 March. Sam Bowers enjoyed three mistrials between May 1968 and January 1969, while Lawrence Byrd received a ten-year prison term for arson. William Smith was convicted of murder and sentenced to life on 19 July 1968. Charles Wilson's jury hung for a mistrial nine days later, but he was convicted and sentenced to life in a second trial. James Lyons won a mistrial on 14 November 1968. In the midst of those proceedings, enraged by Klan threats, Forrest County prosecutor James Duke and his brother, an FBI agent, invaded a Ku Klux saloon at high noon and "called out" their abusers, none of whom opted to fight.[186]

Results in federal court were less impressive. Lawrence Byrd's judge declared a mistrial on grounds that testimony offered by a prosecution witness "could prejudice jurors' minds." Subsequent juries deadlocked at the trials of Sam Bowers, Deavours Nix, Charles Wilson, Cecil Sessum, and three other defendants. Separate panels acquitted Klansmen Travis Giles, James Lyons, and Lester Thornton. Prosecutors dismissed all charges against Mordaunt Hamilton in April 1969, while defendant Emanuel Moss won an indefinite continuance on grounds of poor health.[187]

The big loser, according to FBI-sponsored author Don Whitehead, was Billy Pitts. On 8 March 1968 he pled guilty to murder and arson, receiving a life prison term. He subsequently pled guilty on federal conspiracy charges and to kidnapping Jack Watkins, thereby receiving two more five-year terms. In 1970 Whitehead reported that those several sentences were "being served"—but that claim was not strictly true. Almost thirty years later, the *Clarion-Ledger* revealed that Pitts had served a portion of his federal time but never spent a night in state prison.[188]

Ending the "Second Reconstruction"

Most Americans viewed segregation as a lost cause by 1968, but Alabama's George Wallace was not among them. Running for the White House once again, this time on behalf of the far-right American Independent Party, Wallace combined old-fashioned racism, thinly disguised by "law-and-order" rhetoric, with hawkish foreign policy to woo a broader audience. It worked in Mississippi, where, despite 264,000 registered black voters, Wallace carried 63.5 percent of all ballots cast on 5 November 1968. Four other southern states gave Wallace their electors, thereby helping Republican Richard Nixon defeat Vice President Hubert Humphrey.[189]

In other races, Klansman L.E. Matthews lost his bid for a seat in the state legislature, while Charles Evers ran for Congress, leading his primary field with 40,000 mostly black votes. The Klan immediately put a $15,000 bounty on his head, vowing to kill Evers before election day, but state lawmakers used a different method to restrain him. New legislation mandated a run-off vote if primaries produced no clear winner, and Evers lost the second round when white voters turned out en masse to crush his hopes.[190]

Eight days after the presidential vote, on 13 November 1968, Sam Bowers and the MWK suffered another blow. Frustrated by the failure of state prosecutors to convict his father's killers, Jesse White of Natchez slapped the White Knights with a wrongful-death claim for the murder of Ben White in 1966. The case played out in federal court, where Judge Cox ruled against the Klan and ordered it to pay $1,021,500 in damages. White's family never saw a cent, but the symbolic victory served once again to damage Klan prestige in the Magnolia State.[191]

Another round of elections inspired black candidates and voters in spring 1969. Statewide, 155 African Americans sought public office in 52 cities and towns, 18 of them defeating white opponents on election day. White supremacists refrained from violence but posted signs in various establishments from Fayette to Bay St. Louis, declaring that "All Proceeds from Sales to Niggers Will Be Donated to the Ku Klux Klan." Charles Evers was the season's stand-out winner, defeating Fayette Mayor R.J. Allen by 341 of 641 ballots cast. Sworn in on 3 July, Evers became the foremost black politician in Mississippi.[192]

Klan threats against Evers, a constant since his brother's murder six years earlier, increased dramatically after he was installed as mayor, peaking when Evers ordered a statue of his brother to replace Fayette's traditional bronze Confederate soldier. On 10 September 1969 several anonymous callers warned Evers of an active plot against his life, describing the would-be assassin's car. Evers hit the streets with Fayette's newly appointed black police chief, quickly spotting the car and its driver, Tupelo grocer Dale Walton, a friend of Byron De La Beckwith who deemed the KKK "too liberal" and so defected to lead the Knights of the Green Forest. A search of Walton's car revealed three shotguns, one carbine, and one pistol. Questioned as to his motive, Walton told his captors, "I'm a Mississippi white man."[193]

While Walton sat in jail, unable to produce $10,000 bail, phone tips sent Treasury agents to nab his cohorts who had an illegal submachine gun, at a Natchez motel. Defendant Pat Massengale had served as candidate Jimmy Swan's bodyguard during the 1967 gubernatorial campaign. At the time of his latest arrest, Massengale also was under federal indictment for jury-tampering in the Dahmer conspiracy case. At trial, the three Klansmen received forty-five-day jail terms and were fined $329 each for violating the 1968 Gun Control Act.[194]

The Mississippi White Knights faded into limbo in the latter half of 1969. On 17 July the Fifth Circuit Court of Appeals affirmed the Neshoba conspiracy convictions. Only the U.S. Supreme Court remained, but that body declined to review the case on 27 February 1970. Between those events, on 21 October 1969, Byron De La Beckwith telephoned a covert FBI informant in Florida, introducing himself as a mutual friend of a UKA official in South Carolina. They met at a restaurant, where Beckwith identified himself as a member of a new Mississippi Klan group, the White Knights of the Camellia, then launched into a sales pitch for "guerrilla-type warfare" directed at Jews. According to Beckwith, Sam Bowers sought to form a new alliance whose activities would range from "burning Jewish homes and bombing Jewish synagogues" to "pouring plaster of Paris down the commode of Jewish-owned establishments, restaurants, and such." The informant told G-men that Beckwith spoke "brightly" of "killing certain Jews, Negroes, and extremely liberal whites." Jewish children should be killed "more quickly than elderly Jews," Beckwith said, since the latter could not breed.[195]

Whether or not Beckwith spoke for Bowers, the new campaign never materialized. Eight days after Beckwith's tirade, the Supreme Court abandoned its doctrine of "all deliberate speed" and commanded that Mississippi schools desegregate "at once." Another federal court banned state subsidies to the APWR's all-white academy in Natchez, where public schools desegregated without further violence. On 20 March 1970 the "Neshoba Seven" defendants surrendered and were scattered to federal lockups across the country. Despite Bowers' appointment of L.E. Matthews to lead the MWK in his absence, one White Knight later told author Patsy Sims that the Klan's remaining members burned their robes and disbanded.[196]

CHAPTER 6

"Yesterday, Today, Forever"
(1970–2007)

As Sam Bowers and his Neshoba codefendants exhausted their federal appeals in 1970, some Mississippi whites believed the worst was finally behind them. State convictions in the Dahmer case, the ambush in Meridian, and the decisive (although ultimately fruitless) victory of Ben White's family in their lawsuit against the KKK suggested that the Klan — if not its spirit — had been beaten down for good. Black residents of the Magnolia State were not so easily convinced. And, as they soon discovered, with good reason.

Bullets and Ballots (1970–1972)

Old-style racist violence persisted in the "new" Mississippi. On 12 April 1970 a white mob beat one-armed sharecropper Rainey Pool outside a bar in Louise (Humphreys County), then dumped him into the Sunflower River and left him to drown. Police found his corpse two days later and detained four suspects, one of whom confessed. Indictments followed, but a judge dismissed them on grounds that the confession was improperly obtained. One month later, on 14 May, Jackson police and highway patrolmen fired on unarmed students at all-black Jackson State College, killing two and wounding twelve more. Highway patrol inspector Lloyd "Goon" Jones summoned ambulances to the scene with a radio announcement that "We got some niggers dyin'."[1]

Mississippi's gubernatorial primary season was well underway on 25 May 1971, when drive-by gunmen in Drew killed black teenager Jo Etha Collier on the night of her graduation from a newly integrated high school. Police charged three suspects with murder on 26 May, but sent only triggerman Wesley Parks to trial. He received a five-year sentence on conviction, but served less than three years. Most observers described the shooting as "senseless," but activist Fannie Lou Hamer declared herself "convinced Collier's death was connected with the current voter registration campaign." NAACP spokesman Aaron Henry wired President Nixon to protest a "wave of senseless killing in Mississippi of black citizens by white citizens," complaining that Collier's murder was the "third such killing in less than a week."[2]

The year's gubernatorial candidates ignored recent violence while striking various postures on race. Jimmy Swan warned voters that "[w]e must not allow our children to be sacrificed on the filthy atheistic altar of integration." He brandished Theodore Bilbo's tract

Segregation or Mongrelization at rallies, declaring that "every word he said has come true." Judge Marshall Perry said to his audiences, "I am not ready to surrender. All this talk about getting back into the mainstream. We are already in the mainstream. It's the other people, the enemies of Mississippi, who have departed from the mainstream." Lieutenant Governor Charles Sullivan vowed that blacks "will be able to live in dignity in my Mississippi," while ex-prosecutor William Waller joined Sullivan in a promise of fair employment for all.[3]

In August's first primary, Sullivan beat Waller by a margin of 60,795 votes. Swan ran third with 128,946 ballots (an increase of 4,585 over his 1967 total), while Perry trailed the field. With three weeks left before the second primary, Waller elevated fence-straddling to an art form, defending all-white "seg academies" while simultaneously promising an "administration without bigotry." Charles Evers praised Waller's moderation, yet the Klan also supported him, perhaps because Waller had filed Charles Wilson's unsuccessful appeal in the Dahmer slaying. An unnamed FBI informant also claimed that Sullivan had promised freedom for all imprisoned Mississippi Klansmen within one year of his inauguration. Waller, the informant said, had vowed to free them in six months. Despite support from the Hederman newspaper chain, Sullivan lost September's primary to Waller by 60,716 votes.[4]

Primary victory assured Waller's election in November, but he was not running unopposed. After supporting Waller in the primaries, Charles Evers filed against him as an independent candidate, and thus inspired aging Tom Brady to take one last fling on an unabashed racist platform. Ex-Klansmen Edward McDaniel and L.C. Murray astounded their former comrades by supporting Evers, joining him for a Fayette fund-raiser where they joined hands to sing "We Shall Overcome." Fifty-nine percent of Mississippi's eligible blacks were registered to vote in 1971— some 268,000 in all — but they still comprised only 28 percent of the state's electorate. On 2 November William Waller defeated both rivals; Evers received 172,762 votes, while Brady claimed only 6,653. In the lieutenant governor's race, progressive candidate William Winter easily defeated both future governor Charles Finch and *Southern Review* editor Elmore Greaves. Statewide, fifty-one blacks won election to various local positions.[5]

Once in office, Governor Waller pleased conservatives by gutting Head Start and other federal programs, but his motives may not have been racial. Greenville's Hodding Carter III opined that "Waller wants to control every federal buck he can coming into the state. Power is his first motive." Conversely, Waller vetoed funding for the State Sovereignty Commission in April 1973, a first step toward that body's ultimate dissolution in January 1977. And if Waller had promised freedom to convicted Klansmen, he soon forgot all but one of them: in 1972 former client Charles Wilson received two back-to-back ninety-day furloughs from prison, then gained entry to a full-time work-release program at Southern Mississippi State Hospital. Reporters exposed those acts of favoritism and broadcast Waller's alleged primary-eve vow to the Klan, but Waller ignored them and served out his term, then returned to private practice in 1976.[6]

The 1972 presidential campaign renewed Mississippi's drift into the right-wing Republican column after gunman Arthur Bremer crippled independent favorite George Wallace in Maryland on 15 May. In November, Mississippi gave 78 percent of its votes to incumbent Richard Nixon, thereby participating in his landslide victory over Democrat George

McGovern. After four years' service as an aide to congressman William Colmer in Washington, Trent Lott abandoned the party of his forefathers and rode Nixon's coattails to claim his former boss's seat in the House of Representatives.[7]

Hard Times (1973–1975)

One Klansman who did not mellow with age was self-proclaimed assassin Byron De La Beckwith. After losing his race for lieutenant governor, he joined the Liberty Lobby, an anti–Semitic group based in Washington, D.C., that welcomed Tom Brady as a policy advisor. Beckwith also visited his fellow MWK members, confined at Parchman prison for the Dahmer slaying, and campaigned for their release. In early September 1973 he attended a Citizens' Council rally in Jackson, cheering a racist speech by Alabama's George Wallace.[8]

Two weeks later, on 18 September, Mississippi informant Gordon Clark alerted his FBI handlers to a new bombing plot. The target, A.I. Botnick of New Orleans, served as regional director of the Anti-Defamation League (ADL). Agents alerted New Orleans police, while Clark (allegedly unknown to G-men) also warned Al Binder, one of Jackson's leading Jewish businessmen. On 26 September agents trailed Beckwith to the Mayflower Café, where he placed telephone calls to Clark, Elmore Greaves, and L.E. Matthews. Greaves was not at home, but Clark and Matthews soon arrived, Matthews carrying a bomb which he passed to Beckwith in a paper bag. G-men observed the hand-off, as did Binder, watching from a nearby booth. Agents made no arrests.[9]

At 12:02 A.M. on 27 September — the first day of Rosh Hashanah, celebrating the Jewish New Year — police stopped Beckwith's car on the outskirts of New Orleans. Aside from a pistol tucked under his belt, they found a time bomb with six sticks of dynamite, a carbine, a hunting knife, detached barrels for a rifle and a .50-caliber machine gun, extra ammunition, a box of antique china, and a map of New Orleans with markings that led to A.I. Botnick's home. Initially jailed on concealed weapons charges, Beckwith admitted his prior arrest: "They say I killed a nigger in Mississippi." When asked if he was a Klansman, Beckwith replied, "I've been accused of it. Thank you for your interest."[10]

On 1 October a judge set bond at $150,000 and declared Beckwith indigent. Eight days later, federal prosecutors indicted Beckwith on three counts: possessing an unregistered "destructive device," possessing a bomb with no serial numbers, and carrying a firearm during commission of a felony. Greenwood's civic leaders rallied to Beckwith's defense once again. On 20 October an unnamed businessman paid $36,000 in cash to secure his release, while the mayor, ex-sheriff, and a justice of the peace guaranteed Beckwith's bond. A Leflore County planter flew Beckwith home on his private plane, since De La's car was impounded in New Orleans. Mississippi UKA members launched a fund-raising drive, promising $50,000 for Beckwith's defense, but they never reached their goal. Beckwith himself mailed countless letters soliciting donations for his fight against "a plot to Abolish Beckwith."[11]

Beckwith's trial began on 14 January 1974. An ADL staffer testified that Beckwith had visited the New Orleans office twelve days before his arrest, asking questions about Botnick's schedule. Police described their warnings from the FBI and Beckwith's subsequent arrest. Beckwith claimed that he was in New Orleans to sell his new wife's china (once owned by Jefferson Davis), and that he was unaware of the bomb in his car. Defense witnesses L.E. Matthews and Gordon Clark (still under cover for the Bureau) described their ninety-minute lunch with Beckwith on 26 September, suggesting that others could have planted the bomb in his car while they dined, to murder or frame him. Deprived of Clark's inside knowledge, the integrated jury acquitted Beckwith of all charges on 20 January. Judge Jack Gordon, visibly shocked by the verdict, told Beckwith, "You have literally walked through the valley of the shadow of death."[12]

On 31 January 1974 New Orleans district attorney Harry Connick Sr. announced plans to try Beckwith on state charges of illegally transporting explosives. That trial began on 15 May 1975, before Judge Charles Ward and a jury made up of five black women. Defense attorneys Travis Buckley and Harold Wheeler waived opening statements based on "the presumption of innocence" and called Beckwith to repeat his tale of peddling china in New Orleans. This time, however, jurors failed to buy the frame-up argument. Convicted on 16 May and sentenced to the maximum five-year prison term on 1 August 1975, Beckwith remained free on $10,000 bond pending appeal.[13]

Over the next two years, while his case wound its way through various appellate courts, Beckwith maintained his correspondence with pen pals, including Sam Bowers and Richard Butler, head of the Aryan Nations, who praised Beckwith as "a great Warrior for Christ." In September 1976 he participated in a five-day World Nationalist Congress staged in New Orleans by Klansmen Jesse Stoner, David Duke, James Warner, and others. A month later, Beckwith abandoned his Methodist faith and joined Warner's New Christian Crusade Church, espousing the racist and anti–Semitic tenets of "Christian Identity." On 2 January 1977 the Rev. Buddy Tucker—founder of a group called National Emancipation of the White Seed—ordained Beckwith as a minister of his Temple Memorial Baptist Church, an Identity congregation based in Knoxville, Tennessee.[14]

Louisiana's supreme court upheld Beckwith's conviction on 28 February 1977, but Travis Buckley filed petitions for a second hearing. On 23–24 April, while FBI agents studied reports of Beckwith's plan to found a new Klan in Mississippi, he attended a KKK rally in Pennsylvania. From there, Beckwith moved on to Washington, D.C., lodging with Pauline Mackey of the Liberty Lobby and seeking help from James Eastland on a scheme to sell oil filters to the Pentagon. Louisiana issued a fugitive warrant for Beckwith on 26 April, and FBI informants directed G-men to Mackey's apartment three days later.

Returned to the Pelican State in shackles, Beckwith entered Angola state prison on 18 May 1977 and spent the next thirty-two months in solitary confinement for his own protection. Jesse Stoner visited from time to time, bringing cash, and Beckwith befriended inmate Paul Scheppf, an ex–Marine and Klansman jailed for manslaughter. From prison, Beckwith wrote to National Alliance leader William Pierce: "There is still work to be done by those of us who aren't too liberal to survive, and I can't do what needs doing while I'm in here." With time off for good behavior, Beckwith was released on 13 January 1980, and he returned to his Greenwood mobile home.[15]

Beckwith was not the only Mississippi Klansman suffering hard times in the mid–1970s. Joe Denver Hawkins died in 1974, victim of what his family called "a nigger robbery," and son Danny Joe received a three-year federal prison term for firearms violations that same year, serving thirty months. Also in 1974, Edgar Killen telephoned threats to a woman whose husband he suspected of adultery. Unaware that his call was being tape-recorded,

Killen said, "That son of a bitch will be dead at 8 o'clock, you hear? Folks die for things he did. You understand that? I don't make any mistakes and get the wrong man.... Would you be satisfied with him if somebody would bring him home where you wouldn't recognize him for a week? I want that revenge. I like revenge." Before embarking on a five-month jail term in 1976, Killen granted an interview to author Patsy Sims. On that occasion, Killen denied Klan membership, blamed bombings of "old dilapidated churches" on "outsiders or some leaders of the civil rights movement," and claimed that prosecutors in the Neshoba triple murder "never did prove they found the bodies."[16]

Meanwhile, incidents of Klan-type violence continued. Obie Clark, president of Meridian's NAACP chapter, suspected Klansmen in the deaths of five black Kemper County residents. The first case, in October 1974, involved a man and his three children who reportedly died from accidental carbon monoxide poisoning. Authorities blamed epilepsy for another black man's death, in July 1975, but Clark and a local mortician insisted that all five victims were lynched. The Justice Department rebuffed Clark's complaint with a denial of federal jurisdiction.[17]

Reviving the Empire (1975–1977)

The latter 1970s witnessed a brisk revival of the Ku Klux Klan, initiated by Louisiana's David Duke. An Oklahoma native born in 1950, Duke move to New Orleans with his family in the early 1960s. He entered Louisiana State University in 1968 and there organized the White Youth Alliance, later known as the National Party, collaborating with members of the National Socialist Liberation Front and the National Socialist White People's Party. Duke donned a full-dress Nazi uniform to picket various events on campus and logged two arrests in 1972 for manufacturing firebombs and embezzling money from the Wallace presidential campaign. (Neither charge resulted in conviction.) By 1973 Duke was Louisiana grand dragon for Jim Lindsay's Knights of the KKK. Following Lindsay's (still-unsolved) murder in June 1975, Duke assumed control of the Klan and changed his title from imperial wizard to "national director."[18]

Duke promoted the Klan like no leader before him, barnstorming the media talk-show circuit and presenting his Klan as a nonviolent "civil rights group" for white Christians whose religious "cross-lightings" bore no taint of intimidation. He welcomed Catholics, admitted women to full membership for the first time in Ku Klux history, proselytized among military personnel, and created a Klan Youth Corps for members seventeen and younger. The technique paid dividends, as 2,700 supporters turned out for a 1975 rally in Walker, Louisiana, and third-term governor George Wallace named Duke an honorary colonel of the Alabama state militia. In November 1977 the *Hattiesburg American* gave Duke front-page coverage, under the headline "Ku Klux Klan Turns to Slick Public Relations Strategy to Reach Goals."

Meanwhile, in private, Duke held strategy sessions with Robert Shelton, fugitive Minutemen leader Robert DePugh, and American Nazi Party alumnus James Warner, while peddling Nazi literature and telling his Klansmen, "We say give us liberty and give them [blacks] death." Duke also supported Byron De La Beckwith, calling him "a political prisoner" and "one of the most selfless patriots in this nation" who "should serve as an heroic

DAVID DUKE FOR GOVERNOR
A <u>Real Choice</u> for a Change

Cut the Fat, No Tax Increases

Louisiana has the highest personal tax rate of any Southern state, higher taxes than even Teddy Kennedy's Massachusetts! Hard-working, middle class people are already taxed too much and I say **enough is enough!** Gov. Roemer has tried to raise taxes even more than "Super Taxer," Edwin Edwards. He raised sales taxes and telephone taxes, increased fees, tried to triple income taxes, and tried to destroy the Homestead Exemption; I stand firmly against tax increases on the working person or the small businessman.

Scrub the Budget -- Duke Action vs. Roemer Rhetoric

Gov. Roemer took office promising to scrub Edwards' bloated budget. Edwards' last fat budget was $6.7 billion. Roemer's proposed budget is over $9 billion, a 34% increase from Edwards' already sky-high budget -- in just one term!

A Balanced Budget

Instead of cutting the budget as he promised, Roemer's first act as Governor was to borrow one billion dollars. $500 million was used on the first year's expenditures. He has left us a crushing debt of $700 million that we and our children will pay. Borrowing is not balancing. I will not increase our state debt. I will use the line-item veto to eliminate waste.

Reduce the Size of Government

Big Government has grown by leaps and bounds under Edwards and Roemer. We have twice the number of state employees, per capita, as our neighbor, Texas. And while we have not given our current employees and retirees a fair raise, Big Government continues to expand with more boards, commissions, and employees! Government is out of control! I will implement a hiring freeze and let attrition reduce the size of our top-heavy state bureaucracy.

David Duke led the dominant Klan faction of the 1970s (Author's collection).

example for Americans who want to stop the destruction of our school system and the destruction of white Christian culture and civilization."[19]

Duke's main competition came from Elbert "Bill" Wilkinson, Duke's successor as Louisiana grand dragon. They quarreled over money in August 1975, and Wilkinson defected to lead his own Invisible Empire Knights (IEK) along a more militant path. Firearms were frequently displayed at IEK rallies, with Wilkinson declaring, "These guns ain't for killing rabbits; they're for wasting people." He copied Duke's Klan Youth Corps and told reporters, "I don't mind admitting we want to brainwash these kids." Overtures toward independent Klans from South Carolina to Ohio paralleled violent clashes with black demonstrators in Mississippi, Alabama, and Georgia. Grand Dragon Gordon Gaille made headlines in 1976, seeking a Mississippi charter for his IEK realm, while Robert Shelton designated George Higgins Jr. as the Magnolia State's first UKA dragon since Edward McDaniel, ten years earlier. Duke named no Mississippi officers, although mail-order members helped inflate his bank account.[20]

As for the old MWK, its troops were scattered and demoralized after the prosecutions of 1967–1969. Cecil Price left prison in 1974 and joined an all-white country club in Philadelphia, but he revealed no Klan connections. Sam Bowers, paroled in 1976, returned to Laurel and his Sambo Amusement Company, doubling as a "preacher of Jesus the Galilean,"

Bill Wilkinson (center, in suit) defected from Duke's Klan to lead a more militant group (SPLC).

whom Bowers described as an "Aryan" prophet. One self-described insider told Patsy Sims that the White Knights "were back in business" two days after Bowers left prison, but independent Klan-watchers found no group in Mississippi using that name until 1987.[21]

The ADL has charted Klan membership since World War II, and while no statistics exist for Mississippi in the 1970s, broad estimates and profiles are available. Various Klans claimed 5,000 members nationwide in 1973, increasing to 6,500 two years later. ADL observers at Klan rallies reported that 60–80 percent of KKK members were in their twenties to mid-thirties; 15–25 percent were late thirties or older; and 15 percent were teens. Only 20 percent of identified members were veterans of the 1960s or earlier movements. Female members, mostly wives or girlfriends of Klansmen, comprised 25–33 percent of total membership. Outside of Louisiana, few Catholics responded to Klan membership appeals.[22]

The 1976 presidential campaign offered little hope for hard-core Klansmen. Republican incumbent Gerald Ford was tarred with the brush of Watergate and Richard Nixon's pardon, while Democratic standard bearer Jimmy Carter, although Georgian, was a certified liberal. Another Georgian, arch-segregationist Lester Maddox, won the nomination of George Wallace's American Independent Party, but he reaped only 170,531 votes nationwide. Lyndon LaRouche, assisted by Pennsylvania Klansman Roy Frankhouser at U.S. Labor Party headquarters, did even worse, with only 40,043. Carter's victory brought Mississippi back into the Democratic column by an eyelash — 49.6 percent to Ford's 47.7 — but that proved to be an aberration, not a trend.[23]

Eight months later, Mississippi Klanswomen made their voices heard on the contentious subject of the Equal Rights Amendment. Passed by overwhelming majorities in both houses of Congress, the ERA was ratified by thirty states in 1972. There it stalled, eight states shy of ratification, as conservative women flocked to right-wing author Phyllis Schlafly's STOP ERA movement, founded in October 1972. Ellen Campbell, head of Mississippi's STOP ERA chapter, spoke for thousands of Christian fundamentalists when she declared, "Man is the head of the home. In the societal order of things, he is above the women."

ERA opponents blocked passage in Mississippi's state legislature, while Congress extended the deadline for ratification to 1979, then again to 1982. In 1977 an International Women's Year (IWY) Conference convened in Jackson, bitterly divided by debate over the ERA. Dallas Higgins, the wife of a prominent Klansman, won election to represent Mississippi at the national IWY Conference, where acrimonious quarrels continued. ERA's deadline finally expired on 30 June 1982 — one day before Governor William Winter named Judge Lenore Prather to serve as the first female justice on Mississippi's supreme court.[24]

Violence and Schism (1978–1980)

Mississippi's first significant Klan demonstrations in a dozen years occurred in August 1978. Alfred Robinson's United League of Mississippi (ULM) was busy that summer, boycotting racist merchants and marching against police brutality in Alcorn, Chickasaw, Lee, and Marshall counties. Bill Wilkinson read the headlines and saw an opportunity to expand his Invisible Empire and "restore this government to the white people."[25]

In Okolona, where two grand juries failed to indict the patrolmen who killed an unarmed black youth, Judge H.D. Ross ordered police to frisk all marchers and "suspicious" bystanders for weapons until 24 August, when lawsuits filed by the American Civil Liberties Union and North Mississippi Rural Legal Services overturned his order. Two days later, when Robinson led 350 marchers through Okolona, they confronted both police and robed Klansmen — the latter ostensibly present "in case they try to take over the town." More IEK Klansmen, some sporting shoulder-length hair beneath their peaked hoods, rallied at Tupelo's Convention Hall on 26 August, barring reporters from the gathering. Klansmen assaulted marchers, and drive-by gunmen blasted a vehicle driven by Dr. Howard Gunn, Okolona's ULM leader. Seemingly proud of the mayhem, Bill Wilkinson told journalists, "We hurt some niggers. We shot up Gunn's car and we're not ashamed of it."[26]

The final clash occurred on Thanksgiving Day, 30 November, after 4,000 ULM supporters staged an anti–Klan march through Tupelo. Forty IEK members scrubbed plans to confront the marchers, but someone sabotaged the steering on a ULM bus, causing it to crash on the homeward journey. Elsewhere, Klansmen followed a carload of ULM marchers from Tupelo into Alabama, where they forced the car to stop and extracted its passengers at gunpoint, then beat them with clubs and chains.[27]

Wilkinson's knights staged similar attacks on black marchers in Decatur, Alabama, on 26 May 1979, prompting a lawsuit by the Southern Poverty Law Center (SPLC). Members of the SPLC's Klanwatch project hoped to secure testimony from one of the rioters, a former Mississippi IEK commander and Philadelphia lawman who split with Wilkinson after a "nasty dispute," but the witness eluded them. Two months later, black marchers protesting the violent tactics of Simpson County sheriff Lloyd "Goon" Jones met Klansmen who were armed with baseball bats and signs reading "Support Your Local Police." Jones — who was among the state troopers at Oxford in 1962, and who broadcast the radio alert on dying "niggers" from Jackson State College in 1970 — denied any wrongdoing but acknowledged that blacks had called him Goon "since Freedom Rider days."[28]

Klan ranks expanded during the latter 1970s. ADL observers estimated national membership at 6,000 to 8,000 in 1978, increasing to 10,500 the following year. More significantly, estimates of "non-member sympathizers" around the country increased from 40,000 in 1978 to 100,000 in 1979. The ADL saw "major gains" in Mississippi and five other southern states, while a total of twenty-two states harbored active klaverns. David Duke was the big loser in 1979, convicted of inciting a New Orleans riot, while his active membership dipped to 1,200. On 21 July 1980 Duke met with Bill Wilkinson, hoping to sell his membership list for $35,000, but Wilkinson brought a camera crew to the meeting and publicized Duke's offer nationwide. Three days later, Duke resigned from the KKKK, passing the reins to Alabama's Don Black, and announced formation of a new National Association for the Advancement of White People.[29]

Ronald Reagan recaptured Mississippi for the GOP in 1980 with a speech on states' rights delivered at the Neshoba County Fair. Fifty-one percent of Mississippi voters took the bait, pursuing what one state Republican spokesman called "a second chance to elect Barry Goldwater." Reagan carried all of Dixie except Jimmy Carter's native Georgia, while American Independent Party candidate John Rarick — a former Louisiana congressman named in FBI files as the exalted cyclops of St. Francisville's klavern — polled 41,268 votes nationwide. Violence marred Mississippi's electoral season, as a Klansman's son teargassed black students on a Jackson school bus and police in Burnsville blamed the KKK for a series of shootings that left one man dead and four others wounded.[30]

New Frontiers, Old Tactics (1981–1984)

Don Black had little time to enjoy his new role a imperial wizard. Even before he took command of the struggling Knights, he was embroiled in a plot hatched by David Duke and others that would send him to federal prison along with veteran Mississippi terrorist Danny Joe Hawkins.

The plan — dubbed "Operation Red Dog" — resembled a Hollywood script. Armed Klansmen would invade and conquer a Caribbean island and establish an Aryan paradise, then spend the rest of their lives awash in tax-free money from casinos, brothels, and cocaine sales, while black slaves served their every whim. According to sworn testimony, Texas Klansman Michael Perdue pitched the scheme to Duke in 1979, and Duke recruited Canadian Klan leader Wolfgang Droege and others. First, the would-be commandos fixed their sights on Grenada, then switched to Dominica when ex-prime minister Patrick John expressed interest in toppling his successor, Mary Eugenia Charles. Two members of Canada's Klan-allied Western Guard received $3,000 for a reconnaissance mission. Financial backers of the plot, identified in media reports but never charged, included Mississippi Klansman L.E. Matthews, Canadian neo–Nazi Martin Weiche, and Memphis lawyer J.W. Kirkpatrick.[31]

Operation Red Dog hit its first snag in February 1981 when the original ship's captain and crew recruited by Duke dropped out of the plan. Perdue then posed as a CIA agent and hired Texan Michael Howell to command his one-boat invasion fleet. Howell, in turn, reported the plot to agents of the Treasury Department's Bureau of Alcohol, Tobacco, and Firearms. Dominican police arrested Patrick John on 25 April 1981, but Perdue and his Klansmen still chose to proceed. The ten-man strike force gathered in Louisiana on 27 April, but federal agents sprang from ambush to arrest them and seize their arsenal of weapons and a Nazi flag. Aside from Black, Droege, and Perdue, the ten included Mississippi Klansmen Hawkins, George Malvaney, and William Waldrop Jr. On 7 May 1981 a federal grand jury indicted all ten on charges of violating the Federal Neutrality Act, plus various Customs and firearms violations. David Duke, although subpoenaed by the grand jury, was never charged.[32]

At trial in New Orleans, Michael Perdue turned state's evidence against defendants Hawkins, Black, and Michael Norris of Alabama, portraying himself as a hapless "baby mercenary," blaming everyone but himself for the plot. Don Black cast himself as a "military adviser" who agreed to help "secure" Dominica against communism, a plan based on promises that "the U.S. government was behind us." Defense attorney David Craig portrayed Danny Joe Hawkins as "a redneck, if you will, a Confederate flag-carrying son of the South who wants to fight communism and wants to fight for his country." Prosecutor Lindsay Larson ridiculed such claims, replying, "If they want to fight communism, let them join the U.S. Army." On 20 June 1981 jurors convicted Black and Hawkins; they acquitted Norris based on testimony that he thought the CIA had hired him for the mission. J.W. Kirkpatrick shot himself three days later. Droege and six other defendants pled guilty in separate proceedings.[33]

Bill Wilkinson, while not inclined toward foreign wars, had troubles of his own in 1981. The *Nashville Tennessean* published evidence that Wilkinson had served the FBI as an informant since he joined the Klan in 1974; and while that revelation caused many defections, Wilkinson remained as imperial wizard for another eighteen months. In Jackson that December, Klansmen Kenneth Painter and Larry Walker fired 116 rifle shots into the office of the *Jackson Advocate*, Mississippi's premiere black newspaper. When arrested, one gunman explained: "They had written some articles about myself and some friends." Painter pled guilty and received an eighteen-month jail term. Walker entrusted his fate to a jury and got ten years.[34]

Reports of mayhem and intimidation haunted Mississippi's Ku Klux realm through 1982. July brought the still-unsolved case of teenager Beverly Parnell, murdered in a Meridian warehouse with "KKK" spray-painted on the floor near her corpse. In Laurel, meanwhile, the first black woman to open a state-licensed nursing home received a warning letter: "The KKK is watching you." On Labor Day weekend, David Duke joined leaders of seven rival Klans, the NSRP, and the Aryan Nations for a "unity meeting" at Stone Mountain, Georgia. Together, they forged a short-lived Confederation of Klans, pointedly excluding the UKA and IEK in a bid to avoid "bad publicity."[35]

The year 1983 brought changes in national Klan leadership. In January the IRS slapped Wilkinson's group with a lien for $8,915.76 in back taxes and penalties. Wilkinson filed for bankruptcy, citing debts of $27,219, and ceded the wizard's post to Connecticut Catholic James Farrands. Meanwhile, Identity minister Thomas Robb succeeded Don Black as imperial wizard of the KKKK and moved its headquarters to Harrison, Arkansas. ADL Klanwatchers charted a steady decline in nationwide membership from 11,500 in 1981 to 10,000 in 1982 and 6,500 in 1984. The Farrands IEK regime claimed 2,000 members in twenty-one states, including a small Mississippi klavern.[36]

Tough talk and occasional violence continued despite the decline. In 1983 a Yalobusha County civil rights leader suffered wounds from sniper fire outside his office. February 1984 witnessed a cross-burning at the home of a white farmer who supported a black candidate for public office. Seven months later, a white Jackson resident donned a white hood to harass black children. The stunt cost him his job, the angry ex-employer telling reporters, "It wasn't a joke. I don't see how anybody could do anything so stupid."[37]

The 1984 presidential campaign offered new avenues of expression for white supremacists. Willis Carto, founder of Washington's Liberty Lobby, launched a new Populist Party with Mississippi Klansman Robert Weems as national chairman. Backed by state chairmen like NSRP leader Jerry Pope in Kentucky, Weems told reporters, "We Populists have adopted a tri-partisan approach. We share with Lyndon LaRouche, within both major parties, and through the Populist Party itself."

LaRouche himself was back in the running with localized Klan support and Mississippi running mate Billy Davis, claiming 78,773 votes nationwide for his Independent Democratic Party. Populist candidate (and 1948 Olympic bronze medalist) Bob Richards trailed LaRouche with 66,168 votes, while Delmar Dennis and his American Party collected 13,149. All those were sideshows to the main event, as Ronald Reagan's landslide buried Democratic contender Fritz Mondale in forty-nine states. Mississippi continued its new GOP tradition by giving Reagan 61.8 percent of its votes. Robert Weems soon tired of politics and moved to Washington, D.C., as the Liberty Lobby's research director.[38]

Citizens' Councils Reborn

Retreating on every front since the mid–1960s, the Citizens' Councils of America (CCA) collapsed after longtime member Lester Maddox failed to capture the White House in 1976. Its leaders, nonetheless, could not admit defeat. On 7 March 1985 attorney Gordon Baum hosted a gathering of former CCA leaders in St. Louis, Missouri. Delegates included Maddox, Tut Patterson, Louisiana's John Rarick, and Leonard "Flagpole" Wilson, leader of a 1956 segregationist riot at the University of Alabama. The meeting produced a new Council of Conservative Citizens (CCC), with Baum at the helm and Patterson assigned to write a column for the group's newsletter, the *Citizens' Informer*. Bill Lord, the CCC's new Mississippi leader, was another CCA alumnus from the 1960s.[39]

Rarick was the new group's first link to the Klan, identified in FBI files as a klavern leader from the 1960s, but he was not alone. Soon, SPLC investigators identified CCC members affiliated with the Carolina Knights, the IEK, David Duke's NAAWP, the Populist Party, and William Pierce's neo–Nazi National Alliance. Mark Cotterill, head of the CCC's youth group in Washington, D.C., resigned after the SPLC exposed his ties to Pierce.

Arkansas lieutenant governor Mike Huckabee canceled a CCC speech in 1994 on learning that he was scheduled to share the dais with KKK/Aryan Nations attorney Kirk Lyons. Aryan Nations security chief Vince Reed claims that Baum invited him to dinner in 1995, telling Reed, "I can really use a person like you.... The Jews are going to fall from the inside, not from the outside, and the niggers will be a puppet on a string for us." Baum brands the tale "a total lie," but *did* encourage CCC members to support David Duke's various political campaigns between 1988 and 1992, while CCC member Glayde Whitney wrote the foreword for Duke's autobiography, *My Awakening*. According to the *Clarion-Ledger*, CCC member and Mississippi state senator Mike Gunn received $9,500 through a fake company for writing Duke's gubernatorial fund-raising brochures. In December 1998 DeWest Hooker, self-described "best friend" of American Nazi Party leader George Rockwell, told a Washington CCC audience, "Be a Nazi, but don't use the word." After that story broke, Gordon Baum told the *Washington Post* he supposed "we were just too dang candid" on race.[40]

Despite repeated exposure of such unsavory links and pronouncements, the CCC attracted Mississippi politicians like moths to a flame. The SPLC listed thirty-five Magnolia office-holders linked to the group, ranging from local posts to the state legislature, the governor's mansion, and Congress. Governor Kirk Fordice suffered embarrassment in November 1999 when he addressed a CCC national board meeting and found David Duke peddling neo–Nazi tracts to the audience. Reporters got the story, prompting Gordon Baum to blame "one of the niggers at the front desk." Despite that flap, gubernatorial candidate Haley Barbour still graced a Carroll County CCC barbecue in July 2003. Others who endorsed the CCC include Judge Kay Cobb of the state supreme court, Rep. Webb Franklin, and Rep. Roger Wicker. State legislator Tommy Woods was a particular CCC favorite, telling the SPLC's *Intelligence Report*, "We've had blacks come to our meetings and had no problems." When pressed for names, he could not think of one.[41]

No Mississippi statesman was closer to the CCC, or suffered more for it, than Trent Lott. Elected to the U.S. Senate in 1988, he rose to become the GOP whip in 1995 and Senate majority leader the following year. Despite those achievements, his rebel instincts constantly betrayed him. In 1980, while campaigning for Ronald Reagan in Mississippi with

South Carolina's Strom Thurmond, Lott said, "You know, if we had elected [Thurmond] thirty years ago, we wouldn't be in the mess we are today." Four years later he told the Sons of Confederate Veterans that "The spirit of Jefferson Davis lives in the 1984 Republican Platform." In 1992 Lott told the CCC executive board, "We need more meetings like this across the nation.... The people in this room stand for the right principles and the right philosophy." He welcomed CCC leaders to his Washington office in 1997, then hedged by telling *Time* magazine, "You could say that I favored segregation then. I don't now." A year later, Lott claimed he had "no firsthand knowledge of" the CCC and told the *Washington Post*, "I have made my condemnation of the white supremacist and racist view of this group, or any group, clear." And yet, at Thurmond's one-hundredth birthday celebration in 2002, Lott repeated his old refrain: "When Strom Thurmond ran for president, we voted for him. We're proud of it. And if the rest of the country had followed our lead, we wouldn't have had all these problems over the years, either." Three weeks later, under fire from all sides, Lott resigned as Senate majority leader, saying of his latest gaffe, "I regret the way it has been interpreted."[42]

The CCC apparently learned nothing from its various travails, naming Lester Maddox "Patriot of the Century" and dispatching national spokesman Sam Dickson to David Duke's prison-release party in May 2004. Dickson proudly signed Duke's "New Orleans Protocol," a document supporting "white nationalism." Other signatories included Don Black, Willis Carto, NSRP founder Edward Fields, National Alliance leaders Kevin Strom and David Pringle, and John Tyndall from the neo-fascist British National Party. The New Orleans protocol stressed nonviolence except in "self-defense," but CCC leaders were not always so temperate. After South Carolina member Marshall Catterton was jailed for shooting a black youth who tore up a CCC poster, Gordon Baum told reporters that in a similar situation, he might react "just as Catterton did." Such incidents and statements seemed to help the CCC, which claimed 15,000 members by 1999. The group's strength peaked in Mississippi during 2004, with ten active chapters, and six remained when this book went to press.[43]

Violence and Decline (1985–1989)

Mississippi Klan activity in the latter 1980s consisted mainly of cross-burnings carried out by nocturnal sneak squads. Their targets included a Jackson elementary school, black families in Coldwater and Tylertown, the residence of Marshall County's new black sheriff, and an NAACP youth conference in Long Beach. The action was more serious in Avery, where threats preceded the fiery destruction of a black couple's home on 3 November 1985. Arson was also "strongly" suspected when fire razed the first black frat house at Ole Miss, on 4 August 1988, but police made no arrests. Suspicion naturally fell upon the new White Knights, founded in 1987 with headquarters in Kansas City, although no charges resulted. The new group's *White Beret* newsletter described MWK members—Danny Joe Hawkins among them — as "fanatical ecologists." Nationwide, the ADL pegged Klan membership around 5,500 in 1988.[44]

The Populist Party abandoned any semblance of moderation in 1988, nominating David Duke as its presidential candidate. Ex-Green Beret James "Bo" Gritz initially accepted the party's vice-presidential slot, then changed his mind and ran for a Nevada congressional seat, instead. His replacement, Ralph Forbes, was a former member of the American Nazi Party, founder of the anti–Semitic Shamrock Society, an associate of the Aryan Nations, and a self-styled evangelist whose Sword of Christ radio "ministry" broadcast from Arkansas.

Ole Miss graduate James Meredith endorsed Duke and posed for photos with the ex-wizard, then moved on to a staffer's job with Senator Jesse Helms before resigning and declaring Helms "too liberal." Meredith's son diagnosed those astounding events as symptoms of a craving for attention, "even if it's only for a day." November's balloting sent George H.W. Bush to the Oval Office and predictably disappointed Klan-linked candidates: Duke polled 46,910 votes, Lyndon LaRouche and Billy Miles got 25,530 for their Independent Party, and Delmar Dennis scored 3,476 on his last hurrah with the American Party.[45]

Memories of the Neshoba County murders were revived in 1986 with the election of Susan Akin, granddaughter of an acquitted defendant, to serve as Miss America. Two years later, British director Alan Parker began filming his fictionalized version of the case at various Mississippi locations, with full support from Governor William Allain. Successor Raymond Mabus opposed the project, but reluctantly cooperated to avoid a potential public-relations disaster. After *Mississippi Burning* was released in January 1989, Mabus hired his own PR firm to dispute the film's accuracy. Philadelphia's theater initially refused to show the film, then relented in the face of public outcry. Lawrence Rainey and other ex–Klansmen sued the film's producers for libel, but their case was dismissed. In June 1989, at a twenty-fifth anniversary memorial service in Longdale, Mississippi secretary of state Richard Molpus offered the first (and only) official apology for 1964's triple murder.[46]

As the 1980s ended, SPLC Klan-watchers found two factions active in Mississippi. The Christian Knights, under Grand Dragon Marcus Blanton, owed allegiance to Imperial Wizard Virgil Griffin in North Carolina, while the White Sons of the Confederacy was a native operation run from Poplarville by Jordan Gollub. Jackson neo–Nazi Richard Barrett launched his Nationalist Movement in 1987, quickly expanding to other states on both sides of the Mason-Dixon Line. Scuffles with black demonstrators in Georgia prompted the

Sign announcing a 1980s rally of the Christian Knights in Mississippi (SPLC).

Members of the Christian Knights distribute pamphlets at a Mississippi rally (SPLC).

SPLC to sue Barrett, but jurors cleared his brownshirts of charges that they violated marchers' civil rights.

Meanwhile, ex-army colonel Gordon "Jack" Mohr preached Identity's gospel of hatred from Bay St. Louis via his Crusade for Christ and Country. A longtime associate of the John Birch Society and Michigan Klansman Robert Miles, founder of his own paramilitary Citizens Emergency Defense System, Mohr taught his disciples that "[b]ecause Hitler understood the plans of International Jewry and what they were trying to do to Western Christian civilization, he was marked for destruction by any means, even the murder of countless millions during World War II." Philadelphia vandals sprayed "KKK" on downtown buildings in July 1989, while Natchez Klansmen burned a cross on 15 September at the home of a white man who sold property to African Americans.[47]

New World Disorder (1990–1995)

The face of klannishness changed in the 1990s. In general, Klansmen were more inclined to sport long hair and beards, resembling their Reconstruction forebears more closely than knights of the 1920s through the 1960s. Many turned their backs on mainstream Christianity, preferring the tenets of Identity or forsaking Jesus altogether in pursuit of Nordic paganism. As their ranks thinned, they increasingly forged bonds to "patriot militias," neo–Nazi groups, and teenage racist skinhead gangs.[48]

Neo-Nazi skinheads have collaborated with the KKK since 1985 (SPLC).

Skinheads arrived on the American scene from Britain in 1985, spreading from coast to coast in a wave of teenage angst, racial hatred, and lust for "romantic violence." By 1990 the ADL found active gangs in 109 cities, scattered across 34 states. Some gangs rallied and marched with Klansmen, while others focused mainly on drinking, street-fighting, and crude vandalism. Mississippi's first skinhead clique, the Biloxi-based Confederate Hammer Skins, made headlines in April 1990 when two members were jailed for assaulting patrons at a gay bar. By 1992 the gang claimed chapters in Tennessee and Texas, but its members managed to avoid further incarceration. Police listed no gang affiliation for the quartet of skinheads imprisoned in 1995 for firebombing an interracial couple's home in Richland. A decade later, SPLC researchers found no gangs active in the state.[49]

In 1990, Poplarville's Jordan Gollub renamed his White Sons of the Confederacy, emerging as imperial wizard of the Calvary White Knights of the KKK. The following year, he claimed a satellite klavern in Georgia, expanding to Virginia and West Virginia by 1992. His competition, the Alabama-based Confederate Knights, planted a klavern in Harpersville, led in 1991 by Marcus Blanton, then pulled up stakes and moved to Tylertown. Jack Mohr's Crusade for Christ and Country survived through 1991, replaced the following year by a short-lived Christian Patriots Defense League.[50]

Klan-type incidents continued in Mississippi throughout the early 1990s. On 1 May 1990 police in Forest jailed the father of a local kludd (chaplain) for firing shots at a black driver's car. Two months later, hooded men invaded Picayune's city jail and threatened a black inmate. Grenada vandals defaced a black couple's home on 29 July 1990, then returned to light a cross in the yard two nights later. Small rallies in Decatur and De Kalb produced no more than thirty Klansmen at a time, and the Confederate Knights lost one of their own on 5 October 1991 when "drinking buddies" beat Klansman Jeffrey Smith to death in Tylertown, stealing $700 of Klan money. The night riders who burned a cross at a black man's home in Eudora, on 3 May 1992, found themselves jailed for malicious mischief two months later.[51]

Mississippi *was* changing, but some changes came slowly. In 1991, the first year during which the FBI collected data on hate crimes throughout the nation, only four of Mississippi's eighty-two counties admitted any racist incidents. Relatives of Andre Jones were naturally suspicious in August 1992 when the teenager allegedly hanged himself in Simpson County's jail, administered by the same Sheriff Jones whom Klansmen rallied to support in 1979. The family filed wrongful-death suits in both state and federal court, where they were dismissed in 1995 and 1996, respectively.[52]

Despite his evident conservatism, President George Bush had little to offer the racist far-right in 1992. His public references to a "new world order" fueled conspiracy theories and spawned rogue "militias" nationwide, many associated with their local Klans and neo–Nazi groups. Bo Gritz made peace with the Populist Party, securing its presidential nomination *and* that of the far-right America First Party. Inspired by George Wallace and his defunct American Independent Party, former Nixon aide Howard Phillips campaigned for the Oval Office at the helm of his new U.S. Taxpayers Party, whose national committee included a mixed bag of anti–Semites, militia activists, and a convicted bomber of abortion clinics. Mississippi remained in the GOP column, giving 50 percent of its votes to Bush, versus 41 percent to ultimate winner Bill Clinton. (The remainder went to independent Ross Perot.) Nationwide, Bo Gritz polled 98,918 votes, Phillips claimed 42,960, and Lyndon LaRouche (campaigning from federal prison) received 22,863.[53]

Richard Molpus ran for governor in 1995, and saw his moment of compassion six years earlier become a weapon in the hands of rival Kirk Fordice. While courting votes from the CCC, Fordice condemned Molpus for his 1989 apology at Longdale, assuring Mississippians that it did "no good" to reopen old wounds. "This is the nineties! This is now!" Fordice declared. "We're on a roll! We've got the best race relations in America, and we need to speak positive [sic] Mississippi!" White Mississippi agreed, sweeping Fordice into office with 60 percent of the vote.[54]

Belated Justice

Byron De La Beckwith maintained his pose as a racist celebrity through the 1980s. Remarried in June 1983, he held court for reporters and neo–Nazi admirers from his new wife's home at Signal Mountain, Tennessee, and traveled as the spirit moved him. In 1986 he attended a "Klan Homecoming" at the order's birthplace, in Pulaski, Tennessee. A year later he surfaced in Blackhawk, Mississippi, for one of William Waller's gubernatorial rallies, and surprised his former prosecutor with a cheerful handshake, captured by photographers for Jackson's daily papers. Beckwith's nephew and biographer Reed Massengill says the stunt was designed "to muddy the political waters ... hoping to publicly embarrass Waller and end his political career." If so, it seemed to work: Ray Mabus won the race that year, claiming 90 percent of Mississippi's black ballots.[55]

Despite his hypersensitivity in racial matters, Beckwith failed to notice certain fundamental changes in Mississippi's political landscape. Jackson's *Clarion-Ledger*, once nicknamed the "Klan-Ledger" for its racist editorials, won a Pulitzer Prize in 1983 for a series on public education. Three years later, Magnolia voters— including 12 percent of all whites in the Delta — elected their first black congressman since Reconstruction. In 1987 an African American was crowned Miss Mississippi. During the furor over *Mississippi Burning*, newsman Jerry Mitchell pressed for a reopening of Beckwith's case. Mitchell's headline story of 1 October 1989 revealed that agents of the State Sovereignty Commission had "checked" prospective jurors during Beckwith's murder trials in 1964. Eight days later, at a meeting of Hinds County's supervisors, one board member offered a resolution calling for renewed investigation of the Evers slaying, but no one seconded the motion. Mitchell and the *Clarion-Ledger* next pursued an editorial campaign for justice, drawing wide support. Black spokesmen led by Aaron Henry criticized the state's inaction at a press conference in February 1990.[56]

Quietly, behind the scenes, assistant district attorney Bobby DeLaughter searched for new evidence. In April 1990 he read a biography of Delmar Dennis—*Klandestine*, published in 1975 — that included Beckwith's boast of killing Evers. DeLaughter met Dennis in May and secured his agreement to testify at any future trial. FBI agents stalled DeLaughter for months before delivering their files on Beckwith. While waiting for those documents, DeLaughter found the misplaced murder weapon at the home of his late father-in-law, Beckwith trial judge Russell Moore. At last, in autumn 1990, Hinds County's grand jury convened to consider the case.[57]

Beckwith, secure in Tennessee, exuded confidence. In January 1990 he received an award from the Nation of Yahweh "in recognition of uncommon valor and bravery, in the face of innumerable enemies." Eleven months later, he told a reporter, "God hates mongrels. My people came here to take this country from the red man by force and violence, and that's the way we're going to keep it — by force and violence." News of his latest murder indictment, on 14 December, did not seem to faze him. When officers came to arrest him on 17 December, Beckwith told them, "I'm ready to go, boys. I'm not guilty. Do you want to search me for a bomb?"[58]

Jailed pending extradition, Beckwith reached out through the mails to his supporters on the racist right. He sent out fliers for Jesse Stoner's Crusade Against Corruption ("Praise God for AIDS!") and received $2,000 from Edward Fields of the NSRP. Ex-Klansman Tom Metzger, founder of White Aryan Resistance, offered moral support. Richard Butler wrote to Beckwith from Aryan Nations headquarters, signing his letters "88"—for "HH," or "Heil Hitler." Louisiana gubernatorial candidate David Duke called Beckwith's indictment "a travesty upon justice." A Tennessee judge ordered Beckwith's extradition on 3 October 1991. As De La left for Jackson in handcuffs the following day, Thelma Beckwith asked a reporter, "What the hell is wrong with Mississippi?"[59]

Beckwith's lawyers, who privately called him "despicable," applied for bail in November 1991. At that hearing, Gordon Lackey appeared as a character witness, denying Klan membership, while Beckwith's son blamed his mother for Byron's domestic violence. Prosecutors countered with Beckwith's recent letters of praise to a bank-robbing white-supremacist cult, the Phineas Priesthood, and bond was denied. Judge Breland Hilburn scheduled trial for 10 February 1992. A month before that date, on 14 January, Beckwith's defenders tried again for bail. This time, they submitted eighty-eight affidavits from Beckwith supporters, including Tut Patterson of the CCC and a dozen former members of the MWK (Travis Buckley, L.E. Matthews, and Danny Joe Hawkins among them). Judge Hilburn denied bond again, but rescheduled trial for 1 June. Ex-wizard Sam Bowers, posing as a "Mr. Bancroft," pestered the defense team with legal advice until he was barred from their offices.[60]

Further delays ensued. In April 1992 the defense sought dismissal of Beckwith's indictment on Sixth Amendment grounds, claiming that he had been denied a speedy trial. Judge Hilburn denied that motion on 4 August, while granting a change of venue to DeSoto County, with a new trial date of 20 September. That date in turn was scrubbed, as Mississippi's supreme court considered Beckwith's appeal for dismissal. Oral arguments commenced on 15 October 1992. Two months later, to the day, the court upheld Beckwith's indictment by a narrow vote of four to three. Chief Justice Roy Noble dissented, calling that decision "the worst pronouncement of the law during my tenure ... and [an] egregious miscarriage of justice." On 23 December, Judge Hilburn set Beckwith's bond at $100,000, secured by $12,000 from an anonymous donor. On 4 October 1993 the U.S. Supreme Court declined to review Beckwith's case, thus finally clearing the way for his trial.[61]

After another change of venue, jury selection began in Batesville on 18 January 1994 and was completed eight days later. Sheriff's deputies ejected one Ku Klux old-timer from the courtroom on opening day, and kept a sharp eye out thereafter. Bobby DeLaughter called Delmar Dennis and other witnesses who had heard Beckwith boast of his crime through the years. Beckwith himself had helped the state in August 1992 when he admitted traveling with prosecution witness Peggy Morgan to Parchman state prison for a visit with incarcerated Klansman Cecil Sessum. Beckwith's defenders challenged the veracity of each witness in turn, but failed to sell their case. Jurors convicted Beckwith on 5 February 1994 and he received a life sentence. The state supreme court upheld Beckwith's conviction on 22 December 1997. He died in prison on 21 January 2001.[62]

Déjà Vu (1996–1999)

In one respect, it seemed as if the early 1990s might present a replay of the violent 1960s. Between 1990 and 1995 thirty black churches burned across Dixie, none rating mention in the FBI's annual lists of domestic terrorist incidents. In Mississippi, fire consumed Pike County's Rocky Point Missionary Baptist Church on 5 April 1993, lit by whites who fled the scene shouting, "Burn, nigger, burn!" Three teenage suspects, described by one of their defense attorneys as "young, drunk and crazy," received federal prison terms in that case, but Washington otherwise ignored the problem until 1996, when thirty-five churches burned between January and June. Five of those fires were deemed accidental, including two of Mississippi's seven cases. In the other five — at Hatley, West Point, Ruleville, Satartia, Mount Pleasant, and Central Grove — police made one arrest without revealing a conspiracy. Congress reached the same conclusion, following a one-day "study" of the arson epidemic, and a National Church Arson Task Force found "no evidence of a national conspiracy," in June 1997.[63]

Others strongly disagreed. ADL investigators noted four Klans active in the Magnolia State during 1996, including Thom Robb's Knights of the KKK, the Confederate Knights, the U.S. Klans, and Knights of the Flaming Sword. While none of them were linked to any of the fires by concrete evidence, the skinhead torching of an interracial couple's home at Richmond, late in 1995, suggested possible conspiracy. Atlanta's Center for Democratic Renewal, formerly the Anti-Klan Network, listed nine Mississippi church fires since 1993, and spokesman Noah Chandler blamed "the conspiracy of racism itself." State commissioner of public safety James Ingram disputed those statistics and blamed blacks for five of the church fires reported during 1990–92 (none of which made the CDR's list). As for the latest incidents, two churches burned on 17 June 1996, Ingram regarded both as inconsequential "copycat" crimes. Throughout Dixie, only two arson cases— both from South Carolina, in 1995 — were proved to be the work of Klansmen.[64]

Mississippi's worst act of racist violence in the 1990s did not involve the KKK, but it sprang from similar roots. On 12 April 1996 neo–Nazi drifter Larry Shoemake — who, ironically, had played a walk-on role in *Mississippi Burning*— invaded a Jackson restaurant, shot eight black victims (killing one), then set the place afire and thus committed suicide. A search of his apartment revealed Nazi regalia and a dog-eared copy of *The Turner Diaries*, a racist novel penned by National Alliance leader William Pierce, which had inspired ex–Klansman Timothy McVeigh to bomb Oklahoma City's federal building on 19 April 1995. Like McVeigh, Shoemake was enthralled by the tenets of Christian Identity and obsessed with federal mishandling of the 1993 siege of a religious compound in Texas. Police could not explain how Shoemake had collected weapons valued at some $50,000, when he lived from hand to mouth and rarely held a job.[65]

Eleven months later, a gunman killed Cleve McDowell at his home in Drew, Mississippi. McDowell was the first African American to attend Oxford's James Eastland School of Law (in 1963); but he finished his studies in Texas, then returned to spend three decades as a public defender and civil rights activist in Sunflower County, serving for a time as Mississippi field director of the NAACP. A teenage client of McDowell's confessed to the slaying and pled guilty to manslaughter, then claimed that police obtained his confession through torture. Confusion persists in the case, feeding conspiracy theories, since a local judge issued a gag order twenty minutes after McDowell was found dead, and the state's file on his murder remains sealed to this day.[66]

While SPLC investigators found no active Klans in Mississippi during 1997, there was no shortage of Klan-allied groups in the state. David Duke's NAAWP claimed nine chapters statewide, including offices in McComb and Philadelphia. Richard Barrett ventured from his Nationalist Movement's headquarters in Learned to mount protests at Ole Miss. When an African American candidate sought a seat on the Lauderdale County commission, night riders stoned his Collinsville home and burned a cross in his yard. The National Socialist White People's Party (NSWPP) opened an office in Collinsville, while the Aryan Nations colonized Picayune. In February, a caller claiming membership in the latter group threatened to bomb Jackson's federal building.[67]

The Klan returned to Mississippi in 1998, represented by a Lucedale klavern of the Indiana-based American Knights. On 9 January, Starkville policeman David Lindley was placed on six months probation for wearing his Klan robe on duty. David Duke lost seven of his NAAWP chapters, retaining units in Hazelhurst and McComb, while members of the Mississippi Militia trained for battle around Ocean Springs and the North Mississippi Militia drilled at Southaven. The NSWPP survived on a shoestring budget in Collinsville, while another outside racist group, Matthew Hale's World Church of the Creator, preached its doctrine of "RAHOWA"—*racial holy war*—from Raymond.[68]

In 1999 the KKK and its affiliates enjoyed a minor renaissance in the Magnolia State. Active Klans included the home-grown Southern Knights in Petal; a klavern of Hoosier wizard Jeff Berry's American Knights in Lucedale; and a unit of the Kentucky-based Imperial Klans of America in Sumrall. The American Knights were most publicly active, staging small rallies in Canton on 29 May, and in Philadelphia on 18 September. Meanwhile, the Nationalist Movement endured in Learned and claimed a satellite chapter in Nebraska.[69]

Mississippi Turning

Byron De La Beckwith's tardy murder conviction did not immediately start a trend. Four more years elapsed before state prosecutors reopened Vernon Dahmer's case in Forrest County, once again at the media's urging. On 17 January 1998, Jerry Mitchell informed *Clarion-Ledger* subscribers that confessed killer Billy Pitts had never served a day of his life sentence. When a new arrest warrant was issued, Pitts again offered to testify against Sam Bowers. Two months later, on 12 March, Mitchell revealed that FBI memos from 1968 suggested jury tampering in Bowers' several mistrials. On 28 May 1998, state authorities arrested Bowers, Deavours Nix, and ex–Klansman Charles Noble on charges of murder and arson. State attorney general Mike Moore told CNN, "We want them to have a very, very speedy trial. It's been thirty-two years and we think it's time justice is served."[70]

Bowers faced trial alone on 18 August 1998, represented by longtime colleague Travis Buckley. Assistant D.A. Bob Helfrich opened with a description of the "cowardly" Dahmer attack and named Bowers as its instigator. Buckley granted that the murder was "atrocious," then condemned the proceedings as a media-orchestrated show-trial and urged the integrated jury to shun emotion. Buckley warned that the state would harp on "the burning of [Dahmer's] family, the burning of his house. The witnesses they have are not credible."

Billy Pitts testified that Buckley himself had attended planning sessions for the raid, and Judge Richard McKenzie denied Buckley's call for a mistrial. FBI informant Robert Wilson recalled Bowers gloating: "Look at what my boys did to that Dahmer nigger for me." Another witness to that comment, Klan widow Cathy Lucy, described Bowers as "smiling and jubilant" when he spoke. Deavours Nix testified from a wheelchair with an oxygen tank at his side: "I never heard a racial slur or a threat come from [Bowers]. Sam was a gentle-man at all times." In closing arguments, Helfrich assured the jury that "justice delayed is not justice denied." Buckley countered, condemning the trial as "persecution," but jurors convicted Bowers on 21 August, imposing an automatic life sentence.[71]

Justice was neither swift nor sure for the ex-wizard's codefendants. Deavours Nix died from lung cancer on 19 September 1998 before his trial could convene. Nine months later, on 15 June 1999, a hung jury produced a mistrial for Charles Noble. After repeated delays, the court dismissed all charges against Noble on 16 January 2002. Meanwhile, a Ku Klux website cam-paigned to "!!!Free Sam Bowers!!!" Its message declared that "Sam Bowers and his men stood courageously, at great personal sacrifice and without reward, to preserve Southern Heritage and rights. There is no doubt that Sam Bowers is the greatest and most heroic defender of white people's rights of this era. Hail Sam Bowers!" Unmoved by such efforts, the courts rejected each appeal in turn, and Bowers died in prison, from a heart attack, on 5 November 2006.[72]

Another racial murder case, without specific Klan involvement, inched its way toward trial while Bowers sat in prison. Humphreys County authorities had been less than eager to prosecute Rainey Pool's killers in 1970, but a new grand jury indicted five of the lynch-ers on 31 July 1998. Jurors acquitted one defendant on 30 June 1999, dismissing him as a bystander to the event. A second suspect pled guilty to manslaughter and turned state's evidence against the remaining defendants— all brothers— and thus secured their manslaughter convictions on 13 November 1999. All four received twenty-year terms in state prison, and Mississippi's supreme court rejected their appeals in August 2002.[73]

The 2000 presidential campaign offered little to hard-core Klansmen and neo–Nazis. Howard Phillips, after polling 42,960 votes in 1996, renamed his vehicle the Constitution Party and braced himself for another run. Extremists continued to staff the new party, includ-ing a member of David Duke's latest venture — EURO (the European-American Unity and Rights Organization)— who served as party chairman in Utah. Phillips improved his mar-gin, more than doubling his ballot count to 98,020 in November 2000, but it proved to be his last outing. Mississippi, meanwhile, remained solidly Republican, giving 58 percent of its votes to George W. Bush. Active Klans at the close of the millennium included the Louisiana-based Bayou Knights, with a Brookhaven klavern, and Philadelphia's United White Klans, with chapters in Greenwood and Collinsville. Petal, with fewer than eight thousand residents, boasted two home-grown Klans, the Mississippi White Knights and the Southern Knights.[74]

Lost Cause Warriors (2001–2005)

Mississippi's Klans enjoyed a modest growth spurt as the new millennium began. The several factions launched in 2000 survived in 2001, with the United White Klans claiming a new Union klavern and two more in South Carolina. Setbacks humbled the UWK in 2002, stripping away all but its headquarters klavern in Philadelphia, but Jackson hosted two new

Klans, the Royal Confederate Knights and the White Knights of the Southern Realm of Mississippi. David Duke's EURO planted a chapter at Southaven and staged a "Celebration of Southern Cultural Heritage" in Biloxi on 20 July 2002, promoting the display of Confederate flags. Members of rival orders gathered in Laurel to form a Konfederation of Klans on 9 November 2002, but Thom Robb's KKKK mustered only twelve knights for a march through Biloxi, three weeks later.[75]

Mississippi's Klan front remained fluid in 2003. Gone by mid-year were the Royal Confederate Knights, United White Klans, and White Knights of the Southern Realm. Petal's Southern Knights became the Mississippi Southern White Knights, expanding to plant klaverns in Bay St. Louis and Robinsonville, while the Bayou Knights moved their headquarters to Fulton. New competitors by year's end included a rejuvenated Mississippi White Knights and an ill-defined Klonvocation of Klans staged in Laurel on 8 November 2003. Two Alabama Klans, the Aryan Nations Knights and Orion Knights, claimed chapters in Fulton and Star, respectively. Richard Barrett's Nationalist Movement mounted rallies for the Confederate flag in Oxford, while neo–Nazi rivals set up shop as the National Socialist Movement, in Collinsville. Announcement of an impending Klan rally at Collinsville, broadcast via MemphisSite.com in May 2003, sparked enthusiastic response from self-proclaimed Klansmen anxious to "clean up the town." One anonymous writer declared, "I am very excited about this new meeting and can't wait to attend. Many of us have waited a lifetime for a moment like this as some may say."[76]

By 2004 Mississippi's rival Klans struggled toward a semblance of unity, with less than impressive results. A joint Philadelphia demonstration, staged by the MWK and Orion Knights, lured only fifteen Klansmen on 10 April. A few more appeared when the MWK met with members of the White Knight Alliance in Laurel, seven months later. Fliers from Thom Robb's Knights of the KKK blanketed Marion County in August, but the group claimed no Mississippi klaverns. SPLC investigators listed the year's active Klans as the Bayou Knights (in Fulton and Richton), Petal's MWK (with klaverns in five other states), and the Southern White Knights (in Robinsonville). Grand Dragon Billy Bob Boyle, affiliation undisclosed, brought armed bodyguards to an August rally in Biloxi, protected by police and chain-link fencing as he announced a $50,000 donation "to update the voting machines in Mississippi." At last report, the cash had not materialized.[77]

At mid-decade, the MWK was Mississippi's largest Klan, still headquartered in Petal, with klaverns in Bruce, Oxford, Philadelphia, Star, and Tremont, and three outside the state. The Bayou Knights remained in Richton, while a klavern of the Florida-based Empire Knights operated from Lucedale, replacing the former American Knights. David Duke's EURO maintained a chapter in Ripley, while its leader dodged federal fraud indictments in Europe and Russia. Richard Barrett's Nationalist Movement sponsored a "warrior training camp" at Learned, in September 2005. Two months later, an MWK cross-burning ceremony in Tremont drew more hecklers than Klansmen.[78]

Strange Bedfellows

Nationwide, the far-right "patriot militias" of the 1990s and early 2000s generally welcomed Klansmen and neo–Nazis as members, circulating anti–Semitic literature with their paramilitary training manuals and spicing their anticommunist doctrines with strong doses of racism. SPLC investigators found no active "patriot" groups in Mississippi after 2001, but the Mississippi Militia maintained an Internet Website through 2007, announcing its mission "to safeguard against tyranny and educate the public of their Constitutional duties and heritage of Liberty."[79] The site also posed a rhetorical question, "Are you white suprema-cist?" and replied:

> We seem to be getting asked this one a lot lately. And the answer is NO!!!! NO!!!! But we have always held the belief that these misnomers are forced upon us by those in the media and the government as a way to make the population "disunited." Disunification is the goal of "political correctness," multiculturalism, and ethnic diversity. Each of these lib-eral ideologies seeks to separate "We the People" so that we may not stand united against our "real" common enemies. We are Americans regardless of our ethnic backgrounds and that is our unifying factor.[80]

Meanwhile, spokesmen for a burgeoning "neo–Confederate" movement, led by such groups as the League of the South (LOS) and the Sons of Confederate Veterans (SCV), shunned any pretense of moderation on matters of race and politics. Both groups veered from their historical traditions at the turn of the millennium and charted far-right courses that would bring them into close collaboration with the KKK.

Organized in 1994, the LOS first drew attention for its racism five years later, when charter member David Cooksey, former leader of the Tuscaloosa, Alabama, chapter, wrote online about an interracial rape case: "You see the day is coming when we will NEED a new type of klan. Yes I said Klan!! If push comes to shove I'm for it!... Time has come to stop this crap now! Or would you all like to see your daughters raped???" In March 2000, attor-ney Kirk Lyons, a proud supporter of both the Klan and the Aryan Nations, appeared as a keynote speaker, in Montgomery, for a pro–Confederate flag rally jointly sponsored by the LOS and SCV. In May 2000, after a brawl between blacks and Klansmen in Decatur, Alabama, LOS member Siren Dresch wrote, on the AlaReb Website: "I hope the next group ... is armed and ready to hit an afro between the eyes." In April 2003, after the public nudity of some participants in Biloxi's "Black Spring Break" sparked white outrage, Mississippi LOS leader John Cripps denounced "the cultural barbarism of this group of animals." LOS founder Michael Hill, once a professor at historically black Stillman College in Tuscaloosa, Alabama, called for whites to arm themselves against "these thugs." He added, "Let us not flinch when our enemies call us 'racists'; rather, just reply with, 'So, what's your point?'"[81]

The LOS, which claimed 9,000 members in 2000, boasted other less-than-savory asso-ciations. One of its national directors, Jack Kershaw, was a Citizens' Council veteran and a prominent CCC member, prime mover in the erection of a Nashville monument to Nathan Bedford Forrest, who said in 1998, "Somebody needs to say a good word for slavery." David Cooksey doubled as a leader of the CCC in Alabama. SPLC investigators found that many key LOS officers were also "Christian reconstructionists," part of a sect that advocates replac-ing the U.S. Constitution with Old Testament law (including execution for adultery, witch-craft, and homosexuality).

In 2001, Michael Hill described Al Qaeda's 9/11 terrorist attacks as the "natural fruit" of America's racial diversity. Around the same time, while promoting "Anglo-Celtic cul-ture," Hill called African Americans "a compliant and deadly underclass." Four years later, in Cayce, South Carolina, SPLC reporters revealed that the LOS Southern Patriot Shop was run by David Sutter — also known as "Wulfran Hall," in his capacity as a member of the Aryan Nations "high counsel [*sic*]." Exposure of that neo–Nazi link prompted a change in management, as the shop morphed into an LOS "Southern Cultural Center."[82]

Hill and other LOS leaders created the Southern Party in 1999 as a political vehicle advocating "peaceful secession of the Southern States from the American union and the restoration of an independent Southern nation." That goal seemed impractical, and Hill soon lost control of his brainchild; but the LOS survived the schism. In 2001 the League boasted five Mississippi chapters and staged its eighth national conference in Jackson. Three years later, with two chapters surviving, the LOS sponsored a "Great Revival in the Southern Armies Conference" at Southaven, on 15 June 2004. By 2006, a solitary LOS chapter — one of 101 nationwide — eked out a sparse living in Mendenhall.[83]

The much older Sons of Confederate Veterans, founded in 1896, survived nearly a century before it lapsed into extremism. Early SCV newsletters defended the first KKK and claimed that the United States was "created for whites," but the group generally billed itself as "non-political" and "non-racial." That moderate image suffered in 1953, when leadership passed to William McClain, a staunch segregationist and ally of the State Sovereignty Commission who, as president of Southern Mississippi State University, helped frame Clyde Kennard in 1959. Thirty years later, striving to keep pace with America, the SCV condemned display of Confederate flags by groups espousing "political extremism or racial superiority." In 1990, a new resolution denounced racist groups. An SCV "camp" (chapter) countermarched against Klansmen who displayed the Stars and Bars in 1993, and the following year, SCV leaders expelled "chief of heritage protection" Charles Lunford for delivering a racist speech before the CCC.[84]

All that began to change in 1994, when the League of the South emerged as a new voice of southern "heritage." Four years later, SCV leaders relaxed prior restrictions on collaboration with other organizations, resulting in a near-immediate commingling with the LOS and CCC. Aging rioter and CCC founder Leonard Wilson soon emerged as an SCV officer in Alabama, while the SCV's *Confederate Veteran* magazine sold books sympathetic to the Klan. In 1999 David Duke shared the stage with lawyer Kirk Lyons in Arlington, Virginia, where Lyons urged the SCV to rid itself of "grannies" and "bed-wetters" who opposed political struggle. In January 2000, South Carolina SCV leader Ron Wilson teamed with Lyons to sponsor a Rebel-flag rally; he subsequently joined the board of Lyons's Southern Legal Resource Center and helped Lyons win election to the SCV's national board in August 2000. In Mississippi, during April 2001, the SCV and CCC staged a joint rally supporting display of Confederate flags.[85]

With 31,400 members nationwide, the SCV's transition to a racist group did not go unopposed. Gilbert Jones ran for lieutenant commander of the group's North Carolina division in December 2001, saying, "The SCV has come to a decisive fork in the road.... I think we ought to take the neo–Nazis, the white supremacists, the skinheads and show them to the door." Gilbert lost that election by seventeen votes, but still fought to protect his beloved organization. In August 2002, at the SCV's national convention in Memphis, Lyons supporters shouted Gilbert down and elected Ron Sullivan their national commander by a margin of forty-seven votes. Under the new regime, SCV officers included Leonard Wilson (no relation to Ron) as staff parliamentarian; Charles McMichael of Free Mississippi (see below) as genealogist-in-chief; Allen Sullivant, owner of the Order of White Trash Website, as chief of heritage defense; and CCC founder Gordon Baum as judge advocate general.

In February 2003 the SCV purged several hundred members who had formed a moderate insider's group called Save the Sons of Confederate Veterans. A month later, headquarters severed its ties to the Military Order of Stars and Bars, a group including 1,450 descendants of Confederate officers who opposed the Wilson clique. Kirk Lyons officially welcomed klansmen to the SCV's ranks in March 2004, while the SCV's Heritage Defense Fund bankrolled his fringe legal practice.[86]

Still, resistance continued, led by William Pate in North Carolina and Walter Hilderman III in South Carolina. Pate wrote to friends in the SCV, saying, "The organization is now being led at the national level by angry, misguided bigots and what has charitably been called 'the lunatic fringe.'" Hilderman declared, in November 2004, "We intend to build a movement within the SCV that will identify the extremists and vote them out of office or obtain their resignations. If they are secessionists, let them join the League of the South. If they think racism is a virtue, let them join the Ku Klux Klan."[87]

For the most part, however, such appeals fell on deaf ears. The SCV's extremist ties endured and expanded. Linda Sewell, Alabama spokesperson for the Georgia-based Heritage Preservation Association, meddled in Biloxi's Rebel-flag quarrel during 2002, then accepted a "certificate of appreciation" from the Aryan Knights of the KKK in January 2003 and joined klansmen to picket SPLC headquarters. Even more peculiar was the SCV's bond with Michael Tubbs, a former Green Beret who served four years in federal prison for stealing weapons and explosives from Fort Bragg, North Carolina, to arm his Knights of the New Order. Upon release, Tubbs served as "chaplain" for a Florida SCV camp, led the SCV's "Flags Across Florida" drive (seeking to line state highways with Confederate banners), and doubled as vice chairman of the LOS in northeastern Florida. In October 2004, still serving the SCV, Tubbs led a noisy racist picket line at SPLC headquarters. Another extremist, John Adams, served as Florida's SCV commander and the group's national webmaster until he was fired in 2002 for bombarding the SPLC with pornographic e-mails.[88]

The Magnolia State's neo–Confederate spearhead was Free Mississippi, founded by John Cripps of Lumberton. Formerly the pastor of a tiny "Confederate Presbyterian Church," Cripps served as Mississippi's LOS chairman until 2000, when he unilaterally changed the group's name and opened his storefront Confederate States Research Center in Wiggins. Although an LOS defector, Cripps retained his SCV membership and campaigned for retention of Mississippi's Confederate flag. In 2001 Free Mississippi claimed seventeen chapters statewide, plus a youth group in Laurel. Two years later, the far-right Constitution Party chose Cripps as its gubernatorial candidate, running on a largely "anti" platform that included abolition of Civil Service, welfare, the IRS, and the Food and Drug Administration; repeal of *Roe v. Wade*; elimination of congressional salaries; and American withdrawal from the United Nations. The "positive" aspects of his campaign included religious education in public schools and a vague injunction to "be fruitful and multiply."[89]

Pursuing Justice (2000–2007)

In November 1999, thirty-three years after the fact, federal prosecutors "learned" from ABC's *20/20* television program that Klan victim Ben White was murdered on federal land in the Homochitto National Forest. Ex-FBI agent Bill Dukes, retired to a Gulfport law practice, lamented the revelation, telling Jerry Mitchell, "It's a closed era in Mississippi, and I don't want to be a part of its resurrection." Of White's killers, only Ernest Avants survived at the turn of the century, suggesting to a *20/20* reporter, "If I was tried now, hell, I'd be convicted."[90]

Those words seemed prophetic on 7 June 2000, when G-men arrested Avants for murder on government land. Prosecutor Brad Piggott told reporters, "No time is too late to vindicate our country's repudiation of acts of racial violence. We are committed to bringing to justice those who commit such acts, no matter how long it takes." Still, it was 24 February 2003 before Avants faced trial before Judge William Barbour Jr. Defense attorney Tom Royals acknowledged that his client "ran his mouth a whole lot" and "bragged that he used violence against black people," but he dismissed such claims as boasts without substance. Witness Eddie Waters described his discovery of White's corpse on his (Waters's) twelfth birthday, while retired G-men recalled Avants's confession to killing White. "I shot that nigger," he had said. "I blew his head off with a shotgun." Jurors rejected a defense argument that the agents suffered from faulty memories, convicting Avants of murder on 28 February. While spectator Richard Barrett, head of the Nationalist Movement, complained that "there wasn't any evidence," Judge Barbour issued a sentence of life without parole on 17 June. Avants died in a Texas prison on 14 June 2004.[91]

An even older case was next in line for final reckoning. Surviving relatives of Michael Schwerner, James Chaney, and Andrew Goodman called for reexamination of the case in December 1998, after Jerry Mitchell revealed a comment by Sam Bowers admitting that he thwarted justice in Neshoba County and did not mind going to prison, "because a fellow Klansman got away with murder." State attorney general Mike Moore met with Neshoba district attorney Ken Turner on 25 May 1999, charting the course for a new investigation of the triple slaying. FBI agents reluctantly delivered 40,000 pages from their files in December 1999, while Cecil Price — elected vice president of the local Shriners three years earlier — secretly cooperated with prosecutors. Triggerman Alton Roberts died in 1999, and authorities saw no point in pursuing Sam Bowers through yet another murder trial when he was bound to die in prison for the Dahmer slaying. Instead, they fixed their sights on Edgar Killen, universally regarded as the classic "one who got away."[92]

Killen remained an enigmatic figure in early 2000, still denying Klan membership, complaining to journalists, "I don't have any rights. I have to be a newspaper reporter or a nigger if I want to have rights." Jackson prosecutor Bobby DeLaughter took a different view, writing that Killen "has been and still is" Neshoba's top klansman. Be that as it may, the state had lost a key witness on 1 June 1996, when Delmar Dennis died (the John Birch Society publicly mourned "The Passing of an American Hero"), and it lost another on 6 May 2001, when Cecil Price suffered a fatal accident at his workplace. Meanwhile, Jerry Mitchell named ex–Klansmen Bob Stringer and Ernest Gilbert as new witnesses, then aired a 1967 hold-out juror's refusal to find Killen guilty because she "could never convict a preacher." On 19 July 2001, retired investigator George Metz revealed Killen's admission that he helped clean up the murder scene on Rock Cut Road the morning after Schwerner, Chaney, and Goodman were slain.[93]

Despite the furor, Killen seemed optimistic. In October 2004 he announced a petition drive, launched at Mississippi's State Fair by the Learned-based Nationalist Movement, "opposing Communism, integration and non-speedy trials." Hinds County sheriff Malcolm

McMillan circulated a counter-petition, calling for Killen's indictment. Two months later, the Mississippi Religious Leadership Conference offered a $100,000 reward for final solution of the triple slaying.

On 6 January 2005 Neshoba County's grand jury charged Killen with three counts of murder. He posted bond, then broke both legs while chopping wood at home, thus postponing the start of his trial from 18 April to 13 June 2005. Killen appeared before Judge Marcus Gordon in a wheelchair, entrusting his fate to attorney Mitchell Morgan and an integrated jury. For the first time ever, Morgan granted that Killen had once been a klansman, but he insisted the preacher "was just a bystander in the same organization that a lot of other people were in at the same time and in the same place." Far from serving as the local Klan's "godfather"—a description offered by attorney general Jim Hood in his opening remarks—Morgan insisted that his client merely stood on the sidelines, far removed from any acts of violence.[94]

The prosecution's witnesses suggested otherwise, testifying that Killen directed the triple murder's planning and helped to clean up afterward. A spike in Killen's blood pressure briefly delayed the trial, on 15 June, but he returned to hear his prosecutors read aloud the 1967 testimony offered by Delmar Dennis in federal court. Joseph Hatcher, a former Meridian policeman, recalled Killen telling him where the corpses were buried two months before G-men unearthed them. According to Killen, two workers involved in constructing the dam had found blood on the ground and were promptly "sworn in, or sworn to secrecy, and threatened" by Killen. Killen's siblings testified for the defense, placing him at a family dinner when the murders occurred; but jurors ignored them, convicting Killen of manslaughter on the forty-first anniversary of the slayings. Two days later, Judge Gordon sentenced Killen to the maximum twenty-year term on each count, for a total of sixty years.[95]

Preacher Killen still had one last trick up his sleeve. On 12 August 2005 he claimed that his hands were paralyzed, prompting Judge Gordon to release him from custody on a $600,000 appeal bond. Three weeks later, on 3 September, the *Clarion-Ledger* published a deputy's statement that he had seen Killen driving a car "with no problem." Other officers gave similar testimony at a 9 September hearing, where Judge Gordon revoked Killen's bond and returned him to prison. Neo-Nazi Richard Barrett staged a "Killen Appreciation Day" in Philadelphia, on 18 September, but he played no apparent role in the foundation of a local National States Rights Party chapter, pledged to reestablishment of segregation and repeal of all the 1960s civil rights laws.[96]

Killen's belated conviction briefly roused hopes for a solution to the Wharlest Jackson bombing. Federal prosecutor Dunn Lampton, in Jackson, announced reopening of the case in 2005, then closed the file again, reporting that an FBI investigation revealed the prime suspects were dead. Jerry Mitchell's effort in pursuit of aging Ku Klux killers was rewarded in November 2005, when he received the John Chancellor Award for Excellence in Journalism from the University of Pennsylvania's Annenberg Public Policy Center. Author David Halberstram, speaking for the Center, summarized Mitchell's achievement: "Mitchell pursued these stories after most people believed they belonged to history, and not to journalism. But they did belong to journalism, because the truth had never been told, and justice had never been done. As each of the guilty convictions was finally handed down, it has been news of the highest order, and Jerry was there still covering the story."[97]

"As Long as the White Man Liveth"

Killen's imprisonment appeared to leave the Mississippi Klan in disarray. The SPLC found four active Klans in the state during 2005, including the Bayou Knights (two klaverns), the Orion Knights, the Mississippi White Knights, and the Southern White Knights (two klaverns). MWK imperial wizard Richard Greene urged his klansmen to steer clear of Killen's trial, but opined that "[t]he Klan is far from dead. All this show trial did was wake a sleeping tiger." Jordan Gollub, whose moribund Royal Confederate Knights failed to make the SPLC's list, took a more pessimistic view, telling Jerry Mitchell, "It's a different day and a different time." A ghost joined the debate, as Gollub quoted the late Sam Bowers, declaring in a phone call from prison, "I don't think the KKK is the way to go in the present day."[98]

The following year, Klan-watchers themselves seemed confused by the state of the Invisible Empire. ADL spokesmen found only the MWK still active in Mississippi; it staged an April rally in Amory and burned a December cross-burning in Itawamba County. The SPLC, by contrast, published a statewide survey including the Christian White Knights Church of the KKK in Petal, while the MWK boasted nine Mississippi klaverns and one in Arkansas. Siding with klansmen, where they could be found, were members of the Philadelphia-based NSRP, Richard Barrett's Nationalist Movement, and a chapter of David Duke's EURO in Ripley.[99]

Surprisingly, the Mississippi Klan found its greatest strength online, where a "free nation simulation game" called NationStates invited players to "[b]uild a nation and run it according to your own warped political ideals. Create a Utopian paradise for society's less fortunate or a totalitarian corporate police state. Care for your people or deliberately oppress them. Join the United Nations or remain a rogue state. It's really up to you." One such online creation was the White Knights of Mississippi, described by its anonymous creator as "a largely political yet somewhat paramilitary organization of right-wing Christians." Led by members of the fictional Fabus family, the WKM used its slogan, "Be a man, join the Klan," to recruit 450 million virtual members in eighteen American states, as well as "Mississippian Egypt, Western Sahara, Fabus Island, and Angola." Led by grand dragons in various realms, the WMK took credit for sundry belligerent activities, including wholesale "lynching of political opponents" and staging "massive rallies in support of white causes, almost weekly occurrences of rallies ranging from a few hundred to tens of millions across the Mississippian Federation."[100]

If playing NationStates fueled racist fantasies, the real-world outlook for Mississippi's hooded knights seemed bleak in 2007. Southaven police — pursuing vandals who defaced local homes and mailboxes with condiments and "KKK" graffiti during February — pinned the crime wave on a pair of teenagers with no connection to the Klan.[101] Meanwhile, the sluggish wheels of justice rolled toward one more target in a case from the chaotic 1960s.

Ben White's death was not the only case in which the FBI ignored a homicide on federal land. Henry Dee and Charles Moore had also been slain in the Homochitto National Forest, in May 1964, but thirty-five years elapsed before the Justice Department acknowledged that fact in January 2000. Suspect James Seale, believing that FBI files had been shredded, appeared unconcerned. "I ain't in jail, am I?" he asked Jerry Mitchell. He added, "Have at me. They don't have any more than you have right now — which is nothing." Agents arrested Seale for kidnapping on 24 January, but declined to say why Charles Edwards, who confessed to the crime in 1964, was not indicted with Seale.[102]

Seale soon learned that Edwards planned to testify against him, but the news apparently had little impact. Jailed without bond, Seale stalled his trial for another seven years, filing repetitive appeals based on the five-year statute of limitations for federal kidnapping charges. Finally, on 23 February 2007, Judge Henry Wingate dismissed Seale's final argument, ruling that statutes of limitations were waived when Congress made kidnapping a federal crime, and that repeal of the federal death penalty clause in 1972 did not apply retroactively to cases from earlier years. On 14 June jurors convicted Seale on two counts of kidnapping and one count of conspiracy. Ten weeks later, on 24 August, Judge Wingate declared Seale's crime "unspeakable because only monsters could inflict this." Seale received three life terms, with provision for confinement in a prison where his cancer could be treated.[103]

Seale's conviction was the twenty-third obtained since 1989 in slayings committed during Dixie's "Second Reconstruction." Another hundred homicides, nearly one-third of them from Mississippi, are presently under review by the Justice Department's Civil Rights Division, but assistant attorney general Wan Kim warned survivors and the public against unreasonable hope for sweeping victories.[104]

As 2009 began, the Mississippi White Knights of the KKK continued operations from headquarters in Petal, with seven more klaverns identified in Brookhaven, Bruce, Jackson, Kiln, Philadelphia, Tunica and Tupelo. Klan-watchers also identified one klavern of the United Northern and Southern Knights, but could not pin down its location. Six chapters of the CCC competed for members with single units of the European-American Unity and Rights Organization (in Ripley), the Nationalist Movement (in Learned), and Southaven's Order of St. Andrew. Neo-Confederates made do with one League of the South lodge, in Mendenhall, while overt neo–Nazis joined Raymond's branch of the Creativity Movement.[105]

Statewide, Klansmen sustain themselves with a boast as old as their order itself:

> Yesterday, Today, Forever,
> Since Eighteen Hundred and Sixty-Six,
> the KU KLUX KLAN
> has been riding and will
> continue to do so as long as
> the WHITE MAN LIVETH.[106]

Chapter Notes

Introduction

1. Stanley Horn, *Invisible Empire* (Boston: Houghton Mifflin, 1939), 9; Allen Trelease, *White Terror* (Westport: Greenwood, 1971), 3–5, 430; Wade, *Fiery Cross* (New York: Simon & Schuster, 1987), 31–35.

2. History of the Order, www.uta.edu/student_orgs/kao/rbhistory.html; "Kuklos Adelphon"; "Some notes on Theta's history"; Trelease, 4–5, 21.

3. Carleton Beals, *Brass-Knuckle Crusade* (New York: Hastings House, 1960), 158–159, 293–294; William Percy, *Lanterns on the Levee* (New York: Alfred A. Knopf, 1941), 234.

4. John Blassingame, ed., *Slave Testimony* (Baton Rouge: Louisiana State University Press, 1977), 156, 267; Gladys-Marie Fry, *Night Riders in Black Folk History* (Knoxville: University of Tennessee Press, 1975), 113; Leon Litwack, *Been in the Storm So Long* (New York: Alfred A. Knopf, 1979), 46; Wade, 18, 35.

5. Fry, *Night Riders,* 121; Sally Hadden, *Slave Patrols* (Cambridge, Harvard University Press, 2001), 212–213, 215–216; Trelease, 83; Wade, 37.

6. Avery Craven, *Reconstruction: The Ending of the Civil War* (New York: Holt, Rinehart and Winston, 1969), 91; John Franklin, *Reconstruction After the Civil War* (Chicago: University of Chicago Press, 1961), 25–31; David Sansing, "Governors of Mississippi," mshistory.k12.ms.us./features/feature27/governors_first.htm.

7. Craven, 106–107; W.E.B. Du Bois, *Black Reconstruction* (New York: Russell & Russell, 1935), 432; Eric Foner, *Reconstruction* (New York: Harper & Row, 1988), 193–194; Franklin, 41; Rembert Patrick, *The Reconstruction of the Nation* (New York: Oxford University Press, 1967), 33.

8. Du Bois, 433, 434; Foner, 199; Franklin, 43; Patrick, 33, 60–61; Sansing; Kenneth Stampp, *The Era of Reconstruction* (New York: Alfred A. Knopf, 1965), 78.

9. Lerone Bennett, Jr., *Before the Mayflower* (New York: Penguin, 1988), 477; Patrick, 41, 44, 61; Neal Peirce, *The Deep South States of America* (New York: W.W. Norton, 1972), 167–168.

10. Craven, 119–120; Du Bois, 170–175; Foner, 199; Franklin, 48.

11. Du Bois, 173, 175–176; Litwack, 369; Patrick, 43.

12. Patrick, 42.

13. Du Bois, 171–172; Foner, 10.

14. Du Bois, 177; Foner, 200–201.

15. Franklin, 50; Litwack, 369; Patrick, 44.

16. Bennett, 476; Craven, 121; Litwack, 368; Patrick, 43–44, 61; Sansing; Stampp, 80–81.

17. Bennett, 478.

18. F.Z. Browne, "Reconstruction in Oktibbeha County," *Publications of the Mississippi Historical Society* 13 (1913): 274; Du Bois, 141–142, 432; Franklin, 5, 51; Trelease, xlv–xlvi, 7–9; Wade, 18, 37; Fred Witty, "Reconstruction in Carroll and Montgomery Counties," *Publications of the Mississippi Historical Society* 10 (1909), 132–133.

19. Bennett, 479; Foner, 143; Franklin, 35, 70–72, 121, 198; Otto Olsen, ed., *Reconstruction and Redemption in the South* (Baton Rouge: Louisiana State University Press, 1980), 78; Patrick, 97–101, 103, 116.

20. Jack Hurst, *Nathan Bedford Forrest* (New York: Alfred A. Knopf, 1993), 284–287; Trelease, 14–15; Wade, 37–38.

21. Horn, *Invisible Empire,* 32–33.

22. Ibid., 397.

23. Ibid.

24. Trelease, 14–17; Wade, 409–418.

Chapter 1

1. Foner, *Reconstruction,* 16; Peirce, 166–7.

2. Hurst, *Forrest,* 12–29, 33, 59–60, 67, 71; Ezra Warner, *Generals in Gray* (Baton Rouge: Louisiana State University Press, 1959), 92–93.

3. Hurst, 103, 139–41, 144, 165–178.

4. Hurst, 5, 265–71, 275, 278, 281–2, 285, 341; Trelease, *White Terror,* 26–7, 30, 50.

5. Horn, *Invisible Empire,* 149; Trelease, 88; Witty, "Reconstruction," 129–130.

6. Franklin, *Reconstruction After,* 154; Witty, 129–30.

7. M.G. Abney, "Reconstruction in Pontotoc County," *Publications of the Mississippi Historical Society* 11 (1910): 243–4, 246; Horn, *Invisible Empire,* 145, 148–9; Julia Kendel, "Reconstruction in Lafayette County," *Publications of the Mississippi Historical Society* 13 (1913): 229, 239; Irby Nichols, "Reconstruction in Desoto County," *Publications of the Mississippi Historical Society* 11 (1910): 310; Trelease, 49–50; Witty, 131.

8. Abney, 237; George Leftwich, "Reconstruction in Monroe County," *Publications of the Mississippi Historical Society* 9 (1906): 66; *Testimony Taken by the Joint Select Committee to Inquire into the Condition of Affairs in the Late Insurrectionary States: Mississippi* (hereafter *KKK Testimony*), 1089, 1091–2; Trelease, 298–9; Ruth Watkins, "Reconstruction in Newton County," *Publications of the Mississippi Historical Society* 11 (1910): 210, 220–1.

9. David Chalmers, *Hooded Americanism,* 2nd edition (New York: New Viewpoints, 1981), 15; *KKK Tes-*

timony, 215–16; Hattie Magee, "Reconstruction in Lawrence and Jefferson Counties," *Publications of the Mississippi Historical Society* 11 (1910): 193; Trelease, 88.

10. Chalmers, 15; Franklin, 153; William Gillette, *Retreat from Reconstruction* (Baton Rouge: Louisiana State University Press, 1979), 43; Kendel, 243–44; Trelease, 88.

11. Bruce Allardice, *More Generals in Gray* (Baton Rouge: Louisiana State University Press, 1995), 99–100; Richard Current, *Those Terrible Carpetbaggers* (New York: Oxford University Press, 1988), 322–4; Ben Haas, *KKK* (San Diego: Regency, 1963), 26; "James Zachariah George"; Kendel, 244; Stetson Kennedy, *After Appomattox* (Gainesville: University of Florida Press, 1995), 248; Lester and Wilson, *Ku Klux Klan*, 310; Trelease, 20; Witty, 120, 130.

12. Abney, 236; Brown, 237; Current, 316–17, 322; Foner, 524–25; Kendel, 229–30, 244–6; Albert Kirwan, *Revolt of the Rednecks* (Gloucester: Smith, 1964), 3; *KKK Testimony*, 297–98, 348, 850–51, 910–911, 1160–62; "Lucius Quintus Cincinnatus Lamar"; Olsen, 92.

13. Brown, "Reconstruction in Yalobusha and Grenada Counties," 224, 235–36, 239–243; Browne, "Reconstruction in Oktibbeha County," 275, 287–88; Forrest Cooper, "Reconstruction in Scott County," *Publications of the Mississippi Historical Society* 13 (1913): 111, 127; "Henry Lowndes Muldrow"; Kendel, 229–30, 232–33, 239; *KKK Testimony*, 884; Leftwich, "Reconstruction in Monroe County," 66; Nichols, "Reconstruction in Desoto County," 310–11; "Samuel James Gholson"; Trelease, 88–9, 296, 400; Warner, 103–4; Watkins, "Reconstruction in Marshall County," 163.

14. Abney, 252; W.H. Braden, "Reconstruction in Lee County," *Publications of the Mississippi Historical Society* 10 (1909): 144; Coleman, "Reconstruction in Attala County," 157; *KKK Testimony*, 323; Magee, "Reconstruction in Lawrence and Jefferson Counties," 167; Nichols, 310–11.

15. Fry, *Night Riders*, 162–163; *KKK Testimony*, 279–80, 293, 351, 356–57, 808–19, 899, 1089; Trelease, 298–99.

16. Brown, 235; Coleman, 157; *KKK Testimony*, 558, 564, 567; John Kyle, "Reconstruction in Panola County," *Publications of the Mississippi Historical Society* 13 (1913): 51–2; Watkins, "Reconstruction in Marshall County," 178.

17. Abney, 246–47; Coleman, 157; Fry, *Night Riders*, 129, 132–34, 143; Kendel, 239–40; *KKK Testimony*, 274, 327–28, 343, 467, 483–84, 571, 584, 667, 771, 855 Magee, 193.

18. Abney, 247; Brown, 241; Coleman, 158; Fry, *Night Riders*, 131, 137–38; *KKK Testimony*, 663, 771, 813, 894; Kyle, 52–3; Magee, 194–95.

19. Cooper, 128.

20. *Forest Register*, 1 April 1868.

21. Cooper, 115–18, 128; Kendel, 243; *KKK Testimony*, 5, 573, 718, 1080; Watkins, "Reconstruction in Marshall County," 165, 168, 179.

22. *KKK Testimony*, 580.

23. Brown, 242; Kendel, 242; *KKK Testimony*, iii, iv, xv–xviii, xxix, xxx, xxxi, xxxvi–viii, 1084, 1165; Kyle, 52, 80–1; Watkins, "Reconstruction in Newton County," 220.

24. Braden, 145; Brown, 237–39; Kendel, 241–43; *KKK Testimony*, 708–9, 803–6; Trelease, 275–76, 288–90; Watkins, "Reconstruction in Marshall County," 179–80.

25. Du Bois, *Black Reconstruction*, 142; Peirce, 167.

26. Abney, 250, 252–53; Braden, 145; Brown, 240–42; Cooper, 138–40; Kendall, 240–42; *KKK Testimony*, 823, 1004, 1153, 1165; Watkins, "Reconstruction in Marshall County," 179.

27. Coleman, 158–59.

28. Du Bois, 143; Foner, 429; *KKK Testimony*, 233, 355, 376, 482–83; Hurst, 330; Trelease, 275, 288; Wade, 75, 76.

29. Hurst, 330; Trelease, 288.

30. Hurst, 323–25, 331; *KKK Testimony*, 74, 318; Litwack, *Been in the Storm*, 352; Trelease, 303; Charles Wilson.

31. *KKK Testimony*, 221, 225, 502, 528, 629, 666–67, 823, 921, 1165–66; Trelease, 289.

32. Abney, 233, 238, 247; Coleman, 152–153; Kendel, 229, 239, 251–52; Kyle, 51; Magee, 188; Trelease, 287; Watkins, "Reconstruction in Newton County," 208, 210–11, 220–21.

33. Cooper, 129–30; Current, 174–75; Foner, 426; *KKK Testimony*, 270, 280, 302; Trelease, 287.

34. Braden, 145; Du Bois, 431; Patrick, *Reconstruction of the Nation*, 41; Witty, 122.

35. Bennett, 482; Cooper, 151; Craven, *Reconstruction*, 236; Current, 83–84; Kyle, 29–30; Franklin, 102; Stampp, *Era of Reconstruction*, 169.

36. Current, 84; John Skates, "Constitution of 1868," Mississippi History Now, mshistory.k12.ms.us./features/feature8/1868constitution.html.

37. Current, 112–15; Sansing, "Governors of Mississippi."

38. Brown, 246–50; Craven, 238; Current, 118; Du Bois, 438–39; Kendel, 247–48; Nichols, 299; Trelease, 88.

39. Hurst, 267, 280–82, 298, 300–1; Joseph Kane, *Presidential Fact Book* (New York: Random House, 1998), 112.

40. Current, 121; Kane, 112; Sansing; Trelease, 124.

41. Hurst, 316.

42. Cooper, 155; Du Bois, 440; Foner, 414; Skates.

43. Current, 172–73; Witty, 216.

44. Current, 173–76; Nichols, 303–4; Trelease, 277.

45. Nichols, 304.

46. Bennett, 489; Current, 175–76, 181; Du Bois, 440; Kendel, 248; Olsen, 79–80; Patrick, 142–43; Sansing.

47. Horn, *Invisible Empire*, 146; Olsen, 79–80.

48. Abney, 236–38; Braden, 144–45; Brown, 235–37, 242; Browne, 275–78; Chalmers, 15; Coleman, 156–61; Cooper, 127–31; Franklin, 157; Kendel, 229–33, 242; *KKK Testimony*, i–lx; Kyle, 51–4; Leftwich, 59, 65–7; Magee, 192–95; Nichols, 310–11; Olsen, 81; Trelease, 88, 276; Watkins, "Reconstruction in Marshall County," 173–76; Watkins, "Reconstruction in Newton County," 216–22; Witty, 130–33.

49. *KKK Testimony*, 78–80, 102–5, 249–52; Nichols, 310–11; Trelease, 127, 137, 275–76, 290–91.

50. *KKK Testimony*, xxxvi–xxxviii, 1074–75, 1078–79, 1086, 1088, 1152; Nichols, 310–11; Trelease, 275, 288; Watkins, "Reconstruction in Marshall County," 160, 163, 178–81, 195–96.

51. *KKK Testimony*, 268–69, 356–57, 363, 462, 676–77, 779, 849, 921; Leftwich, 67; Trelease, 276, 287, 296–97, Wade, 65–8.

52. *KKK Testimony*, xxxvi–xxxviii, 230, 423, 674–675, 719–21, 774–75, 1038–40, 1045–46; Trelease, 276, 288.

53. *KKK Testimony*, xv–xvii, 114, 165–66, 230, 256–57, 477–78, 501–2, 523–26, 528, 539, 569, 583, 589, 629, 707–8, 883–84.; Trelease, 275–76.

54. Browne, 275–279, 281–285; *KKK Testimony,* xv–xvii, xxxvi–xxxvii, 230, 325–42, 467, 486, 493, 587–88, 601, 640, 643–46, 650, 699, 783, 824, 840, 871, 987, 1024–25 1106–7, 1150; Trelease, 288; Watkins, "Reconstruction in Newton County," 210, 213–14, 216–18, 219–22.

55. Abney, 253; Kendel, 229–33, 235, 237–39, 247, 251–53, 260, 263; Kyle, 40–1, 51–4, 79–81; Trelease, 274–75.

56. Abney, 233, 236–38, 243–44, 246–53, 258; Horn, *Invisible Empire,* 152–155; *KKK Testimony,* 1089–93, 1101–2, 1104–5; Trelease, 295.

57. Abney, 251, 253; Braden, 135, 144–45; Brown, 214, 227–28, 235–39; "Galusha Pennypacker"; *KKK Testimony,* 588.

58. Coleman, 152–53, 156–61; *KKK Testimony,* 588; Witty, 116, 119, 129–32.

59. Chalmers, 15; Cooper, 101–2, 110–11, 127–31, 138–141, 200, 203, 205; Current, 117–18, 317–18; Franklin, 157; Trelease, 88.

60. *KKK Testimony,* 302; Magee, 163, 192–95; Trelease, 88.

61. Horn, *Invisible Empire,* 154–155; *KKK Testimony,* 345, 583–84, 633–634, 794, 991, 989, 1086, 1106–7; Trelease, 289, 295–96.

62. Braden, 145; Chalmers, p 19; Horn, *Invisible Empire,* 357–58; Cooper, 130; Hurst, 325–26; Trelease, 184–85.

63. Horn, *Invisible Empire,* 356–59; Trelease, 179–80.

64. Braden, 144; Current, 186; Franklin, 167; Horn, *Invisible Empire,* 145–46; Leftwich, 65–6; Trelease, 298.

65. Horn, *Invisible Empire,* 155–156; *KKK Testimony,* 864–65; Trelease, 277–78, 299.

66. Abney, 238, 251; Brown, 237; Kendel, 247; *KKK Testimony,* 1089, 1093, 1099; Leftwich, 67; Trelease, 274–75, 296; Witty, 116, 130–32.

67. Foner, 366–68; Franklin, 112–13, 139; Horn, 149.

68. Abney, 258; Kendel, 260; *KKK Testimony,* 282, 662–63, 676, 899; J.S. McNeilly, "The Enforcement Act of 1871 and Ku Klux Klan in Mississippi," *Publications of the Mississippi Historical Society* 9 (1906): 149; Trelease, 293–94; Wade, 64.

69. Cooper, 129, 193–94; Horn, *Invisible Empire,* 149; *KKK Testimony,* 326–27, 493, 1150.

70. *KKK Testimony,* 265–98; Leftwich, 59; Wade, 64–8.

71. Brown, 239, 364–65; *KKK Testimony,* 18–19, 76, 94, 260, 283, 329, 402, 477–78, 502, 539, 587, 601, 699–700, 989, 1021, 1150; Trelease, 293–94.

72. *KKK Testimony,* 64–5, 78–80, 101–5, 122–23, 249–52; McNeilly, 126–33; Trelease, 290–91.

73. Current, 180; Horn, *Invisible Empire,* 159–62; *KKK Testimony,* 39, 41, 105–6; McNeilly, 126–33; Trelease, 291–93.

74. Current, 186–87; Horn, *Invisible Empire,* 159–62; *KKK Testimony,* 10, 23–53, 127–64; McNeilly, 126–33; Trelease, 290–93; Wade, 88.

75. McNeilly, 126–133; Trelease, 292.

76. Bennett, 489–91; Stephen Cresswell, "Enforcing the Enforcement Acts," *Journal of Southern History* 53 (August 1987): 421–22; McNeilly, 119–22.

77. Bennett, 489, 491–92; Current, 187.

78. Cresswell, 432; *KKK Testimony,* 817–18, 1147–67; Watkins, "Reconstruction in Newton County," 213–14, 221

79. Brown, 237; Kendel, 243; *KKK Testimony,* 1086–1100.

80. Cresswell, 424–26, 430–31, 433–34; Horn, *Invisible Empire,* 172–76; Kendel, 244–246; *KKK Testimony,* 936–87; McNeilly, 140–44; Trelease, 399–400.

81. Hurst, 338; *KKK Testimony,* i–lx; Leftwich, 67–8; McNeilly, 135–40, 170–71; Trelease, 391–98.

82. Hurst, 313–315, 337–344; Kennedy, *After Appomattox,* 210–17; *KKK Testimony, Miscellaneous and Florida,* 3–41.

83. Abney, 249–50; Browne, 276, 283–86; Foner, 457; Gillette, 30, 44; Trelease, 412–13.

84. *KKK Testimony,* 677–79, 1017–21, 1089–91; Trelease, 299.

85. *KKK Testimony,* 257–58, 477, 501, 1067, 1138–39, 1141, 1145; Trelease, 299.

86. Cresswell, 430; Du Bois, 441; Nichols, 305–306; Sansing; Trelease, 287–288; Watkins, "Reconstruction in Marshall County," 192–93.

87. Browne, 291–92; Cresswell, 426; Kane, 113–14; Sansing; Watkins, "Reconstruction in Marshall County," 163, 187–88.

88. Bennett, 495; Cresswell, 434–35; Current, 307–9; Du Bois, 432, 441, 444; Gillette, 44; Kennedy, 234–36; Olsen, 85–86; Sansing.

89. Craven, 240; Current, 309, 311; Gillette, 182.

90. Current, 326; Gillette, 229–30; Leftwich, 70–1; Olsen, 92.

91. Brown, "Reconstruction in Yalobusha and Grenada Counties," 227, 235; Donald, 454, 456; Gillette, 153–54; Horn, *Invisible Empire,* 166–67; Kennedy, *After Appomattox,* 237–38; Nichols, 310–11; Olsen, 86–7, 90–6; Stampp, 201–2.

92. Current, 314–17; Foner, 558–59; Franklin, 197; Gillette, 150; Kendel, 264.

93. Current, 314–17; Foner, 558–59; Gillette, 150–53; Olsen, 96–9.

94. Current, 314–17; Foner, 558–59; Gillette, 150–53.

95. Kennedy, *After Appomattox* 244; Olsen, 101, 106.

96. Brown, 251–252; Donald, 455–58; Kendel, 250, 263; Kyle, 71–6; Leftwich, 71–82; Patrick, 159–60.

97. Bennett, 497–99; Brown 257; Cooper, 140–41; Current, 317–18; Foner, 559–62; Gillette, 153–65; Kennedy, 237–46; Stampp, 209–10.

98. Brown, 227, 235; Cooper, 174–75; Foner, 559–62; Hurst, 367–68; Kennedy, 237–47; Nichols, 310–11; Stampp, 202–3; Witty, 119–20.

99. Browne, 287–91; Current, 324–26; Foner, 559–62; Franklin, 223–24; Kennedy, 248–50; Stampp, 202–3; Watkins, "Reconstruction in Marshall County," 160.

100. Creswell, 430, 437; Du Bois, 685–86; Gillette, 44.

101. Current, 324–25; Foner, 562; Franklin, 224; Sansing.

102. Brown, 252–53; "Henry Lowndes Muldrow"; Kane, 121; Kirwan, 6; "Lucius Quintus Cincinnatus Lamar"; Nichols, 307–8; William Randel, *The Ku Klux Klan: A Century of Infamy* (London: Chilton, 1965), 44.

103. Cresswell, 429–30; "Henry Lowndes Muldrow"; Stanley Hirshson, *Farewell to the Bloody Shirt* (Chicago: Quadrangle, 1962), 22–7; Kane, 122; "Lucius Quintus Cincinnatus Lamar"; Randel, 87; Witty, 134.

104. Gillette, 376.

105. Bennett, 500; Foner, 580–81; Kane, 122; Kennedy, 272–280; Patrick, 266.

106. Bennett, 488–89, 495–96; Craven, 229; Du Bois, 447; Franklin, 136; Neil McMillen, *Dark Journey* (Urbana: University of Illinois Press, 1990), 36.

107. Du Bois, 450; Olsen, 89, 101; Patrick, 145, 147; Stampp, 178–79.

108. Cooper, 128–29, 203, 205; Cresswell, 430–31; Current, 117; Franklin, 113; Trelease, 88–9, 296–97.

109. Horn, *Invisible Empire,* 375; Hurst, 345.

Chapter 2

1. Foner, *Reconstruction,* 588–90, 594.

2. Kirwan, *Revolt,* 24–5; James Wells, *The Chisolm Massacre* (Washington: Chisholm Monument Assoc., 1878).

3. Gillette, 347; Kirwan, 45–6.

4. Cresswell, "Enforcing the Enforcement Acts," 427; James Loewen and Charles Sallis, eds., *Mississippi: Conflict and Change* (New York: Random House, 1974), 179; Clark Miller, "Let Us Die to Make Men Free," PhD diss., University of Minnesota, 1983, 186; "Samuel James Gholson"; Harvard Sitkoff, *A New Deal for Blacks* (New York: Oxford University Press, 1978), 4; Ruth Watkins, "Reconstruction in Marshall County," *Publications of the Mississippi Historical Society* 12 (1912): 160; Watkins, "Reconstruction in Newton County," 210–11, 220.

5. Hirshson, *Farewell,* 43; Logan, *Betrayal of the Negro,* 31

6. Bennett, 501; Hirshson, 65, 68; Miller, 54–55.

7. Current, *Those Terrible Carpetbaggers,* 416; Hirshson, 154; "James Zacariah George"; Miller, 52, 54–5.

8. Miller, 66–7, 75–7, 107–8, 118–20.

9. Kane, *Presidential Fact,* 123, 127–8; Logan, 35–6.

10. Julia Brown, "Reconstruction in Yalobusha and Grenada Counties," *Publications of the Mississippi Historical Society* 12 (1912): 58, 228–9; "James Ronald Chalmers"; "James Zachariah George"; Kirwan, 9–10; Loewen and Sallis, 179; Miller, 180–1; Wilson, "Mississippi Chinese."

11. Miller, 187, 243, 245.

12. Ibid., 242, 245, 257.

13. Ibid., 258.

14. Ibid., 267–8.

15. Hirshson, 112–13; Kirwan, 10;

16. Hirshson, 113.

17. Cresswell, "Enforcing the Enforcement Acts," 430, 432; "James Ronald Chalmers."

18. Hirshson, 120–1; Loewen and Sallis, 179–80; Miller, 371–2, 375.

19. Miller, 380–3, 385–9.

20. Cresswell, "Enforcing the Enforcement Acts," 435; Kane, 137; Miller, 406–7, 429.

21. "Edward Cary Walthall"; "Henry Lowndes Muldrow"; Hirshson, 154–6; "Lucius Quintus Cincinnatus Lamar."

22. Current, 409–10.

23. Miller, 434–7.

24. Hirshson, 153–4; Gustavus Myers, *History of Bigotry in the United States* (New York: Random House, 1943), 163–91; Wade, 114.

25. Bennett, 502; Hirshson, 165; Kane, 138, 143; Kennedy, *Jim Crow Guide,* 178; Richard Kluger, *Simple Justice* (New York: Alfred A. Knopf, 1976), 73, 77–8; "Lucius Quintus Cincinnatus Lamar."

26. Miller, 448, 466.

27. McMillen, *Dark Journey,* 226; Miller, 512–14, 518.

28. McMillen, 52, 232; Miller, 529.

29. Terrence Finnegan, "Lynching and Political Power in Mississippi and South Carolina," in *Under Sentence of Death,* edited by W. Fitzhugh Brundage, 189–218 (Chapel Hill: University of North Carolina Press, 1997), 194–5; Miller, 529–33.

30. Finnegan, "Lynching" 194–5; Miller, 534–6.

31. Miller, 537–40.

32. Cresswell, "Enforcing the Enforcement Acts." 432; Miller, 545–50; Stewart Tolnay and E.M. Beck, *A Festival of Violence* (Urbana: University of Illinois Press, 1995), 182.

33. Browne, "Reconstruction in Oktibbeah County," 292; "Henry Lowndes Muldrow"; "James Zachariah George"; Logan, 65–6; McMillen, 39; Sansing, "Governors of Mississippi."

34. Loewen and Sallis, 188.

35. McMillen, 43; Miller, 629; Peirce, 169.

36. Stetson Kennedy, *Southern Exposure* (Garden City: Doubleday, 1946), 37; Kirwan, 48, 50; McCarty, "Farmers, the Populist Party, and Mississippi"; Tolnay and Beck, 175–80.

37. Finnegan, 205; Kane, 147–8; Kirwan, 94; Loewen and Sallis, 190–1; Miller, 636, 649, 654.

38. Kennedy, *Southern* Exposure, 41; Kirwan, 95–6; Loewen and Sallis, 190–1; Tolnay and Beck, 175–80.

39. Kane, 152, 159, 165, 171; McCarty, "Farmers, the Populist Party, and Mississippi."

40. Kennedy, *Southern Exposure,* 44–5.

41. Ibid., 46; Myers, 193.

42. Beals, *Brass-Knuckle,* 297; Myers, 194–5.

43. Myers, 196–8, 205; Wade, 144.

44. Kirwan, 45–6; Trelease, 420; Wade, 114–15.

45. William Holmes, "Whitecapping: Anti-Semitism in the Populist Era," *American Jewish Historical Quarterly* 43 (March 1974): 245–7, 250.

46. Ibid., 247–8.

47. Ibid., 248.

48. Finnegan, p 206–7; Holmes, 248–50, 256; McMillen, 120.

49. Holmes, 250–2.

50. Ibid., 252–5.

51. Ibid., 255–8.

52. Ibid., 258–60.

53. William Holmes, "Whitecapping: Agrarian Violence in Mississippi, 1902–1906," *Journal of Southern History* 35 (May 1969): 167–9; McMillen, 120.

54. Holmes, "Whitecapping: Agrarian Violence," 169–70; McMillen, 120.

55. Holmes, "Whitecapping: Agrarian Violence," 170–1.

56. Ibid., 171–3.

57. Ibid., 173–4.

58. Ibid., 175–80; Loewen and Sallis, 195.

59. Holmes, "Whitecapping: Agrarian Violence," 181–4.

60. "Dunning School"; Foner, 609.

61. Browne, 291; Victoria Bynum, *The Free State of Jones* (Chapel Hill: University of North Carolina Press, 2001), 148; Foner, 609; Kendel, "Reconstruction in Lafayette County," 263; Kyle, 52, 78, 81; Hattie Magee, "Reconstruction in Lawrence and Jefferson Counties," *Publications of the Mississippi Historical Society* 11 (1910): 168, 195; Watkins, "Reconstruction in Marshall County," 199; Watkins, "Reconstruction in Newton County," 222.

62. Abney, "Reconstruction in Pontotoc County," 246; Braden, "Reconstruction in Lee County," 145; James Garner, *Reconstruction in Mississippi* (Baton Rouge: Louisiana State University Press, 1901), 378;

McNeilly, "The Enforcement Act," 125; Watkins, "Reconstruction in Newton County," 220; Witty, "Reconstruction," 134.

63. Chalmers, *Hooded Americanism*, 23; Wade, 122–3, 125.

64. Stephen Cresswell, "Was Mississippi a Part of Progressivism?" Mississippi History Now. mshistory. k12.ms.us/features/feature53/progressive.htm.

65. John Barry, *Rising Tide* (New York: Simon & Schuster, 1998), 124; Cresswell, "Was Mississippi a Part of Progressivism?"; Phillip Dray, *At the Hands of Persons Unknown* (New York: Modern Library, 2002), 417; "James Kimble Vardaman"; Kirwan, 144–6; Reinhard Luthin, *American Demagogues* (Boston: Beacon, 1954), 46; Peirce, 170.

66. Bynum, 151; Finnegan, 204–5; Ginzburg, *100 Years of Lynchings*, 253; *Lynchings by State and Race*, 1; McMillen, 229–30, 234; Peirce, 169; Tolnay and Beck, 38.

67. Ginzburg, 62–3; Kay Mills, *This Little Light of Mine* (New York: Plume, 1993), 29–31; Frank Shay, *Judge Lynch* (New York: Washburn, 1938), 103–5.

68. Kirwan, 152; Adam Nossiter, *Of Long Memory* (Reading: Addison-Wesley, 1994), 88.

69. Loewen and Sallis, 194; McMillen, 13, 62, 192, 226.

70. Barry, 124; Kirwan, 180; Loewen and Sallis, 197; Luthin, 46; McMillen, 6; "Theodore Gilmore Bilbo."

71. Pete Daniel, *The Shadow of Slavery* (New York: Oxford University Press, 1973), 102–3; Logan, 387; McMillen, 226; NAACP, *Thirty Years of Lynching*, 78–9.

72. Kirwan, 217–18; Loewen and Sallis, 198–9; Luthin, 47; McMillen, 176.

73. Barry, 129–30; Kirwan, 217–18; Loewen and Sallis, 200; Luthin, 48

74. William Doyle, *An American Insurrection* (New York: Anchor, 1962), 53; Dray, 417–18; McMillen, 121.

75. Chalmers, 25–6.

76. Chalmers, 25–6; Wade, 119, 125–7, 136.

77. "Leo Frank," Wikipedia.

78. Myer, 199–203; Wade, 144.

79. "Leo Frank"; Myers, 205–6; Wade, 143–4.

80. Chalmers, 29; Haas, *KKK,* 42–3; Myers, 216–17; Wade, 140–3.

81. Chalmers, 29–30; Haas, 42–3; Myers, 217; Arnold Rice, *The Ku Klux Klan in American Politics* (Washington: Public Affairs, 1962), 1; Wade, 140–5.

82. Wade, 146–7, 428, 430.

83. Richard Damms, "Loyalty and Dissent in Mississippi During the Great War, 1917–1918," Mississippi History Now; "James Kimble Vardaman"; Myers, 208–9.

84. Chalmers, 31; Damms; Wade, 148, 150.

85. McMillen, 272–3, 305–6; 315; NAACP, *Thirty Years of Lynching*, 80, 105.

86. Luthin, 54; Peirce, 171.

87. Wade, 149, 151.

88. Bynum, 151–2; Dray, 257; McMillen, 228–9, 305–6; Shay, 93

89. McMillen, 305–6; NAACP, *Burning at Stake in the United States*, 4–9.

90. Kane, p180; Peirce, 172; Wade, 151.

91. Chalmers, 31; Peirce, 204; Rice, 5.

92. New York *World* (19 Sept. 1921), 1; Wade, 153–4.

93. Chalmers, 34; Wade, 154–6.

94. Chalmers, 35; Wade, 157.

95. Chalmers, 35–8; Rice, 59; Wade, 161–6.

Chapter 3

1. Ben Edmonson, "Pat Harrison and Mississippi in the Presidential Elections of 1924 and 1928," *Journal of Mississippi History* 33 (November 1971): 333.

2. Laura Bradley, "Protestant Churches and the Ku Klux Klan in Mississippi During the 1920's," master's thesis, University of Mississippi, 18; "Movement on Foot to Start Ku Klux Klan"; "Mysterious Ku Klux Klan Again Gains Prominence."

3. Bynum, *The Free State of* Jones, 165–6; Chalmers, *Hooded Americanism*, 66, 68; "Ku Klux Klan Invades Jackson Tuesday"; Rice, *The Ku Klux Klan in American Politics*, 49.

4. Bradley, "Protestant Churches and the Ku Klux Klan," 15–16.

5. Bradley, 51–2.

6. Bradley, 11; Haas, *KKK,* 61–2; Jackson, *Ku Klux Klan in the City*, 237; "Ku Klux Membership Falls"; Rice, 13.

7. Wade, 427.

8. Ibid., 428.

9. Bradley, 24; Nancy MacLean, *Behind the Mask of Chivalry* (New York: Oxford University Press, 1994), 7.

10. Ibid., 25.

11. Ibid., 13, 25–6, 48.

12. Percy, *Lanterns on the Levee*, 234.

13. Kathleen Blee, *Women of the Klan* (Berkeley: University of California Press, 1991), 25–8, 30–1.

14. Ibid., 157–8, 160–1.

15. Wade, 420.

16. Ibid., 432.

17. Barry, *Rising Tide*, 142.

18. Bradley, 31–4, 44–5; Bynum, 166; MacLean, 8.

19. Bradley, 33, 63–4; Wade, 168, 176–7.

20. Bradley 38–9.

21. Ibid., 27–8, 37, 39, 41–3 48.

22. Lewis Baker, *The Percys of Mississippi* (Baton Rouge: Louisiana State University Press, 1983), 100–1; Bradley, 12–13.

23. Bradley, 14–16.

24. Ibid., 16.

25. Rice, 49.

26. Barry, 180; Bradley, 39, 47.

27. Bradley, 43–4, 49–51, 68.

28. Ibid., 34–5.

29. Wade, 428–9.

30. MacLean, 49, 132, 140, 238.

31. Bradley, 8, 10–12; Percy, 234; Wilson, "Italians in Mississippi."

32. Bradley, 20; MacLean, 135, 137, 144–5.

33. Bradley, 12, , 17–18, 20–1.

34. Wade, 430.

35. Wade, 433.

36. Stetson Kennedy, *Jim Crow Guide* (Boca Raton: Florida Atlantic University Press, 1990), 30; MacLean, 132, 134, 140.

37. Kennedy, *Jim Crow Guide* 30–1; MacLean, 132.

38. Jacquelyn Hall, *Revolt Against Chivalry* (New York: Columbia University Press, 1979), 155; Bynum, 152.

39. Baker, 101; Bradley, 18; Bynum, 152; Rice, 132.

40. "Rich Planter Leads Mississippi Klansmen."

41. Bradley, 18; Bynum, 166; "S.D. Redmond Target of Ku Klux Klan Threat."

42. "S.D. Redmond Target of Ku Klux Klan Threat."

43. McMillen, *Dark Journey*, 159–60; "S.D. Redmond Target of Ku Klux Klan Threat."

44. "Klan Warns Firemen to Leave Jobs."
45. Ralph Ginzburg, *100 Years of Lynchings* (New York: Lancer, 1962), 147–9; "Klan Warns Firemen to Leave Jobs"; McMillen, 159–60.
46. McMillen, 315, 325.
47. Ginzburg, 160, 165, 171, 180; McMillen, 234.
48. Charles Payne, *I've Got the Light of Freedom* (Berkeley: University of California Press, 1995), 18–19; Shay, *Judge Lynch*, 106.
49. Percy, 269; Daniel, *Shadow of Slavery*, 151–7.
50. Bradley, 65; Edmonson, 333–4; Glenn Feldman, *Politics, Society, and the Klan in Alabama, 1915–1949* (Tuscaloosa; University of Alabama Press, 1999), 213–14, 260–1; Luthin, *American Demagogues*, 59.
51. Bradley, 26, 40–1, 51, 65–6; Chalmers, 289; Wade, 249–50.
52. Bradley, 25, 53, 55, 71.
53. Ibid., 55–9, 68–71.
54. Barry, 144; Bradley, 23–4, 37; Percy, 231–2.
55. Baker, 143–4; Barry, 143; Percy, 232.
56. Barry, 146; Percy, 232–3.
57. Baker, 95; Barry, 146.
58. Barry, 146.
59. Barry, 147, 149; Percy, 233.
60. Baker, 108–9; Chalmers, 60–4; Percy, 235–6.
61. Baker, 103–4; Barry, 149.
62. Baker, 106–7.
63. Ibid., 107.
64. Chalmers, 111, 198, 200; Wade, 165.
65. Chalmers, 68; Luthin, 55; Rice, 48–9.
66. Baker, 109; Barry, 149–50; Brenda Poke, Greenville Public Library, e-mail of 28 February 2006.
67. Baker, 105–6; Barry, 150; Bradley, 37, 54–5.
68. Baker, 110; Barry, 153; Percy, 237–41; Poke e-mail, 28 February 2006.
69. Bradley, 22–3.
70. Baker, 111; Edmonson, 335–6.
71. Edmonson, 338; Paul Gillette and Eugene Tillinger, *Inside Ku Klux Klan* (New York: Pyramid, 1965), 50–2; Kane, *Presidential Fact,* 185–6; Rice, 81.
72. Butler, "How 'Al' Smith Fared," 244–5; John Carlson, *The Plotters* (New York: E. Dutton, 1946), 51–2; Chalmers, 69; Luthin, 56, 58–9.
73. "Grover C. Nicholas Injured"; "Bloodhounds Lead to Arrest."
74. "Bloodhounds Lead"; "Nicolas [*sic*] Murder" [hereafter Scrapbook], 1.
75. Scrapbook, 1–2, 5, 7.
76. Scrapbook, 5, 7.
77. Scrapbook, 2.
78. Scrapbook, 2–3.
79. Scrapbook, 3.
80. Scrapbook, 3–4.
81. Scrapbook, 5, 7–8.
82. Scrapbook, 6, 8, 11, 15, 22.
83. Scrapbook, 9, 36, 40.
84. Scrapbook 10, 16, 19.
85. Scrapbook, 10.
86. Scrapbook, 16, 18.
87. Scrapbook, 20, 23–4, 28.
88. Scrapbook, 32–3, 49.
89. Scrapbook, 37–41.
90. Scrapbook, 42–5.
91. Scrapbook, 49, 55.
92. Chalmers, 68; Scrapbook, 56.
93. Butler, 245; Chalmers, 68; Edmonson, 342.
94. Edmonson, 341–4.
95. Ibid., 345–7.

96. Edmonson, 348–9; Rice, 88.
97. Edmonson, 348–50; Luthin, 60.
98. Kane, 192; McMillen, 66–7.
99. Chalmers, 68.
100. Feldman, *Politics, Society, and the Klan,* 213–14.
101. Ibid., 260–1.
102. Bynum, 172; "White Floggers Out on Bond."
103. Jessie Ames, *The Changing Character of Lynching* (Atlanta: Commission on Interracial Cooperation, 1942), 23–5; Finnegan, "Lynching and Political Power," 35; Ginzburg, 215–16, 227; Payne, 7–15; Shay, 93–4.
104. Ginzburg, 231; Shay, 245; Sitkoff, *New Deal for Blacks,* 241, 247–8.
105. Dray, *At the Hands of Persons Unknown,* 321–2; Hall, 173, 215–16.
106. Dray, 359–60; Ginzburg, 203; Shay, 106.
107. Sitkoff, 117, 240.
108. Myrlie Evers and William Peters, *For Us, the Living* (Garden City: Doubleday, 1967), 17; Loewen and Sallis, *Mississippi,* 239; Luthin, 63; Maryanne Vollers, *Ghosts of Mississippi* (Boston: Little, Brown, 1995), 8–9.
109. Luthin, 68; Sitkoff, 117–18, 122.
110. James Cobb, *The Mississippi Delta and the World* (Baton Rouge: Louisiana State University Press, 1995), 49: Peirce, 172.
111. Chalmers, 307.
112. Wade, 259.
113. Chalmers, 307; Kane, 198–201.
114. Peirce, 171, 208; Sitkoff, 36.
115. McMillen, 160; Sitkoff, 36.
116. Richard Hofstadter and Michael Wallace, eds., *American Violence* (New York: Vintage, 1970), 177; McMillen, 134, 136–7; Sitkoff, 171.
117. Chalmers, 319–21; Sitkoff, 179–80.
118. Ames, *Changing Character of Lynching,* 2; Chalmers, 318, 322–3; Wade, 265–6.
119. "James Oliver Eastland"; Peirce, 172; Robert Sherrill, *Gothic Politics in the Deep South* (New York: Grossman, 1968), 203.
120. Luthin, 68.
121. John Dittmer, *Local People* (Urbana: University of Illinois Press, 1995); Payne, 13–14; Sitkoff, 231.
122. Wade, 273–4.
123. Chalmers, 323–4; Haas, 91.

Chapter 4

1. Chalmers, *Hooded Americanism,* 325; Haas, *KKK,* 92; House Committee on Un-American Activities, *Present-Day Ku Klux Klan Movement* [hereafter *HUAC Report*], 9; Michael Newton, *The Ku Klux Klan* (Jefferson, NC: McFarland, 2007), 383.
2. Carlson, *The Plotters,* 51–2; Kennedy, *Klan Unmasked,* 190–1; Kennedy, *Southern Exposure,* 325; Rice, 112.
3. Dray, *At the Hands of Persons Unknown,* 418; Kennedy, *Klan Unmasked,* 139–40; Newton, 172; Rice, 112.
4. Dernoral Davis, "Medgar Wylie Evers and the Origin of the Civil Rights Movement in Mississippi," Mississippi History Now; Dittmer, 1–3; Vollers, *Ghosts,* 31–3.
5. Dittmer, 1–3; Dray, 418; Kennedy, *Jim Crow Guide,* 158; Loewen and Sallis, 239; Luthin, *American Demagogues,* 70–1.
6. Dittmer, 6; Payne, *I've Got the Light,* 31, 448.
7. Dittmer, 1–3, 5; Evers and Peters, *For Us, the*

Living, 26; Walter Lord, *The Past That Would Not Die* (New York: Harper & Row, 1965), 27; Vollers, 31–3.

8. Dittmer, 1–4, 8; Dray, 418; Loewen and Sallis, 239; Luthin, 73.

9. Cobb, *Mississippi Delta,* 49; Peirce, 200–1.

10. Bennett, 542–5; Chalmers, *Hooded Americanism,* 326; Dittmer, 24.

11. Bennett, 544–5; Yasuhiro Katagiri, *The Mississippi State Sovereignty Commission* (Jackson: University of Mississippi Press, 2001), xxii–xxv; McMillen, *Dark Journey,* 235; Morgan, "Presidential Elections"; Newton, 234.

12. Jack Davis, *Race Against Time* (Louisiana State University Press, 2001), 153; Kane, *Presidential Fact,* 211–12; Morgan; Newton, 234; Peirce, 191.

13. House Committee on Un-American Activities, *Activities of Ku Klux Klan Organizations in the United States* [hereafter *HUAC Hearings*], vol. 5, 2818.

14. Arnold Forster, *A Measure of Freedom* (Garden City: Doubleday, 1950f), 24; Haas, 103–4.

15. Feldman, 312–13; Forster, *Measure of Freedom,* 14; Gillette and Tillinger, 74, 82; Rice, 115.

16. Gillette and Tillinger, 74–89.

17. "Klan Moves into Mississippi." *New York Times,* 26 March 1950; advertisement for commemorative plate, http://www.kkklan.com/restrikes.htm, accessed 14 July 2005.

18. Davis, "Medgar Wiley Evers"; Davis, "When Youth Protests"; Evers and Peters, *For Us, the Living,* 86–7; Payne, 48–9; Vollers, 41.

19. Numan Bartley, *The Rise of Massive Resistance* (Baton Rouge; Louisiana State University Press, 1969), 46, 50; Kane, 219; Katagiri, xxv; Morgan.

20. Bennett, 375–6.

21. James Cook, *The Segregationists* (New York: Appleton-Century-Crofts1, 1962), 4; Evers and Peters, *For Us, the Living,* 109, 111; Katagiri, xxix; McMillen, *Citizen's Council,* 15.

22. Doyle, *An American Insurrection,* 54, 60.

23. Kennedy, *Jim Crow Guide,* 98–9; John Martin, *The Deep South Says "Never"* (New York: Ballantine, 1957), 27, 123–4; Neil McMillen, *The Citizens' Council* (Urbana: University of Illinois Press, 1971), 16, 26–8, 118.

24. Cook, 54; Kennedy, *Jim Crow Guide,* 98–9; Lord, 66–7; Martin, 28–30.

25. Katagiri, xxx; Florence Mars, *Witness in Philadelphia* (Baton Rouge: Louisiana State University Press, 1977), 57; McMillen, *Citizens' Council,* 18; Peirce, 174.

26. Cook, 153–5; McMillen, *Citizens' Council,* 118; Newton, 146, 170–1.

27. McMillen, *Citizens' Council,* 256–7; Wade, 300.

28. Reed Massengill, *Portrait of a Racist* (New York: St. Martin's Griffin, 1996), 149–50; Newton, 61, 157–8.

29. Ira Harkey, *The Smell of Burning Crosses* (Jacksonville, MS: Harris-Wolfe, 1967), 104; *HUAC Report,* 11.

30. Bartley, 76–7, 211; Cook, 85, 89; Evers and Peters, *For Us, the Living,* 175–6; Katagiri, xxxiv, 4–6; Mills, *This Little Light of Mine,* 32.

31. Bartley, 181; Cook, 85, 89; Doyle, 55; Sarah Rowe-Sims, "The Mississippi State Sovereignty Commission," Mississippi History Now.

32. Evers and Peters, *For Us, the Living,* 133; McMillen, *Citizens' Council,* 235–6; Sherrill, *Gothic Politics in the Deep South,* 176.

33. Sarah Bullard, ed., *Free at Last* (Montgomery: Southern Poverty Law Center, n.d.), 36; Evers and Peters, *For Us, the Living,* 154; McMillen, *Citizens' Council,* 216–17; Lord, 66–7; Jack Mendelsohn, *The Martyrs* (New York: Harper & Row, 1966), 2–3 Vollers, 58–62.

34. Dittmer, 53–4; Evers and Peters, *For Us, the Living,* 156–8; Mendelsohn, 8–10; Vollers, 58–60.

35. Bullard, *Free at Last,* 38–9; Vollers, 63–4.

36. Bullard, *Free at Last,* 40–1; Dray, 424–8; Paul Hendrickson, *Sons of Mississippi* (New York: Alfred A. Knopf, 2003), 7–8, 111; Vollers, 65–7.

37. Dray, 429–32; Ginzburg, 243; Mars, 67–8.

38. Evers and Peters, *For Us, the Living,* 177–81; McMillen, *Citizens' Council,* 216–17; Mendelsohn, 15; Vollers, 67–9.

39. Davis, 160; Dittmer, 32; Payne, 34–40, 138–9.

40. "Cong. Thompson pushes for cold case unit"; Evers and Peters, *For Us, the Living* 180; Mitchell, "Forgotten murders"; Anne Moody, *Coming of Age in Mississippi* (New York: Dell, 1971), 132–3.

41. Seth Cagin and Philip Dray, *We Are Not Afraid* (New York: Macmillan, 1988), 174–5; Lord, 66–7; McMillen, *Citizens' Council,* 235–6, 254–6.

42. "Cong. Thompson pushes for cold case unit"; Evers and Peters, *For Us, the Living,* 204; Mitchell, "Forgotten murders"; Martin, 134; Sherrill, 177.

43. Moody, 134–7; Andy Lewis, e-mail to the author, 12 July 2007; Peter Rinaldi, e-mail to the author, 8 September 2006.

44. *HUAC Report,* 48; Massengill, 149–50; William McCord, *Mississippi: The Long, Hot Summer* (New York: W.W. Norton, 1965), 37; Jack Nelson, *Terror in the Night* (Jackson: University Press of Mississippi, 1993), 26; Vollers, 52; Don Whitehead, *Attack on Terror* (New York: Funk & Wagnalls, 1970), 22.

45. Bartley, 164–7; Bennett, 556; Kane, 221; Kennedy, *Jim Crow Guide,* 158; Morgan.

46. Bartley, 203; "Cong. Thompson pushes for cold case unit"; Evers and Peters, *For Us, the Living,* 204; Mitchell, "Forgotten murders"; Rice, 121–2.

47. "Cong. Thompson pushes for cold case unit"; Evers and Peters, *For Us, the Living,* 204; Mitchell, "Forgotten murders"; *HUAC Report,* 58–9; Michael Newton and Judy Newton, *Racial and Religious Violence in America* (New York: Garland, 1991), 445.

48. Bartley, 212; Davis, "Medgar Wiley Evers"; Katagiri, 41; Kennedy, *Jim Crow Guide,* 106; Nossiter, *Of Long Memory,* 42, 47, 96; O'Reilly, *Racial Matters,* 179–80; Vollers, 74–5.

49. Dray, 434–5; Smead, *Blood Justice,* 32–5, 39–40.

50. Bullard, *Free at Last,* 118; Dray, 436–7; Thomas Parker, ed., *Violence in the United States* (New York: Facts on File, 1974), 11–12; Smead, 97.

51. Dray, 436–7, 442; Parker, 11–12.

52. Katagiri, 118; Smead, 201.

53. Dittmer, 340–1; Doyle, 49–50, 52; Nossiter, 69; Sherrill, 174, 178, 183–5; Smead, 171; Sumners, *Governors of Mississippi,* 129–30.

54. Nossiter, 92–3; Peirce, 184; Smead, 171.

55. "Cong. Thompson pushes for cold case unit"; Mitchell, "Forgotten murders"; Moody, 187–8, 224.

56. "Cong. Thompson pushes for cold case unit"; Dittmer, 79; Evers and Peters, *For Us, the Living,* 204, 211–14; Mitchell, "Forgotten murders."

57. Bennett, 383–4, 559–61; Arnold Forster and Benjamin Epstein, *Report on the Ku Klux Klan* (New York: ADL, 1966), 20.

58. Davis, "When Youth Protests"; Dittmer, 85–6, 179.

59. Bennett, 561; Cook, 28; Kane, 227–8.

60. Kane, 128; Morgan; Rice, 124–9.

61. Lord, 85; Parker, 18.

62. "Civil Rights Timeline"; Davis, "When Youth Protests"; Dittmer, 87; Nossiter, 47; Vollers, 81.

63. Bennett, 563–4; Cagin and Dray, 121; "Civil Rights Timeline"; Dittmer, 90–1, 95.

64. Cagin and Dray, 131, 139; Davis, "When Youth Protests"; Dittmer, 103; *HUAC Report* 16, 20–3.

65. Davis, 162–3; Hendrickson, 227; Mitchell, "A Crime Not Forgotten."

66. Taylor Branch, *Parting the Waters* (New York: Simon & Schuster, 1988), 503–4, 528–9; Cagin and Dray, 151–2; Dittmer, 106; Mendelsohn, 25–7.

67. Branch, *Parting Waters*, 508–11; Cagin and Dray, 152–4; "Civil Rights Timeline"; Dittmer, 109; Lord, 85; Mendelsohn, 29–31.

68. Newton and Newton, *Racial and Religious Violence,* 454; Parker, 24; Peirce, 180.

69. Bullard, *Free at Last,* 50–1; Cagin and Dray, 154; Evers and Peters, *For Us, the Living,* 204; Newton and Newton, 454; Salter, *Jackson, Mississippi,* 37–8.

70. Branch, *Parting Waters,* 633–7; Cagin and Dray, 151–2, 180, 187–8; Mills, 36–9, 46; Newton and Newton, 455.

71. Cook, 3.

72. Bennett, 568–9; "Civil Rights Timeline"; Dittmer, 140; Parker, 30–1; Salter, 40.

73. Russell Barrett, *Integration at Ole Miss* (Chicago: Quadrangle, 1965), 98; Doyle, 81, 98–9, 128–9; Lord, 184.

74. Michael Dorman, *We Shall Overcome* (New York: Delacorte, 1984), 83–4; Doyle, 92, 98–9, 128–9, 134, 186–7; Vollers, 94.

75. Dorman, 29, 49; Doyle, 99; Parker, 32; Sherrill, 268, 281.

76. Doyle, 186–7; Lord, 219; Parker, 30–3.

77. Bennett, 568–9; "Civil Rights Timeline"; Dorman, 81, 114; Doyle, 162–6, 215–16, 277–8, 280–1; *HUAC Hearings,* vol. 3, 2689.

78. Bennett, 568–9; Dorman, 114–15, 188–9, 264–6; Lord, 230.

79. Epstein and Forster, *Report on the KKK,* 30; Lord, 238; Vollers, 96.

80. *HUAC Report,* 58–9; Jerry Mitchell e-mail to the author, 24 January 2006; Mitchell, "A Crime Not Forgotten"; James Silver, *Mississippi: The Closed Society* (New York: Harcourt, Brace & World, 1966), 125; Vollers, 95.

81. Harkey, 140–1, 146–8; Hendrickson, 51–6, 59–60, 156–8.

82. Harkey, 140–3, 146–8, 153–5, 161–2; Hendrickson, 62.

83. Hendrickson, 63–4.

84. Moody, 286; Parker, 34; Michelle Hudson e-mail to the author, 24 February 2006.

Chapter 5

1. Howard Ball, *Murder in Mississippi* (Lawrence: University Press of Kansas, 2004), 32–3; *HUAC Report,* 29, 44; *HUAC Hearings,* vol. 3, 2799; Sims, *The Klan,* 241; Vollers, *Ghosts,* 210; Whitehead, *Attack on Terror,* 22–4.

2. Davis, *Race Against Time,* 164; Dittmer, 216; *HUAC Report,* 29, 48, 127–8; *HUAC Hearings,* vol. 3, 2677.

3. Ball, 33; Cagin and Dray, *We Are Not Afraid,* 245; Chalmers, *Backfire,* 53, 56; *HUAC Report,* 44; Mars, *The Deep South,* 120; Massengill, *Portrait of a Racist,* 334; Sims, 258; Wade, 334; Whitehead, 24.

4. Cagin and Dray, 245; *HUAC Report,* 44; *HUAC Hearings,* vol. 3, 2677.

5. Taylor Branch, *Pillar of Fire* (New York, Simon & Schuster, 1998), 240; DeLoach, *Hoover's FBI,* 164; *HUAC Report,* 44, 46, 163; *HUAC Hearings,* vol. 3, 267–8, 2736, 2745–6; Whitehead, 177.

6. *HUAC Report,* 131–2; Nelson, *Terror in the Night,* 113.

7. Massengill, 216; Mitchell, "A Crime Not Forgotten"; Nelson, *Terror,* 63; Wade, 324–5; Whitehead, 23–4.

8. Wade, 334.

9. Davis, *Race,* 235–6; Hendrickson, *Sons,* 229; Katagiri, *Sovereignty Commission,* 177–9; Shirley Tucker, *Mississippi from Within* (New York: Arco, 1965), 28.

10. Davis, *Race,* 190; *HUAC Hearings,* vol. 3, 2800; Katagiri, 177–9; Nelson, *Terror,* 81; Tucker, 28–9.

11. Davis, *Race,* 198.

12. "Cong. Thompson pushes for cold case unit"; Dittmer, 187; Mitchell, "Forgotten murders."

13. Dittmer, 146–7; Branch, *Parting,* 715–16.

14. Bennett, 570; Branch, *Parting,* 717; Branch, *Pillar of Fire,* 69; Cagin and Dray, 191–2; Hendrickson, 88, 90; *HUAC Hearings,* vol. 3, 2678; Massengill, pp 119–20; Nossiter, *Of Long Memory,* 122; Parker, *Violence in the U.S.,* 35.

15. Branch, *Pillar,* 71; Dittmer, 150; Hendrickson, 88; Massengill, 120; Parker, 35–6; Payne, *I've Got the Light,* 220–1, 466.

16. Payne, 202–5.

17. Branch, *Parting,* 781–2; Dittmer, 192–3; Parker, 36; Payne, 278–9.

18. "Civil Rights Timeline"; Nossiter, 84–5; Parker, 37–8; Salter, viii–ix.

19. Dorman, *We Shall Overcome,* 216; Bobby DeLaughter, *Never Too Late* (New York: Scribner, 2001), 38; Massengill, 135–6, 140, 321; Mendelsohn, *The Martyrs,* 72; Payne, 287–9.

20. Mendelsohn, 74l Payne, 289; Salter, 187–8.

21. DeLaughter, 44, 47; Dittmer, 166; Massengill, 145; Vollers, 133–4, 147–9.

22. Massengill, 150–6; Anthony Villano and Gerald Astor, *Brick Agent* (New York: Quadrangle, 1977), 90–3.

23. DeLaughter, 48; Evers and Peters, *For Us, the Living,* 33–4; Massengill, 156, 159; Parker, 40; Vollers, 154.

24. Evers and Peters, *For Us, the Living,* 333–4; Massengill, 17, 37, 43–6, 59, 65, 75; Vollers, 21, 241.

25. Massengill, 73, 92, 106–8, 110; Nossiter, 90, 119–20; Parker, 40; Vollers, 51, 77, 79, 89.

26. Massengill, 114, 117, 166; Nossiter, 123–4; Vollers, 77.

27. Harkey, *Burning Crosses,* 193–4; Massengill, 163–4, 169, 171; McMillen, *Citizens' Council,* 360; Mendelsohn, 84; Payne, 287–9; Vollers, 157, 163–4.

28. Evers and Peters, *For Us, the Living,* 367–8; Massengill, 180–1, 201; Mendelsohn, 84; Nossiter, 108–9; Parker, 40; Payne, 287–9; Vollers, 160, 163–4.

29. Evers and Peters, *For Us, the Living,* 368–9; Massengill, 206–9, 214–15; Nossiter, 136; Vollers, 203–5.

30. Massengill, 209, 214–15; Nossiter, 134; Payne, 322–3; Vollers, 217–18.

31. Chalmers, *Backfire,* 56; Cagin and Dray, 429; DeLaughter, 50; *HUAC Hearings,* vol. 3, 2700; Massengill, 173, 212–14, 224, 228; Nossiter, 120; Vollers, 209–10.

32. DeLaughter, 51, 150; Massengill, 135–6, 149–50, 346; Vollers, 154, 225–6.

33. Dittmer, 173; Forster and Epstein, *Report*, 31; Parker, 51; Salter, 231–3.

34. *Mississippi*, 305; Cagin and Dray, 211–12; Chalmers, *Backfire*, 91–2; Dittmer, 199; Peirce, 183.

35. Davis, *Race*, 161–2; *HUAC Hearings*, vol. 3, 2799–2800; Ladd, "Evolution of a Man"; Payne, 223.

36. Davis, *Race*, 166; Dittmer, 215–16, 266–7; Moody, *Coming of Age*, 339; Payne, 298–9.

37. Branch, *Parting*, 921; Branch, *Pillar*, 222–3; Cagin and Dray, 228; Forster and Epstein, *Report*, 33; Mendelsohn, 37; Payne, 299–300.

38. Branch, *Pillar*, 240; Davis, *Race*, 166; Dittmer, 215–17; Charles Marsh, *God's Long Summer* (Princeton: Princeton University Press, 1997), 57; Newton and Newton, *Racial and Religious Violence*, 464.

39. "Cong. Thompson Pushes for Cold Case Unit"; Davis, *Race*, 174; Dittmer, 215–16; *HUAC Hearings*, vol. 4, 2935; Mitchell, "Forgotten Murders"; Sims, 245.

40. Dittmer, 232; Katagiri, 144.

41. Cagin and Dray, 264; Dittmer, 224; *HUAC Hearings*, vol. 4, 3023; Katagiri, 163; Mars, 80–2; Marsh, 58; O'Reilly, 160–1.

42. Ball, 8; Dittmer, 266; Mills, 109.

43. Ball, 55; Marsh, 58; O'Reilly, 160–1.

44. Mississippi White Knights, "Twenty Reasons."

45. Branch, *Pillar*, 240; Cagin and Dray, 389; Davis, *Race*, 166; Dittmer, 215–16; Forster and Epstein, *Report*, 34; *HUAC Hearings*, vol. 4, 3023; *HUAC Report*, 112; Marsh, 58; McCord, *The Long, Hot Summer*, 48.

46. *HUAC Report*, 169–71.

47. Mills, 109.

48. Bullard, *Free*, 64–5; Ladd; Mitchell, "Justice on the Way"; Whitehead, 99–100.

49. Bullard, *Free*, 64–5; *HUAC Hearings*, vol. 3, 2804, 2810; *HUACH Hearings*, vol. 4, 2942–3; Ladd; Mitchell, "Justice on the Way"; Parker, 60.

50. Ladd.

51. Ball, 34; Branch, *Pillar*, 240; *HUAC Hearings*, vol. 4, 3023.

52. *HUAC Hearings*, vol. 3, 2588; *HUAC Report*, 30, 71–2, 127–8.

53. DeLoach, 179–80; Dittmer, 255; Mitchell, "Klan Kidnapping"; Whitehead, 111–24.

54. Dittmer, 237; Marsh, 58.

55. Katagiri, 177–8.

56. *HUAC Hearings*, vol. 3, 2713–15, 2720, 2827; *HUAC Hearings*, vol. 4, 2936; *HUAC Report*, 44; Sims, 242; Whitehead, 1–9.

57. Ball, 55; Cagin and Dray, 256–64; Whitehead, 30–6.

58. Ball, 7–8; Cagin and Dray, 373; Mars, 76–8.

59. Ball, 36–8; Cagin and Dray, 36–7, 263–4; DeLaughter, 168; Mars, 101–2; Mitchell, "Stringer Recalls"; Sherrill, *Gothic Politics*, 193.

60. Ball, 57–8; Cagin and Dray, 1–5, 38; Dittmer, 247; Katagiri, 163; Mars, 123–4; Mitchell, "Stringer Recalls."

61. Ball, 60–3; Cagin and Dray, 7–14; Katagiri, 164; Mitchell, "Stringer Recalls"; Parker, 62–3.

62. Ball, 60–3; Cagin and Dray, 249, 278–301.

63. Branch, *Pillar*, 366; Parker, 62–3; O'Reilly, 165.

64. Branch, *Pillar*, 367–8; *HUAC Report*, 122; Parker, 62–3; Vollers, 216.

65. Branch, *Pillar*, 430; DeLoach, 185; Nelson, *Terror*, 85–6; O'Reilly, 169; Parker, 62–3.

66. Cagin and Dray, 358; Carter, *Politics of Rage*, 223; Whitehead, 79–80.

67. Cagin and Dray, 358–9.

68. DeLoach, 183; Nelson, *Terror*, 85–6, 89; O'Reilly, 173; Parker, 62–3.

69. Chalmers, *Hooded*, 384–5; DeLoach, 177, 183; *HUAC Report*, 73; Payne, 316; Spofford, *Lynch Street*, 43.

70. Cagin and Dray, 346–7; DeLoach, 191–3; Mars, 121–3.

71. Ball, 73–8; Branch, *Pillar*, 440; Cagin and Dray, 394, 406–7; DeLoach, 190; Mitchell, "Experts"; Parker, 62–3; Whitehead, 125–39.

72. Cagin and Dray, 406–7; Mitchell, "Experts"; Mitchell, "Spy Agency."

73. Cagin and Dray, 407–8.

74. Cagin and Dray, 428; Mars, 107–10.

75. Branch, *Pillar*, 498; Cagin and Dray, 435; DeLoach, 194–5; Mars, 129.

76. Branch, *Pillar*, 196; DeLoach, 196; Mars, xv–xvi, 132, 135–8; Parker, 63–4.

77. Ball, 93–6; Branch, *Pillar*, 508; Cagin and Dray, 377, 432, 434, 436; Mars, 140; Parker, 63–5; Silver, *Closed Society*, 325; Whitehead, 179.

78. Cagin and Dray, 435, 437; *HUAC Hearings*, vol. 3, 2678–9; Parker, 63–5; Silver, 293–4; Whitehead, 191.

79. Ball, 81; *r*, 111–12; Dittmer, 267; Forster and Epstein, *Report*, 34–5; Holt, *Summer That Didn't End*, 207–10; *HUAC Hearings*, vol. 4, 3023; *HUAC Report*, 65; Parker, 61, 71; Whitehead, 167–9.

80. Branch, *Pillar*, 371–3; Katagiri, 191.

81. Dittmer, 267; *HUAC Hearings*, vol. 4, 2981; Tucker, 86.

82. "Civil Rights Timeline"; McCord, 85–7; Silver, 329; Vollers, 226–7.

83. Branch, *Pillar*, 395; Dittmer, 276–9; Holt, 215, 217–18, 220, 223–4; Payne, 211–12; Silver, 330–1.

84. Branch, *Pillar*, 394; "Cong. Thompson Pushes for Cold Case Unit"; Forster and Epstein, *Report*, 36; Holt, 215–16, 218–19, 233; McCord, 87; Mitchell, "Forgotten Murders"; Parker, 71; Whitehead, 100.

85. Branch, *Pillar*, 394; Carter, *So the Heffners Left McComb*, 9, 29, 68–71.

86. Dittmer, 268; Forster and Epstein, *Report*, 36; Holt, 214, 218, 222–3; *HUAC Hearings*, vol. 3, 2839–42; *HUAC Hearings*, vol. 4, 2968, 3023; *HUAC Report*, 112–13; *Mississippi Black Paper*, 84; Parker, 71; Tucker, 86.

87. Forster and Epstein, *Report*, 37; Holt, 211, 213, 217, 221, 223–4, 226–7; McAdam, *Freedom Summer*, 84; *Mississippi Black Paper*, 84; Parker, 71–2.

88. Hendrickson, 91.

89. Austin, "On Violence and Nonviolence"; Dittmer, 267, 267; Holt, 223; *Mississippi Black Paper*, 84.

90. Ball, 81; Dittmer, 278–9; Forster and Epstein, *Report*, 36; Holt, 228–9, 234, 236, 240–1, 248; *HUAC Hearings*, vol. 3, 2741; Parker, 72; Payne, 211–12, 217.

91. Holt, 227, 234, 236–7; *HUAC Hearings*, vol. 4, 2927, 2968, 3023.

92. Branch, *At Canaan's Edge*, 349; Davis, *Race*, 168, 172–4; Forster and Epstein, *Report*, 36; Holt, 229, 231, 236–8, 245; *HUAC Report*, 100.

93. Dittmer, 270; Holt, 237–8, 243–4; *HUAC Hearings*, vol. 4, 2968.

94. Forster and Epstein, *Report*, 36; Holt, 240–1, 249; *HUAC Hearings*, vol. 4, 2968; Mars, 111–16; McAdam, 129; McCord, 122–3; Parker, 72.

95. McAdam, 129.

96. Cagin and Dray, 386; Dittmer, 251; Mars, 111; O'Reilly, 171; Whitehead, 103.

97. DeLoach, 167, 176, 178.

98. Nelson, *Terror*, 93–4; Theoharis, *Spying on Americans*, 140–1.

99. Nelson, *Terror*, 94.

100. Churchill and Vander Wall, *COINTELPRO Papers*, 33, 50–1, 304; Nelson, *Terror*, 91.

101. O'Reilly, 202.

102. Forster and Epstein, *Report*, 37; Holt, 251; *HUAC Hearings*, vol. 4, 2968; *HUAC Report*, 114; Parker, 72.

103. Ball, 81–2; Dittmer, 306–7; Forster and Epstein, *Report*, 38; *HUAC Hearings*, vol. 3, 2741; *HUAC Hearings*, vol. 4, 3023; Newton and Newton, 477; Parker, 72; Tucker, 52.

104. Cagin and Dray, 266; DeLoach, 193–47; Forster and Epstein, *Report*, 27, 38; Mars, 117–18; Parker, 73; Vollers, 221; Whitehead, 175–7, 187.

105. Branch, *At Canaan's*, 320; Davis, *Race*, 173; Forster and Epstein, *Report*, 38; Hendrickson, 24, 31–2, 228, 237–8; Parker, 73; Tucker, 24.

106. Davis, *Race*, 186.

107. Branch, *Pillar*, 495; Dittmer, 305–7; Forster and Epstein, *Report*, 38; *HUAC Hearings*, vol. 4, 3023–4; *HUAC Report*, 111; McCord, 122–3; Parker, 72–4.

108. Dittmer, 266–7, 303, 312, 493; Forster and Epstein, *Report*, 38; *HUAC Hearings*, vol. 4, 3049; *HUAC Report*, 103–5, 108–9, 111; Whitehead, 167–9.

109. Dittmer, 311; Forster and Epstein, *Report*, 24; *HUAC Hearings*, vol. 3, 2838; Parker, 74; Silver, 334–7.

110. Whitehead, 169–71.

111. Parker, 74.

112. Dittmer, 323; Forster and Epstein, *Report*, 39; Holt, 180; *HUAC Hearings*, vol. 3, 2741; *HUAC Hearings*, vol. 4, 2937; *HUAC Report*, 114; Parker, 73.

113. Forster and Epstein, *Report*, 26, 39; *HUAC Hearings*, vol. 3, 2734–5; *HUAC Hearings*, vol. 4, 2927, 2938; Parker, 73; Whitehead, 188–9.

114. Davis, *Race*, 177; Whitehead, 225–6.

115. Whitehead, 225–30.

116. Holt, 180–1; O'Reilly, 185–9.

117. Chalmers, *Hooded*, 382–3; Kane, *Presidential Fact*, 237; Morgan; Peirce, 192.

118. Cagin and Dray, 441; Mitchell, "Suspects"; Parker, 65; Whitehead, 207–8.

119. Whitehead, 208–10.

120. Ball, 96–7; Parker, 65.

121. Ball, 97–100; Branch, *Parting*, 508; Forster and Epstein, *Report*, 26; Mars, 225–7; Salter, 69; Vollers, 84.

122. *HUAC Hearings*, vol. 3, 2703–4; Whitehead, 220–3.

123. "Cong. Thompson Pushes for Cold Case Unit"; *HUAC Hearings*, vol. 4, 2927; Mitchell, "Forgotten Murders."

124. Hendrickson, 50; Nossiter, 77–9.

125. Branch, *Pillar*, 597; "Cong. Thompson Pushes for Cold Case Unit"; Forster and Epstein, *Report*, 39–40; *HUAC Hearings*, vol. 3, 2700, 2740–1; Mitchell, "Forgotten Murders"; Parker, 118.

126. Goodman, *The Committee*, 465–7; *HUAC Report*, 1.

127. Goodman, 465–70; *HUAC Hearings*, vol. 3, 2683–2865; *HUAC Hearings*, vol. 4, 2901–3055; *HUAC Report*, 1–2; Vollers, 223–4.

128. Davis, *Race*, 181; Goodman, 470–1; *HUAC Report*, 60–2.

129. Chalmers, *Hooded*, 387; Forster and Epstein, *Report*, 7; Hendrickson, 268.

130. *HUAC Hearings*, vol. 3, 2678–9, 2700, 2741; *HUAC Hearings*, vol. 4, 2906.

131. "Civil Rights Timeline"; DeLaughter, 161; *HUAC Report*, 85; Nossiter, 179; Whitehead, 230–2.

132. *HUAC Hearings*, vol. 3, 2588; *HUAC Report*, 85; Katagiri, 177–9; Whitehead, 230–2.

133. *HUAC Hearings*, vol. 4, 2928; Mars, 185–92, 194–5.

134. Katagiri, 190–1.

135. DeLaughter, 150, 161; Massengill, 226–7, 242.

136. "Cong. Thompson pushes for cold case unit"; *HUAC Hearings*, vol. 3, 2810–13; *HUAC Hearings*, vol. 4, 2906, 2928; *HUAC Report*, 102–3, 114; Mitchell, "Forgotten Murders"; Silver, xxiii–xxiv.

137. Davis, *Race*, 180–3, 215–16; Dittmer, 354; Parker, 119–20; Whitehead, 229–30.

138. Branch, *At Canaan's*, 349; Davis, *Race*, 180–3; Dittmer, 354–5; *HUAC Hearings*, vol. 4, 3054; Parker, 173.

139. "Cong. Thompson pushes for cold case unit"; *HUAC Hearings*, vol. 3, 2588, 2741–2; *HUAC Hearings*, vol. 4, 2902–4, 2928; *HUAC Report*, 85, 100, 153–4; Mitchell, "Forgotten Murders"; Parker, 120–1.

140. Branch, *Pillar*, 58–9; Dittmer, 180–1; Nelson, *Terror*, 28; Parker, 164, 173; Peirce, 184; "2 Agents of FBI Shot At"; Whitehead, 235.

141. Branch, *Pillar*, 606–7; Parker, 164–5; Whitehead, 235–7.

142. Branch, *Pillar*, 608; Chalmers, *Backfire*, 80–1; Whitehead, 238–40, 246–7.

143. Branch, *Pillar*, 608; *HUAC Report*, 103–4, 131; Parker, 164–6; Whitehead, 246–9, 251.

144. "Dying to Vote in Mississippi"; Klopfer, "Murders Around Mississippi."

145. Branch, *At Canaan's*, 452; "Civil Rights Timeline"; Newton and Newton, 491; Parker, 173; Whitehead, 238.

146. Branch, *At Canaan's*, 475; Chalmers, *Backfire*, 69; Dittmer, 392; Doyle, *An American Insurrection*, 299; Gibson, "A Shooting"; Mitchell, "Last Days"; Parker, 166–7.

147. Massengill, 241; Mitchell, "Last Days."

148. Branch, *At Canaan's*, 476; Ladd; Mitchell, "Last Days."

149. Branch, *At Canaan's*, 481–2; Bullard, *Free*, 88; Mitchell, "Last Days"; Parker, 173–4.

150. Branch, *At Canaan's*, 483, 488; Cagin and Dray, 382; Chalmers, *Backfire*, 67; Mars, 210–11; Newton and Newton, 492; Parker, 168.

151. Chalmers, *Backfire*, 92; Flowers, "Southern Plain Talk," 44; Hendrickson, 268; *HUAC Report*, 18, 30; Mars, 217–19, 224; Newton and Newton, 494; Sims, 239; Whitehead, 257–8.

152. Branch, *At Canaan's*, 627; Dittmer, 395–6, 404–6; *HUAC Report*, 153; Parker, 169–71.

153. Katagiri, 199–200.

154. Mars, 213, 219–20; Jerry Mitchell, e-mail to the author, 29 June 2005.

155. Branch, *At Canaan's*, 581; Bullard, *Free*, 90–1; Davis, *Race*, 201–2; Parker, 199–200; Whitehead, 230.

156. Davis, *Race*, 201–2; Evers, *No Fear*, 190–1; Parker, 199–200.

157. DeLaughter, 130; Massengill, 245–6; Vollers, 226–7.

158. Branch, *At Canaan's*, 481–2; Hendrickson, 239–40; Minor, 233–4.

159. Katagiri, 204–5; Nossiter, 156–9; Sumners, 136–7; "3 Mississippi Whites Held."

160. Massengill, 245–7; Nossiter, 156–9; Silver, 327; Sumners, 136–7.

161. Hendrickson, 239–40; Katagiri, 204–5; Massengill, 251; Peirce, 187; Sumners, 136–7; Vollers, 226–7.

162. Ball, 107–10, 118; Cagin and Dray, 441; Mars, 225–6.

163. Ball, 118; Cagin and Dray, 441; Mars, 225–6; Parker, 66; Whitehead, 251.

164. Whitehead, 251–2.

165. Whitehead, 252–6.

166. Ball, 120–2; Branch, *At Canaan's*, 643; Cagin and Dray, 445–7; Parker, 67–8; Whitehead, 260.

167. Ball, 121–2; Whitehead, 267.

168. Ball, 132–3; Cagin and Dray, 450; Mitchell, "Justice: Behind Closed Doors"; Parker, 67; Whitehead, 280–1.

169. Ball, 232.

170. Branch, *At Canaan's*, 647; Cagin and Dray, 451; Mars, 268; Parker, 67–8; Whitehead, 283.

171. Nelson, *Terror*, 29–30, 142–6; Tarrants, *Conversion of a Klansman*, 56–7.

172. Nelson, *Terror*, 24–5, 29–30, 139, 145–6; Tarrants, 2, 5, 34, 40–1, 46–7, 52–3; Whitehead, 287–8.

173. Peirce, 224–5.

174. Whitehead, 285–6.

175. Nelson, *Terror*, 80–1, 269; Whitehead, 285–6.

176. Branch, *Pillar*, 609; Dittmer, 417–18; Nelson, *Terror*, 61, 65–7, 73; Tarrants, 56–8.

177. Branch, *Pillar*, 609; Nelson, *Terror*, pp.79, 139–40; Tarrants, 59.

178. Chalmers, *Backfire*, 82; Nelson, *Terror*, 103, 106–7, 123, 126–7, 132–4; Whitehead, 289–90.

179. Nelson, *Terror*, 46, 60–1.

180. Nelson, *Terror*, 119; U.S. House of Representatives, *Report of the Select Committee on Assassinations*, 494–6.

181. Bennett, 584; Chalmers, *Backfire*, 82; Nelson, *Terror*, 115, 120–1; Tarrants, 61; Vollers, 229–30; Whitehead, 289–90.

182. Nelson, *Terror*, 50, 60–1, 136, 147.

183. Nelson, *Terror*, 139, 150–1, 159, 168–71; Vollers, 229–30.

184. Chalmers, *Backfire*, 85; Nelson, *Terror*, 17–22, 186–7, 201–2, 205, 220–3, 239–42.

185. Branch, *Pillar*, 609; Chalmers, *Backfire*, 80–1, 91–2; Whitehead, 256, 302–3.

186. Branch, *At Canaan's*, 712; Branch, *Pillar*, 609–10; Parker, 166; Whitehead, 302–4.

187. Whitehead, 303–4.

188. Branch, *At Canaan's*, 712; "Civil Rights Timeline"; Newton, *Ku Klux Klan*, 108; Whitehead, 303–4.

189. Kane, 246; Morgan; Peirce, 192.

190. Evers, *No Fear*, 233–4; Nelson, *Terror*, 187; Nossiter, 181.

191. Bullard, *Free*, 88' Mitchell, "Last Days."

192. Evers, *No Fear*, 241–5; Nossiter, 181; Peirce, 183, 188.

193. Evers, *No Fear*, 261–5; Nossiter, 184.

194. Evers, *No Fear*, 262–5; Nossiter, 184; "3 Mississippi Whites Held."

195. DeLaughter, 211; Mars, 268–9.

196. Bennett, 589; Davis, *Race*, 229–36; Mars, 269–70.

Chapter 6

1. Bennett, 590; Brown, "Trial Begins"; "Civil Rights Timeline"; Peirce, 216–17; Spofford, 89.

2. Bennett, 594; Klopfer, Emmett Till Blog; "A Senseless Killing."

3. Nossiter, *Of Long Memory*, 159–63; Peirce, 188.

4. Katagiri, *Sovereignty Commission*, 220–1; Newton, *Ku Klux Klan*, 256; Nossiter, 162–3; Sumners, 140.

5. Davis, *Race*, 278; Katagiri, 220–1; Nossiter, 160; Peirce, 189, 192; Vollers, *Ghosts*, 247–8.

6. "Civil Rights Timeline"; Doyle, *An American Insurrection*, 306; Newton, *Ku Klux Klan*, 256; Peirce, 272; Rowe-Sims; Vollers, 306.

7. "Chester Trent Lott"; Kane, *Presidential Fact*, 247–8; Morgan; Peirce, 189.

8. Massengill, *Portrait of a Racist*, 263; Nossiter, 139–41.

9. Massengill, 266; Nelson, *Terror in the Night*, 250; Nossiter, 139–41; Vollers, 231–2.

10. Massengill, 267; Nossiter, 140–1; Vollers, 234–6.

11. Massengill, 269; Vollers, 237–8.

12. Massengill, 269–72; Nossiter, 141; Vollers, 238–9.

13. Massengill, 272–4; Nossiter, 141; Vollers, 240.

14. Massengill, 275–8.

15. DeLaughter, *Never Too Late*, 198; Massengill, 279–81, 284, 287, 291; Nossiter, 141; Vollers, 241.

16. Ball, *Murder in Mississippi*, 139–40; Mitchell, "Suspects"; Nelson, *Terror*, 269; Sims, 249–57.

17. Sims, 237.

18. ADL, *Extremism on the Right*, 19; Newton, *Ku Klux Klan*, 64–5, 123.

19. ADL, *Extremism*, 72–3; ADL, *Hate Groups*, 20; ADL, "KKK Tries for a Comeback," 9–10; Hendrickson, *Sons*, 77; Massengill, 269–70; Newton, *Ku Klux Klan*, 64–5.

20. ADL, *Extremism*, 16, 153; ADL, *Hate Groups*, 20–1; Newton, *Ku Klux Klan*, 89–90, 120; Sims, 235–6.

21. Ball, 138–9; Branch, *At Canaan's*, 647; Nelson, *Terror*, 270; Sims, 235–6; SPLC *Intelligence Report* No. 101, 36.

22. ADL, *Hate Groups*, 4; ADL, "KKK and Neo-Nazis," 1; ADL, "KKK: 1978," 1; ADL, "KKK Tries for a Comeback," 7; Suall and Lowe, "Hate Movement," 348.

23. Kane, 262–3; Morgan.

24. Spruill and Wheeler, "The Equal Rights Amendment and Mississippi."

25. Chalmers, *Hooded Americanism*, 408; Neier, "Black Marchers," 265–6; Wade, 376.

26. ADL, "KKK Comeback," 4; Neier, 265–6; Wade, 376–7.

27. Wade, 377.

28. Spofford, 43, 89, 178–9; Stanton, *Klanwatch*, 178–9.

29. ADL, *Extremism*, 72–4; ADL, *Hate Groups*, 4; ADL, "KKK Comeback," 2–3; ADL, "KKK and Neo-Nazis," 1; ADL, "KKK: 1978," 1; Newton, *Ku Klux Klan*, 64–5, 123; Suall and Lowe, 348.

30. Cagin and Dray, *We Are Not Afraid*, 454; Kane, 271; Chris Lutz, *They Don't All Wear Sheets* (Atlanta: Center for Democratic Renewal, 1987), 58; Morgan; Newton, *Ku Klux Klan*, 245.

31. "Alleged Backer of Plot"; "Klansmen Are Among 10 Indicted"; "Operation Red Dog."

32. ADL, *Extremism*, 20; "FBI Arrests 10"; "Klansmen Are Among 10 Indicted"; "Operation Red Dog."

33. "Alleged Backer"; Newton, *Ku Klux Klan*, 226; "Sentences Passed"; "2 Guilty in New Orleans."

34. ADL, *Extremism*, 21, 154; ADL, *Hate Groups*, 13; Lutz, 58.

35. ADL, *Extremism*, 73–4; Culpepper, "Body Found

in Warehouse"; Culpepper, "Sister Identifies Slain Teen"; Lutz, 58; Newton, *Ku Klux Klan*, 123; SPLC *Intelligence Report* No. 47, 7.

36. ADL, *Extremism*, 21; ADL, *Hate Groups*, 4; ADL, "KKK and Neo-Nazis," 1; Newton, *Ku Klux Klan*, 89–90; Suall and Lowe, 348.

37. Lutz, 57.

38. "Far Right Strategy in the Elections"; "Front Man for Fascism"; Kane, 272; Morgan.

39. "Sharks in Mainstream," 22–3; SPLC *Intelligence Report* No. 105, 37, 47–8.

40. Newton, *Ku Klux Klan*, 245; "Sharks in the Mainstream," 24–6.

41. Beirich and Moser, "Communing with the Council," 11, 13, 17–18; "Sharks in the Mainstream," 21–2, 25.

42. Beirich and Moser, 11; "Chester Trent Lott"; Doyle, 306; "Trent Lott's 'Uptown Klan.'"

43. Beirich and Moser, 11, 13; "Sharks in the Mainstream," 21, 23; SPLC *Intelligence Report* No. 117, 58; SPLC *Intelligence Report* No. 125, 55.

44. ADL, *Hate Groups*, 4; Bennett, 624; Lutz, 58; SPLC *Intelligence Report* No. 47, 33.

45. ADL, *Extremism*, 1, 57; "Front Man for Fascism"; Hendrickson, 116, 177, 276–7; Kane, 283–4; Morgan.

46. Ball, 143; DeLaughter, 99; Nossiter, 227–9, 231.

47. ADL, *Extremism*, 116–17; *Forsyth County, Ga. v. Nationalist Movement* (505 U.S. 123); "Nationalist Movement"; SPLC *Intelligence Report* No. 47, 25–6.

48. ADL, "Neo-Nazi Skinheads"; Suall and Lowe, 347–62.

49. ADL, "Hate Groups and Black Church Arsons—State By State"; ADL, "Neo-Nazi Skinheads"; "; SPLC *Intelligence Report* No. 59, 16; "; SPLC *Intelligence Report* No. 125, 56.

50. SPLC *Intelligence Report* No. 54, 17–18; SPLC *Intelligence Report* No. 59, 16–17.

51. SPLC *Intelligence Report* No. 54, 22–4, 26; SPLC *Intelligence Report* No. 59, 28; SPLC *Intelligence Report* No. 62, 14; SPLC *Intelligence Report* No. 63, 12.

52. "Mississippi Jail Lynchings"; SPLC *Intelligence Report* No. 62, 7.

53. Burghardt, "Neo-Nazis Salute," 28–30; "Front Man for Fascism"; Kane, 293–4; Morgan; Moser, "Our Terrible Swift Sword," 52.

54. Ball, 144.

55. DeLaughter, 198; Massengill, 3–4; Nossiter, 142; Vollers, 256–9.

56. DeLaughter, 24; Vollers, 259–60, 262–4, 278.

57. "Civil rights timeline"; DeLaughter, 107–14, 143–4; Nossiter, 142, 244; Vollers, 279.

58. "Civil Rights Timeline"; DeLaughter, 131; Massengill, 6; Nossiter, 142; Vollers, 286.

59. DeLaughter, 190; Massengill, 9–10, 299; Nossiter, 142; Vollers, 295.

60. DeLaughter, 206; Massengill, 305, 313–14; Nossiter, 246; Vollers, 296–301.

61. Massengill, 314–15; Nossiter, 247–8; Vollers, 314–15, 321–2, 328.

62. "Civil Rights Timeline"; DeLaughter, 221, 253–81; Nossiter, 249–51, 254; Vollers, 303–8, 331, 337, 377–8.

63. Booth, "In Church Fires"; Beau Grosscup, *The Newest Explosions of Terrorism* (Far Hills, NJ: New Horizons, 1997), 114–15; "List of Black Church Fire Investigations"; "Two More Black Churches Destroyed by Fire."

64. ADL, "Hate Groups and Black Church Arsons";

Booth; "Former Klansmen Plead Guilty in Church Fires"; Fumento, "A Church Arson Epidemic?"; "Klansmen Must Pay $38m for Church Arson."

65. Mitchell, "Battle by the Book."

66. Klopfer, "Murders around Mississippi."

67. SPLC *Intelligence Report* No. 89, 11, 29, 32–3, 48.

68. SPLC *Intelligence Report* No. 90, 28, 44; SPLC *Intelligence Report* No. 93 40–2; SPLC *Intelligence Report* No. 93, 30.

69. SPLC *Intelligence Report* No. 94, 49; SPLC *Intelligence Report* No. 95, 40; SPLC *Intelligence Report* No. 97, 32–3, 35, 59.

70. "Civil Rights Timeline"; "Klan Leader Faces New Trial in 1966 Firebombing."

71. "Former KKK Leader Convicted of 1966 Murder"; "Former Klan Leader Faces Murder Trial for Fifth Time"; "Witness: Klan Leader Ordered 1966 Slaying of NAACP Official."

72. Gall, 36; "Civil Rights Timeline"; "Ex-Klansman Charged In '66 Race Slaying Dies"; "Klansman Imprisoned for Bombing Dies."

73. "Civil Rights Timeline"; "Trial Begins in 1970 Death of Black Man"; *Caston v. State*, 823 So. 2d 473 (Miss. 2002).

74. Kane, 293; Morgan; Moser; SPLC *Intelligence Report* No. 101, 36–7.

75. ADL Archive of Extremist Events by State; SPLC *Intelligence Report* No. 105, 34–5; SPLC *Intelligence Report* No. 109, 39, 41, 72.

76. ADL Archive of Extremist Events by State; SPLC *Intelligence Report* No. 113, 38–40; www.memphisite. com/forums/Collierville/posts/145.html.

77. ADL Archive of Extremist Events by State; Campbell, "Something Stinks"; SPLC *Intelligence Report* No. 115, 47; SPLC *Intelligence Report* No. 116, 55; SPLC *Intelligence Report* No. 117, 53.

78. ADL Archive of Extremist Events by State; SPLC *Intelligence Report* No. 121, 53–4, 58.

79. Mississippi Militia; SPLC *Intelligence Report* No. 106, 35; SPLC *Intelligence Report* No. 109, 49.

80. Mississippi Militia.

81. "A League of Their Own," 13–14, 16–17.

82. "A House Divided," 47; "A League of Their Own," 16; SPLC *Intelligence Report* No. 106, 5; SPLC *Intelligence Report* No. 119, 57.

83. ADL Archive of Extremist Events by State; "Southern Party"; SPLC *Intelligence Report* No. 105, 37; SPLC *Intelligence Report* No. 125, 57.

84. "A House Divided," 44–6; SPLC *Intelligence Report* No. 101, 3.

85. "A House Divided," 46–50; Beirich and Potok, "A War Within," 38; SPLC *Intelligence Report* No. 101, 3.

86. "A House Divided," 44; Beirich and Potok, 37, 40; SPLC *Intelligence Report* No. 109, 2; SPLC *Intelligence Report* No. 110, 5; SPLC *Intelligence Report* No. 114, 5.

87. Beirich and Potok, 37–8, 44–5.

88. Beirich, "SCV Standoff," 30–1; SPLC *Intelligence Report* No. 109, 3; SPLC *Intelligence Report* No. 116, 4.

89. "A House Divided," 49; Moser, 54–5; SPLC *Intelligence Report* No. 105, 37; SPLC *Intelligence Report* No. 111, 20.

90. "Civil Rights Timeline"; Mitchell, "Grand Jury Examining Evidence in '66 Death"; Mitchell, "'66 Klan Slaying Not Only Killing on Federal Property."

91. "Avants Dies in Federal Prison"; "Civil Rights Timeline"; "Feds Charge Mississippi Man with Civil

Rights-Era Murder"; "Judge Issues Life Sentence in 1966 Racial Slaying"; Mitchell, "Avants Found Guilty in '66 Klan Killing"; Mitchell, "Ex-Agent Testifies Against Avants"; Mitchell, "Jury Selection in Avants Case Ordered Closed"; Mitchell, "Man Who Spotted Body Testifies."

92. Ball, Murder 139–40, 145, 154–5; "Civil Rights Timeline."

93. Ball, 139–41, 145–6, 154–5; "Civil Rights Time-line"; DeLaughter, 162; Mitchell, "Activist Slayings Reopened"; Mitchell, "New Witnesses Surface in Probe of '64 Killings"; Mitchell, "Suspects in 1964 Civil Rights Slayings Put Past Behind Them"; "'64 Case Dying with Witnesses."

94. Carrillo, "$100,000 Reward for Mississippi's Infamous Civil Rights Murders"; "Edgar Ray Killen"; Myers, "Killen Trial Will Proceed as Scheduled"; Ryan, "Defense: Killen a 'Bystander' in the Klan."

95. Dewan, "Jury Hears Mother of Rights Worker Slain in 1964"; "Edgar Ray Killen"; Hart, "41 Years Later, Ex-Klansman Gets 60 Years in Civil Rights Deaths"; Hart, "Mississippi Man Called Architect of 1964 Killings"; Oziewicz, "Klansman Guilty in 1964 Slayings"; Pettus, "Siblings Provide Alibi for Ex-Klansman"; Pettus, "Trial in '64 Klan Killings Hits Snag."

96. ADL Archive of Extremist Events by State; "Edgar Ray Killen"; SPLC *Intelligence Report* No. 121, 58.

97. "Civil Rights Timeline"; "Investigative Reporter Mitchell Tapped for Chancellor Award."

98. Mitchell, "Will KKK fade into history?"; "; SPLC *Intelligence Report* No. 121, 53–4.

99. ADL, "Ku Klux Klan Today"; SPLC *Intelligence Report* No. 125, 53, 55.

100. White Knights of Mississippi Profile.

101. SPLC *Intelligence Report* No. 126. 63.

102. "Civil Rights Timeline"; "Ex-deputy, Thought to Have Been Dead, Arrested in 1964 Murders"; Mitchell, "'Justice on the way'"; Mitchell, "'64 Suspect in Klan Murders Scoffs at Reinvestigation Talk"; Pettus and Jordan, "Charges Laid in '64 Race Killings."

103. "Mississippi: Kidnapping Charges Stand in 1964 Case"; Mitchell, "3 Life Terms for Seale"; Pettus, "Seale Gets 3 Life Terms for '64 Killings."

104. Mitchell, "3 Life Terms for Seale."

105. SPLC, *Intelligence Report,* no. 133: 53–57.

106. Chalmers, *Hooded Americanism,* 438.

Bibliography

Abney, M.G. "Reconstruction in Pontotoc County." *Publications of the Mississippi Historical Society* 11 (1910): 229–69.

Alexander, Charles. *The Ku Klux Klan in the Southwest*. Lexington: University of Kentucky Press, 1965.

Allardice, Bruce. *More Generals in Gray*. Baton Rouge: Louisiana State University Press, 1995.

"Alleged Backer of 'Invasion' of Dominica Kills Himself." *New York Times*, 23 June 1981, p. A14.

Ames, Jessie. *The Changing Character of Lynching*. Atlanta: Commission on Interracial Cooperation, 1942.

Anti-Defamation League. Archive of Extremist Events by State. www.adl.org.

_____. *Extremism on the Right*. New York: ADL, 1983.

_____. "Hate Groups and Black Church Arsons—State by State." New York: ADL, 1996.

_____. *Hate Groups in America*. New York: ADL, 1998.

_____. *The KKK and the Neo-Nazis*. New York: ADL, 1984.

_____. "The Ku Klux Klans: 1978." *Facts* (March 1978).

_____. The Ku Klux Klan Today. www.adl.org/learn/ext_us /kkk.

_____. "The Ku Klux Klan Tries for a Comeback." *Facts* (November 1979).

_____. "Neo-Nazi skinheads: A 1990 status report." *Terrorism* (1990): 243–75.

Austin, Curtis. "On Violence and Nonviolence." Mississippi History Now. mshistory.k12.ms.us/features/feature24/ms_civil_rights.html.

"Avants Dies in Federal Prison." WLOX-TV (Biloxi, Mississippi), 16 June 2004.

Baker, Lewis. *The Percys of Mississippi*. Baton Rouge: Louisiana State University Press, 1983.

Ball, Howard. *Murder in Mississippi*. Lawrence: University Press of Kansas, 2004.

Barkun, Michael. *Religion and the Racist Right*. Chapel Hill: University of North Carolina Press, 1997.

Barrett, Russell. *Integration at Ole Miss*. Chicago: Quadrangle, 1965.

Barry, John. *Rising Tide*. New York: Simon & Schuster, 1998.

Bartley, Numan. *The Rise of Massive Resistance*. Baton Rouge: Louisiana State University Press, 1969.

Beals, Carleton. *Brass-Knuckle Crusade*. New York: Hastings House, 1960.

Beckett, R.C. "Some Effects of Military Reconstruction in Monroe County, Mississippi." *Publications of the Mississippi Historical Society* 8 (1904): 177–86.

Beirich, Heidi. "SCV Standoff." *Intelligence Report* 115 (Fall 2004): 29–31.

Beirich, Heidi, and Bob Moser. "Communing with the Council." *Intelligence Report* 115 (Fall 2004): 11–18.

Beirich, Heidi, and Mark Potok. "A War Within." *Intelligence Report* 108 (Winter 2002): 36–45.

Belfrage, Sally. *Freedom Summer*. New York: Viking, 1965.

Bennett, Lerone, Jr. *Before the Mayflower*. New York: Penguin, 1988.

Blassingame, John, ed. *Slave Testimony*. Baton Rouge: Louisiana State University Press, 1977.

Blee, Kathleen. *Women of the Klan*. Berkeley: University of California Press, 1991.

"Bloodhounds Lead to Arrest of Negroes." *Clarksdale Register* 17 (October 1925): 1.

Booth, Williams. "In Church Fires, a Pattern but No Conspiracy." *Washington Post*, 19 June 1996, p. A1.

Braden, W.H. "Reconstruction in Lee County." *Publications of the Mississippi Historical Society* 10 (1909): 135–46.

Bradley, Laura. "Protestant Churches and the Ku Klux Klan in Mississippi During the 1920's." Master's thesis, University of Mississippi, 1962.

Branch, Taylor. *Parting the Waters*. New York: Simon & Schuster, 1988.

_____. *Pillar of Fire*. New York: Simon & Schuster, 1998.

Bridges, Tyler. *The Rise of David Duke*. Jackson: University Press of Mississippi, 1994.

Brown, Julia. "Reconstruction in Yalobusha and Grenada Counties." *Publications of the Mississippi Historical Society* 12 (1912): 214–82.

Brown, Timothy. "Trial Begins in 1970 Death of Black Man." *Amarillo (Texas) Globe-News*, 12 November 1999.

Browne, F.Z. "Reconstruction in Oktibbeha County." *Publications of the Mississippi Historical Society* 13 (1913): 273–298.

Bullard, Sarah, ed. *Free at Last*. Montgomery: Southern Poverty Law Center, n.d.

_____. *The Ku Klux Klan*. 4th edition. Montgomery: Southern Poverty Law Center, 1991.

Burghardt, Tom. "Neo-Nazis Salute the Anti-Abortion Zealots." *Covert Action Quarterly* 52 (Spring 1995): 26–33.

Busbee, Westley F. *Mississippi: A History*. Wheeling, Ill: Harlan Davidson, 2005.

Bushart, Howard, John Craig and Myra Barnes. *Soldiers of God*. New York: Pinnacle, 1998.

Butler, Hilton. "How 'Al' Smith Fared in Mississippi." *Nation* 125 (14 September 1927): 244–245.

Bynum, Victoria. *The Free State of Jones*. Chapel Hill: University of North Carolina Press, 2001.

Cagin, Seth, and Philip Dray. *We Are Not Afraid*. New York: Macmillan, 1988.

Campbell, Dennis. "Something Stinks, but It's Not in Denmark." ChronWatch. http://72.14.203.104/ search?q=cache: YyoEsdBLcN4J:www.chron watch.com/content/contentDisplay.asp%3Faid% 3D9033+mississippi+%2B+%22grand+ dragon%22&hl=en.

Camejo, Peter. *Racism, Revolution, Reaction, 1861–1877*. New York: Monad, 1976.

Carillo, Karen. "$100,000 Reward for Mississippi's Infamous Civil Rights Murders." *Amsterdam News,* 27 December 2004.

Carlson, John. *The Plotters*. New York: E.P. Dutton, 1946.

_____. *Undercover*. New York: E.P. Dutton, 1943.

Carter, Dan. *The Politics of Rage*. 2d edition. Baton Rouge: Louisiana State University Press, 2000.

Carter, Hodding. *So the Heffners Left McComb*. Garden City: Doubleday, 1965.

Caston v. State, 823 So. 2d 473 (Miss. 2002).

Chalmers, David. *Backfire*. Lanham, MD: Rowman & Littlefield, 2003.

_____. *Hooded Americanism*. 2nd edition. New York: New Viewpoints, 1981.

_____. "The Ku Klux Klan in Politics in the 1920s." *Mississippi Quarterly* 18 (Fall 1965): 234–47.

"Chester Trent Lott." Biographical Directory of the United States Congress.bioguide.congress.gov/ scripts/ biodisplay.pl?index=L000447.

Churchill, Ward, and Jim Vander Wall, *The COINTELPRO Papers*. Boston: South End, 1990.

"Civil Rights Timeline." *Jackson Clarion-Ledger,* 26 February 2003.

Classen, Steven. *Watching Jim Crow*. Durham: Duke University Press, 2004.

Cobb, James. *The Mississippi Delta and the World*. Baton Rouge: Louisiana State University Press, 1995.

Coleman, Edward Jr. "Reconstruction in Attala County." *Publications of the Mississippi Historical Society* 10 (1909): 147–61.

"Cong. Thompson (D-MS) Pushes for Cold Case Unit at Justice Dept." Mississippi Link. www.mississippilink.net/index.php?id=839.

Cook, James. *The Segregationists*. New York: Appleton–Century-Crofts, 1962.

Cooper, Forrest. "Reconstruction in Scott County." *Publications of the Mississippi Historical Society* 13 (1913): 99–221.

Craven, Avery. *Reconstruction: The Ending of the Civil War*. New York: Holt, Rinehart and Winston, 1969.

Cresswell, Stephen. "Enforcing the Enforcement Acts." *Journal of Southern History* 53 (August 1987): 421–40.

_____. "Was Mississippi a Part of Progressivism?" Mississippi History Now. mshistory.k12.ms. us/features/feature53/progressive.htm.

Culpepper, Kay. "Body Found in Warehouse." *Meridian Star* 19 July 1982: 1.

_____. "Sister Identifies Slain Teen." *Meridian Star,* 20 July 1982, p. 1.

Current, Richard. *Those Terrible Carpetbaggers*. New York: Oxford University Press, 1988.

Damms, Richard. "Loyalty and Dissent in Mississippi During the Great War, 1917–1918." Mississippi History Now. mshistory.k12.ms.us/features/ feature64/Great_War.htm.

Daniel, Pete. *The Shadow of Slavery*. New York: Oxford University Press, 1973.

Davis, Dernoral. "Medgar Wiley Evers and the Origin of the Civil Rights Movement in Mississippi." Mississippi History Now. mshistory.k12.ms.us/ features/feature45/medgar_evers.htm.

_____. "When Youth Protest: The Mississippi Civil Rights Movement, 1955–1970." Mississippi History Now. mshistory.k12.ms.us/features/feature 21/civilrights.html.

Davis, Jack. *Race Against Time*. Baton Rouge: Louisiana State University Press, 2001.

Dees, Morris. *A Season for Justice*. New York: Scribner's, 1991.

Dees, Morris, and James Corcoran. *Gathering Storm*. New York: HarperPerennial, 1996.

DeLoach, Cartha. *Hoover's FBI: The Inside Story by Hoover's Trusted Lieutenant*. Washington, D.C.: Regnery Pub, 1995.

Dewan, Shaila. "Jury Hears Mother of Rights Worker Slain in 1964." *New York Times,* 18 June 2005.

Dewan, Shaila, and Jerry Mitchell. "A Klan Confession, but Not to 1964 Civil Rights Murders." *New York Times,* 16 June 2005, p. A18.

Delaughter, Bobby. *Never Too Late*. New York: Scribner's, 2001.

Dittmer, John. *Local People*. Urbana: University of Illinois Press, 1995.

"Dominica Coup Plot Described in Court." *New York Times,* 18 June 1981, p. A9.

Donald, David. "The Scalawag in Mississippi Reconstruction." *Journal of Southern History* 10 (November 1944): 447–460.

Dorman, Michael. *We Shall Overcome*. New York: Delacorte, 1964.

Doyle, William. *An American Insurrection*. New York: Anchor, 1962.

Dray, Phillip. *At the Hands of Persons Unknown*. New York: Modern Library, 2002.

Du Bois, W.E.B. *Black Reconstruction*. New York: Russell & Russell, 1935.

"Dunning School." Wikipedia. en.wikipedia.org/ wiki/Dunning_School.

"Dying to Vote in Mississippi." www.buzzle.com/ editorials/11–28–2005–82529.asp.

"Edgar Ray Killen." Wikipedia. en.wikipedia.org/ wiki/Edgar_Ray_Killen.

Edmonson, Ben. "Pat Harrison and Mississippi in the Presidential Elections of 1924 and 1928." *Jour-*

nal of Mississippi History 33 (November 1971): 333–50.

"Edward Cary Walthall." Biographical Directory of the United States Congress. bioguide.congress.gov/scripts/biodisplay.pl?index=W000111.

Epstein, Benjamin, and Arnold Forster. The Radical Right. New York: Vintage, 1967.

_____. Report on the John Birch Society 1966. New York: Random House, 1966.

Evers, Charles, and Andrew Szanton. Have No Fear. New York: John Wiley & Sons, 1997.

Evers, Myrlie, and William Peters. For Us, the Living. Garden City: Doubleday, 1967.

"Ex-Klansman Charged in '66 Race Slaying Dies." New York Times, 20 September 1998.

"Far Right Strategy in Elections." The Monitor. www.skepticfiles.org/socialis/farright.htm.

"Feds Charge Mississippi Man with Civil Rights-era Murder." CNN, 8 June 2000.

Feldman, Glenn. Politics, Society, and the Klan in Alabama, 1915–1949. Tuscaloosa: University of Alabama Press, 1999.

Finnegan, Terrence. "Lynching and Political Power in Mississippi and South Carolina." In Under Sentence of Death, edited by W. Fitzhugh Brundage, 189–218. Chapel Hill: University of North Carolina Press, 1997.

"Fire at Black Church in Maryland Ruled Accidental." CNN, 19 June 1996.

Foner, Eric. Reconstruction. New York: Harper & Row, 1988.

Footlick, Jerrold, and Anthony Marro. "G-men and Klansmen." Newsweek 86 (25 August 1975): 74–5.

"Former KKK Leader Convicted of 1966 Murder." CNN, 21 August 1998.

"Former Klan Leader Faces Murder Trial for Fifth Time." CNN 18 August 1998.

"Former Klansmen Plead Guilty in Church Fires." CNN, 14 August 1998.

Forster, Arnold. A Measure of Freedom. Garden City: Doubleday, 1950.

Forster, Arnold, and Benjamin Epstein. Report on the Ku Klux Klan. New York: ADL, 1966.

_____. The Troublemakers. Garden City: Doubleday, 1952.

Forsyth County v. Nationalist Movement, 505 U.S. 123 (19 June 1992).

Franklin, John. Reconstruction After the Civil War. Chicago: University of Chicago Press, 1961.

Fry, Gladys-Marie. Night Riders in Black Folk History. Knoxville: University of Tennessee Press, 1975.

Fumento, Michael. "A Church Arson Epidemic?" Wall Street Journal, 8 July 1996.

"Galusha Pennypacker." Wikipedia. en.wikipedia.org/wiki/Galusha_Pennypacker.

Garner, James. Reconstruction in Mississippi. Baton Rouge: Louisiana State University Press, 1901.

Garrow, David. Bearing the Cross. New York: Morrow, 1986.

Gibson, Christine. "A Shooting—and the Civil Rights Movement Changes Course." AmericanHeritage.com.www.americanheritage.com/events/articles/web/20060606-james-meredith-education-ole-miss-columbia-segregation-martin-luther-king-black-power-march.shtml.

Gillette, Paul, and Eugene Tillinger. Inside Ku Klux Klan. New York: Pyramid, 1965.

Gillette, William. Retreat from Reconstruction. Baton Rouge: Louisiana State University Press, 1979.

Ginzburg, Ralph. 100 Years of Lynchings. New York: Lancer, 1962.

Goodman, Walter. The Committee. New York: Farrar, Straus and Giroux, 1968.

Goodwyn, Lawrence. The Populist Movement. Oxford: Oxford University Press, 1978.

Grossup, Beau. The Newest Explosions of Terrorism. Far Hills, NJ: New Horizons, 1997.

"Grover C. Nichols Injured by Axe Blow." Clarksdale Register, 16 October 1925: 1.

Haas, Ben. KKK. San Diego: Regency, 1963.

Hadden, Sally. Slave Patrols. Cambridge: Harvard University Press, 2001.

Hall, Jacquelyn. Revolt Against Chivalry. New York: Columbia University Press, 1979.

Harkey, Ira. The Smell of Burning Crosses. Jacksonville, MS: Harris-Wolfe, 1967.

Hart, Ariel. "41 Years Later, Ex-Klansman Gets 60 Years in Civil Rights Deaths." New York Times, 24 June 2005.

Hart, Lianne. "Mississippi Man Called Architect of 1964 Killings." Los Angeles Times, 16 June 2005.

"Hate Groups and Black Church Arsons—State by State." Anti-Defamation League press release, 20 June 1996.

Hendrickson, Paul. Sons of Mississippi. New York: Alfred A. Knopf, 2003.

"Henry Lowndes Muldrow." Biographical Directory of the United States Congress. bioguide.congress.gov/scripts/biodisplay.pl?index=M001068.

Herbers, John. "Mississippi Hints Policing Accord." New York Times, 27 June 1964, p. 10.

Hilton, Bruce. The Delta Ministry. New York: Macmillan, 1969.

Hirshson, Stanley. Farewell to the Bloody Shirt. Chicago: Quadrangle, 1962.

History of the Order. www.uta.edu/student_orgs/kao/rbhistory.html.

Hofstadter, Richard, and Michael Wallace, eds. American Violence. New York: Vintage, 1970.

Holmes, William. "Whitecapping: Agrarian Violence in Mississippi, 1902–1906." Journal of Southern History 35 (May 1969): 165–85.

_____. "Whitecapping: Anti-Semitism in the Populist Era." American Jewish Historical Quarterly 43 (March 1974): 244–61.

Holt, Len. The Summer That Didn't End. New York: Morrow, 1965.

Holthouse, Davie. "'Heritage' for Sale." Intelligence Report 119 (Fall 2005): 57.

"Hooded Horsemen Gallop Out of the Past in a Sudden Revival of the KKK." Life 58 (23 April 1965): 28–35.

Horn, Stanley. Invisible Empire. Boston: Houghton Mifflin, 1939.

House Committee on Un-American Activities. Activities of Ku Klux Klan Organizations in the United States. 5 vols. Washington: U.S. Government Printing Office, 1966.

_____. The Present-Day Ku Klux Klan Movement.

Washington: U.S. Government Printing Office, 1967.

"A House Divided." *Intelligence Report* 105 (Spring 2002): 44–50.

Huie, William. *Three Lives for Mississippi*. New York: WCC, 1965.

Hurst, Jack. *Nathan Bedford Forrest*. New York: Alfred A. Knopf, 1993.

"Investigative Reporter Mitchell Tapped for Chancellor Award." *Editor & Reporter*, 22 November 2005.

"Investigators Search for Clues in Mississippi Fires." CNN 18 June 1996.

Jackson, Kenneth. *The Ku Klux Klan in the City, 1915–1930*. New York: Oxford University Press, 1967.

"James Kimble Vardaman." Biographical Directory of the United States Congress. bioguide.congress.gov/scripts/biodisplay.pl?index=V000070.

"James Ronald Chalmers." Biographical Directory of the United States Congress. bioguide.congress.gov/scripts/biodisplay.pl?index=C000272.

"James Zachariah George." Biographical Directory of the United States Congress. bioguide.congress.gov/scripts/biodisplay.pl?index=G000127.

Joshi, S.T., ed. *Documents of American Prejudice*. New York: Basic, 1999.

"Judge Issues Life Sentence in 1966 Racial Slaying." *St. Petersburg Times*, 18 June 2003, p. 1.

"Jury Convicts 72-year-old Man in 1966 Slaying of Black Sharecropper." CNN, 28 February 2003.

Kane, Joseph. *Presidential Fact Book*. New York: Random House, 1998.

Kaplan, Jeffrey. *Encyclopedia of White Power*. Walnut Creek: AltaMira, 2000.

_____. "Leaderless Resistance." *Terrorism and Political Violence* 9 (Autumn 1997): 80–95.

Katagiri, Yasuhiro. *The Mississippi State Sovereignty Commission*. Jackson: University Press of Mississippi, 2001.

Kendel, Julia. "Reconstruction in Lafayette County." *Publications of the Mississippi Historical Society* 13 (1913): 223–71.

Kennedy, Stetson. *After Appomattox*. Gainesville: University Press of Florida, 1995.

_____. *Jim Crow Guide*. Boca Raton: Florida Atlantic University Press, 1990.

_____. *The Klan Unmasked*. Boca Raton: Florida Atlantic University Press, 1990.

_____. *Southern Exposure*. Garden City: Doubleday, 1946.

Key, Valdimer. *Southern Politics in State and Nation*. New York: Random House, 1949.

Kirwan, Albert. *Revolt of the Rednecks*. Gloucester, MA: P. Smith, 1964.

"Klan Leader Faces New Trial in 1966 Firebombing." CNN, 28 May 1998.

"Klan Moves into Mississippi." *New York Times*, 26 March 1950, p. 49.

"Klan Warns Fireman to Leave Jobs." *Chicago Defender*, 3 September 1921, p. 1.

"Klansman Imprisoned for Bombing Dies." CNN, 5 November 2006.

"Klansmen Are Among 10 Indicted in Plot on Caribbean Island Nation." *New York Times*, 8 May 1981, p. A16.

"Klansmen Must Pay $38m for Church Arson." BBC News, 25 July 1998.

Klopfer, Susan. Emmett Till Blog. hungryblues.net/2005/06/15/why-doesnt-mississippi-da-mark-duncan-want-assistance-from-the-doj/.

_____. "Murders Around Mississippi." neshobanews.blogspot.com/2005/06/birdia-keglar-lynched-jan.html.

Kluger, Richard. *Simple Justice*. New York: Alfred A. Knopf, 1976.

Knebel, Fletcher, and Clark Mollenhoff. "Eight Klans bring new terror to the South." *Look* 21 (30 April 1957): 59–60.

"Kuklos Adelphon." Wikipedia. en.wikipedia.org/wiki/Kuklos_Adelphon.

"Ku Klux Klan Invades Jackson Tuesday." *Yazoo City Herald*, 7 July 1922, p. 1.

"Ku Klux Membership Falls from 8,904,871 in 1925 to 34,694 Now." *Washington Post*, 2 November 1930, M1.

"Ku Klux's Record of Atrocities Grow." *The (New York) World*, 19 September 1921, p. 1.

Kyle, John. "Reconstruction in Panola County." *Publications of the Mississippi Historical Society* 13 (1913): 9–98.

Ladd, Donna. "Evolution of a Man: Lifting the Hood in South Mississippi." *Jackson Free Press*, 26 October 2005, p. 1.

"A League of Their Own." *Intelligence Report* 99 (Summer 2000): 13–17.

Leftwich, George. "Reconstruction in Monroe County." *Publications of the Mississippi Historical Society* 9 (1906): 53–84.

"Leo Frank." Wikipedia. en.wikipedia.org/wiki/Leo_Frank.

Lester, John, and David Wilson. *Ku Klux Klan, Its Origin, Growth, and Disbandment*. New York: Neale, 1905.

Levitas, Daniel. *The Terrorist Next Door*. New York: Thomas Dunne, 2002.

"List of Black Church Fire Investigations." CNN, 8 June 1996.

Litwack, Leon. *Been in the Storm So Long*. New York: Alfred A. Knopf, 1979.

Loewen, James, and Charles Sallis, eds. *Mississippi: Conflict & Change*. New York: Random House, 1974.

Logan, Rayford. *The Betrayal of the Negro from Rutherford B. Hayes to Woodrow Wilson*. New York: Da Capo, 1997.

Lord, Walter. *The Past That Would Not Die*. New York: Harper & Row, 1965.

"Lucius Quintus Cincinnatus Lamar." Biographical Directory of the United States Congress. bioguide.congress.gov/scripts/biodisplay.pl?index=L000030.

Lumpkin, Benjamin, and Thomas Malone. *Full Report of the Great Ku Klux Trial in the United States Circuit Court at Oxford, Miss*. Memphis: W.J. Mansford, 1871.

Luthin, Reinhard. *American Demagogues*. Boston: Beacon, 1954.

Lutz, Chris. *They Don't All Wear Sheets*. Atlanta: Center for Democratic Renewal, 1987.

MacLean, Nancy. *Behind the Mask of Chivalry.* New York: Oxford University Press, 1994.

Magee, Hattie. "Reconstruction in Lawrence and Jefferson Counties." *Publications of the Mississippi Historical Society* 11 (1910): 163–97.

Mars, Florence. *Witness in Philadelphia.* Baton Rouge: Louisiana State University Press, 1977.

Marsh, Charles. *God's Long Summer.* Princeton: Princeton University Press, 1997.

Martin, John. *The Deep South Says "Never."* New York: Ballantine, 1957.

Marx, Andrew, and Tom Tuthill. "1978: Mississippi organizes." *Southern Exposure* 8 (Summer 1980): 73–6.

Massengill, Reed. *Portrait of a Racist.* New York: St. Martin's Griffin, 1996.

McAdam, Doug. *Freedom Summer.* New York: Oxford University Press, 1988.

McCarty, Kenneth. "Farmers, the Populist Party, and Mississippi." Mississippi History Now. mshistory.k12.ms.us/features/feature42/ populistparty.html.

McCord, William. *Mississippi: The Long, Hot Summer.* New York: W.W. Norton, 1965.

McIlhany, William. *Klandestine.* New York: Arlington House, 1975.

McMillen, Neil. *The Citizens' Council.* Urbana: University of Illinois Press, 1971.

_____. *Dark Journey.* Urbana: University of Illinois Press, 1990.

McNeilly, J.S. "The Enforcement Act of 1871 and Ku Klux Klan in Mississippi." *Publications of the Mississippi Historical Society* 9 (1906): 109–71.

Mendelsohn, Jack. *The Martyrs.* New York: Harper & Row, 1966.

Miller, Clark. "'Let Us Die to Make Men Free,' Political Terrorism in Post-Reconstruction Mississippi, 1877–1896." PhD diss., University of Minnesota, 1983.

Mills, Kay. *This Little Light of Mine.* New York: Plume, 1993.

Mills, Nicolaus. *Like a Holy Crusade.* Chicago: Ivar R. Dee, 1992.

Minor, Bill. *Eyes on Mississippi.* Jackson: J. Prichard Morris, 2001.

Mississippi Black Paper: Fifty-Seven Negro and White Citizens' Testimony of Law and Order and the Corruption of Justice in Mississippi. New York: Random House, 1965.

Mississippi Constitutional Militia. www.constitution.org/mil/ms/mil_usms.htm.

"Mississippi/Federal Government to Reopen 1964 Klan Assassination Case." Associated Press, 6 February 2000.

"Mississippi Jail Lynchings." *Revolutionary Worker* 979 (25 October 1998). rwor.org/a/v20/970–79/ 979/miss.htm.

"Mississippi: Kidnapping Charges Stand in 1964 Case." *New York Times,* 23 February 2007.

Mississippi Militia. www.mississippimilitia.com.

Mitchell, Jerry. "Activist Slayings Reopened." *Jackson Clarion-Ledger* 8 February 2000, p. 1.

_____. "Avants Found Guilty in '66 Klan Killing." *Jackson Clarion-Ledger,* 1 March 2003, p. 1.

_____. "Battle by the Book." *Intelligence Report* 93 (Winter 1999): 12–13.

_____. "A Crime Not Forgotten." *Jackson Clarion-Ledger,* 6 January 1998, p. 1.

_____. "Ex-agent Testifies Against Avants." *Jackson Clarion-Ledger,* 28 February 2003, p. 1.

_____. "Experts: Autopsy Reveals Beating." *Jackson Clarion-Ledger,* 4 June 2000, p. 1.

_____. "The Forgotten Killings." *Jackson Clarion-Ledger,* 5 February 2005, p. 1.

_____. "Grand Jury Examining Evidence in '66 Death." *Jackson Clarion-Ledger,* 8 February 2000, p. 1.

_____. "Jury Selection in Avants Case Ordered Closed." *Jackson Clarion-Ledger,* 25 February 2003, p. 1.

_____. "Justice: Behind Closed Doors." *Jackson Clarion-Ledger,* 7 May 2000, p. 1.

_____. "Justice Department Attorney Observes Grand Jury Testimony." *Jackson Clarion-Ledger,* 9 February 2000, p. 1.

_____. "'Justice on the Way.'" *Jackson Clarion-Ledger,* 25 January 2007, p. 1.

_____. "Klan Kidnapping Foreshadowed Murders." *Jackson Clarion-Ledger,* 10 September 2000, p. 1.

_____. "The Last Days of Ben Chester White." *Jackson Clarion-Ledger,* 23 February 2003, p. 1.

_____. "Letters to Sheriff Reveal Story Behind Battle for Civil Rights." *Jackson Clarion-Ledger,* 28 May 2000, p. 1.

_____. "Makeup of Jury for Avants Trial to Be Announced Today." *Jackson Clarion-Ledger,* 26 February 2003, p. 1.

_____. "Man Who Spotted Body Testifies." *Jackson Clarion-Ledger,* 27 February 2003, p. 1.

_____. "New Witnesses Surface in Probe of '64 Killings." *Jackson Clarion-Ledger,* June 2000, p. 1.

_____. "Rita's Story." *Jackson Clarion-Ledger,* 18 June 2000, p. 1.

_____. "'64 Suspect in Klan Murders Scoffs at Reinvestigation Talk." *Jackson Clarion-Ledger,* 23 January 2000, p. 1.

_____. "'66 Klan Slaying Not Only Killing on Federal Property." *Jackson Clarion-Ledger,* 14 January 2000, p. 1.

_____. "Spy Agency Took Aim at N.Y. Pathologist." *Jackson Clarion-Ledger,* 4 June 2000, p. 1.

_____. "Stringer Recalls 'Elimination' Plan." *Jackson Clarion-Ledger,* 14 May 2000, p. 1.

_____. "Suspects in 1964 Civil Rights Slayings Put Past Behind Them." *Jackson Clarion-Ledger,* 21 May 2000, p. 1.

_____. "3 Life Terms for Seale." *Jackson Clarion-Ledger,* 25 August 2007.

_____. "Will KKK fade into history?" *Jackson Clarion-Ledger,* 15 July 2005, p. 1.

Moody, Anne. *Coming of Age in Mississippi.* New York: Dell, 1971.

Moore, Edmund. *A Catholic Runs for President.* New York: Ronald, 1956.

Morgan, Chester. "Presidential Elections: Mississippi's Voting History." Mississippi History Now. mshistory.k12.ms.us/features/feature7/elections.html.

Moser, Bob. "Our Terrible Swift Sword." *Intelligence Report* 111 (Fall 2003): 52–6.

"Movement on Foot to Start Ku Klux Klan." *Hattiesburg American,* 26 January 1921, p. 1.

Murphy, Robert. "The South fights bombing." *Look* 23 (6 January 1959): 13–17.

Muse, Benjamin. *Ten Years of Prelude.* New York: Viking, 1964.

Myers, Debbie. "Killen Trial Will Proceed as Scheduled." *Neshoba Democrat,* 6 January 2005, p. 1.

Myers, Gustavus. *History of Bigotry in the United States.* New York: Random House, 1943.

"Mysterious Ku Klux Klan Again Gains Prominence." *Hattiesburg American,* 8 February 1921, p. 8.

NAACP. *Burning at Stake in the United States.* New York: NAACP, 1919.

_____. *M Is for Mississippi and Murder.* New York: NAACP, 1956.

_____. *Thirty Years of Lynching in the United States.* New York: NAACP, 1919.

"Nationalist Movement." Wikipedia. en.wikipedia. org/wiki/Nationalist_Movement.

Neier, Aryeh. "Black marchers bring out the Klan." *Nation* 227 (23 September 1978): 265–7.

Nelson, Jack. *Terror in the Night.* Jackson: University Press of Mississippi, 1993.

Newton, Michael. *The Ku Klux Klan.* Jefferson, NC: McFarland, 2007.

Newton, Michael, and Judy Newton. *Racial and Religious Violence in America.* New York: Garland, 1991.

"Nicholas [*sic*] Murder and Coleman Lynching Trials, Etc., Oct. 1925–Feb. 1926." N.p.: n.d.

Nichols, Irby. "Reconstruction in DeSoto County." *Publications of the Mississippi Historical Society* 11 (1910): 295–316.

Nieburh, Reinhold. *Mississippi Black Paper.* New York: Random House, 1965.

Nossiter, Adam. *Of Long Memory.* Reading: Addison-Wesley, 1994.

Olsen, Otto, ed. *Reconstruction and Redemption in the South.* Baton Rouge: Louisiana State University Press, 1980.

"Operation Red Dog." Wikipedia. en.wikipedia. org/wiki/Operation_Red_Dog.

O'Reilly, Kenneth. "*Racial Matters.*" New York: Free, 1989.

Oziewicz, Estanislao. "Klansman Guilty in 1964 Slayings." *Toronto Globe & Mail,* 22 June 2005.

Parker, Thomas, ed. *Violence in the United States.* New York: Facts on File, 1974.

Patrick, Rembert. *The Reconstruction of the Nation.* New York: Oxford University Press, 1967.

Patterson, Barbara. "Defiance and dynamite." *New South* 18 (May 1963): 8–11.

Payne, Charles. *I've Got the Light of Freedom.* Berkeley: University of California Press, 1995.

Peirce, Neal. *The Deep South States of America.* New York: W.W. Norton, 1972.

People Against Racist Terror. "Front Man for Fascism." www.nizkor.org/frp.cgi/people/g/frp.py? people/g/gritz.bo/ gritz.PART.

Percy, William. *Lanterns on the Levee.* New York: Alfred A. Knopf, 1941.

Pettus, Emily. "Seale Gets 3 Life Terms for '64 Killings." Associated Press, 24 August 2007.

_____. "Siblings Provide Alibi for Ex-Klansman." *Washington Post,* 19 June 2005.

_____. "Trial in '64 Klan Killings Hits Snag." *Houston Chronicle,* 16 June 2005.

Pettus, Emily, and Lara Jordan. "Charges Laid in '64 Race Killings." *Toronto Star,* 25 January 2007.

Randel, William. *The Ku Klux Klan: A Century of Infamy.* London: Chilton, 1965.

Reed, Roy. "3 Mississippi Whites Held in Alleged Plot to Assassinate Evers." *New York Times,* 11 September 1969, p. 19.

Rice, Arnold. *The Ku Klux Klan in American Politics.* Washington: Public Affairs, 1962.

"Rich Planter Leads Mississippi Klansmen." *Chicago Defender,* 6 August 1921, p. 2.

Ridgeway, James. *Blood in the Face.* New York: Thunder's Mouth, 1990.

Rogers, William. "Lucius Quintus Cincinnatus Lamar." Mississippi History Now. mshistory. k12.ms.us/features/feature69/Lamar_pf.htm.

Roig-Franzia, Manuel. "After Nearly 40 Years, a Guilty Verdict." *Washington Post,* 1 March 2003, p. 1.

Rose, Douglas, ed. *The Emergence of David Duke and the Politics of Race.* Chapel Hill: University of North Carolina Press, 1992.

Rose, Thomas, ed. *Violence in America.* New York: Vintage, 1970.

Rowe-Sims, Sarah. "The Mississippi State Sovereignty Commission." Mississippi History Now. mshistory.k12.ms.us/features/feature35/sovereignty.html.

Ryan, Harriet. "Defense: Killen a 'Bystander' in the Klan." Court TV, 16 June 2005.

"S.D. Redmond Target of Ku Klux Klan Threat." *Chicago Defender,* 12 November 1921, p. 1.

Salter, John. *Jackson, Mississippi.* Hicksville, NY: Exposition, 1979.

Salter, Sid. "Message Found in Killen's Sentence." *Neshoba Democrat,* 29 June 2005, p. 1.

"Samuel James Gholson." Biographical Directory of the United States Congress. bioguide.congress. gov/scripts/biodisplay.pl?index=G000149.

Sansing, David. "Governors of Mississippi." Mississippi History Now. mshistory.k12.ms.us/features/feature47/governors_first.htm.

Schardt, Arlie. "A Mississippi Mayor Fights the Klan." *Reporter* 34 (27 January 1966): 39–40.

"A Senseless Killing." *Time* (7 June 1971). www.time. com/time/magazine/article/0,9171,905129, 00.html?promoid=googlep.

"Sharks in the Mainstream." *Intelligence Report* 93 (Winter 1999): 21–6.

Shay, Frank. *Judge Lynch.* New York: Washburn, 1938.

Sherrill, Robert. *Gothic Politics in the Deep South.* New York: Grossman, 1968.

Silver, James. *Mississippi: The Closed Society.* New York: Harcourt, Brace & World, 1966.

Sims, Patsy. *The Klan.* New York: Stein & Day, 1978.

Sitkoff, Harvard. *A New Deal for Blacks.* New York: Oxford University Press, 1978.

"'64 Case Dying with Witnesses." *Jackson Clarion-Ledger,* 17 November 2002.

Skates, John. "The Constitution of 1868." Mississippi History Now. mshistory.k12.ms.us/features/feature8/ 1868constitution.html.

Smead, Howard. *Blood Justice.* New York: Oxford University Press, 1986.

"Some Notes on Theta's History." Archives of Phi Gamma Delta. www.phigam.org/history/Magazine/ThetaHistory.htm>.

"Southern Party." Wikipedia. en.wikipedia.org/wiki/Southern_Party.

Spofford, Tim. *Lynch Street.* Kent: Kent State University Press, 1988.

Spruill, Marjorie, and Jesse Wheeler. "The Equal Rights Amendment and Mississippi." Mississippi History Now. mshistory.k12.ms.us/features/feature37/era_ms.html.

Stampp, Kenneth. *The Era of Reconstruction.* New York: Alfred A. Knopf, 1965.

Stanton, Bill. *Klanwatch.* New York: Grove Weidenfeld, 1991.

Suall, Irwin, and David Lowe. "The Hate Movement Today." *Terrorism* 10 (1987): 345–64.

Sumners, Cecil. *The Governors of Mississippi.* Gretna: Pelican, 1980.

Tarrants, Thomas, III. *The Conversion of a Klansman.* Garden City: Doubleday, 1979.

"Theodore Gilmore Bilbo." Biographical Directory of the United States Congress. bioguide.congress.gov/scripts/biodisplay.pl?index=B000460.

Theoharis, Athan. *Spying on Americans.* Philadelphia: Temple University Press, 1978.

"3 Mississippi Whites Held in Alleged Plot to Assassinate Evers." *New York Times,* 11 September 1969, p. 19.

Till-Mobley, Mamie, and Christopher Benton. *Death of Innocence.* New York: Random House, 2003.

Tolnay, Stewart, and E.M. Beck. *A Festival of Violence.* Urbana: University of Illinois Press, 1995.

Trelease, Allen. *White Terror.* Westport: Greenwood, 1971.

"Trent Lott." Wikipedia. en.wikipedia.org/wiki/Trent_ Lott#Resignation_from_Senate_Leadership.

"Trent Lott's 'Uptown Klan.'" *Nation,* 11 December 2002. www.thenation.com/blogs/thebeat?bid=1&pid=208.

Tucker, Shirley. *Mississippi from Within.* New York: Arco, 1965.

Tuskegee Institute. *Lynching by States and Race, 1882–1959.* Tuskegee: Department of Records and Research, 1959.

"2 Agents of FBI Shot At; 7 Seized at Cross Burnings." *New York Times,* 5 January 1966, p. 12.

"2 Guilty in New Orleans for Plot on Dominica Invasion." *New York Times,* 21 June 1981, p. 22.

"Two More Black Churches Destroyed by Fire." CNN, 18 June 1996.

U.S. Congress. *Joint Select Committee to Inquire into the Condition of Affairs in the Late Insurrectionary States.* 13 volumes. Washington: Government Printing Office, 1872.

U.S. House of Representatives. *Report of the Select Committee on Assassinations.* New York: Bantam, 1979.

Villano, Anthony, and Gerald Astor. *Brick Agent.* New York: Quadrangle, 1977.

Vollers, Maryanne. *Ghosts of Mississippi.* Boston: Little, Brown, 1995.

Wade, Wyn Craig. *The Fiery Cross: The Ku Klux Klan in America.* New York: Simon & Schuster, 1987.

Warner, Ezra. *Generals in Gray.* Baton Rouge: Louisiana State University Press, 1959.

Watkins, Ruth. "Reconstruction in Marshall County." *Publications of the Mississippi Historical Society* 12 (1912): 155–213.

_____. "Reconstruction in Newton County." *Publications of the Mississippi Historical Society* 11 (1910): 205–28.

"'We love Negroes, in their place—like shinin' shoes, etc.'" *Life* 58 (23 April 1965): 33.

Wells, James. *The Chisolm Massacre.* Washington: Chisolm Monument Association, 1878.

"White Floggers Out on Bond." *Pittsburgh Courier,* 10 May 1930, p. 3.

"White Knights of Mississippi Profile." Nation States. forums3.jolt.co.uk/showpost.php?p=733 8157&postcount=1.

Whitehead, Don. *Attack on Terror.* New York: Funk & Wagnalls, 1970.

Wilson, Charles. "Italians in Mississippi." mshistory.k12.ms.us/features/feature55/italians.htm.

_____. "Mississippi Chinese: An ethnic people in a biracial society." Mississippi History Now. mshistory.k12.ms.us/features/feature33/chinese.html.

"Witness: Klan Leader Ordered 1966 Slaying of NAACP Official." CNN, 19 August 1998.

Witty, Fred. "Reconstruction in Carroll and Montgomery Counties." *Publications of the Mississippi Historical Society* 10 (1909): 115–34.

Woodward, C. Vann. *The Strange Career of Jim Crow.* New York: Oxford University Press, 1974.

Wooten, James. "Inquiry on FBI in Klan Death Urged." *New York Times,* 8 April 1970, p. 28.

Zanden, James. "The Klan revival." *American Journal of Sociology* 65 (March 1960): 456–62.

Index